Transoceanic America

OXFORD STUDIES IN AMERICAN LITERARY HISTORY

Gordon Hutner, Series Editor

Transoceanic America

RISK, WRITING, AND REVOLUTION
IN THE GLOBAL PACIFIC

Michelle Burnham

OXFORD
UNIVERSITY PRESS

OXFORD

UNIVERSITY PRESS

Great Clarendon Street, Oxford, OX2 6DP,
United Kingdom

Oxford University Press is a department of the University of Oxford.
It furthers the University's objective of excellence in research, scholarship,
and education by publishing worldwide. Oxford is a registered trade mark of
Oxford University Press in the UK and in certain other countries

First Edition published in 2019

Impression: 1

Published in the United States of America by Oxford University Press
198 Madison Avenue, New York, NY 10016, United States of America

British Library Cataloguing in Publication Data
Data available

Library of Congress Control Number: 2018967503

ISBN 978-0-19-884089-3

Printed and bound by
CPI Group (UK) Ltd, Croydon, CR0 4YY

for Mara and Jana

When writers begin a book, its future shape can be hard to predict. But its past influences are often just as hard to discern. *Transoceanic America* is, in a number of ways, not the book I planned to write when I began it, and I have often found myself trying to figure out exactly how I ended up at the particular scholarly intersection where literary novels, political revolution, and commercial mathematics meet in the context of a global eighteenth-century Pacific. In this list, math surely requires the most explanation. Although I have been writing and thinking about economics and early American literature for some time, math seemed to be taking a step too far, and I've had more than a few well-meaning friends, family members, and colleagues give me quizzical or concerned looks upon learning that some of my research for this book involved reading about math and numbers. These were people well aware that I have never been able to balance my checkbook, that I routinely failed to help my children with their algebra homework, and that my eyes glaze over with a blank and faraway stare whenever someone asks a question whose answer requires calculating numbers. Why would an arithmophobe like me willingly set out to learn and write about the history of math, calculation, and numbers?

My effort to answer this question reminded me of the last job I had before leaving the workforce to attend graduate school. In 1987, I worked as a proofreader for a Boston financial information firm that, in the early days of the personal computer, began to digitize the quarterly company reports that informed stockholders about the recent and anticipated performance of their shares. My job entailed comparing the printed company stock market reports with their computerized printouts to confirm that the numbers and the words were inputted accurately, and to correct the printout if they were not. As dull as these reports were, after scanning page after page of them, day after day and week after week, I began to realize that for those who understood their language, syntax, and plot, these apparently mundane lists of numbers actually comprised a narrative, a story whose excitements or dangers were buried inside those numbers. 1987 was also the year of the stock market crash known as Black Monday, and in its wake I began to sense the power held by those who could understand and manipulate this language of finance. My commute to this job took me each day on a walk past Boston's Federal Reserve Bank building, and I remember looking up at its countless floors, trying to imagine how many employees filled that much office space and wondering: what do they do in there, exactly? I was prompted to ask this question not only as a result of the reports I was reading, but because then-Federal Reserve Bank chairman Alan Greenspan was routinely credited in the wake of Black Monday with rescuing the U.S. economy from what everyone at the time fully expected to be a second Great Depression. In more recent years, Greenspan has been positioned not as an economic hero but as the villain who ushered in our current era of massive inequality, financial corruption, and the marketization of everyday life.

In retrospect, proofreading stock market reports may have been one driving force in my decision two years later to enter graduate school, where I focused on words. The advanced degree I went on to earn led me, at least eventually, to a university teaching position at Santa Clara University, located in Silicon Valley. I arrived here, exactly a decade after the 1987 economic crash, to the boom that would later be dubbed the dotcom bubble. As an assistant professor of English, I was well on the margins of this economic bonanza. But I absorbed enough stories from those working in the technology sector to recognize that the narrative centerpiece of high-tech boom culture at that time was the unwavering conviction that their company's software or hardware product was going to change the world. It was impossible to pull this rhetoric of cultural revolution and social improvement away from the fantasy of personal enrichment woven into it. I remember being told that the repetitive noise of a small airplane flying back and forth over my neighborhood at irritating times of night was the CEO of one behemoth tech company, whose wealth had granted him special privileges to practice flying his personal jet in and out of San Jose's airport. It is now two decades later, and most of these early Silicon Valley fantasies have been replaced by employment anxieties and growing homelessness. At the time, however, everyone believed that they, too, might one day be that jet-flying billionaire, just as a decade before that everyone seemed confident that Alan Greenspan would save us all. In the end, it has been exactly my lack of facility with numbers that made me fascinated by the material and narrative power they have over us, and I am convinced that scholars and students in the humanities need to intervene in the construction of those narratives. Numbers appear to be disinterested and abstract; they absolutely are not.

It's much more obvious why I've turned to the Pacific in this project, given my location in Silicon Valley. Not too long after I arrived at Santa Clara University, one of my colleagues gifted me a small volume published by Heyday Books containing excerpts from the Frenchman Jean-François Galaup de La Pérouse's account of his 1787 visit to Monterey, California. I had never heard of La Pérouse, and it occurred to me that in the decade or so I'd been studying and writing about early American literature and culture, I had never really wondered what was going on in California during the period I regularly teach and write about. The Heyday edition led me to locate the Hakluyt Society's edition of La Pérouse's entire, three-volume narrative. If the Heyday edition alerted me to the entirely new fact that a Frenchman visited the Spanish mission on the coast of California in the year that the Constitution was being ratified in Philadelphia, the Hakluyt Society volume was a revelatory entry into the expanse and diversity of the eighteenth-century Pacific world. La Pérouse's journal was filled with stunning accounts of Chile, Lituya Bay, Kamchatka,

Formosa, Samoa Islands, Botany Bay, and more. My journey from that point forward into the literary, historical, cultural, and commercial world of the early Pacific is documented better in the contents and footnotes of the chapters that follow than I could possibly do here. It is not too much to say, however, that it has changed entirely my understanding of early America.

It has also changed my understanding of American literary history, especially as this new spatial framework within which to situate American texts and figures exposed the limitations of an older temporal framework for narrating the history of early American literature. While conducting research for this book, I was continuing to teach an annual introductory American literature survey course that covered American writing from its beginnings to 1865. As long as I have been teaching it, American literature anthologies have begun with Native American storytelling traditions and Spanish conquistadors, rather than with the New England Puritans—the result of scholars in the fields of early American literature and history who have challenged the idea that colonial North America was a mere incubator for the U.S. nation that would form much later. Instead, the continent was filled with indigenous peoples even as it became increasingly occupied over the colonial period by British, French, and Spanish colonial outposts and settlements, and with Africans forcibly transported to the Americas and sold as slave labor.

I became increasingly aware, however, that the reorientation that brought such wholesale changes to the first two-thirds of the course's chronology seemed to have made a far slighter dent in its final third—which tended moreover to take up a disproportionate two-thirds of the course time. As the report "A Survey of Survey Courses" by Maurice Lee in a 2014 issue of the journal *J19* observes, the nineteenth-century texts taught in American literature surveys remain profoundly canonical, barely changed from an earlier curricular age despite the wealth of extraordinary scholarship that points in other directions. This data confirmed my own sense that I was teaching one (global, multilingual) narrative about America for one half of the course and another (national, English-only) narrative for its second half. I didn't know quite what to do about that (or even if I should do something about it) but I came to realize that the key to this narrative disjunction was the American Revolution, which occupied the temporal space between these two halves.

At about the same time as I was asking these questions and beginning the research for this book, I was drafted to help design a pilot course for a newly required core curriculum sequence for incoming first-year students called Cultures and Ideas. The two-course sequence would replace what had been a traditional Western Civilization unit with a more global framework, and the research and discussions around course development introduced me to new histories that began to have a curious effect on the American literature courses I continued to teach. It made me more consciously aware of the global contexts for the texts and figures I assigned in class, but it also made it harder and harder for me to separate the Atlantic from the Pacific, because in the course of thinking and reading about both of them it was increasingly clear that they were conceptually and materially connected to each other throughout the revolutionary period. It's the story of that connection—and the difference that connection might make for the way we tell the story of American literary and cultural history—that *Transoceanic America* endeavors to tell.

There has never been an academic book that did not take too long to write, and this one is no exception. While a number of unanticipated professional and personal interruptions have prolonged its gestation beyond the birth date I had hoped for it, it's also the case that researching and writing this book has regularly brought me a sense of joy and escape. Those sensations, I'm also aware, have been made possible by networks of collegiality, friendship, and professional and institutional support. The special collections holdings, fellowship support, and staff expertise at a number of research libraries made this book what it could not possibly have been otherwise. An Andrew W. Mellon fellowship at the Huntington Library gave me the opportunity to read widely and deeply in early Pacific travel writing. An ASECS-sponsored fellowship at the American Antiquarian Society allowed me unprecedented access to early American mathematics textbooks as well as many adjacent numerical genres, and their staff provided incomparable research support while also nurturing a community of scholars. In between these two research fellowships, a briefer visit to the British Library gave me access to additional texts about the eighteenth-century Pacific. Finally, a fellowship at the University of Sydney's United States Studies Centre gave me the time, space, and intellectual community needed to wrestle two resistant chapters to the mat and head toward the finish line. I am especially grateful to Paul Erickson, Laura Wasowicz, Ashley Cataldo, and Tracey Kry at the AAS; and to Paul Giles, Aaron Nygeres, Rodney Taveira, and Thomas Adams at the USSC. In addition to its material and human resources, the USSC fellowship provided the invaluable perspective of working on and thinking about this project from the other side of the Pacific.

I have had the good fortune to present work in progress from this book in a number of venues and professional organizations over the past years, including the Society for Early Americanists, C19, the American Studies Association, the American Association for Eighteenth-Century Studies, the American Literature Association, and the Modern Language Association. I am especially thankful for the careful readings of selected chapter drafts by Philip Barnard, Lance Bertelsen, Jim Egan, and Tim Watson. Christine Skwiot was an early interlocutor on this project and transoceanic studies more generally; I have deeply appreciated sharing work and dialogue with her. For other opportunities to share work in progress from this book, I thank Juliane Braun and Ben Fagan at the German Historical Institute and Auburn University; Jim Kearney and the Early Modern Center at the University of California, Santa Barbara; Ignacio Lopez-Calvo and Christina Lux at the University of California, Merced's Humanities Center; Andrew Ferris, Sarah Rivett, and Wendy Warren at Princeton University's Early American Seminar; Kate Fullagar at Macquarie University's History Department; Teresa Toulouse at the University of Colorado, Boulder; Hester Blum at Pennsylvania State University's Center for American Literary Studies; the organizers of the "Beyond Sweetness" conference at the John Carter Brown Library; and Becky McLaughlin in the English Department at the University of South Alabama.

Grants from the Provost office at Santa Clara University made many of my research trips possible. In addition, a course release for research provided special assistance in the early stages of this book, as did sabbaticals both early and later in the writing process. The staff of Archives and Special Collections at Santa Clara University's library has been a partner in this project, beginning with its former director Deborah Whiteman. When Deborah brought me our copy of Cook's voyages from the vault, she started a conversation that led to a long and fruitful pedagogical partnership that introduced undergraduates to the archives. That partnership has been continued, enhanced, and expanded by current director Nadia Nasr.

My student research assistant, Nicole Bator, spent many hours scouring early periodical databases for materials about the Pacific, and I am grateful to her and to the Office of the Provost for a grant through the Faculty-Student Research Assistant Program to support this collaboration. I want also to thank the Department of Women's and Gender Studies, the American Studies working group, and the Department of English at Santa Clara University for opportunities to share work in progress from this project. While attempting to finish this book, I spent three years as Chair of the English Department, and I am enormously grateful to my then associate chairs, Terry Beers and Julie Chang, whose sturdy dependability and clear-eyed vision helped keep our leadership stool from tipping over. During those years my writing was also supported by our departmental "Shut Up and Write" group, which met in both virtual and face-to-face formats, and included colleagues Julie Chang, Jackie Hendricks, Maria Judnick, Claudia MacIsaac, Danielle Morgan, Trish Serviss, Robin Tremblay-McGaw, and Julia Voss. Similarly, the campus-wide "Shut Up and Write" group, facilitated by the incomparable Eileen Razarri Elrod, Vice Provost for Faculty Development, has provided many hours of quiet time and space in which to write, balanced with the invigorations of scholarly community (also food).

Outside of that context, Eileen Elrod has read and commented on more than one chapter draft over the years, as have my fellow Americanist colleagues Julie Chang and Juan Velasco. I reserve special thanks to Naomi Andrews, who may have read more of this book in early versions than anyone else, whose feedback has been unfailingly helpful, and whose conversation and friendship have been sustaining. The fact that so many of the people who have supported my research and writing process are also the people who have provided me the most encouragement when that progress has been interrupted or stalled is a testament to my extraordinary good fortune in friends and colleagues.

In 2009, at the conclusion of the Society of Early Americanists' memorable conference in Bermuda, I was graciously offered space in a taxi cab by a fellow conference participant who was likewise on his way to the airport. That companion traveler turned out to be Gordon Hutner, which is how this book ended up in his incredibly able and patient editorial hands. My thanks to Paul Giles and an anonymous reader for Oxford University Press whose incredibly helpful feedback and advice made this book much better than it would have been, to Aimee Wright at OUP for guidance through the final stretch, and to Seemadevi Sekar for copyediting oversight.

For assistance securing digital images and permissions, I thank staff members at the Library of Congress, the American Antiquarian Society, the Wellcome Library, Columbia University Library, Stanford University Library, Santa Clara University Library, Harvard University Archives, the National Library of Australia, the British Museum, the University of Pennsylvania Press, and the Huntington Library. I am grateful to Tanya Chiykowsky-Rathke for creating the maps that appear in the Epilogue. Material from some chapters appeared elsewhere in earlier versions. Some of the content in the Introduction and Epilogue appeared in *Turns of Event: Nineteenth-Century American Studies in Motion*, edited by Hester Blum, and I thank the University of Pennsylvania Press for permission to use that material here. Chapter 1 appeared in an earlier version in *Early American Literature* (Volume 46, no. 3. Copyright © 2011 by the University of North Carolina Press. Used by permission of the publisher. www.uncpress.org). Portions of Chapter 3 are reprinted by permission of the Modern Language Association of America, from *PMLA* 128.4 (2013). Chapter 7 appears here in revised form from its earlier appearance in *Legacy: A Journal of American Women Writers*, published by the University of Nebraska Press.

The genre of academic book acknowledgments traditionally separates institutional support and resources from personal and family ones, often creating the perception that our loved ones patiently tolerate our absences on research trips to distant locations or extended disappearances into campus offices for writing time. My own experience has instead been one of work-life confusion that has been by turns sustaining and complicated, exasperating and fun. My family crossed the North American continent and both oceans with me over the course of four research visits for this book. I am incredibly grateful for the willing division of childcare responsibilities with their father, which made these expeditions in no small part possible. My daughters were aged seven and ten on the first of these expeditions, and fifteen and eighteen on the last. They have kindly tolerated my mathematical failings, accompanied me on dog beach adventures along the Pacific, and permanently revolutionized my world for the better. I dedicate this book to Mara and Jana.

{ CONTENTS }

{ LIST OF FIGURES }

Introduction

TRANSOCEANIC AMERICA

When the ship *America* arrived in the port of New York from Calcutta in 1796, among its crew was a Salem, Massachusetts resident named Nathaniel Hathorne, and among its cargo was a two-year-old elephant from Bengal, India. The elephant was the first of its kind ever to set foot in America. As might be expected, she arrived amidst considerable fanfare and was soon available to view, for the cost of 25 cents, on the corner of Broadway and Beaver Street. In the logbook he kept during the voyage, the ship officer Hathorne did not remark on the unusual animal until they reached St. Helena—an island situated between the continents of South America and Africa, nearly in the middle of the south Atlantic. He recorded then that the *America* picked up a cargo of twenty-three sacks of coffee on the island, as well as food supplies such as pumpkin, cabbages, and fish for the crew. In an additional note titled "ELEPHANT ON BOARD," he mentions that they brought on to the ship "greens for the elephant" who, according to later mythology, had until then been subsisting on beer because she consumed too much of the ship's fresh drinking water.

Hathorne was, of course, the father and namesake of the nineteenth-century author, who would be born eight years after the elephant's arrival. By 1830, Hawthorne Jr. added a "w" to the spelling of his last name, and that name has since become indelibly associated with the town of Salem and its regional New England history. By contrast, Hathorne Sr. was a globetrotter who traveled on numerous long and risky voyages across and between the world's oceans, first to the East Indies and later to the West Indies. He died on one of the latter in 1808—in Suriname, South America, where he succumbed to yellow fever. He left a wife and four children behind in Salem, including Nathaniel Jr., who was four years old at the time. The elephant by that point had traveled on tours throughout the eastern U.S., and went on to outlive her first chronicler by eight years. The son meanwhile spent the years of his youth reading through his father's East India logbooks, where he must have happened upon the elephant anecdote.[1]

Why do we know so much more about the son's imaginary nineteenth-century custom house than we do about the father's very real eighteenth-century import? What if the story of Hathorne the mariner, the island of St. Helena, and the Indian elephant were as familiar to us as the story of Hawthorne the author, the New England town of Salem, and the *Scarlet Letter*? American literature and culture have always been integrated within complex and wide-ranging networks that spanned the entire globe—beginning long before 1796 and continuing ever since. But our most often-repeated stories about America have tended instead toward a surprising geographical insularity as well as narrative linearity. As a result, we are as familiar with the New England town of Salem as we are ignorant of the Atlantic island of St. Helena, and far more aware of Hawthorne's Puritan forebears than of the regular travels to Calcutta and Suriname taken in the eighteenth century by men like his father.

The field of American literary studies was inaugurated in the 1960s with a nar-rative that stitched together the pioneering Harvard University-based work of Perry Miller and F. O. Matthiessen with a thread that ran from Puritan New England in the 1620s and 1630s to transcendentalist New England in the 1850s. That narrative thread maintained its linear consistency by being further fastened to the intervening eighteenth-century events of the Great Awakening and the American Revolution. Scholars of American literature have in many ways thoroughly rewritten this narrative since the 1980s by vastly expanding its geographical reach, recovering non-canonical texts, and complicating its cultural assumptions. Yet it often feels as if the effects of this newer narrative have done little to dislodge that older narrative from the public imagination and the secondary school curricula that reproduce it. Perhaps that is in part because, as Kendall A. Johnson points out, Matthiessen's "erasure of the China trade" persists even in the more recent scholarly revisions of American literary history that otherwise upend and expand the limited narrow-ness of his canon. By bringing attention to China and the East, Johnson aims to reconfigure our assumptions about nineteenth-century American literature begin-ning in about the 1840s.[2]

Transoceanic America: Risk, Writing, and Revolution in the Global Pacific aims to further redress this imbalance by tracing the narrative debt owed by the literary genre of the novel to the explosion in transoceanic global commerce in the age of revolutions. It joins recent efforts by scholars such as Wai Chee Dimock, Lawrence Buell, Paul Giles, Lisa Lowe, Stephen Shapiro, Caroline Levander, and others to build a global account of and approach to American literature.[3] It differs from other such efforts by focusing specifically on oceans, and in particular on the kinds of transoceanic connections between the Pacific and Atlantic that carried shipmen like Hathorne and imports like the elephant between the world's continents. In doing this, I draw on recent Pacific studies and oceanic studies scholarship from a variety of fields, as well as the few but critical scholarly works that have begun to think and read transoceanically.[4] I use the term "transoceanic" throughout this book to refer to connections between oceans, and while many of the voyages con-sidered here did circulate through the Indian Ocean as well as the Atlantic and Pacific, my focus is specifically on connections between the Pacific and Atlantic waters that touch American shores. A transoceanic approach like this one has the advantage of encouraging a materialist focus on the goods and bodies that moved across and between oceans; of engaging with the financial mechanisms that, in making such movement possible, also established the foundations of global capitalism; and of possessing a greater detachment from the geopolitical boundaries of nations and continents in favor of the fluidity of empires and oceans. This aquatic approach to American studies is also something like the geographic equivalent to a photographic negative, producing a shift in perspective that revises the terms and alters the features of what had been a clear and familiar image of the globe and of America's place in it; this approach attempts to reverse what Russell and Stephens describe as the "negative hallucination" brought on by the continental bias that has rendered water and island systems invisible within American studies.[5]

The long spatial reach of *Transoceanic America* is perhaps offset by its more contracted temporal frame. My focus here is on the roughly fifty years between 1770 and 1820, and on the intertwined commercial, political, and literary developments that accompanied the period's explosion in global maritime travel and exploration as a host of scientific and commercial voyages mutually dedicated to discovery and profit forever connected the Pacific to the rest of the world's oceans, including the Atlantic. It's also a period referred to as the "age of revolutions," when political upheavals began to transform and reshape the world and its peoples. One of those revolutions, of course, gave birth to the United States of America, an event whose prominence in nation-centered histories has often determined which texts, writers, and events we include in (and which we silently omit from) our literary and cultural narratives. Seen from the perspective of more than one ocean, however, that event and its Atlantic counterparts begin to take on new meanings and positions within less national and more global narratives. Finally, this is also a period marked by the consolidation of the novel as modernity's foremost literary genre. By entering into American literary and cultural history at this crucial revolutionary juncture point— but doing so from a transoceanic perspective that links the Pacific and Atlantic worlds—I bring unexpected texts and writers into dialogue with more familiar ones, in order to pry apart some of the assumptions that have long held these histories together and to imagine new ways of narrating them that better acknowledge the relationship of the North American landmass (and the various American literatures that emerged from it) to the rest of the globe.

Because the geographical scope of this book is transoceanic and its historical focus is on those transitional decades around the Revolution and Independence, my use of the words "America" and "American" often seem to mean both less and more than they should. There is admittedly a geographical as well as historical lack of distinction to the term as I use it in this book, since it very often crosses the historical and political boundary between colonialism and nationalism, even as it sometimes (but not always) includes a hemispheric awareness of the larger Americas. My use of "American literature" throughout this project is meant to invoke an American literary history that acknowledges and foregrounds rather than resolves or conceals those uncertainties. As Levander notes, the term "American literature" itself "exceeds the neat containers—disciplinary, national, linguistic, and regional—that we and higher educational institutions have developed over the last century to organize, sort, and systematize knowledge."[6] In this sense, the failed coherence of both American literary history and Pacific studies share boundary problems that, I submit, should instead be seen as opportunities for new global approaches to literary and cultural history.

How might we understand the relatively new genre of the novel in relation to other kinds of genres—including those preoccupied with various forms of numerical calculation—that emerged to facilitate transoceanic commerce? What do early American novels look like (and which works even count as early American novels) if we approach them from this new framework? What network of connections— between Salem and Calcutta, St. Helena and New York, Canton and Philadelphia, Hawai'i and Boston—do we begin to see when we read American literature in a maritime global context? And how might those connections alter our traditionally linear narratives of revolutionary change?

America between Oceans

The late eighteenth-century East Indies trade that brought the elephant to New York along with a shipload of global products and sailors was the result of centuries of prior efforts by Europeans to reach Asia and its markets. A transoceanic retelling of American history might begin with an unusual map (see Figure A.1) that

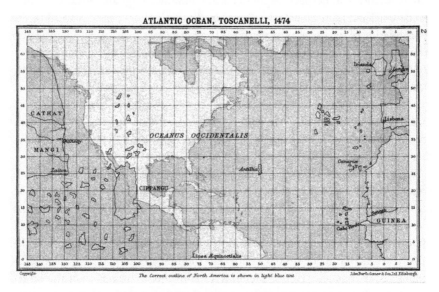

FIGURE A.1. *Transoceanic America. "Atlantic Ocean, Toscanelli, 1474." J. G. Bartholomew,* A Literary and Historical Atlas of North and South America *(London: J. M. Dent, 1911; rev. ed., 1930). Courtesy, Department of Special Collections, Stanford University.*

appeared in J. G. Bartholomew's 1911 *Literary and Historical Atlas of America*.[7] This composite map superimposes a premodern map by Toscanelli onto a modern cartography of the Atlantic world. The earlier 1474 map was drawn, of course, without any knowledge of the existence of the Americas, and the effects of combining pre-Columbian with post-Columbian geography are at once fascinating and disorienting. Narratives of American literature and history like to begin with what was wrong about this older map, and scholars such as Peter Hulme and others have taught us to understand that it was the power of mistaken maps like Toscanelli's that convinced Columbus that Cuba was really Cathay, and that Hispaniola must be Japan.[8] Anecdotes about Columbus's cartographic and continental confusion now usually circulate as humorous early modern warnings about the failure to ask for directions or the humiliating consequences of bad geography. But this perspective only encourages students and scholars alike to ignore what is most revealing about this story—the incredible intensity of Europe's desire to reach Asia, not only in 1492 but also for centuries after. It's as though the East Indies fall off the map as soon as the West Indies appear on it.

The same is true for our narratives of American literature and culture, from which the Eastern hemisphere is likewise absent, especially before the late nineteenth century. It is easy to assume that during an age of sail, the enormous distance between the Americas and Asia meant the two landmasses had little connection to or communication with each other. But seafaring has long connected the world's continents in spite of these distances. Evidence suggests that, even long before Columbus, Polynesian travel was sophisticated and extensive enough to constitute what James Belich describes as a "staggering Neolithic globalization," driven by what Nicholas Thomas describes as "voyages of settlement" that have been misread as "accidental voyages." Mary Louise Pratt meanwhile insists that the Americas have been imaginatively separated from "the Afro-Eurasian world system" only because we have "naturalized" the "geographic integrity of the territory" to which the latter refers.[9] By the time Columbus set off westward across the Atlantic in the late fifteenth century, "Asian productivity and Asian markets...were prime movers" of commodity flows about the globe, and it was precisely the desire to reach those East Indian ports and markets that drove his voyage.[10] Explorers and navigators moreover continued to search for a western water route to the East—even through the obstruction of the North American continent—for centuries afterward. In other words, recognizing the Americas has long meant forgetting Asia, despite the fact that America continued in many ways to be managed, understood, and recorded through Europe's sustained interest in reaching the products and markets of the East. This forgetting of Asia (and of a globally positioned America) happened at the hands of the nation-centered narratives that have dominated our histories. As Gary Okihiro points out, "America's very origins and its subsequent expansion...was the result of a transoceanic and transcontinental journey to India embarked upon by Europeans"—a perspective we lose unless we remember to pay attention to Asia and its peoples.[11]

Transoceanic America adopts a context for American literary studies that takes seriously what may be unintentionally right about Bartholomew's disorientingly liquid map, in which the Atlantic and Pacific oceans appear to compete for exactly the same water as they blend across a continental America that is both in the middle of it all and yet not quite there. This book invokes oceanic connection across and around a half-present continent as a model for reading American literature in materialist global context, an approach that also raises questions about which texts and figures belong to the category of American literature. *Transoceanic America* brings together an unusual assortment of genres made up of travel narratives about the Pacific, mathematical texts and other number-dominated genres, and novels about revolution. All of these circulated during a half-century in which scientific expeditions headed to the Pacific in search of cartographic, botanical, and ethnographic knowledge, followed quickly by commercial voyages in search of Asian and Pacific commodities such as fabrics, teas, and porcelain, or whales, sandalwood, and sea cucumber. Narratives about these expeditions were reprinted and translated, often in abridged or collected book form, and also frequently excerpted and serialized in periodicals. At the same time, travel narratives from earlier centuries and their representations of the Pacific world were made newly available to reading publics around the Atlantic, who were awash in news of the Pacific.

This rich world of eighteenth- and nineteenth-century writing about the Pacific has long drawn the attention of scholars working in English and other European literary and cultural studies but has remained absent from American literary histories, presumably because their authors are for the most part not American.[12] This preoccupation with authors' national identities has meant that American literary studies typically recognize the Pacific only with the arrival of Herman Melville, missing as a result a rich earlier archive of international texts and connections that, ironically, were among his most influential reading material. We have overlooked, as it were, both the elephant and the boat on which it moved. A preoccupation with national identity affects assumptions about geography as well as authorship, and the absence of Melville from this book (along with his well-known contemporaries like Hawthorne) is an intentional effort to correct this imbalance by opening up American literary history to greater transoceanic cultural, commercial, and textual contexts. Histories of American literature have neglected these earlier materials because the period's identification with Atlantic revolutions and nation-building has always distanced and marginalized the Pacific. The centuries-long history of contact between the Americas, Asia, and the transpacific has been especially overlooked, as Kariann Akemi Yokota notes, "during the colonial and post-Revolutionary periods" of American history. For Rosemarie Zagarri, too, the East or the Pacific has been routinely relegated to anecdotal status in "[t]he story of the United States in the period from 1776 to 1860," which focuses instead "on the country's internal developments, problems, and issues."[13]

Even as a recent spate of excellent historical studies of the revolutionary and early national periods have begun to move beyond the eastern seaboard of North America to explore both indigenous and transnational histories in the continent's central and western domains, their geographic scope seldom reaches beyond the eastern Pacific.[14] An important handful of early American literary studies have begun to recognize the Pacific and the East in the work of long-studied authors.[15] But our knowledge of Jefferson's connection to Lewis and Clark's continental journey to the Pacific still vastly exceeds our awareness, for instance, of his earlier involvement with John Ledyard's (ultimately failed) attempt to reach the western U.S. from the other way around—crossing the Pacific by way of Russia. Similarly, we remember Benjamin Franklin's travels to France while forgetting his connection to the Polish-Hungarian count Maurice Benyowsky, who escaped from a Siberian prison into the Pacific and went on to take part in the American Revolution. And we forget, too, that such canonical revolutionary American texts as Thomas Paine's *Common Sense* or Jefferson's "Declaration of Independence" showed up in ports around the Pacific, where they had been carried on ships traveling between and across oceans.

The texts and figures chosen to populate American literary and cultural histories are determined by the narrative plots of those histories. In fact, it is precisely during the revolutionary decades that the storylines of American and European histories diverge because at that moment their plots become fundamentally incompatible with each other. American history focuses on the Revolution and the nation's founding fathers just as European history shifts away from the Atlantic and its North American colonies to the imperial Pacific. As Michael A. McDonnell cogently explains: "[b]etween 1760 and 1820, Europeans swarmed around the globe during a period of dramatic imperial expansion. At the heart of this movement was a 'swing to the east' as European attention and interest moved away from the old Atlantic world and refocused on new prizes and riches in the Indian and Pacific Ocean world," where European empires tried out "lessons learned from imperial projects in the Atlantic" in new regions of the globe.[16] Kathleen Wilson observes that "the period of the American war forced into the English national consciousness the contradictions, inequities, and atrocities perpetuated in the name of national identity and obscured by the fire and fury of imperial expansion." Precisely at the time when British publics began raising serious questions about the role of violence in relation to what C. A. Bayly describes as the empire's "overseas despotisms," an American narrative coalesces around a story invested in celebrating freedom while forgetting the violence of settler colonialism.[17] It's as if the signifying chains holding these independent narratives of European imperialism and American nationalism intact make it impossible to bring their terms together. As a result, we have been prevented from asking what revolutionary nation-building and transoceanic commerce-building might have to do with each other, much less what the two together might have to do with the literary genre of the novel.

Atlantic → Pacific → Transoceanic

The Atlantic world framework that has so powerfully reoriented the field of American studies over the past several decades would seem to have given a new kind of centrality to the ocean. But several scholars have pointed out that the apparently aquatic focus on the Atlantic remains in many ways undermined by a persistent terrestrialism. Despite the shift in categories from nation to ocean, the Atlantic paradigm is sustained by a land-based imaginary in which the ocean figures predominantly as a liquid road that connects solid pieces of land to each other—what Philip E. Steinberg describes as "a space of connection that merely unifies the societies on its borders." The result is too often an Atlantic in which one "never gets wet" or an approach to oceanic studies that, in Kären Wigen's words, "rarely peers beneath the waves."[18] Felipe Fernández-Armesto has used the term "rimlands" to describe this model's reliance on those stretches of "land at the water margin," terrestrial spaces devoid of that "complex, four-dimensional materiality" that Steinberg so evocatively identifies with oceanic space.[19]

If the Atlantic often hasn't been imagined in watery enough terms, the Pacific has usually been accused of being far too watery. By leading scholars to overlook the ocean itself, the rimlands model provides Atlantic studies with a container whose boundaries, however vague, satisfyingly mark the limits of the field. The Pacific, on the other hand, lacks rimlands defined enough even tentatively to hold together the borders of its sprawling liquid world. One of the conventional refrains within Pacific studies has been its supposed lack of coherence caused by the absence or fragmentation of terrestrial edges. As Adam McKeown explains, it has been difficult to "imagine a coherent Pacific world," largely because it is made up of such "vast distances and great diversity of peoples" whose movement moreover frequently reaches far "beyond the borders of the Pacific."[20] The Pacific seems too porous to hold together; everywhere one looks, it overflows.

An additional effect of this rimlands orientation, however, is to disconnect the oceans from each other. That separation appears especially strange as soon as one considers that the movement of water itself is incapable of such distinction: after all, oceanic water only merges, melds, and mixes with more water—with bays and inlets, with rivers, gulfs and seas, but also with other oceans. Perhaps, then, the best way to "restore the ocean to Atlantic history"[21] is to restore the Atlantic itself to its global transoceanic connections. Okihiro reminds us of the maritime tradition of American historical narrative that offered a more global orientation than the agrarian tradition with which it competed, but he also emphasizes the importance of turning this maritime lens toward the Pacific in ways that challenge "the binaries of Old and New World and white and black" in order to position Americans as "equally a continental and an oceanic peoples, both an Atlantic and a Pacific civilization."[22] Even the vast body of scholarship on the slave trade, for example, that has given such crucial shape and force to the Atlantic studies model has been recently invigorated by new work excavating the long history of slavery in and along the

Pacific—including the reach of the Atlantic slave trade into Pacific waters along with the Pacific's own networks of maritime-terrestrial enslavement and exploitation.[23] Etsuko Taketani has unearthed a literary and cultural tradition of "black Pacific narrative" from the early twentieth century when America emerged as a "bioceanic" empire. However, recent studies on the slave trade's Pacific reach by Greg Grandin, Stacey Smith, and Jean Pfaelzer together with work by Matt Matsuda, Kate Fullagar, and David Igler on the early Pacific dramatically extend the history of these material and imaginary interracial alliances within and against empire.[24]

If the Pacific has been missing from studies of the Atlantic world, the Atlantic has also been too little integrated into Pacific literary studies. Historically, scholars have made various attempts to impose imaginary boundaries within the Pacific, often by dividing it into geographical subregions or historical eras, whether characterized by national histories or disciplinary categories. The names for these regions have, as Damon Salesa notes, proliferated: "Oceania, Asia-Pacific, the Pacific Basin, the South Pacific or South Seas...or the Pacific Islands." Others have used national or linguistic categories to differentiate between, say, Spanish, French, British, or American Pacifics. More recently, however, a handful of scholars have embraced and celebrated the Pacific's leaky or amphibian qualities, its lack of distinct boundaries, whether geographical or national. In his groundbreaking and influential work, Epeli Hauʻofa observes that Pacific island peoples have long engaged in a kind of "world enlargement" that makes "nonsense of all national and economic boundaries, borders that have been defined only recently, crisscrossing an ocean that had been boundless for ages before Captain Cook's apotheosis."[25]

Recent interdisciplinary work builds on the insights of Hauʻofa to open up new possibilities for mapping and narrating the Pacific, providing ways as well to reimagine global relations in more oceanic terms. As Salesa insists, "all seas are connected, and there are no neat limits," since everywhere "[i]n the Pacific it was, and is rare for the meeting of land and water to translate into a simple boundary."[26] Matsuda likewise rejects fantasies of an isolated, unified, or empty Pacific for an alternative model of multiple Pacifics that are layered, busy, and in motion. Borrowing Hauʻofa's conception of the Pacific as a "sea of islands" characterized by "a crowded world of transits, intersections, and transformed cultures," Matsuda describes a multitude of Pacific worlds that "are not synonymous with just one declared and defined 'Pacific,' but with multiple seas, cultures, and peoples, and especially the overlapping transits between them."[27] Similarly, many of the compelling stories in the early Pacific—such as the China trade, whaling, or Russian fur trading—"often cross, relocate or fall in the cracks between these bigger categorisations of island, rimland, and trans-Pacific spaces."[28]

Scholars such as Kate Fullagar, Elizabeth DeLoughrey, and Christine Skwiot have meanwhile begun unearthing the transoceanic ligatures by which this Pacific remained in dialogue and contact with its Atlantic counterpart, recognizing how these oceanic histories have intersected with, borrowed from, or responded to each other. DeLoughrey adopts Kaumu Brathwaite's non-linear model of "tidalectics" as "an 'alter/native' historiography to linear models of colonial progress" that resists "the synthesizing telos of Hegel's dialectic by drawing from a cyclical model, invoking the continual movement and rhythm of the ocean."[29] Such a model, she argues, is needed to read transoceanic archives. This is the expansive, multiple, and unruly Pacific that *Transoceanic America* puts into dialogue with the Atlantic during the late eighteenth and early nineteenth centuries.

The Liquidities of War Capitalism

Although the arrival of an elephant in an eighteenth-century North American port was highly unusual, the animal's fascinating novelty differed more in degree than in kind from the teas, spices, fabrics, furniture, carpets, porcelain, and other products that poured from the Indian and/or Pacific oceans into Atlantic ports during this period. Like these other products, the elephant's transportation across thousands of saltwater miles was driven by an interest in profit. Even before Hathorne announced her presence in his shipboard logbook, the elephant appeared in correspondence surrounded by the mundane language of numbers. Jacob Crowninshield, captain of the *America*, wrote to his brothers (who were also running ships to India on behalf of the family's Salem-based shipping company) that "We take home a fine young elephant two years old, at $450.00. It is almost as large as a very large ox, and I dare say we shall get it home safe, if so it will bring at least $5000.00." Crowninshield's anticipated profit margin of over 1100 percent turned out to be an underestimate, as records indicate that the elephant sold for an astonishing $10,000.[30]

In this respect, the story of the elephant is little different from that of the sacks of coffee and tea or crates of porcelain and other household goods that were carried and counted, and whose value was calculated as they moved across oceans on ships whose crewmembers endured voyages that lasted many years. Global commerce took place amidst tremendous risks—as Hathorne Sr.'s demise indicates—experienced across vast oceanic distances and prolonged periods of time that were managed through a host of numerical calculations: navigational, financial, meteorological, temporal, hydrographic, actuarial. Such calculations were designed to make it increasingly possible to reduce the risks of transoceanic travel and commerce necessary to achieve the pleasures and rewards of profit. While travel narratives and maritime logbooks tended already to be number-laden genres, there were also numerous print industries dedicated to instructing a remarkable range of readers—from sailors and merchants to schoolchildren and housewives—in how to make sense of and manipulate numbers. The numerical pedagogies in genres such as mercantile manuals, mathematical textbooks, and insurance handbooks play a perhaps surprising role in this book, which is after all largely concerned with the literary genre of the novel.

Margaret Cohen has recently made a stirring case for the novel's maritime origins, locating the genre's deep roots in the dangers and crafty problem-solving that attended sea travel.[31] Yet the presence of numerical record-keeping in the annals of maritime travel has gone largely unaccounted for in proportion to its narrative record-keeping. Even though numbers themselves tend to be absent from novels, their calculative residue is, I maintain, the very stuff that differentiates novelistic from other kinds of narrative. The especially long distances and durations of transoceanic voyages only heightened the strangely paradoxical status of numbers, which performed routine and mundane calculations on the one hand while producing anxious and exhilarating speculations on the other. That strangely affective alliance of boredom and anticipation, of the ordinary with the unexpected, is precisely what characterizes novels and their narratives of protracted suspense. And that alliance is created by numbers in the service of a capitalism that has always been global.

In his book *Empire of Cotton: A Global History*, Sven Beckert gives the name "war capitalism" to nineteenth-century industrial capitalism's predecessor, and he does so in order to foreground the centrality of violence, both private and state-sanctioned, to its practices. That violence made the expansion of global capitalism possible at the hands of European empires that navigated oceans in pursuit of commodities, markets, and labor. War capitalism was ignited by transoceanic access, made possible by the maritime achievements of Columbus's 1492 Atlantic voyage and Vasco da Gama's 1497 voyage into the Indian Ocean. The effects of these two voyages "fed on one another" as the gold and silver raided from Mexico, Peru, and Brazil were used to purchase highly desirable Asian products; as Beckert puts it, "domination in Asia dovetailed with expansion into the Americas." By beginning his narrative with the British East India Company and its "wave of expropriation of labor and land" rather than with John Locke's celebration of property rights, Beckert locates what he calls "capitalism's illiberal origins" in a "joint venture of private capital and increasingly robust states."[32] Although Beckert's focus does not often reach the Pacific, the Pacific fits neatly into his model. Bernard Smith has pointed out, after all, that Captain James Cook was "Adam Smith's first and perhaps greatest global agent," for he offered the inhabitants of the Pacific the choice "between exploitation and extermination."[33]

Beckert's insights correspond with those of Lisa Lowe, who brings British archives about Asia to bear on American and Atlantic histories of slavery and race in her global study, *The Intimacies of Four Continents*. Lowe too identifies a narrative whose fifteenth-century beginnings in the so-called "discovery" of the "new world" culminate in the late eighteenth and early nineteenth centuries, when modern liberalism is put in the service of gaining access to and controlling global resources and markets.[34] For Lowe as for Beckert, violence is a central feature of the world of intercontinental intimacy that emerges over those ensuing three centuries. Both scholars emphasize as well the accompaniment of physical force by the coercion of bureaucratization, which took the form of rules and regulations—and also of numbers. For Beckert "the invention of financial instruments" combined with "the muscle of armed trade," just as for Lowe a newer "economic rationality" coexisted with rather than replaced an older mode of "colonial conquest."[35]

These strategies played out across oceans as much as they did on land; as Margaret Cohen insists, "saltwater transport networks…functioned as the circuitry of global capitalism and European imperialism."[36] War capitalism possessed in this sense dual liquid components: a physical movement across oceanic water that also demanded financial liquidity. By relying on numbers to span oceans in pursuit of goods, the liquidities of war capitalism lengthened but also (somewhat paradoxically) tightened temporality, producing a calculus of risk which offset the dilemmas of short-term losses by positioning them within the dynamics of long-term profit. This is the transoceanic bath in which the intertwined institutions of capitalism, revolution, and the novel were cultured. Buried in the novel form is therefore something close to a "business sublime" whose excitements and agonies are—no less than Wall Street activity is today—suspended on financial tools and mathematical formulas too intricate, confusing, and boring for most of the public even to recognize, much less understand. But those tools and formulas also configure relationships between humans in ways that make exploitation and violence surprisingly easy to overlook, or even accept, under the conditions of narrative expectation.

The violence of war capitalism played out in fields and factories throughout the Atlantic world, but also on shipboards, on coastlines and islands, and at trading posts in the Pacific world—where it most often left its mark on the bodies of indigenous peoples, sailors, and women as they assisted or obstructed the profitable movement and exchange of goods. The attention paid to women throughout the chapters of this book may seem out of proportion to their actual presence in the early Pacific and the writings that document ventures to and encounters in the region. After all, we are frequently reminded that ships were the province of men, spaces that explicitly banned the presence of women. But as Patty O'Brien has convincingly argued, because "indigenous women were at the forefront of contact" in the Pacific, they were "also at the forefront of negotiating with colonizers and their expectations."[37] Enmeshed everywhere in episodes of material exchange for goods and for sex, indigenous women were subject to frequent and often devastating violence, even as they appeared in European accounts of the Pacific in much more mythic and idealized forms. And despite the fact that European or American women weren't (with a few unusual exceptions) aboard these visiting ships, they were directly affected by their voyages. As the situation of Elizabeth Manning Hathorne makes abundantly clear—the widowed mother left behind in Salem, after the death of her husband Nathaniel in Suriname, to care for four Hathorne children—the results of these voyages always traveled home to women whether their husbands (or brothers or sons) returned or not. Indeed, it was in part for such reasons that women were often encouraged to learn the accounting and calculation skills taught by mathematical textbooks and accounting manuals. Because women and their bodies are frequently at the center of simultaneously violent and profitable encounters in the Pacific, both as objects and as causes, their presence provides a crucial counterpoint to the disembodiment associated with numbers and calculations, helping to expose the role those numbers play in global war capitalism.

Transoceanic America argues that, by failing to look beyond the more conventional maps and narratives of the revolutionary period, we have overlooked the East and the Pacific, as well as the violence concealed by the calculus of risk that enabled ships from Europe and America to get to those distant locations. This book therefore addresses the politics of narrative time within global capitalism by first shifting dominant assumptions about geographical space during the age of revolutions. In doing so, it contributes to recent work on the intersection of commerce, finance, and literary form in the long eighteenth century.[38] The narrative form of the novel is a product of this transoceanic world of global commerce and its dynamic calculus of risk, which drives the genre's anxiously coiled narratives of anticipation—whether or not those novels had any overt concern with the Pacific or even the maritime world.

Lines → Circles → Spirals

Perhaps the two most popular after-images of the Pacific left behind by voyage narratives were those of economic bonanza and sexual license (as if the region were the Las Vegas of the late eighteenth century, with Polynesian islands standing in for brothels and Cantonese trading factories serving as the equivalent of slot machines). At least since Bougainville's account of Tahiti, Polynesia became associated with easy access to sexual partners and with a remarkably open expression of sexuality. The 1774 New York edition of John Hawkesworth's narrative of Cook's first voyage, for example, opens with a fold-out illustration of a "Dramatic Interlude & Dance given by the Indians of Ulietea, performed by two Women and six Men with three Drums." The engraving—produced by soon-to-be Patriot Paul Revere for an edition published by Loyalist printer John Rivington—represents two topless Native women dancing in grass skirts before eight observing men in robes on the left, while other men play instruments on the right.[39] Enticing accounts of sexual license and economic windfall by those on these voyages are often disassociated from the scientific data collected by them. We foreground and celebrate that data whenever we refer to these as voyages of "discovery" engaged in the reputedly disinterested search of new knowledge. In practice, however, it was impossible to disconnect these commercial, sexual, and scientific engagements from each other. Indeed, the Pacific simultaneously developed a reputation as a place of extraordinary violence, a site where, as fur trade historian James R. Fichter puts it, "American and Native leaders both acted with appalling brutality for profit," where a spiraling dynamic of violence, distrust, and retribution led to a cycle of massacres and killings.[40] The political, commercial, and sexual exchanges initiated by these voyages produced considerable damage—cultural, demographic, ecological, and corporeal—along with the pleasures of profit and sex.

It is perhaps these unavoidable encounters with damage, disaster, and misery in the transoceanic Pacific that have made it difficult to invest its histories with the kind of narrative continuity and linearity that has characterized Atlantic histories. Balboa's 1513 sighting and naming of the "South Sea" has never launched a story about the Pacific in the way that Columbus's 1492 Caribbean landing has for the Atlantic, in part because Europeans had such trouble, and for so long, in navigating and making sense of the Pacific. Even Magellan's 1521 Pacific crossing couldn't generate the kind of imperial momentum and European triumphalism that characterized accounts of Columbus's Atlantic crossing. Joyce Chaplin notes that well until the later eighteenth century, the Pacific exerted a kind of "constant, fatal erosion of European mariners and their ships." That made it far harder in the Pacific to hide the sensations of misery and experiences of loss that, as Kathleen Donegan has recently argued, were also characteristic of so many of Europe's first experiences in an Atlantic North America.[41] The unavoidable confrontation with disaster and failure in the transoceanic context of the revolutionary era has the advantage of exposing the dependence of linear narrative's pleasurable expectation on often-repressed episodes of cyclical violence.[42]

Jorge Cañizares-Esguerra chides U.S. historical narratives for their "annoyingly optimistic narratives of 'American exceptionalism'" and calls for "a balance between the patriotic excesses that characterize the historiography of the North and the tragic visions that dominate the historiography of the South" by finding "stories of both misery and redemption throughout the Western Hemisphere."[43] *Transoceanic America* pursues such a narrative rebalance by insisting on a transoceanic rather than Atlantic or hemispheric perspective. The eighteenth-century phenomena of capitalism, revolution, and the novel are all animated by a subtle narrative pairing of damage with pleasure, of violence with profit. *Transoceanic America* asks that we position these three modern developments within a specifically maritime globalism whose extraordinary temporal and spatial distances promoted a new narrative dynamics of expectation that took shape in the context of a calculus of risk, where the expectation of future profits buried the pain of present losses.

Scholars working on the Pacific and the transoceanic seem to agree that new narrative models are needed to tell these stories. Matsuda's embrace of the Pacific's aquatic geography, for instance, calls for another kind of temporality as well, one defined less by a linear and progressive trajectory held together by the solidity of land and more by an episodic assemblage whose pieces are connected through multiple trans-local ties and movements. Salesa similarly outlines an alternative genealogy for the Pacific derived from indigenous notions of space and time that understand archipelagic polities as "a kaleidoscopic weave of maritime places, constantly being made and unmade ... like a moving and changing map, like the ocean itself." This geography drives Hau'ofa's embrace of the non-linear temporalities of traditional peoples as well, which produce narratives in which memories of the past, for example, sometimes appear up ahead in the future.[44] A special issue of the *Pacific Historical Review* on transpacific history likewise insists on the "messiness of the transpacific" and on the "multidirectional, multilayered, and multisited" stories emerging from such a mobile and layered space.[45]

A transoceanic spatial framework invites a more cyclical temporal framework to replace the conventionally linear and progressive narratives of American history. These tell stories that are satisfying both in their continuity (in unifying themes, for example, of American independence or freedom) and in their logic of improvement or advance, of progress made over time. But these very narrative structures are, in fact, the products of global war capitalism and the transoceanic space on which it was carried out. Paul Carter, in his remarkable history of Australia, offers a spatial alternative to the traditional temporal mode of historical narrative. He points out that the latter, linear approach, which "pays attention to events unfolding in time alone, might be called imperial history" and its primary purpose "is not to understand or to interpret: it is to legitimate." It moreover performs that legitimation through a "logic of cause and effect" whose chronology satisfyingly narrates "the emergence of order from chaos." Carter proposes instead a spatial history that takes the "form of non-linear writing" in order to be able to "explore the lacuna left by imperial history."[46]

Some literary historians have made similar appeals for anti-linear approaches, especially in our efforts to narrate global literary histories. Stephen Shapiro, for instance, has advanced the possibilities of a cyclical literary history attuned to the long waves of global capital that would allow us to recognize alignments and shared features among texts from otherwise very different historical periods or geographical areas. Geraldine Heng has argued that a globally reinvigorated literary history will require us to "not see historical time as a linear progression from premodernity to modernity fissured by a break, but instead view history as offering repetitions with change."[47] *Transoceanic America* similarly finds an alternative to traditional narrative linearity in the temporality of rotation—the micro-cycles or spirals, if you will—that so often characterized episodes of transoceanic commercial, political, and literary development in the revolutionary age. The enlivening anticipation or dread with which we tend to read novels (or with which we respond to financial investments, or to efforts at radical political change) are themselves the products of episodic cycles or spirals of violence and victory, pain and pleasure, exploitation and excitement. I read novels about revolution in this book in ways that expose these non-linear narrative features, features that are made legible through the context of war capitalism's transoceanic dimensions.

The Voyage Ahead

Part I of *Transoceanic America*, "Connecting the Pacific and the Atlantic," consists of three chapters that establish the textual, commercial, and political ties between the two oceans during the age of revolutions. I consider the relationship between narrative and numbers, both in the genre of Pacific travel writing and in various numerical genres—including mathematics, bookkeeping, navigation, and insurance—that feature a global, transoceanic scope. I locate in these genres a new narrative temporality that animates financial, political, and novelistic narrative during this period. That narrative temporality suspends a linear and progressive plot across episodes of cyclical violence that result from the movement of goods (such as fur, silk, and silver) and bodies (especially women, the indigenous, and sailors) within a transoceanic and transnational geography. The chapters in Part I establish the ways in which these non-fiction genres helped to connect the Atlantic and Pacific for readers during the revolutionary age as part of a larger world of global traffic. They also establish how calculations across transoceanic time and space contributed to a narrative dynamics of risk and promise that informed revolutionary plots, novelistic plots, and financial plotting.

Chapter 1, "Narrative: Trade and Time in Early Pacific Travel Writing," engages with a transnational archive of popular Pacific travel narratives published during the late eighteenth and early nineteenth centuries. The accounts of these long-distance voyages embed the pleasures of speedy expectation—whether of geographical discovery, cultural encounter, or commercial profit—within an otherwise dreary prolongation, for these texts record in considerable detail multi-year expeditions that navigated vast oceanic spaces. The result is a narrative dynamic of expectation that works to mask or minimize the violent transoceanic movement of goods and bodies accompanying these voyages' profitable returns. This logic of calculation, I propose, relies on a new understanding of numbers and risk that might be thought of as prolonged promise, one shared by the new genre of the novel.

The violent short-term losses that attended risky transoceanic commerce were masked but also abetted by the interrelated long-term logics of calculation and speculation. Chapter 2 considers more carefully the role played by numbers in the production of this narrative expectation. "Numbers: Calculation and Speculation in the Eighteenth-Century Novel" turns to several numerical genres from the period—including mathematical textbooks, accounting manuals, and insurance handbooks—that place both male and female readers in a global, transoceanic world of goods and exchanges. These genres taught strategies of calculation as a response to risk, but they also worked together with genres of speculation like the lottery handbill to produce narrative and financial anticipation. These largely prose-devoid texts are actually filled full of plot: they might be said to "calculize" narrative by putting numbers in the service of storytelling. And they are surprisingly, even astonishingly, global in orientation. This pedagogy of calculation, in which urgency and prolongation offset each other in a coiled tension, also drove the suspenseful narratives of novels. Because novel plots and novel reading shared with mathematical genres strategies for determining promise and risk, they provided an affective training ground for managing prediction and disappointment as well as for calculating probability and danger.

Pacific travel writing from the period also offered constant reminders, however, that the blithe disembodiment of numerical calculation and speculation usually obscured the violent embodiment of exploitation and desire.[48] Chapter 3, "Politics: Violence and Gender in the Revolutionary Pacific," returns to a close reading of Pacific travel narratives to identify in them a remarkable yet overlooked record of uprisings and rebellions—especially by indigenous peoples in response to European arrival, but also by shipbound sailors. These Pacific events have remained well outside even the most global accounts of the revolutionary age, partly because they do not observe the narrative expectations associated with the political category of revolution. This chapter uncovers a Pacific counterpart to the revolutionary Atlantic and argues for a more transoceanic emplotment for revolution, one whose narrative is less linear than episodic and one that is held together by anti-imperialist insurrection rather than by nation formation. Acknowledging the terms of this revolutionary Pacific revises our narratives of the revolutionary Atlantic, while politically connecting the two oceans in the long and wide encounter between European empires and indigenous peoples around the globe. It also foregrounds the bodies of women as embodied sites through which to locate the violent effects of war capitalism and its relationship to commercial calculation and revolutionary politics. As scholars including Patty O'Brien, Kathleen Wilson, and Margaret Jolly have observed, episodes of violence in the Pacific often collect around the paired appearance of women and goods, around sexual and commercial exchange—sparking anti-imperial responses within what amount to rotating cycles of brutality.

Together, these three chapters establish the literary, commercial, and political connections between the Pacific and Atlantic worlds during the revolutionary age, thus establishing a transoceanic context for reading novels from the period, whether those novels directly concern the sea or not. Part II of *Transoceanic America*, "Reading Novels across Oceans," brings that context to bear on four novels about revolution published during the thirty-year period between 1778 and 1808. One of these fictional texts is explicitly set in the Pacific while the others take place in the Atlantic and/or Caribbean. But their tales of revolutionary societies—in the imaginary Pacific colony of Armoseria, and the real Atlantic locations of Philadelphia, Jamaica, and Haiti—are all made legible in new ways by reading them within the intertwined commercial, political, and literary contexts that connect the Pacific with the Atlantic. Each of these locations is characterized by spectacles of excess whose local performance depends on transoceanic mercantile and maritime networks. Reading these novels in a transoceanic context helps to reveal a late eighteenth- and early nineteenth-century imperial culture of pleasurable consumption that concealed its own dependence on global relations of exploitative violence. In her study of the sea novel, Cohen notes the absence of maritime novels from this period and suggests that this curious gap must have been filled instead by the kinds of non-fiction travel narratives I engage with in Chapter 1. But I'm interested in the ways in which novels from this period—whether or not the ocean and sea travel are part of their content—are formally plotted precisely on the developments in narrative temporality that occupy their non-fiction counterparts. While driven by apparently linear plots that draw readers anxiously along toward uncertain futures, these novels also contain explicit engagement with non-linear cyclical plots and narrative structures. In fact, all of these novels might be seen to return revolution to its older, astronomical definition of rotation rather than its more familiar association with a dramatic linear break and change. My titles for the four chapters in Part II—circles, coils, cycles, and circuits—emphasize these non-linear narrative engagements with rotation and repetition.

Chapter 4, "Circles: Seduction and Revolution in *The Travels of Hildebrand Bowman*," recovers and reads this long-forgotten pseudonymous novel, published in 1778, in the context of the global marketplace, transoceanic empire, and political revolution. Ostensibly an account by a sailor left behind in New Zealand on Cook's second voyage, Bowman's *Travels* allegorizes the American Revolution by relocating it in the south Pacific and associating it with indigenous anti-colonial uprisings against Europeans, especially the Grass Cove massacre by the Maori. The novel positions revolution as a response to a transoceanic world of excess and inequality, and represents seduction as one of many damaging forms of global consumption. In Bowman's *Travels*, as in so many novels of the period, women's bodies mediate global and economic (and not just national or sexual) anxieties, while anti-imperial revolt is placed in a global commercial rather than a national political context. As its protagonist circles the aquatic globe, the novel also satirically turns eighteenth-century narratives of human development from a line into a circle, exposing stories of human progress as illusions that conceal painful repetitions.

Women's bodies also expose the violence of global revolution and transoceanic commerce in Charles Brockden Brown's *Ormond; or the Secret Witness*. Chapter 5, "Coils: Financial Speculation and Global Revolution in Charles Brockden Brown's *Ormond*," establishes the political and economic contexts for the far-flung geographical references that have largely been overlooked in Brown's 1799 novel. The novel is set in Philadelphia when it was the U.S. hub of commerce to the East Indies and populated by merchants whose extravagant wealth was acquired by investing in risky Pacific trade and shipping ventures. Brown's villain Ormond is based on such contemporary merchants and transoceanic travelers, including the controversial international revolutionary Count Maurice Benyowsky, who was associated with economic speculation, political revolution, and sexual seduction in the Pacific. Brown's tightly coiled narrative spirals forward seemingly to nowhere, maintaining an exhausting tension between urgency and deferral. As it does so, his plot points toward the ways in which transoceanic commerce and its pursuit of profits and pleasures exacts violent costs on the bodies of the laboring poor and women, both in the U.S. and in the Asiatic East.

Commodities such as furs, porcelain, and silk often dominate histories of Atlantic merchants in the early Pacific. Chapter 6, however, turns to the surprisingly competitive transoceanic trade in plants, pursued as lucrative medicines, foods, and ornamental luxuries. I read William Earle's 1800 novel *Obi*, set during a slave uprising in British Jamaica, in the context of transoceanic botanical transplantation. "Cycles: Atlantic Slavery and Pacific Botany in William Earle's *Obi*" focuses on the novel's representation of plants and plantations during a historical moment in which botanists, merchants, and ship captains regularly profited from the transportation of seeds and plants between the Pacific and Atlantic oceans. William Bligh, for instance, finally delivered breadfruit trees from Tahiti to Jamaica in the wake of the mutinous rebellion against him in the Pacific. I situate the novel's anti-slavery critique alongside political and natural histories of Jamaica, the botanical-revolutionary poetry of Erasmus Darwin, and the voyages of Bligh and others. Darwin aligns the political cyclicality of revolution with the ecology of the natural world, identifying revolution as the political expression of the earth's organic and economic imbalance. Earle similarly positions Atlantic slavery and the plantation system as violent practices of transplantation disguised as benevolent commerce, a destructive cycle his novel exposes.

Chapter 7 turns to another novel set in the West Indies and written in a period when Atlantic trade routes were being aggressively extended through exploration and commerce into the Pacific. Leonora Sansay's 1808 *Secret History; or the Horrors of St. Domingo* is set in post-revolutionary Haiti. Like *The Adventures of Hildebrand Bowman* thirty years earlier, Sansay's novel attends to figures of consumption and cannibalism that evoke the space of the Pacific in a lucrative, exotic, and obscene world of capitalist appetite. "Circuits: Female Bodies and Capitalist Drive in Leonora Sansay's *Secret History*" establishes the interwoven forms of political, economic, and domestic violence in the novel, paying particular attention to the ways in which bodies of women expose the implication of short-term desires within a long-term system of global capitalist drive whose relentless circuits generate violence and inequality. In Sansay's Saint Domingue, these circuits produce both revolutionaries and coquettes, risk-taking figures who turn against those who helped bring them into being. Compared to the other novels examined here, the Pacific is least explicitly present in the plot and text of *Secret History*, but this novel is perhaps most explicitly aware of the ways in which circuits of desire are caught up in circuits of commerce and profit that, by 1808, are inescapably transoceanic and tragically destructive.

Early America was regularly infused by peoples and objects from the Pacific. It was, after all, Chinese tea that got thrown into Boston harbor, while products from Asian markets were in the homes of many elite North American colonists and printed accounts of the Pacific regularly circulated among a more diverse audience in American books and periodicals. The Pacific and its peoples were central to the increasingly interconnected late eighteenth-century globe, when the Pacific and the Atlantic were tied together in a variety of critical, and surprisingly intimate, ways. *Transoceanic America* asks how our understanding of America and our narratives about it change once we expand our view of American literary and cultural history to include, from the very beginning, not just the terrestrial continent or hemisphere but the aqueous globe. It pursues answers to those questions by adopting a transoceanic approach to the revolutionary period rather than an American-centered approach to the early Pacific. That decision has resulted in an uneasy kind of commitment to and alliance with the interdisciplinary field of American studies. Starting with oceans and empires rather than with continents and nations has led me at times into close proximity to those spaces and peoples we traditionally define as or associate with early America and Americans; at other times this navigational decision has left me at what feels a great distance from these recognizable landmarks.

Transoceanic America offers a paradigm for American literary and cultural studies in which the Atlantic and Pacific Oceans are recognized as a vast and intertwined waterworld characterized by networks of ongoing commercial, political, and textual ties. As historian Peter Coclanis observes, the "degree of separation between the 'Atlantic World' and the rest of the world is chronically overstated"; in a recent interview titled "Are We All Global Historians Now?," David Armitage specifies that "one of the futures of Atlantic history is precisely joining it to other oceanic and trans-regional histories" in order to "think about the interrelations between these oceanic arenas and how in some sense they add up to a global or proto-global history."[49] Such transoceanic reorientations may allow us to approach Okihiro's view of the U.S. "not only as a center with its own integrity but also as a periphery and fluid space of movements and engagements that resist closure and inevitable outcomes."[50] My Epilogue, "Towards a Transoceanic American Literary History," returns to the question about how we narrate American literary history with which this Introduction opens, and suggests ways in which episodic and cyclical forms might better serve us than the linear and progressive ones with which we are familiar. We can take recent scholarship on the Pacific as an exemplary starting point here. Matsuda has argued that the Pacific must be understood not as a unified entity but through "particularities," and we might aim at a literary history that tells particular transoceanic episodes within a global literary history whose form refuses to take the shape of a coherent whole or neatly to conform to a straight narrative linearity. I advocate for a global American literary history oriented toward archival exploration rather than textual accumulation. Like the oceanic histories described by Hau'ofa, each of the chapters in this book tracks interconnections between regions and disciplines, and follows movements between land and sea. Like water itself, these chapters take on form and shape as a result of the texts with which they engage, even when those texts concern non-maritime material. These readings locate the presence of the Pacific in the Atlantic, and of the Atlantic in the Pacific, and in doing so establish a global materiality to narrative in the transoceanic age of revolutions.

PART I

Connecting the Pacific and the Atlantic

Narrative

TRADE AND TIME IN EARLY PACIFIC
TRAVEL WRITING

In his 2001 novel, *American Gods*, Neil Gaiman regularly interrupts the central plot to imaginatively recreate distant moments in the long historical past of the American continent. One of these interludes, titled "Coming to America: 1778," abruptly takes readers from the present-day Pacific coast city of San Francisco to the Atlantic world of the eighteenth century to tell the story of African twins who are sold into slavery by their uncle. Wututu and her twin brother Agasu survive the Middle Passage only to be sold in slave markets in the Americas, where they are separated from each other and then sold and renamed by new owners several times over, each of them subjected to repeated violence. The story follows the pair from their entrance into slavery in 1778, when the American Revolution would have been in its third year, until Agasu's death in 1802, two years before the end of the Haitian Revolution. Over the intervening years Agasu is sold to work on a sugar plantation in St. Domingue, where despite having lost one arm to a spider bite, he helps to plan and fight in the colony's 1791 slave revolution. His sister is by then a slave in a New Orleans home and a healer who has one withered arm. The connection between the two is sustained through Africa and the god Elegba, and when Agasu dies, Wututu feels his death in her own body.

Gaiman precedes this story with a reflection on the relationship between numbers, narrative, and empathy. "We need individual stories," he remarks, for "[w]ithout individuals we see only numbers: a thousand dead, a hundred thousand dead, 'casualties may rise to a million.' With individual stories, the statistics become people." Detailed narrative, he suggests, humanizes the abstraction of numbers, as readers confront and grapple with the violent transatlantic history of slavery, for example, through the story of Wututu and Agasu. But he quickly pauses to note that narrative's power is also always limited, indeed fundamentally insufficient, for even when narrative turns some numbers into individuals, "the people continue to suffer in numbers that themselves are numbing and meaningless." The suggestion is that despite its power, fiction is never powerful enough to change the conditions of suffering it describes, and that its effect on readers remains temporary at best. "Fiction allows us to slide into these other heads, these other places, and look out through other eyes," Gaiman remarks, but despite our sense of connection to these others, readers always "stop before we die, or we die vicariously and unharmed, and in the world beyond the tale we turn the page or close the book, and we resume our lives." We retreat onto a kind of island where we remain insulated from these other, more painful lives, lives which fiction has coated for us with "a smooth, safe, nacreous layer" that allows them to "slip, pearl-like, from our souls without real pain." Readers of fiction are, for Gaiman, oysters who process nasty particles of grit and disgorge them as pearls.[1]

One of the arguments of *Transoceanic America* is that when fiction—particularly in its long form of the novel—processes suffering through narrative storytelling, as Gaiman describes in the preceding paragraph, it does so not despite numbers or in opposition to them, but rather in concealed collaboration with them. It also suggests that the development and dynamics of this relationship between narrative suspense and numerical speculation, between words and numbers, might be tracked through the transoceanic connections between the Atlantic and Pacific oceans during the late eighteenth century—a period when ships moved with increasing regularity between the world's oceans and when novels came to dominate the literary world of fiction. That maritime global movement was facilitated by numerical calculations that unsuspectedly animate the narratives describing those long voyages. Readers around the Atlantic—including merchant investors and would-be mariners, but also the public at large—absorbed these popular narratives about the Pacific world, processing their grit into pearls much like Gaiman's metaphorical oysters. This chapter begins to explore and untangle the narrative mechanisms by which this engaging and unsettling process works, mechanisms that emerged as a way to manage the risk entailed by sailing between the world's oceans.

When we imagine late eighteenth-century America today, however, we almost never imagine the Pacific, which has arrived rather late, and somewhat slowly, to the study of early America. In a 2005 *Common-place* issue focused on early America and the Pacific, historians Edward Gray and Alan Taylor advocate adopting for the Pacific something like the Atlantic studies paradigm which moves "beyond nations and states as the defining subjects of historical understanding, turning instead to large scale processes" that might account for the effects of "disease, migration, trade, and war" in the Pacific as well as in the Atlantic. David Igler similarly insists that, like the Atlantic, the early Pacific was "international before it became national" and bemoans the fact that most scholarship on the Pacific to date has instead relied on a national framework, leaving "too little of this work ... cast in a comparative, transnational, or transoceanic mold."[2] Igler's transoceanic invitation urges a global maritime approach that moves beyond the exchanges and processes *within* each of these oceans to consider the connections *between* them as well. This chapter examines late eighteenth- and early nineteenth-century Pacific travel writing as the dominant print product of precisely such a transoceanic context, and it does so by taking into account Margaret Cohen's reminder that "cross-ocean travel" constituted "the theater of global capitalism,"[3] a liquid stage that was filled with both risks and rewards.

The first European to see and describe the Pacific was Vasco Núñez de Balboa, who arrived on foot in 1513 with Native American guides.[4] But it wasn't until several years later, in 1519, that Magellan's navigational feat of rounding Cape Horn at the tip of South America opened up European access to the Pacific in unprecedented ways. These competing starting points offer a good reminder that land-based narratives seldom serve Pacific history well. They are also an important reminder that for centuries the Pacific was, for Europe and for European America, invariably connected to the world's other oceans. The desire to gain access to Asian markets and products drove the earliest European voyages into the Pacific, where they arrived motivated to locate the so-called Northwest Passage that was believed to connect the Atlantic with the Pacific through a series of waterways in the upper reaches of the North American continent. Pacific coast entrances to such a passage were reported by Juan de Fuca and Bartholomew de Fonte and were eagerly sought after—with varying degrees of eagerness and skepticism—by explorers from Martin Frobisher and Francis Drake to James Cook and George Vancouver.[5] The myth of the Northwest Passage endured despite growing evidence against its existence because its discovery would have provided European ships with a quicker and less contested route to Asia and its desirable trade goods.

Such a passage was of course never found, but the many voyages that set out either to prove or disprove its existence did in fact end up connecting the two oceans—not through the simple geography of a Northwest Passage, but through the complicated commercial, political, and textual networks these efforts established. Published accounts of these voyages represent a fascinating and substantial transnational archive that as yet has barely been touched by early American literary scholars.[6] I am not interested in making any claims about the "Americanness" of these texts. Although a small proportion of them were written by men who could be identified as American, the national identity of their authors is one of the least revealing features of these narratives. Privileging that identity has moreover had a tendency to obscure the participation of these texts in a transnational and multi-linguistic dialogue carried out in part through translation and reprint practices. I want to insist that the study of American literature and culture needs to engage with early transnational Pacific travel texts in the same way that it has with early transnational Atlantic texts—not because they should be considered in any special way American but because the transoceanic imagination in these narratives provides an indispensable global context for understanding the literature and culture of the period. In fact, the transoceanic and intercontinental sweep of this early Pacific material offers one way to bring the two models of transatlantic and hemispheric early American studies into greater dialogue with each other in a global framework.[7] While even earlier Pacific travel accounts warrant consideration in their own right, I pay particular attention to those that appeared in the revolutionary period spanning the late eighteenth and early nineteenth centuries—an era whose literary and cultural history has never been asked to accommodate the pressures of this particular transoceanic archive, and whose traditional focus on nation formation has in fact made it especially resistant to such material. Overcoming such resistance, however, allows us to consider the unexpected global context for the literary genre of the novel (a line of inquiry I develop in Chapter 2) and for the politics of revolution (the focus of Chapter 3).

The current chapter begins with a brief transnational survey of Pacific travel writing between approximately 1760 and 1820, a period of international competition for scientific discovery and commercial profit that provided the impetus for these voyages and the publication of narratives about them. I pay particular attention to the subgenre of the state-sponsored Pacific travel narrative, including the dynamics of trade and time embedded within its textual and narratological features. Time and trade are crucially contingent on each other in this context because the often enormous returns of profit and knowledge from these voyages were only made possible by their lengthy duration. It took anywhere from three to six years to travel through the Atlantic, past Cape Horn, and across and around the Pacific on voyages seeking new lands, resources, and trade goods. It took just as long or longer on routes that passed the Cape of Good Hope and traveled through the Indian Ocean to reach and explore the Pacific. As a result, the sense of expectation and anticipation generated by these voyages and texts depended on considerable patience and prolongation. But that temporal prolongation also worked to mask or minimize the violence that accompanied such returns, including the violent trans-oceanic movement of desirable goods (such as fur, silk, and silver—the pursuit of which drove many of these voyages) and of bodies (especially the indigenous, women, and sailors—whose capacities for labor or sex were exploited in the effort to reach and possess those goods). The narrative dynamics of this calculative logic rely on a new understanding of numbers and risk that subsumed violence and loss within the mechanics of long-run calculations. It's impossible to separate the textual, commercial, and political features that contribute to this dynamic, and these elements will combine and engage with each other in a variety of ways over the course of the three chapters that make up Part I of this book, chapters that work together to understand the ways in which textual narrative, financial numbers, and political resistance collaborate within the transoceanic dynamics of war capitalism that inhabits the literary world of novels.

Pacific Travel and Pacific Travel Writing

Atlantic–Pacific connections were not new to the late eighteenth century. European ties to the Pacific were established at least as early as the Portuguese settlement on the Chinese island of Macao in 1557, which linked Portugal through a lucrative regular trade in silks, silver, and spices with China, Japan, India, and the Moluccas (or Spice Islands). The following decade, Spain established a regular route between the Atlantic and the Pacific when it conquered the Philippines and established the galleon trade in 1565, which saw several ships every year leave Acapulco with

Mexican silver to exchange in Manila for popular Asian trade goods. Spices, porcelain, and silk were in turn transported back to Acapulco, through the Caribbean, and across the Atlantic into Spain. Matt Matsuda describes the galleon trade as "the heart of the global economy," which began to "connect Europe and the Americas to the real provider of treasure: China."[8] Those connections between oceans and continents were further extended over the following centuries through a series of imperial and commercial voyages undertaken on behalf of states or merchants in the West—on ships populated by Spanish, Dutch, French, Russian, English, Portuguese, U.S., and indigenous peoples.

At the end of the sixteenth century, the Dutch launched a series of mercantile voyages into the Pacific, establishing a trading post at Batavia in Java (now Jakarta in Indonesia) and inaugurating a vigorous spice trade in the East Indies. The Dutch extended their presence to the south Pacific in the seventeenth century with Tasman's voyages to Van Diemen's Land (or Tasmania) and New Zealand and, early in the eighteenth century, with Roggeveen's expedition in search of the Australian continent. Meanwhile, the privateering efforts led by English figures such as Francis Drake and Woodes Rogers sought to intercept the Spanish ships loaded with silver from American mines that crossed the Pacific for trade in Asia. Those privateers also brought some of the most widely circulating stories of the Pacific to Europe in the form of travel narratives that often underwent multiple translations and reprints.

The historian J. C. Beaglehole has categorized the sixteenth century in the Pacific as Spanish, the seventeenth century as Dutch, and the eighteenth century as French and English. Of course, this neat taxonomy simplifies what recent scholars have recognized as the more complex and consistent internationalism of the region.[9] By the second half of the eighteenth century especially, there was an explosion in Pacific travel, trade, and exploration by the Russians, the Spanish, the English, the French, and the Americans—each of whom made regular contact not only with each other but with an astonishing array of Pacific peoples and lands, from the Kamchatka peninsula in eastern Siberia to the trade ports of Macao and Canton in China, from the coasts of Alaska and California to the Philippines, Indonesia, New Guinea, Australia, and numerous Polynesian island systems including Tahiti, Hawai'i, Samoa, Fiji, and the Marianas.

Much of this late eighteenth-century activity in the Pacific was launched when Russian fur trading expeditions began moving across the Bering Sea to the Aleutian and Kodiak islands in the 1740s, as well-established fur trapping and trading practices in Siberia expanded further to the east. That expansion was driven by the Chinese desire for furs, which were exchanged at Kyakhta—a trading site on the border of Mongolia that had opened in the 1690s—for Asian teas, silks, spices, and porcelain.[10] As these Russian voyages extended east across the far north Pacific and then south along the northwest American coastline, buoyed by the forced labor of expert indigenous Kodiak and Aleutian sea otter hunters, the Spanish began to grow fearful of possible Russian encroachments on their territory.

In response, Spain sent the Portolá expedition by land into Alta California in 1769, establishing an extensive mission system and also imagining Monterey as a possible port for Asian trade. By the end of that century, Spain had also sent the Anza settlement expedition north by land to Monterey and San Francisco, and expeditions by sea led by Mourelle and Bodega, and Malaspina.[11]

As the Spanish were responding to the Russian presence along the North American coastline in the 1760s, both the English and the French were sponsoring ambitious voyages of discovery to the Pacific. France entered the Pacific with Bougainville's circumnavigation of the globe in 1766, while the English sent no fewer than three expeditions during that same decade: by Byron in 1764, by Wallis and Carteret in 1766, and by Cook in 1768. These voyages were followed up by two more expeditions by Cook in the 1770s, by the Frenchman La Pérouse's circumnavigation in the 1780s, and by Vancouver's English voyage in the 1790s. By the late 1780s and throughout several subsequent decades, the Pacific was also traversed by numerous British, American, French, and Russian commercial voyages seeking profits from the lucrative China trade as well as from sealing and whaling. During the late eighteenth century, then, a multinational array of goods and bodies moved with some regularity around the Pacific Ocean, its American and Asian coastlines, and Polynesia. Even the population of a single ship seldom conformed to the singularity of national identity that Beaglehole ascribes to entire centuries. The Pacific routes these ships carved out were, of course, situated within transoceanic maritime trade networks that linked the Pacific with the Atlantic through the exchange of European finished goods such as cookware, clothing, and firearms for Chinese teas, silks, and porcelains, primarily by way of sea otter pelts trapped and traded on the American northwest coast.

All of these voyages, of course, generated a considerable amount of writing. If the Pacific has been neglected by historians of early America, as Gray and Taylor note, it has been even more neglected by scholars working in early American literary studies. This neglect is in spite of the fact that this international explosion in Pacific travel was accompanied by an equally international print explosion in Pacific travel writing. Writings by privateers like Drake and Dampier had already interested readers around the Atlantic in the Pacific, but written accounts of the region really exploded in the second half of the eighteenth century, when Britain began sponsoring global circumnavigations—first by John Byron on the *Dolphin* in 1764, and again by Samuel Wallis in 1766.

The most dominant subgenre within Pacific travel writing of the period were narratives of the large state-sponsored European expeditions and the collections of earlier international voyages that motivated and guided them. The state-sponsored Pacific expeditions were preceded, however, and likely inspired by Charles de Brosses's historical collection of Pacific travel narratives. In the following review of the kinds of texts that made up this quite popular late eighteenth-century genre, I focus in particular on narratives that circulated in English translation or that were originally published in English. De Brosses's collection was first published in

France in 1756, for example, but it appeared in English by John Callander a decade later, in 1766—the year of Wallis's voyage. *Terra Australis Cognita: or, Voyages to the Terra Australis, or Southern Hemisphere, during the Sixteenth, Seventeenth, and Eighteenth Centuries* collected into multiple volumes accounts of several centuries of Spanish, Dutch, Portuguese, and English voyages. Callander's edition translated de Brosses's material into English, but it also silently excised all mention of the book's original French editor and even "substitut[ed] England for France"[12] throughout the volume. As a result, it efficiently argued that the English nation was in the best position "to advance the Knowledge of Geography and Navigation" and hoped that the book itself would help "to promote the Commercial Interests of *Great Britain*, and extend her Naval Power."[13] Callander's appropriative edition appears to have launched an English boom in Pacific travel and Pacific travel writing that lasted through the remainder of the eighteenth and into the beginning of the nineteenth century.

Numerous English travel compilations followed Callander's translation. These included, among others, two volumes of early Spanish and Dutch Pacific voyages edited by Alexander Dalrymple and published in 1770–1; John Hawkesworth's 1773 collection of the English voyages of Byron, Wallis, Carteret, and Cook; William Coxe's *Account of the Russian Discoveries Between Asia and America*, published in 1780 and in a revised and updated edition in 1787; George William Anderson's 1784 *A New, Authentic, and Complete Collection of Voyages Round the World*, which collected English eighteenth-century Pacific voyages; Christopher Smart, Oliver Goldsmith, and Samuel Johnson's *The World Displayed; or, a Curious Collection of Voyages and Travels, Selected and compiled from the writers of all nations*, published in London in 1759–61 in a massive twenty-volume set; and James Burney's *A Chronological History of the Discoveries in the South Sea or Pacific Ocean*, published in five volumes between 1803 and 1817. There were also continued translations of Pacific travel narratives into English during these decades; for example, Bougainville's voyage was published in London in 1772, the Spanish voyage of Mourelle and Bodega in 1781, and La Pérouse's voyage around the world in 1798.

These titles circulated in England along with a burgeoning wave of multi-media cultural productions about the Pacific. Inspired in large part by the return of a celebrated figure like Joseph Banks to London after Cook's first expedition, and the extended visit in England by the Polynesian Native Mai following Cook's second expedition, these productions included poems, plays, scientific treatises, scientific collections, paintings, engravings, and periodical reports and reviews that depicted and assessed the cultural and natural worlds of the wider Pacific, including its indigenous peoples and their exchanges with visiting Europeans. As Gillian Russell has pointed out, British exploration of the Pacific coincided with "the tremendous expansion in the mechanisms and forums of publicity in metropolitan culture," including a proliferation of journals and magazines, museums and theaters, and salons and coffee houses.[14] News from and representations of the Pacific circulated widely through these various outlets to reach a diverse audience, far beyond those

members of the elite able to afford the print editions of Pacific voyages that appeared
in multiple volumes and in larger formats. The new mechanisms of celebrity
culture helped leave behind an extensive archive of eighteenth-century materials
that makes it possible to assemble a rich and extensive reception history of Pacific
travel narratives and reports, especially in London.

Evidence for the reception of Pacific travel writing in early America is, by
contrast, far harder to come by. There was no local version of Joseph Banks nor any
tour by a Pacific islander like Mai. Yet in some ways that discrepancy makes North
American interest in the Pacific during this period all the more remarkable.
Evidence for that interest exists in the publication history of these narratives,
which can tell us quite a bit about who might have read about Pacific voyages, even
if it's not always clear exactly how those readers used or responded to their content.[15]
The volumes by Callendar/de Brosses, Dalrymple, and Coxe mentioned above did
not see American editions, but the Hawkesworth volume was printed in 1774 in
both New York City and Philadelphia, only a year after its appearance in London.
The New York edition was also reprinted in Annapolis, Maryland, and may have
appeared or circulated much more widely, judging by the original plans for the
edition described by the printer James Rivington. On March 16, 1774, Rivington
published an advertisement soliciting patrons for funds to publish an affordable
American edition of Cook's first narrative. The ad begins by noting that those
wishing to purchase the London edition of *The Late Voyage Round the World* "must
give THREE GUINEAS for it," and Rivington claims that this "excessive price" has
inspired him to propose "a complete edition of that work, copied line after line
from the London edition." Rivington's ad concludes by listing a series of printers
who should be sent the names of those interested in sponsoring the edition. That
list includes printers located in New York, Philadelphia, Boston, New Haven,
Annapolis, Charleston South Carolina, and Dominica, Antigua, and St. Croix and
St. Christopher in the West Indies. The book, he explains, would be printed using
"copperplate cuts engraved in New York" on "paper manufactured in this country."
In order further to entice subscribers, Rivington's two-page appeal offers a detailed
condensation of the narrative's exciting contents and insists that the "voyages of
Lord Anson, Shelvocke, Woodes Rogers, and Dampier, which have been hitherto
held in high estimation, are none of them so interesting and entertaining as this of
Captain Cook."[16] This reference to earlier Pacific maritime narratives suggests
Rivington knew that American readers were familiar with these accounts, even if
hesitant to spend the money on this more recent and rather expensive title.

When it appeared in 1774, Rivington's volume appears to have done for the
Pacific in North America what Callendar's did for it in England, for the following
three-to-four decades saw the steady publication of American editions of Pacific
travel narratives, with versions of one or more of the Cook voyages tending to
dominate. In addition to the three 1774 editions of Hawkesworth mentioned
above, *Early American Imprints* catalogs twelve editions of one or more of Cook's
voyages published between 1783 and 1818 in the cities of Philadelphia, Worcester,

New York, Boston, Hartford, and Hudson—including one written by Connecticut native John Ledyard (who sailed on Cook's third voyage and returned to the United States with widely circulated plans to profit from the Pacific fur trade) and another attributed to John Rickman, identified on the title page only as "an officer on board the *Discovery*." These publication sites suggest that merchants in port cities—especially those interested in prospects for commercial investment in the kind of profitable Pacific trade foregrounded by Ledyard—may have been among the audience for these narratives.

But it's also clear that prospective sailors for Pacific seal-hunting voyages were also among this audience, since these crews were drawn largely from the New York and New England regions. The town of Hudson, New York, offers a particularly instructive example. Hudson might otherwise appear a relatively obscure and unlikely location for the publication of a Pacific travel title, but the town was founded by Nantucket seafarers and, as James Kirker explains, it "provided the majority of sealers from the state of New York."[17] This detail suggests that sailors (but also their families) may have been among the primary readers of editions like this one, which is described as "Faithfully abridged from the Quarto edition" and which runs to a comparatively brief ninety-six pages. Its compressed content features descriptions of exotic and beautiful Pacific birds, coral, fruit, and women, and describes Polynesian dances, feasts, ceremonies, and exchanges of goods between European sailors and Pacific islanders, including an especially extensive description of dancing women in Otaheite (Tahiti). A woodcut of dancing Polynesian women occupies the very first page of the 1774 Rivington edition of Hawkesworth's Cook narrative, suggesting that it was exotic (and perhaps even erotic) adventure rather than geographical or commercial discovery that drove interest in these titles.

Most American editions were shorter, abridged, one-volume books. A translation of the La Pérouse voyage into English appeared in Boston in 1801 (published under the spelling La Peyrouse) in abridged form, for example. Only one American edition of Cook's narratives (printed in 1796 in New York) ran as long as four volumes, while the 1797 Boston edition and the 1814 New York edition were two volumes each. Exceptions to this trend toward brevity were William Fordyce Mavor's compilation, *An Historical Collection of the Most Celebrated Voyages, Travels, and Discoveries* (published in 1802, and reduced from its original twenty volumes in London to fourteen volumes published in Philadelphia); and the Smart, Goldsmith, and Johnson collection noted earlier in this section, which appeared in its first American edition in Philadelphia in 1795–6 in a more modest eight rather than twenty volumes. Mavor's introduction explains that the narratives included have been "divested as far as possible, of technical phrases and cumbrous minutiae," and furthermore asserts that "we have written with an eye to youthful innocence and female delicacy" so that the pages "will not offend." He claims space for the collection "in the pocket, the parlor, or the library" and hopes that it will also be available in "schools and seminaries for either sex."[18] These comments indicate that the collection was designed both to entertain and to instruct, and that it explicitly aimed at both male and female readers—including the young, and schoolchildren in particular.

Narratives of the state-sponsored maritime expeditions discussed throughout this section were quickly followed by commercial voyages. Before long, it seemed as though merchants outfitted ships nearly as quickly as readers purchased books, sending trading and hunting ships to the Pacific from England, the United States, Spain, France, Portugal, and even Sweden and Denmark. Merchant groups from across Europe—and increasingly, beginning in the 1780s, from North America as well—set out in search of profits from seals, whales, sandalwood, or bêche-du-mer from Pacific waters and islands, as well as teas, fabrics, spices, and porcelain from the Chinese market in Canton. The 1784 publication of the narrative of Cook's third voyage in particular prompted simultaneous booms in Pacific commerce and in publishing about the Pacific. The first edition of the narrative reportedly "sold out within three days" and was followed not only by numerous editions and translations that circulated throughout Europe and America but by "unofficial published narratives" penned by various officers and men on the voyage.[19] It was no coincidence that the first U.S. ship to travel to the Pacific, the *Empress of China*, left New York harbor for Canton that same year, in 1784.

While the voyages by and narratives about Cook tend to dominate this publication and reception history, numerous lesser-known voyages and experiences in the Pacific—including those by ship captains, castaways and captives, disgruntled or impoverished sailors, missionaries, and merchants—also made it into print during the last decade of the eighteenth century and the first two decades of the nineteenth: the Polish Count Benyowsky's exploits in Siberia and the Pacific were published in 1790; James Colnett's Pacific whaling narrative in 1798; James Wilson's missionary voyage to the south Pacific in 1799; William Moulton's account of shipboard tyranny and William Broughton's exploration voyage, both in 1804; John Jewitt's Nootka captivity narrative in 1807; John Turnbull's commercial voyage in 1810; David Porter's U.S. expedition in 1815; shipwreck narratives by the Scotsman Archibald Campbell and the American Daniel Foss in 1816; the sailor Samuel Patterson's account of Fiji in 1817; and officer Amasa Delano's account of his merchant ship voyages (the source for Melville's *Benito Cereno*) in 1818.

Books, however, were only one print source for news of Pacific voyages, for their content was more readily accessible in American periodicals throughout this period. Magazines regularly included excerpts from Pacific travel narratives, often published serially over a number of issues. They also often printed reviews of these books which circulated their content among a wider audience than the books themselves would have reached. A narrative of Wallis's voyage around the world, for example, appeared serialized in three issues of *The Royal American Magazine* in 1774, while a review of the translation (into English from German) of Von Staehlin's collection of Russian discoveries, *Account of the New Northern Archipelago*, appeared in *Pennsylvania Magazine* in 1776. A report on the futility of searching for a Northwest Passage appeared in *The New-Haven Gazette, and the Connecticut*

Magazine in 1786, and excerpts from La Pérouse's dispatches to France were printed in *The Massachusetts Magazine* in 1789.[20] This very partial representation of such excerpts, reprints, and reviews indicates considerable interest by revolutionary-era North Americans in news from the Pacific—an interest that has been occluded by the tendency of literary and cultural histories of America to focus during this period on the Revolution and print productions immediately related to it, like Thomas Paine's *Common Sense.*

Profit and Prolongation

With the glaring exception of the three expeditions led by Captain James Cook, few of the accounts described above have received much in the way of sustained scholarly attention, and even fewer are available in modern editions. Rather than make a case for any single one or more of these texts, however, I read examples here of the particular subgenre of the state-sponsored voyage narrative in order to identify and contextualize some of its textual and narratological features. We might take John Callander's national appropriation of de Brosses's French collection as a model for the way in which these texts often replicated in print the intense international competition that characterized the voyages themselves, which sought to make claims to new scientific discoveries on the one hand and lay claims to considerable commercial profits on the other. In fact, the goals of disinterested scientific knowledge and self-interested commercial gain were always intricately entangled with each other; in most cases, the state-sponsored circumnavigations publicly announced goals of scientific discovery (such as tracking the transit of Venus, or locating the great southern continent, or charting new coastlines) while also secretly pursuing commercial goals (such as identifying new trade goods, or locating sites for the establishment of trading posts, or competing in already established trade networks).[21] As John Mack puts it, "*inquisitiveness* and *acquisitiveness* were intimate bedfellows" in eighteenth-century voyages between the Atlantic and the Pacific.[22]

Whatever the ostensible reasons for sailing into it from the Atlantic, the Pacific became synonymous with exceptionally long periods of time, with the experience of waiting many years to learn of or reap the results of these endeavors. These trips demanded enormous patience even as they excited considerable expectation, since profit and discovery alike depended on the prolonged duration of these very promising, and extraordinarily risky, voyages. While most thinking about temporality in literary studies comes from narratology and studies of the novel, I turn to the textualization of late eighteenth-century Pacific trade and travel to investigate a particular mode of narrative temporality that—by combining patient duration with impatient expectation—might be thought of as prolonged promise. Accounts of Pacific travel are characterized, I argue, by modes of narrativizing risk that reflect a new eighteenth-century conception of numbers and time, and that work to conceal the violence and loss that was an almost inevitable by-product of these voyages.

The experience of Pacific travel repeatedly emphasized that there was no profit without prolongation. When Vitus Bering's 1740 voyage returned to Russia, the results appeared disastrous: one ship had been lost entirely, along with half of its men, and Bering himself died of illness on an uninhabited island in the sea that now bears his name. The returns from the voyage included only some survivors, a reconstructed ship, and some pelts from the sea otters they had consumed as food while stranded on islands in the north Pacific. When those pelts, however, later proved to be highly profitable in the China market, Russian merchants began to outfit subsequent expeditions in exclusive pursuit of sea otter fur along the islands and coastlines of the American far northwest. The past losses of Bering's voyage became dwarfed by the prospect of future profits. This calculus continued to characterize Russia's presence in the region. The fur hunting expedition of Ivan Solov'ev on the ship *St. Paul* in 1771–2 was disastrous by human measures: twenty-two of seventy-two crew members died and countless Aleuts were massa-cred in a series of violent encounters. Commercial measures, however, marked the venture a resounding success; as Claudio Saunt explains, "the ship had collected 681 foxes, 188 sea otters, and 60 otter tails. The high price of furs in distant Kyakhta made the cost of hunting on the Aleutians worth the expense—at least to the *St. Paul*'s merchant owners."[23]

Although it was the Russians who extended and exploited this Pacific fur trade over the subsequent decades, it was the travel narrative of James Cook's third voyage that circulated news of its profitability to western Europe and the United States. Its eager reception by the reading public in 1784 has long been attributed to its description of Cook's death at the hands of Sandwich (or Hawai'ian) Islanders. But it may well have been another passage altogether that marked the book's central moment of narrative engagement for late eighteenth-century readers— namely, the description of the sailors' extraordinary profits by selling in China the sea otter skins acquired from Natives of North America's northwest coast. While the account of Cook's death—and the rather grisly descriptions of attempts to recover portions of his cannibalized body for purposes of identification and burial—has taken on a rather mythic status in cultural memory, the account of income from the Asian fur trade took on an equally gripping and mythic dimension for eighteenth-century readers and speculators.

Indeed, the spectacle of the violent murder and reported cannibalization of James Cook's body on a beach in the Pacific really should be seen as circulating *together with* the spectacle of immense profits made by some sailors and merchants on that voyage. These paired images—of violence and profit, of cannibalization and accumulation—together illustrate the rotating cycle of exploitation and resist-ance that characterized the trade circuits that webbed across the Pacific and that also connected that ocean by commercial and political cords to the Atlantic. But these paired images—the fixed spectacle of a ruined human body and the flurried spin of actual or potential wealth—illustrate as well the strangely allied temporal attitudes of static endurance with restless impatience, of horrified engagement with abstract calculation.

It was just after Cook's death in Hawai'i that the *Resolution* (led on the remainder of its voyage by Captain James King) arrived on the northwest coast of North America. Like the Russians several decades earlier, the sailors discover that the furs possessed by the northwest coast Natives "produce a high price; and the natives, from their mode of life, require few articles in return. Our sailors brought a quantity of furs from the coast of America, and were both pleased and astonished on receiving such a quantity of silver for them from the [Russian] merchants" who were in the region.[24] The full significance of these furs, however, isn't realized until much later, when the men arrive in Asia. In Canton, one sailor "disposed of his stock" of sea otter furs "for eight hundred dollars; and a few of the best skins, which were clear, and had been carefully preserved, produced a hundred and twenty dollars each." The sale of these "best skins" amounted to a return of £90 on an investment of 1 shilling, or a profit of an astonishing 1800 percent.[25] Two sailors jumped ship altogether in the hopes of returning to the fur islands, "seduced by the hopes of acquiring a fortune," while those who remained on the ship had added to their ragged English clothing "the gayest silk and cottons that China could produce."[26]

Once this narrative appeared in print, the quick calculation of these numbers sent numerous men and ships on lengthy expeditions into the Pacific from Europe and the United States—including that inaugural Pacific voyage of the *Empress of China*. As though to help readers with those numbers, this passage is accompanied by a fairly detailed calculation of the mathematical progress of profits from Pacific furs that takes into account both time and distance:

> notwithstanding the merchants have so extravagant a profit upon these imported goods [primarily clothing and cookware], they receive still a greater advantage from the sale of the furs at Kiachta, a considerable market for them on the frontiers of China. In Kamtschatka, the best sea-otter skins usually produce about thirty roubles a-piece; at Kiachta, the Chinese merchant gives more than double that price, and disposes of them again at Pekin for a much greater sum; after which, an additional profit is made of many of them at Japan. If then, the original value of a skin at Kamtschatka is thirty roubles, and it is afterwards transported to Okotsk, thence by land thirteen hundred and sixty-four miles to Kiachta, thence seven hundred and sixty miles to Pekin, and after that, to be transported to Japan, what a lucrative trade might be established between Kamtschatka and Japan, which is not above three weeks sail from it at the utmost![27]

This extended addition of distances and times across multiple points of exchange closes with a fantasy of gaining all of the profit from those exchanges with almost none of the travel between them. But even without stops at these numerous trade sites within Asia, the distances involved were unimaginably long. The ships making the route between Boston, the northwest coast, and Canton became known for delayed desire, both economic and sexual.

These voyages were identified on the one hand with "lucrative profits," since the return on investment for these voyages could be anywhere from 200 to over 2000 percent, and on the other hand with "exotic stopovers," primarily in Hawai'i, where one visitor explained "[w]omen can be considered one of the commodities that these islands abundantly furnish to visiting ships."[28] George Vancouver, who arrived on the northwest coast in the 1790s, encountered an assortment of English, American, and French ships all "collecting the skins of sea-otter and other furs." He also reported that the cost of sea otter skins was "at least an hundred per cent. dearer" than they had been on his last visit (when Vancouver was a member of Cook's third expedition), and finds an English ship searching for inland sources for fur since "the price of skins [was] so exorbitant on the sea-coast."[29] The speediness of the escalations and pleasures described in these texts is in strange contrast to the utter sluggishness of the journeys themselves, although it was precisely the combination of these antithetical tempos that characterize their narratives. These texts shared this temporal duality with the calculative logic of economic investment that motivated and underwrote the voyages themselves and whose terms were especially magnified by the enormous distances, durations, risks, and profits entailed by expeditions to the Pacific.

Duration and Expectation

Temporal prolongation is materially evident in the most obvious feature shared by the vast majority of these Pacific travel books: their size. By eighteenth-century standards, Pacific travel collections tended to be large tomes in every respect, notwithstanding the American preference for abridgment: they were bulky and heavy; they were wide, tall, and thick; and they typically consisted of multiple volumes. The collection edited by Alexander Dalrymple, for instance, was made up of two such heavy volumes. The Hawkesworth collection took up three substantial volumes, as did the Vancouver voyage alone, while Burney's history of Pacific travel ran to five unwieldy volumes of about 600 pages each. The size of these books is, of course, in some part a measure of the length and breadth of the voyages themselves. Their temporal duration was emphasized in titles that almost invariably ended with a serial listing of the years during which the journey was under way. The title of Anderson's collection of English Pacific voyages, for example, begins *A New, Authentic, and Complete Collection of Voyages Round the World*, and concludes with *And successively performed In the Years 1768, 1769, 1770, 1771–1772, 1773, 1774, 1775–1776, 1777, 1778, 1779, 1780.* One American edition of Cook's narrative appeared as *Captain Cook's Three Voyages to the Pacific Ocean. The first performed in the years 1768, 1769, 1770 and 1771: the second in 1772, 1773, 1774 and 1775: the third and last in 1776, 1777, 1778, 1779 and 1780.* Vancouver's travel narrative is called *A Voyage of Discovery to the North Pacific Ocean, and Round the World…performed in the years 1790, 1791, 1792, 1793, 1794, and 1795.* The English edition of Bougainville's travels was titled *A Voyage Round the World. Performed by Order of His Most Christian Majesty, In the Years 1766, 1767, 1768, and 1769*, while La Pérouse's read *A Voyage round the World performed in the Years 1785, 1786, 1787, 1788*. This insistence on sequentially listing each year of the voyage not only advertises but seems to perform the drawn-out temporality of the voyages themselves.[30]

The sense conveyed by these titles of an extensive, almost tedious, duration is often replicated within the texts themselves, which are typically organized as chronological records that take regular note of the ship's location, navigational direction, weather conditions, and nautical details. Sometimes these mundane details, very often recorded in numerical form, are in fact significant scientific findings that challenge, confirm, or complicate the results of earlier expeditions—such as revising information about the exact location of particular islands or filling in the gaps of incomplete charts from earlier voyages. On the one hand, then, these texts are characterized by a temporal duration marked most often by a rather tedious repetition and prolonged regularity, an extended plodding onward in which, from a navigational standpoint, slow progress is being made but, from a narrative standpoint, nothing really happens. On the other hand, these texts were both framed and punctuated by a sense of anticipation, by an expectant sense of promise and urgency.[31] They were *framed* by expectation because they were motivated by the pursuit of new knowledge and wealth, by the conviction that the extraordinary costs of these voyages would result in even greater returns over the long term, and because international competition for such discoveries gave these voyages a sense of special urgency. And they were *punctuated* by expectation because each successive encounter with a new landscape and new peoples might yield profitable products and pliable partners for trade as well as new information and discoveries. They might also yield unexpected conflicts or pleasures.

The pace of these narratives reflects this tension between dilation and acceleration. The narratologist Gérard Genette calculates narrative speed according to the proportion of temporal duration to textual length, so that the "speed of a narrative" is determined by "the relationship between a duration (that of the story, measured in seconds, minutes, hours, days, months, and years) and a length (that of the text, measured in lines and in pages)."[32] Because the navigational portions of Pacific travel narratives typically cover a long expanse of time in a proportionally short number of pages, by Genette's structuralist metric they would be described as fast or accelerated. But although significant expanses of time may be covered in these pages, the pace of the narrative from most readers' point of view is experienced instead as profoundly slow. Indeed, reader-oriented narratology—which understands plot not as "fixed structures, but rather a structuring operation peculiar to those messages that are developed through temporal succession"—would describe these sections of the text as slow or dilatory because they generate little or no sense of expectation or desire. If for Peter Brooks "plot is, most aptly, a steam engine,"[33] the plot of the Pacific voyage narrative too often seems to drift at sea like a preindustrial sail waiting for the wind to pick up. It was not only cost, therefore, that accounts for the proliferation of later, abridged versions of these texts, but also the excision of these navigational or scientific details from earlier, more official and comprehensive editions of these narratives.

But signs of expectation and scenes of excitement in fact do interrupt the steady regularity of curt entries and dry navigational records, most often at moments when the crew makes landfall, giving way to an intensification of detailed descriptions of the land, its produce, its inhabitants, and the crew's interactions with them. Such moments of encounter typically represent an inversion of the proportion of textual length to temporal duration that characterize the navigational sections of the narrative. While only a few days or even hours may pass, the narration of that time often takes up a large number of pages. The narrative pace for readers accordingly speeds up, often quite dramatically, and plotting itself shifts from a largely *geographical* activity (i.e. determining the shape of this coastline, filling in the gaps of geographical knowledge on this map) to a *narrative* dynamic (i.e. wondering what will happen next, now that the ship has anchored offshore, hoping to trade for food and profitable goods with the Natives, who are approaching in canoes, and may or may not be carrying weapons). The routine navigational calculations that make the safe completion of these voyages possible are therefore framed by the expectant economic and political calculations that underwrote these voyages, and also interrupted by the often frantic social calculations that characterized commercial and cross-cultural encounters during the voyage itself.

Another way of understanding this tension in narratological terms is to see it as what Anne Thell, drawing on Genette, calls a "competition between mimesis and diagesis." In the former the quantity of information overwhelms the voice of the informer, while in the latter this proportion is reversed. She describes an early Pacific travel narrative like William Dampier's as turning to diagetic narrative in order to provide some momentum by which to offset an otherwise stagnant mimetic report.[34] Editors of these narratives often found themselves caught between the inclusion of navigational details—which provided crucial data for subsequent explorers and travels (and that sometimes allowed a nation to boast of its discoveries)—and general readers' relative lack of interest in such information. Editors tended to solve this problem by defending narrative tedium in the name of science, eliminating it in the name of entertainment, or some combination of the two. Vancouver, writing in the 1790s, apologizes for the repetitiveness of his narrative but argues that its aim is not entertainment but scientific accuracy. Callander's 1766 volume explained that the editor has removed "intermediate things" and "other things which often tire the reader," although the style has been preserved since it is "utility, and not elegance of style, that is to be looked for here." Thell describes this type of account as "withhold[ing] the kind of details that create" what Defoe described as "Story," which was desired by "such Readers who never intend to go to sea."[35] James Burney admitted that "If half the account of a voyage is found to consist of figures and mathematical dissertation, what reader will not wish that this part had been published separate?," and John Turnbull promises readers not to include "technical extracts of our log book" in his *Voyage Round the World*.[36] Indeed, Turnbull's 1810 volume departs substantially in feel and tone from the vast majority of Pacific travel accounts published in the preceding half-century by abandoning all features of the log book other than temporal progression through a sequential narrative, resulting in a volume with a far less scientific and far more subjective voice and perspective than its forebears.

Interestingly, Turnbull's 1810 narrative actually returns in this respect to some of the features of one of the earliest collections of Pacific narratives, John Hawkesworth's edition of Cook's first voyage, published together with the earlier English voyages of Byron, Wallis, and Carteret. Hawkesworth's 1773 volume was both quite popular and quite controversial, and it was both of these things because of his editorial decision to write the account of Cook's narrative in the first person and to transform what one scholar calls the "plain if sometimes awkward prose of [Cook's] journal" into "a continuous and homogeneous narrative."[37] While Hawkesworth's technique certainly increased narrative pace and heightened reader interest, it also gained many critics in the eighteenth century and since who objected to its elevation of narrative entertainment over scientific detail, its sacrifice of truth to desire—including erotic desire associated with the volume's attention to the sexual experiences of Banks on Tahiti. Reaction to Hawkesworth's editorial decision was strong enough that his experiment was not soon repeated, and even Turnbull avoids the singular in favor of the plural first person.

Ultimately, most of these volumes employ a kind of editorial calculus designed to balance the redundant tedium of navigational or geographic details with the accelerated drama of discovery and exchange, to punctuate prolongation with promise. Hawkesworth suggests as much when he announces that "those who read merely for entertainment will be compensated [for the dry geographical or navigational content] by the description of countries which no European had before visited, and manners which in many instances exhibit a new picture of human life."[38] Despite his critics, Hawkesworth's textual decisions actually reveal a great deal about the narrative mechanics of expectation in travel writing. Indeed, accounts of Pacific travel and trade had in common with the genre of the novel developing in the Atlantic world at the same time this dynamics of prolonged promise, a narrative temporality that helps to explain the popularity of these non-fiction texts with readers unfamiliar with and uninterested in the routine details of navigation.[39] It was, moreover, precisely this protracted suspense of time, this temporal duration, that worked to mask the violence of profit-seeking, a violence that was played out most often on the bodies of indigenous peoples, women, and sailors in the distant and exotic regions of the Pacific. Thell suggests that Hawkesworth's mistake was in exposing "the imaginative machinery that structures travel relation in even non-fictional accounts," for he failed to "factor into his project the shock" that readers felt upon coming into such close contact with the "sex and violence" detailed in his version of the voyage.[40] Hawkesworth's narrative of the Pacific, in other words, may have laid war capitalism too bare, failing to mask its brutal corporeal consequences within a calculus of risk.

The Calculus of Risk

As Alan Taylor's brief history of the Russian presence in the north Pacific makes clear, the profitability of these trading voyages depended not just on long periods of time but on multiple acts of violence against the Natives and their environment. These included initial attacks with firearms on Aleut villages, taking women and children hostage in order to compel the men to hunt furs, sexually enslaving the women during the months that the men were at sea hunting pelts, and eventually decimating the region's sea otter population through indiscriminate overhunting.[41] The French and English travelers and traders who worked the northern Pacific fur trade later in the century often condemned the behavior of their Russian (as well as their Spanish) predecessors in the Americas and offered a patient and pacifist commerce as an antidote to rapid and violent conquest. The de Brosses/Callander collection, for example, imagined the discovery of an immense southern continent that would serve as "an advantageous market for all our wares, such as cloths, glasses, paper, spirits, and all the species of toys that were so greedily sought after by the *Indians* of the West, in the days of Columbus." And yet the French (or English, if one reads Callander's edition) need precisely to "avoid avarice and cruelty" such as was practiced by the Spanish, since "[e]xperience has taught us, that a solid and well-regulated commerce should form our principal object in those distant climes, and not the conquest of large kingdoms." The best method of ensuring the Natives' "useful dependence, is, to take care, that they shall always find it for their advantage, to exchange the product of their country for that of ours." The volume argues that such a design was best driven by kings or republics, not by merchants or trading companies who "have nothing in view but a quick return of profit" and who therefore would be unwilling to take the risks "where the success is uncertain and the profits at a distance."[42]

Ships entered the Pacific from the Atlantic throughout this period and brought back with them news about the Pacific that circulated to Atlantic audiences in books and periodical excerpts. While the mercantile voyages foregrounded commercial profits as their motive, the state-sponsored circumnavigations publicly announced and pursued scientific goals of navigational, geographic, botanical, or astronomic discovery. But this distinction remained confused at best. The state-sponsored scientific voyages also, sometimes secretly, pursued critical commercial goals that included identifying new trade goods or locations for establishing trading posts or strategies for competing in already established trade networks. Likewise, a mercantile whaling voyage like that of James Colnett could see itself as contributing to the advancement of science: "though my former voyages were principally undertaken with the views of commercial advantage, I was never inattentive to the advancement of nautical science." And while the state-sponsored expeditions perceived themselves as engaged in a competitive race with other nations to reach particular destinations, confirm or deny various geographical theories, or lay claim to new discoveries, national boasting could appear in the commercial context as much as it did in the scientific one, such as when Colnett announces that "the known spirit of enterprise and speculation, possessed by the British merchants...is not equaled, by those of any other nation."[43]

Arguments about the virtues of commerce absolutely saturate late eighteenth-century Pacific travel narratives, which frequently repeat the assumption that commerce offered an antidote to the violence of conquest and just as frequently issued instructions that indigenous peoples be treated with respect and fairness precisely in order to enable profitable and long-lasting trade relations. Turnbull's 1800 voyage was inspired by his observation, on a 1799 voyage to China, "that the Americans carried on the most lucrative trade to the north-west of that vast continent" and found merchants willing to invest in the opportunity to replicate the Americans' financial success. He argues that

> [t]here are few dangers, and still fewer difficulties, which can deter men of enterprise from any pursuit which they consider as the means of independence. If the colder moralist, in his abstract reasoning, brand this desire with the name of a pernicious avidity, the practical philosopher, tempering the conclusions of his reason by the modes of life, considers it in a more favourable point of view, hailing it as the grand moving impulse of commerce, and effectually the means of improving the whole condition of life.[44]

Vancouver likewise announces that the "spirit of discovery" has resulted in a "reciprocity of benefits" between Europe and "the less-enlightened of our species," those "people of the newly-discovered countries" who have been supplied with "iron, copper, useful implements, and articles of ornament" in exchange for their supply of animal skins and other useful "articles of a commercial nature" that have been sought after by "traders who now resort to their shores from Europe, Asia, and the eastern side of North America" for the "purpose of establishing new and lucrative branches of commerce between North West America and China."[45] Hawkesworth explains in the dedication to his travel compilation that rather than pursue the motive of conquest the English king has rather acted "from more liberal motives" and has proceeded "not with a view to the acquisition of treasure, or the extent of dominion, but the improvement of commerce and the increase and diffusion of knowledge."[46]

Dalrymple's collection opens with a romantic glorification of Columbus and Magellan as "heroes who went in quest of *New Lands*" and he dedicates his book to their followers who, like them, will be "*Undeterr'd* by DIFFICULTIES, / And / *Unseduc'd* by PLEASURE" and able to "*persist* through *every* Obstacle." European inter-imperial rivalries drove these discoveries, which were opportunities to "invigorate the hand of industry by opening new vents for manufactures, and by a

New Trade to encrease the active wealth and naval power of the country."[47] Howard T. Fry explains that for Dalrymple, the "progress of science and of commerce"[48] were paired goals—as they were for the Pacific explorers of all nations who carried his volumes on their ships. Dalrymple urged British explorers in the Pacific to adopt methods of peaceful commerce rather than the strategies of "*territorial dominion*" that had characterized earlier Spanish efforts in the Americas. The goal of establishing "colonies, whether to dispossess the native inhabitants, or to people desart wilds and woods, are as different from discoveries," he insists, "as *day* from *night*."[49] Vancouver similarly predicts that Spanish control over this region will fall to those more prepared to engage in "an amicable commercial intercourse" that would take advantage of "a well-conducted trade, between this coast and China, India, Japan, and other places," especially trade in the sea otter skins that are such "a profitable article of traffic."[50]

Those who recorded late eighteenth- and early nineteenth-century global circumnavigations often couched their economic motives within a self-proclaimed dedication to scientific discovery, portraying themselves explicitly as scientists rather than conquerors or even as settlers. Dalrymple's rejection of Spanish strategies of "pillage and conquest," for example, was buttressed by his conviction that a policy of trade "would have brought them far greater wealth in the end."[51] Patient commerce is more profitable than immediate conquest. But these were scientists operating in the interests of merchants, their capital, and the states that protected and fostered those interests. Their narratives repeatedly depict or lay claim to a self-discipline designed to avoid the violent effects of war capitalism, although their narratives also invariably describe their resort to precisely such violence. The narratives therefore reveal that commerce didn't so much eliminate violence as conceal it within a narrative temporality of prolonged promise. For instance, Hawkesworth warns readers that the pages of his collection do record "the destruction of poor naked savages, by our firearms, in the course of these expeditions, when they [these 'savages'] endeavoured to repress the invaders of their country."

While Hawkesworth is certain that his readers will share his "regret" about such destruction, he also claims that it is an unavoidable evil, since "resistance will always be made, and if those who resist are not overpowered, the attempt must be relinquished." The other alternative, he suggests, is simply not to attempt such "discoveries" if they result in abuse and violence. But, he argues, "If it is not lawful to put the life of an Indian in hazard, by an attempt to examine the country in which he lives, with a view to increase commerce or knowledge; it is not lawful to risk the life of our own people in carrying on commerce with countries already known." Hawkesworth's justification here uses a calculus of risk that legitimizes the use of force or violence in controlling resistance by Pacific peoples to England's commercial goals. "It seems reasonable to conclude," Hawkesworth determines, "that the increase of knowledge and commerce are ultimately common benefits; and that the loss of life which happens in the attempt, is among the partial evils which terminate in general good."[52] Violence gets buried inside a calculation, counted as one risk within a prolonged but profitable equation. Short-term losses are effectively canceled out by long-term gain.

By emphasizing the long-term general benefits of short-term individual risks, Hawkesworth's commercial calculus expresses a fundamentally mathematical mentality that, as Lorraine Daston notes, gradually came to dominate late eighteenth-century thinking about risk and certainty. Associated with a group of thinkers Daston calls the probabilists, this logic entailed "an altered conception of time and numbers" that differed considerably, she explains, from the "founders of the early life insurance societies [who] believed that more members enrolled over more time meant more risk." In contrast to this logic of the insurers, the probabilists "thought in terms of symmetric deviations from an average that would cancel one another out over the long run. The insurers equated time with uncertainty, for time brought unforeseen changes in crucial conditions; the probabilists equated time with certainty, for time brought the large numbers that revealed the regularities underlying apparent flux."[53] These two competing conceptions of time actually work together in late eighteenth-century narratives of Pacific travel.

If Hawkesworth's commercial calculus most often resembled that of the probabilists, his editorial calculus—to which I now return—remained that of the insurers, since it is the accumulation of each particular, individual detail that will engage readers, not the general results or averages over time. Such detailed description is, according to Hawkesworth, akin to reading a novel. In a passage that reads very much like the one by Neil Gaiman that opens this chapter, Hawkesworth notes that "it is from little circumstances that the relation of great events derives its power over the mind," for those who read "[a]n account that ten thousand men perished in a battle, that twice the number were swallowed up by an earthquake, or that a whole nation was swept away by a pestilence . . . without the least emotion" are those very same readers "who feel themselves strongly interested even for Pamela, the imaginary heroine of a novel that is remarkable for the enumeration of particulars in themselves so trifling, that we almost wonder how they could occur to the author's mind."[54] Jonathan Lamb perceptively argues that Hawkesworth's narrative particularity serves "to neutralize and exploit the aggression that will masquerade as the reader's pious outrage at this excess," that the magnification of particulars "insist[s] on the hazard, in order to neutralize the reader's aggression."[55] Particularist description generates the kind of engagement and expectation associated with novel reading, and it was largely to be found in these travel accounts in the descriptive and often dramatic encounters and exchanges with Native peoples. For Lamb, the details of risk alone in such scenes work to justify the violence of Cook's men and his expedition; I am arguing, however, that such scenes need to be read within the long temporality of the narrative itself, that the narrative expanses between such episodes neutralized risk because they stretched it out over time.

Such scenes also highlight the immediacy and scale of risk in a way analogous to the perspective of the early insurers described by Daston, who saw particular risks and their costs accumulating dangerously over time. Such descriptions may have made for exciting reading material, but it was not conducive to the confidence necessary to promote and resource trade, especially under the conditions of risk that attended such extensive distances and periods of time. And indeed, a Pacific travel narrative that excised all the tedious navigational and geographical details associated with the log book, leaving behind only a series of expectant engagements with particular peoples, may well have resembled those very conquest narratives that the defenders of commerce's virtuous pacifism so aggressively positioned themselves against—as the response to Hawkesworth's volume seems to attest. By contrast, duration and its sense of repetitious tedium created a protracted space and time that allowed uncertain risks and their often violent results to be averaged and canceled out.

Pacific travel narratives therefore play out in their dynamics of trade and time what Lorraine Daston describes as "an altered conception of time and numbers" that took place over the course of the eighteenth century: what seemed to be the multiplication of risk (because it appeared that more and more risks accumulated over a longer period of time) came instead to be seen as its minimization (because in fact these risks tended to average out over time).[56] Goods and bodies moved within a transoceanic and transnational geography in which the short-term uncertainties of risk and loss were absorbed by the prolonged certainty of long-run calculations. It is crucial to recognize that this view of risk *only makes sense from the perspective of the insurer or investor*, not from that of the individuals (such as the sailors or the indigenous peoples, including women, they regularly encounter) whose bodies endure the consequences of such risk (I turn more closely to this perspective and these experiences in Chapter 3). The narrative qualities of prolongation and duration in these Pacific travel narratives provided, in this sense, the risk pool needed by probabilist thinking to neutralize hazard and loss. Scenes of detailed desire and danger may have loaned the narrative's prolonged tedium some measure of uncertain anticipation, but the text's otherwise tedious sections just as importantly minimized through temporal prolongation the violence and exploitation associated with the particularities of commercial exchange and colonial contact in and around the early Pacific.

Lamb has recognized this duality in writing about the Pacific, noting the presence of both "reverie" and "frenzy" in Pacific writing and recognizing that the beach is a "site of loss as well as gain and risk as well as profit."[57] In her study of the novel in the context of the sea, Cohen too emphasizes the riskiness of maritime travel, which demanded resources of craft that became a crucial ingredient in novelistic narrative. The dangerous unpredictability of the sea meant that sailors repeatedly confront utterly urgent problems (like a storm, or a reef, or a leak), which they are compelled to solve, using whatever limited resources they possess, before the ship sinks. Cohen finds in Defoe's *Robinson Crusoe* a narrative "compression" of details and events from what had been in earlier maritime travel narratives the "uncategorized enumeration of anything noteworthy presented in the order in which it was encountered during the voyage." Defoe thus excises all the details in a ship's log or journal that might assist future voyagers but that do not necessarily "serve the episode or expectation." For Cohen, this strategy generates the "unity of action and adventures of problem-solution" that we associate with novelistic narrative, including a greater focus on singular acts and actors while amplifying the sense of danger by drawing out the steps taken to solve it.[58]

It is just as important to recognize, however, that these suspenseful micro-dilemmas are contained within the equally suspenseful macro-relations that sustain the sea voyage in the first place; as Cohen herself notes, craft at sea operated "in service of profit and conquest" as it also provided material for "nationalism and capitalism back on land."[59] These dilemma-riddled voyages are undertaken in order to transport commodities across extraordinary distances and exchange them for other goods that—upon successful return across the same expansive and risk-filled time and space—will yield profits that substantially offset costs. The crafty ingenuity of the sailors and navigators are, to be sure, performed in service to the survival of themselves and their crewmates, but their expressions of craft also served the merchant investors or states on whose behalf they found themselves at sea in the first place. Those investors in turn sent ships, sailors, and goods to sea over and over again, so long as they yielded profitable results. The detailed adventures at sea that accrue along the way thus operate as individualized micro-performances of the risky venture of land-based capital that frames and enables, at a macro level, the entire voyage. Novels share this dual temporality, drawing suspenseful expectation not just from clever solutions to short-term technical crises but from the longer-term investment relations that underwrite the enterprise (or the plot) as a whole. The calculations of risk that keep the ship (as well as the story) afloat depend on the coordination of these two temporalities.

These late eighteenth- and early nineteenth-century Pacific travel narratives represent a body of texts that press at the limits of scholarly models for literary and historical study in a number of ways. Their accounts of international contact in the early Pacific—along with their international publication and translation histories—would seem to make them excellent candidates for inclusion in the transnational and multilingual refiguration of early American literature and history, except that their transoceanic and global scope has left them outside of the Atlantic studies and hemispheric studies models that have replaced earlier nationalist narratives of this period. Moreover, these texts enjoyed their greatest circulation and popularity during the revolutionary and early republican periods in American history, decades that are still represented in current literary anthologies predominantly by texts from the Atlantic seaboard about revolution and nation-building. While a transnational framework has informed the inclusion of translated multilingual travel writings in several early American literary anthologies, those selections have remained largely limited to material from the Atlantic and from the prerevolutionary period—despite the fact that many of these early voyages aimed for Asia and that the greatest surge of interest in this genre was during the last decades of the eighteenth century. In other words, dominant narratives of early American literary history have made it difficult to recognize, much less accommodate, Pacific travel texts and the region of the Pacific, even when these texts and this region are clearly connected with the contemporaneous Atlantic. What Pacific travel texts have to teach us about narrative temporality may therefore ultimately be of value not only in rereading literary texts from the period but in rethinking the roles of expectation and prolongation in dominant narratives of American literary and cultural history.

The two temporal formulations that intersect in Pacific travel writing, for example, correspond not only to two narrative speeds and two mathematical orientations, but also to two definitions of revolution: understood astronomically, revolution is the drone of repetition (analogous to the prolonged duration of narrative, and to the minimized risk of the probabilists); understood politically, revolution is the promise of upheaval (analogous to the speedy anticipation of particular description, and to the accumulated risks of the early insurers). Lisa Lowe observes that Rousseau's *Social Contract* used spatial and temporal distance to conceptually isolate colonial slavery from eighteenth-century Europe, to eliminate the intimacy between them that her book works to recognize by engaging with textual materials and historical experiences from the globe's four continents.[60] Combined with temporal expanse, spatial distance becomes a space of forgetting—a space in which links of cause and effect can be stretched so thin as to become illegible. Those expanses are at the same time compressed, simplified, by numerical systems of calculation that obfuscate further the often violent coercion that characterizes the human relations within them—whether this takes place on ships, coastlines or plantations, or in ports or factories.

Numbers often invite boredom when they take the form of complex equations or specialized knowledge. But numbers also excite interest, and even extreme engagement, especially at points when they begin to multiply: when, for instance, $450 turns into $10,000 by way of a two-year-old elephant from India, described in the Introduction, who traveled across thousands of saltwater miles. The combination of these two functions of numbers—bored detachment and expectant engagement—serves as a resource for liberalism and capitalism. As Chapter 2 shows, that combination also serves as a resource for the narrative dynamic that drives novels. While this chapter has attended to the hidden role of numbers in the explicitly narrative genre of Pacific travel writing, the next one turns to the hidden role of narrative in a series of explicitly numerical genres that served as conventional reading material for those who undertook those voyages, as well as for those who read about them.

Numbers

CALCULATION AND SPECULATION IN
THE EIGHTEENTH-CENTURY NOVEL

In his 2011 *New Yorker* article, "Farther Away," novelist Jonathan Franzen recounts being dropped off by boat on the Pacific island called Masafuera in an attempt to relive the fictional Robinson Crusoe's eighteenth-century experience as an isolated castaway. Masafuera was called Juan Fernandez in Daniel Defoe's time, and later renamed Alejandro Selkirk after Crusoe's real-life prototype was discovered there by the English privateer Woodes Rogers in 1709, a decade before Defoe's novel was published. Located 500 miles off the coast of Chile, the island, which is about 19 square miles of mostly steep rock, is indeed geographically isolated and appears rather inhospitable to human life. It is at least as uninhabited by humans today as it was in Defoe's time. However, by the end of the eighteenth century it briefly became an unexpectedly busy hub for ship captains carrying out the then-lucrative global business in seal furs. Inspired by the narratives of Rogers and others, increasing numbers of ships left crews of men on Masafuera to kill the animals (who visited the island annually in enormous numbers to birth their young) before carrying the fur to Canton, where it fetched a great profit. When a Boston ship captained by Amasa Delano arrived there in 1800, for example, a total of fourteen ships were anchored around the island. Four years later, the sailor William Moulton reported that it was populated by 200 people, most of them deserters from American and English ships who "gave the whole of their voyages to get out of the clutches of their tyrants."[1]

Franzen spends a surprising amount of time during his lonely and solitary episode on Masafuera thinking about the genre of the novel, and while awaiting his flight home he shifts from the adventures of *Crusoe* to the domestic plot of *Pamela*. In remarking that "Pamela Andrews isn't everything and more. She's simply and uniquely Pamela," he echoes an appreciation for the engaging features of the novel form that, as we saw in Chapter 1, John Hawkesworth sought to replicate in his controversial version of Captain Cook's first Pacific voyage.[2] Perhaps because of his interest in the fictional Crusoe's isolation, Franzen misses the actual island's surprisingly busy commercial history, dominated by the risk-laden trade in seal furs that offered potentially extraordinary profits to investors and merchants while incurring substantial costs to laborers and the environment. Yet when Franzen summarizes Catherine Gallagher's work on the origins of the novel, he emphasizes precisely the genre's engagement with calculating risk: "When business came to depend on investment, you had to weigh various possible future outcomes; when marriages ceased to be arranged, you had to speculate on the merits of potential mates. And the novel, as it was developed in the eighteenth century, provided its readers with a field of play that was at once speculative and risk-free."[3] Like business ventures or prospective marriages, novels were speculative because their narratives were propelled by a series of alternative futures with varying degrees of potential, danger, and appeal. But unlike businesses or marriages, novels were risk-free because they weren't real.

The previous chapter examined how this calculus of risk operated within Pacific travel narratives to manufacture a sense of expectant engagement, where it reflected developments both in mathematical thinking and in novelistic storytelling. Financial investment and novelistic narrative share a feeling of extended anticipation, a sensation of suspense whose underlying calculus of risk—as outlined in the preceding chapter—cancels out the hazards of short-term uncertainties through the promises of long-term gain. This chapter turns more explicitly to the realm of numbers to understand better how they were used and encountered in everyday eighteenth-century contexts, and how those uses might have generated the sensations of anticipation and suspense more often associated with novels.[4] Many scholars have by now explored the interconnected developments of novelistic fiction and speculative finance during the eighteenth century, but most have done so without looking closely at how most readers at the time learned to understand and manipulate numbers—especially in relation to the expanding world of global trade made possible by transoceanic travel. Elizabeth Dillon has noted that "the horizon of probability explored in the novel—namely, the *speculative* nature of fictional realism—is linked to the development of the world market,"[5] and it bears remembering that this world market came into shape at the hands of long maritime voyages to fantastically distant locations like the south Pacific island of Masafuera and the trading posts of Canton. Greg Grandin has pointed out that such locations were for many late eighteenth-century Americans in closer imaginative reach than their own continent on the other side of the Allegheny mountains.[6] That's in part because readers regularly encountered these Pacific locations in the many translated, reprinted, abridged, and excerpted travel narratives discussed in the previous chapter.

But they also encountered these locations, and learned about the commercial goods and products that came from them, in a wide variety of pedagogical genres that taught them how to use numbers. Crusoe's apprenticeship in maritime life begins with a sea captain who instructs him to gain "a competent Knowledge of the Mathematicks," and James Cook is introduced in the Boston edition of his collected narratives as someone who "learned arithmetic, book-keeping, &c. and is said to have shewn a very early genius for figures."[7] What did it mean to have mathematical knowledge during this period, and how did such knowledge intersect with the novel's newly "*speculative* nature"? This chapter focuses less explicitly on the geography of the Pacific than on the methods of calculation and the strategies of speculation that made it desirable and possible for ships and crews to get to those distant locations and back. Some of the same kinds of numerical methods and strategies that made the entire transoceanic enterprise possible were regularly learned by a surprisingly wide range of Americans during this period. I focus in particular on the relatively common mathematical and accounting textbooks that were popular in late eighteenth- and early nineteenth-century America, but consider as well some of their more technical counterparts such as insurance and navigation manuals. These books reveal that learning about numbers often encouraged ordinary people to imagine themselves taking part in a global market-place created by the movement of ships transporting desirable goods to and from ports and markets around the world. I place these more mundane genres in dialogue with what was perhaps their most enticing counterpart: the numerical handbills that accompanied the sale of lottery tickets. Read together, these everyday number-dominated genres reveal how the static dependability of calculation and the dynamic uncertainty of speculation combined to generate the kind of disem-bodied and expectationist narrative found in the plots of novels—a narrative that, as Gallagher and others have insisted, encouraged an especially intense reader identification with character and an especially riveting reader engagement with the uncertainties of plot.[8]

Numerical Genres and Global Trade

Eighteenth-century books on mathematics, insurance, accounting, and navigation regularly trafficked in each other's knowledge pool. John Hamilton Moore's *The New Practical Navigator* (1799), for example, focuses on navigation and the skills in geometry and trigonometry needed for it, but also includes an example of how to write and record a ship's journal, explanations of insurance and bookkeeping, and an exchange table of world currency. Likewise, books devoted to mathematics often also offered instruction in how to write bills, understand insurance, keep books, or enter into joint stock agreements. Perhaps the most radical example of this cross-generic combining is George Fisher's enormously popular *American Instructor: or, Young Man's Best Companion*. Versions of Fisher's book had been circulating in England for two decades already when, in 1748, it entered the colo-nial American market, where printers inserted the modifier *American* into his title.[9] *American Instructor* looks like a hodgepodge how-to manual, beginning with instructions on letter-writing and ink-making before turning to lessons and exercises in arithmetical calculation. The book then shifts to instruction on double entry bookkeeping, geometry, and navigation before delivering assorted information about geography, history, and medicine—including a list of English monarchs and English plantations, instructions on how to graft fruit trees and cure ailments, and details on how to make pickles and wine.

The volume's apparently disparate contents, however, are in fact neatly held together by its commitment to preparing "the young Man's Mind for Business"—precisely the kind of learning that Cook was said to have excelled at and that Crusoe's sea captain urged him to seek out. Fisher's book concludes, for example, with a telling reminder that "Money is of a prolific generating Nature. Money can beget Money, and its Offspring can beget more, and so on…The more there is of it, the more it produces every Turning, so that the Profits rise quicker and quicker." This image of almost magically proliferating wealth is followed by what might appear to be a strangely contradictory warning: "Beware of thinking all your own that you possess, and of living accordingly. 'Tis a Mistake that many People who have Credit fall into."[10] While enticing his readers with the image of money accumulating in rapid succession and expanding in geometric proportions, Fisher quickly reminds those readers that this money is (at least in part) fictional, not so much wealth itself as a wealth effect produced by credit relations which make one appear to possess more than one actually does. Readers are being asked here simultaneously to perform a headlong calculation in which money generates "more" and "more" at a "quicker and quicker" speed, and to resist the very pull of that seductive temporality, to hold back from participating in a future that, while exhilaratingly full, has in fact not yet arrived (and may, in fact, turn out to be quite empty once it actually does arrive). Understanding and operating within such a world required combining skills in arithmetic, bookkeeping, and navigation with knowledge about geography, travel, and writing, particularly since business was becoming an increasingly global affair.

Among these overlapping late eighteenth- and early nineteenth-century calculative genres, books on mathematics had by far the largest audience and circulation. Mathematical textbooks and manuals from this period addressed a wide and diverse audience, from prospective accountants, farmers, and schoolchildren to accomplished merchants, navigators, and surveyors, and they included both men and women. The subscribers to Michael Walsh's 1801 *New System of Mercantile Arithmetic* explain that its contents will not only "accomplish the student for commerce, [but] are also extremely well adapted to assist and inform the merchant, the mariner, and the trader in their various occupations." The book is alternately recommended in its opening pages "to fit a youth for the business of the Compting-House," to serve "the purposes of a well-informed merchant," and to assist "the ship-master and supercargo."[11]

But Walsh's book competed with a host of other mathematical manuals; in fact, there were so many of these books available that it became common for them to begin with an apology for contributing yet another volume on arithmetic to what was clearly a saturated market. The preface to Erastus Root's 1795 *An Introduction to Arithmetic for the use of Common Schools*, for example, notes that "almost innumerable are the volumes, which have been written on Arithmetic—they continue to be frequently poured in upon the public; yet the subject has, for a long time, been exhausted." Likewise, Nicolas Pike's 1788 *New and Complete System of Arithmetic, composed for the use of the citizens of the United States* begins by noting that it hardly seems necessary to add yet another arithmetic book to the market "when Authors are so multiplied" and when "it may be imagined there can be nothing more than the repetition of a Subject already exhausted."[12] Despite entering into an already competitive market in 1801, however, Walsh's volume enjoyed astonishing success: it was republished in a variety of editions and locations a total of fourteen times following its initial 1801 appearance. The second, 1803, edition followed what its Newburyport printer Edmund Blunt described as the "rapid sale" of its first edition, only to be quickly followed by "ten thousand copies" of a third, 1804, edition made necessary because "in the very short period of its existence two extensive impressions have been circulated through the country, and orders are already received for a large proportion of the third."[13] A fourth edition of "twenty thousand copies" followed in 1806.

Walsh's book did reach out to an especially mixed audience of merchants, mariners, mathematicians, and schoolchildren—in contrast, say, to Root's arithmetic book which was aimed only at the latter, and even more explicitly those at "common schools" in need of "an easy, accurate, and *cheap* volume, containing all the Arithmetical knowledge necessary for the Farmer or Mechanic."[14] But the success of Walsh's volume may be most attributable to the global and transnational sensibility it maintained in comparison to many other mathematics books circulating at the same time. James Maginess identified the disparity between these audiences in his own *New, Copious, and Complete System of Arithmetic*, when he noted that "People in the interior of the country may, perhaps, object to the length of the chapter on Exchange; but upon a little reflection, they will find, that the historical instruction which it contains, will amply compensate for its room; to *merchants on seaboard*, it will be indispensable." Indeed, the preface to the third edition of Walsh's book explains that its section on exchange has been even further expanded, "the importance of which will easily be seen by Merchants whose remittances may *travel through several countries*."[15]

A closer look at the sample mathematical problems included in these books reveals divergent pedagogies for their different audiences, from the nationalist orientation of textbooks aimed at future farmers and artisans, to the global orientation of those aimed at future merchants and navigators. Nicolas Pike's book, for example, contained such initial math problems as "General Washington was born in 1732; what is his age in 1787?" or "The Massacre at Boston, by the British Troops, happened, March 5th, 1770, and the Battle at Lexington, April 19th, 1775; How long between?" Among its sample problems, Erastus Root's volume asks students to calculate the total population of the United States by adding together the listed population figures for each of its states and to calculate the daily salary of the president of the United States if his annual salary is $25,000.[16]

By contrast, compare the following representative questions from Walsh's text: "How many lbs. of Coffee at 1s7 per lb. may be bought for £.8 12 7?" or "If a chest of Hyson tea, weighing 79 lb. neat, cost £.32 11 9 what is it per lb.?" or "A ship's company of 15 persons is supposed to have bread to last their voyage, allowing each 8 ounces per day—when they pick up a crew of 5 persons in distress, to whom they are willing to communicate, what will the daily allowance of each person then be?"[17] Exercises in both Pike's and Walsh's volumes share of course the same goal of teaching students the basic principles of addition, subtraction, or division. But the details in their respective questions reveal that Root and Pike place students and readers in a nationalist scene of calculation, while Walsh places them in a transnational one where they are asked to calculate the cost of products that have traveled to a place like Newburyport, Massachusetts (where the first five editions of his book were published) from as far away as the West Indies and China. In fact, Walsh's questions implicitly position readers (or at least their investments) on ships, and more specifically on ships undertaking long-distance, transoceanic voyages. Walsh's textbook brought the kinds of calculations used by mariners and merchants to reach and exchange goods in far-flung locations around the world home to those seeking to understand and manipulate the numbers and goods pouring in from around the globe.

Walsh's section on "Exchange," for example, includes details about currency and weight conversions in China, Manila, Ceylon, and Japan, and invites students to calculate what "1897 bags of sugar amount to" if in Manila they weigh "139 piculs 1 arobe 17 ½ lb. at 6 dollars per arobe."[18] Two problems from later in the volume illustrate slightly more complex mathematical calculations, but do so within a similarly global geography of goods: "C has nutmegs worth 7s. 6d. per lb. in ready money, but in barter he will have 8s.; D has tobacco worth 9d. per lb.; how much must he rate it per lb. that his profit may be equal to C's?"; and "A has tea which he barters with B at 10d. per lb. more than it cost him, against cambrick which stands B in 10s. per yard but he puts it at 12s.6d.; I would know the first cost of the tea."[19] On the one hand, these questions ask readers to perform calculations in order to generate numerical answers that match those listed at the conclusion of each question, as math textbooks still do today. But these questions are also inviting readers to inhabit a place where nutmeg from the East Indian spice islands meets tobacco from the tidewater South, or where tea from China meets cambric cloth that might have come from India or Europe. Such texts placed their readers in a transoceanic commercial world where calculation fed on even as it underplayed speculation.

It was precisely this relationship between calculation and speculation that George Fisher maintained when he invited the readers of his *American Instructor* to indulge in the promise of profit only then to warn them about the risk of credit. Novels and transoceanic travel narratives shared this uneasy relationship between promise and risk with the number-laden genres that began to fill up the late eighteenth-century print market. *The Dictionary of Merchandise*, published in Philadelphia in 1805, was a mercantile encyclopedia of global goods, a pocket guide that trained readers to trade in commodities from around the world. The volume represents an Enlightenment exercise in knowledge collection that describes, in alphabetical order, a vast range of natural products and their uses. Entries include the acacia shrub from Egypt and Arabia, acajou nuts from Jamaica, agaric from Muscovy and Tartary, aloe "from the island of Socotora in the Indian ocean," and the cochineal insect from Mexico.[20] One kind of advice offered in its descriptions was how to purchase and prepare the best quality merchandise. Human hair, for example, should be "neither too coarse, nor too slender" and it can be made to curl "by first boiling and then baking it," while the best agaric "ought to be large, white and loose." At the same time, descriptions included information about the demand for and profit from these products. Sugar, for instance, is identified as "one of the most valuable plants in the world" since the "quantity consumed in Europe is estimated at nine millions sterling," while tea "has become almost a necessary of life in several parts of Europe" as consumption in Britain has increased from 700,000 pounds in the early part of the eighteenth century to 20,000,000 pounds at the end.[21] Even these excerpts from a very few of the book's entries demonstrate both the extraordinary spatial dimensions carved out by the movement of goods in the age of revolutions and the extraordinary capacity for profitable growth in their circulation.

The Pacific travel narratives discussed in Chapter 1 often described these kinds of exotic and popular products, and the genre's multiplying numbers participated in both the calculative and the speculative. The 1784 collection of British voyages published by George William Anderson, for example, observes that the Philippine "islands are extremely well situated for trade; all the rich merchandize of India is sent from hence to America, and the treasures of Mexico and Peru are brought hither annually, by which exchange, it is said, they make a profit of 400 per cent." Among the items transported through this route are "spices, Chinese silks, and manufactures, particularly silk stockings, of which no less than 50,000 pair have been shipped in one cargo."[22] Merchants and mariners are virtually invited here to pose and solve their own mathematical equation of the sort found in contemporaneous arithmetic books (if 50,000 pairs of silk stockings are sold at a profit of 400 percent, how much might an investor make?). The example from the narrative of Cook's third voyage, cited in the previous chapter, similarly invites readers to perform a calm calculation within which the fever of speculation rises, as the best sea otter skins gain a profit of $120 each in Canton, offering the possibility of nearly 1800 percent profit.[23] Based on the surprising number of ships parked around the tiny island of Masafuera at the end of the eighteenth century, many readers followed these calculations by joining crews destined for the Pacific.

But that fever could and often did break, as George Fisher warned. Voyagers in the wake of Cook, for instance, complained that the price for furs had dropped dramatically in Canton, as runaway speculation drove overhunting. The French explorer La Pérouse notes that the value of the furs his expedition members sold in China "was a tenth of what it would have been when captains Gore and King arrived at Canton" and "one could get only twelve to fifteen piastres for fur of the same quality which, in 1780, would have fetched more than a hundred."[24] The mathematical calculations sailors and merchants might have performed after reading narratives like Cook's or those collected by Anderson turned out to be far more unstable and uncertain than their numerical results seemed to suggest.

Scholars of probability today locate the emergence of new ideas about expectation in the insurance policy, also known as an aleatory contract.[25] James Allen Park called it, in his 1799 *System of the Law of Marine Insurances*, "a contract of speculation."[26] Even more explicitly than travel narratives, insurance manuals made clear just how tightly long-distance maritime commerce was tethered to the financial mechanisms of risk management. Park begins his volume, for instance, by observing that "wherever foreign commerce was introduced, insurance must have soon followed as a necessary attendant," and Samuel Marshall's two-volume 1810 *Treatise on the Law of Insurance* similarly claims that "maritime commerce, carried to any considerable extent, must necessarily draw after it the contract of insurance, from the desire natural to all men to be protected against the accidents of fortune."[27] Dillon explains that the system of contract—of which the insurance policy was one—shared with the new genre of the novel a logic that is both actuarial and probabilistic, for it "entails an epistemic shift toward a belief in probability—not simply toward empiricism, but toward a kind of deliberative intelligence oriented toward navigating future (and thus fictive) possibilities."[28] Insurance contracts taught risk-takers to imagine a variety of possible futures through numbers; novels did the same through words. But both did so by bringing together the empirical and the possible, the definite and the unlikely, the calculative and the speculative. When readers encountered number-filled passages in voyage narratives, did they imbue them with the fantastic possibility of the lottery scheme or the steady empiricism of the multiplication table? I'm suggesting that for readers of Pacific travel narratives, as well as for readers of novels, every calculation was also a speculation.

Calculative Certainty and Numerical Tables

Pacific-bound exploration voyages carried a host of skilled scientists—including botanists, astronomers, hydrographers, and geographers—who gathered data, samples, and measurements from distant and exotic locations around the globe. That information was then used to populate charts, maps, systems, and dictionaries that were characterized by qualities of order, stability, symmetry, and, perhaps most of all, proportion. Systems associated with Enlightenment thinking such as Linnaean taxonomy or alphabetic encyclopedias like *The Dictionary of Merchandise* provided ways to codify the massive influx of knowledge pouring in from Europe's explorations around the globe, from places like Jamaica or Patagonia, Batavia or New Zealand, China or Manila. A 1748 illustration from *Universal Magazine of*

FIGURE 2.1. *Proportionality and balance in the Enlightenment classroom. "The First Lecture in the Sciences of Geography and Astronomy."* Universal Magazine of Knowledge & Pleasure, *1748. Courtesy, American Antiquarian Society.*

Knowledge and Pleasure titled "The First Lecture in the Sciences of Geography and Astronomy" (see Figure 2.1) visualizes such orderly arrangement. The image depicts an instructor teaching four students in a room filled with globes and posters representing systems for understanding and navigating the planet. The accompanying article emphasizes the use of calculation to understand the satisfying proportionality of the world: "This globe which you find distinguished into so many different parts is artificially divided into 360 degrees, each of which degree contains 60 geographical miles."[29] This numerical proportionality is replicated spatially, as the article goes on to explain that the zodiac cuts the equator into twelve equal pieces through which the sun passes during each of the twelve months. The two tropic circles (Cancer and Capricorn) are balanced out with two polar circles (Arctic and Antarctic) and its five zones are organized such that the middle torrid zone is flanked on either side by two temperate zones and above and below by two frigid zones at either pole.[30] The sense of ordered coherence offered in prose is visually repeated in the accompanying image: in it there are four globes, four posters (all containing circles), and four students (also standing in a circle). A similar scene, depicting a classroom filled with globes and charts, appears opposite the title page of Fisher's *American Instructor*, suggesting that what one needs to know about the world can be calculated using the tools provided in the pages of his book.

The numerical tables found in mathematical textbooks, mercantile manuals, and navigation guides were equivalents to the geographical and astronomical models of order and proportion in this image. Numeration tables, addition or multiplication tables, tables of exchange, tables of interest rates, tables of roots, and tables of latitudes and longitudes all made numbers appear orderly, stable, consistent, and dependable. These tables conveyed, even in their visual form, the pleasures of proportionality. Walsh's table of integers and decimals, for example, illustrates visually the balance described in words: "as whole numbers increase in a tenfold proportion from units to the left hand, so decimals decrease in the same proportion to the right"[31] (see Figure 2.2). Whether their numbers ascend or descend, tables offered an image of pleasing proportionality accompanied by steady, dependable, and exponential increase. The multiplication table is a perfect example of this regular pyramidal increase, which is visualized with particular clarity in the unique table from John Vinall's *Preceptor's Assistant*, where the elimination of duplicate numbers amplifies the slope of numerical ascent (see Figure 2.3). The table of powers offers an even more dramatic example by virtue of the exponential magnitude of gain it represents (see Figure 2.4). In the numerical table, the dependable pleasures of proportion meet and temper the unstable excitements of profit. Embedded within its logical, static, and orderly container, in other words, was that giddy prospect of runaway accumulation described by Fisher,

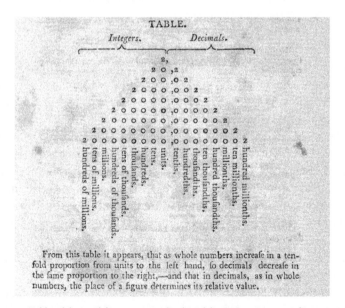

FIGURE 2.2. *Table of decimal fractions. Michael Walsh,* A New System of Mercantile Arithmetic *(Newburyport [MA], 1801). Courtesy, American Antiquarian Society.*

20 MULTIPLICATION OF WHOLE NUMBERS.

BY this rule we find the product of any two numbers, with the affiftance of the fubjoined table,
which the pupil fhould get very perfectly by heart.

TABLE.

1	2	3	4	5	6	7	8	9	10	11	12
2	4	6	8	10	12	14	16	18	20	22	24
3		9	12	15	18	21	24	27	30	33	36
4			16	20	24	28	32	36	40	44	48
5				25	30	35	40	45	50	55	60
6					36	42	48	54	60	66	72
7						49	56	63	70	77	84
8							64	72	80	88	96
9								81	90	99	108
10									100	110	120
11										121	132
12											144

Note. A table of the above form, I have found to
be much preferable to any other, as the fcholar is not fo
likely to be puzzled, as when the whole fquare is filled,
and confequently the table doubled.

MULTIPLICATION OF WHOLE NUMBERS.

To multiply a whole number by a whole number.

RULE.

MULTIPLY every figure of the multiplicand
by every figure of the multiplier, fetting the
firft figure of every line, (in the work) under the multiplying figure, putting down what is under or over ten
or tens, and carrying 1 for every ten to the next product.

Examples.

FIGURE 2.3. *Multiplication table. John Vinall,* The Preceptor's Assistant *(Boston, 1792). Courtesy, American Antiquarian Society.*

in which money begets more money quicker and quicker so that the "more there
is of it, the more it produces every Turning."

But these practical genres also counteracted such frenzy by bringing order to
the dizzying array of mercantile purchases, debts, and loans that marked everyday
experience in the marketplace, or to the equally unpredictable confluence of
maritime winds, directional changes, and shifting tides that characterized life at
sea. The merchant's account book and the captain's log book shared the goal of

TABLE OF POWERS.

Roots,	1	2	3	4	5	6	7	8	9
Squares,	1	4	9	16	25	36	49	64	81
Cubes,	1	8	27	64	125	216	343	512	729
Biquadrates,	1	16	81	256	625	1296	2401	4096	6561
Sursolids,	1	32	243	1024	3125	7776	16807	32768	59049
Square cubes,	1	64	729	4096	15625	46656	117649	262144	531441
Second sursolids,	1	128	2187	16384	78125	279936	823543	2097152	4782969
Biquadrates squared	1	256	6561	65536	390625	1679616	5764801	16777216	43046721
Cubes cubed,	1	512	19683	262144	1953125	10077696	40353607	134217728	387420489
Sursolids squared,	1	1024	59049	1048576	9765625	60466176	282475249	1073741824	3486784401

FIGURE 2.4. *Table of powers. James Maginness,* A New, Copious, and Complete System of Arithmetic, for the Use of Schools and Counting-Houses, in the United States of America *(Harrisburg, PA, 1821). Courtesy, American Antiquarian Society.*

using numbers to fix one's exact financial status in time or geographical location in space. Bookkeeping manuals which taught merchants how to record their accounts, and navigation manuals which taught shipmasters how to keep their journals, essentially offered instruction in producing the stability and dependability promised by such tables—but belied by the everyday scenarios they sought to bring under control.

The calculation problems posed in these volumes worked much like the tables themselves did, by bringing order, stability, consistency, and dependability to what were fundamentally unruly scenarios. Proportionality was fundamentally a fiction that covered over the perpetual presence of risk and uncertainty, the possibility that one might, at any moment, go belly up, become bankrupt or shipwrecked, end up in debtors' prison or stranded alone on a deserted island. The earlier math problems from the Walsh book, for example, which staged scenes of calculation among a global array of goods, quietly represented the scenario of exchange as a stable site of proportionality, fairness, and equality. The question about bartering nutmegs for tobacco, for example, asks readers to calculate the value merchant D should charge merchant C so that each merchant's "profit" is precisely "equal" (meaning here proportional, so that each merchant makes an amount exactly proportional to the other, despite the different starting values per pound of nutmegs and tobacco). Similarly, the question about exchanging tea for cambric supposes an exact proportionality between the profits of merchants A and B. The question is basically asking this: If we know how much profit B made on his cloth by selling it at a higher rate than he purchased it for, how much did A initially pay for his tea if his selling rate is exactly proportional to B's? The pleasure of proportion depends here on an assumed practice of fairness and equality.

Questions like these illustrate what all of these math textbooks call the "Rule of Three," which "teaches, from three numbers given, to find a fourth, that shall be in the same proportion to the third as the second is to the first."[32] There are two kinds of proportion: direct and inverse. As Walsh explains, "Whereas in the Rule of Three Direct, more requires more, and less requires less, in this rule [the rule of inverse, rather than direct, proportion] more requires less and less requires more."[33] The earlier coffee and tea questions are examples of "direct proportion" (assuming that the cost per unit remains the same, how much of each product can you buy if you have more money?). The question about having to share bread rations on a ship with more people than initially planned, on the other hand, is an example of "inverse proportion" (if the amount of bread remains the same, and each shipboard member gets an equal amount of bread, how much will they each get now that there are more of them on the ship?).

It is the kind of crisis scenario summoned by this rule of inverse proportion— in which more requires less and less requires more—that, I suggest, often drives the narratives of novels. Indeed, the ship with limited rations that picks up additional shipwrecked passengers sounds exactly like the plot of a novel. The biggest difference between the novel plot and the math problem is the unspoken assumption of fairness and equality undergirding the latter, where no one is going to take more than his share of the bread, no one is going to charge more for her product than anyone else, and no one is going to misrepresent his costs or values. As soon as we lose the implied fairness and equality in Walsh's math problems about merchants A and B and merchants C and D, we leave the world of a math textbook for one of a novel. Mathematical learning, in other words, routinely eliminated that sensation of speculative risk that always accompanied calculation on transoceanic voyages, even as they often gestured toward speculation's profitable results.[34] The fair and stable scene of calculation presumed by schoolbook scenarios becomes a serviceable novel plot precisely when the element of speculation is openly acknowledged.

The very same issue of the *Universal Magazine* that contains the article and illustration on geographical and astronomical learning also contains a piece titled "The Ways to Raise a Fortune; or, the Art of Growing Rich," which advises the pursuit of "trade as the most natural and likely method of making a man's fortune, for we all know that there are more and greater estates got on the *Exchange*, than at court." But this writer goes on to warn about "the misconduct of those traders, who by their vicious lives, neglect of business, prodigality, or incapacity for trade, frustrate the happy means, which a kind providence has put into their power to make them rich."[35] The author quotes a gentleman observing the problems with young men attempting to make a fortune through trade, including the " 'vanity of trading deep, before their heads are well settled for trading at all: A man in this case may attend to his business with all imaginable care and anxiety; yet ruin himself, and injure all concerned with him. This wrong turn of mind springs from an idle desire of growing rich in a hurry' " and resorting to " 'a kind of random credit, undersellings, ill-finished commodities, &c. But this is one of the phantoms that flies the over-arduous pursuer, and makes him embrace a cloud for *Juno.*"[36]

This lecture describes and warns about speculative behavior leading to danger- ous losses and absurd fantasies, much as Fisher warned his pupil-readers about the error of mistaking credit for cash, or of "thinking all your own that you possess." The instabilities and fictions of speculation, however, tend to get hidden within the apparent stability and factuality of calculation. William Jackson's bookkeeping manual repeatedly emphasizes the accuracy and reliability of the practice of dou- ble-entry accounting, yet at one point issues the following surprising instruction: if, despite following all of the rules, there is a difference in the amounts of the creditor and debtor columns and the mistake cannot be found and corrected, then one must "debit the account to profit and loss for what you have, more than the balance of the account shews, or credit the account by profit and loss for what is wanting of the said balance, and then close the account by balance for what you find in cash."[37] In other words, add or subtract as needed to ensure that the two columns do in fact agree, and continue on with one's calculations and record- keeping as if there never were an inconsistency.

The world of navigation produced similar promises of numerical precision quietly intercepted by utter uncertainty. Navigation manuals, like mathematics textbooks, are filled with tables and, like bookkeeping manuals, instruct on how to produce a scientific and error-proof record. Thus the navigational "log-book," as described by John Hamilton Moore, "is marked in columns for hours, knots, fathoms, courses, winds, leeway, transactions; and under it the columns for courses, distances, northings, or southings, eastings, or westings, the latitude by dead reckoning, latitude by observation, meridianal distance, difference of longitude, longitude in, and in the last, bearing and distance of the land."[38] Thomas Haselden explains in *The Seaman's Daily Assistant* that the purpose of keeping a ship's jour- nal is so that "at any Time you may be able to know what Latitude and Longitude the Ship is in."[39] But Haselden goes on to address the situation in which "you have made all the proper Allowances you can, such as for Variation, Lee-way, Currents, &c. and still find that your Latitude by Dead-Reckoning will not agree with the Latitude by Observation."[40] In such cases, Haselden's advice for the log-keeping mariner is the same as Jackson's advice for the account-keeping merchant: elimi- nate the discrepancy between the two recorded numbers by allowing the dead- reckoning data to take the place of the observational data and continue on as if there never was an inconsistency. Even pages upon pages of carefully recorded and aligned numbers cannot, it seems, eliminate the presence of uncertainty, whose appearance must quickly be erased.

Joseph Huddert's description of trade winds in *The Oriental Navigator* participates in a similarly couched admission of uncertainty; he explains that "there is gener- ally an interval of calm between the Trade winds and the opposite winds in high latitudes" and then goes on virtually to cancel out any possibility of measuring or predicting such a pattern by noting that "it is scarce probable that human foresight will ever be able to form any tolerable idea respecting the duration of winds, or the time of their change."[41] All of these calculative genres generate in their tabular contents a highly appealing image of scientific predictability and dependability. Their textual contents work to confirm such dependability but occasionally destroy it altogether by acknowledging exceptionality, unpredictability, and inequality. Thomas Dilworth's *Schoolmasters Assistant* goes so far as to refuse to include any tables that show the conversion values of foreign currency "partly because all those *Tables*, which I have met with, which shew the Value of *Foreign Coins* in *English Mony*, are very erroneous" but even more so because "the *Value* of *Foreign Species*…in every *Country* is unsettled, and therefore such *Coins* are subject to vary in their *Prices*, as the *Merchants* find an Opportunity to profit by them."[42] Because currency values change so often and so unpredictably, the stability and accuracy of the numbers aligned in these tables are really something closer to fiction. Similarly, the dependability of numbers presented in the tables and answer keys of arithmetic books or accounting manuals is in striking contrast to the insecurity of numbers in the context of actual trade or travel or investment (which most of these books were preparing their readers to participate in, in the first place).

Speculative Risk and Lottery Schemes

These numerical genres inadvertently reveal the unreliability and changeability of numbers even as they repeatedly insist on their accuracy and dependability. They similarly attach themselves to the trustworthy empiricism of numbers in the world of mathematics while distancing themselves from the corrupt instability of numbers in the world of gambling. Marshall's *Treatise on the Law of Insurance*, for example, carefully differentiates an insurance policy from a gambling wager and condemns gaming for "pointing out a speedy, though hazardous mode of accumulating wealth" that "produces a contempt for the moderate, but certain, profits of sober industry."[43] Similarly, Jackson's text on bookkeeping includes a sample waste-book entry on income derived from a successful bet on a horse race, only to announce that this detail "ought never to have been admitted into a Book of this Kind, because, no Person concerned in Trade ought ever to meddle with Gaming." He insists that "raising money by Gaming,…by which one Man's Gain is directly in proportion to another's Loss, and the Advantage is in no Sense mutual, I scruple not to pronounce absolutely wrong and Iniquitous." Part of the problem with gambling for Jackson and Marshall—as with speculation for Fisher—is that it breeds financial impatience (it "never fails to give a person a Dislike to sober Industry, as too slow a Mode of raising Money") and leads toward financial ruin (as "the temptation to risk greater and greater sums is hardly to be resisted").[44] For Jackson and Marshall both, gaining wealth through trade takes time, labor, and patience to yield "moderate, but certain" future profits; gaining wealth through gaming magnifies the risk precisely by shrinking the time. But the *Universal*

Magazine writer who warned about the young businessman who traded too deep and ended up mistaking a cloud for the god Juno, suggests that some traders operate exactly like gamblers.

There was one other location besides books on mathematics, accounting, navigation or insurance where numerical tables could be found during the late eighteenth and early nineteenth centuries: the scheme contained in lottery handbills. Lotteries were a regular feature of everyday life in the early United States, as they were used to raise funds for purposes as diverse as supporting private colleges and public schools, building bridges and libraries, improving public roads and causeways, raising money for factories, businesses, and hospitals (such as the scheme to "enable the Proprietors of the Hartford Woollen Manufactory to procure Machines, Implements, and to increase their Stock, in order to render the Business more extensively useful to the Community"[45]) and even to promote literature or distribute cash or jewelry. The 1795 handbill for the Harvard College Lottery, for example, advertised 25,000 tickets to be sold at $10 apiece (see Figure 2.5). The "Scheme" depicting the various prizes and their value shows two columns, one whose numbers increase substantially and one whose numbers correspondingly decrease in proportion to the former. At the top of that "Scheme" is a single grand prize ticket worth $25,000, while at the bottom are 7,300 tickets that will win a mere $16 each. Of course, unrepresented in the scheme at all (in fact, noted only at the very bottom of the sheet, as if reluctantly to acknowledge a likelihood of loss that the scheme itself does not want to own) are the nearly 19,000 tickets—otherwise known as blanks—that will win absolutely nothing at all.

From a visual standpoint, the lottery scheme's pyramidal shape resembles exactly that of mathematical tables representing factors, powers, or interest. But whereas mathematical tables were perceived as representing disinterested and dependable empirical facts, lottery schemes were perceived as dangerous devices that would snare unwitting citizens into debt, despair, crime, and even death. The lottery scheme might be thought of as the corrupt and irrational counterpart to the mathematical table's virtuous hyper-rationality, and the anti-lottery literature that circulated in response to these handbills and tickets reinforced this perception. The popular tale *Wonderful Advantages of Adventuring in the Lottery!*, for example, tells the story of the pious John Brown, who lives a comfortable life with his wife and son and is employed as a servant to a wealthy merchant. Tempted by a handbill inviting "all who had a mind to be rich in a hurry, to seize the lucky hour of adventuring in the wheel of fortune; shewing them how many thousand pounds they would be sure to get for one guinea!," Brown proceeds to ignore his wife's appeals to religion and reason by buying one ticket. Of course, one ticket quickly becomes six tickets to increase his chances, whereupon he is furthermore tricked into buying an insurance policy on his tickets.[46]

Brown's formerly calm and satisfied demeanor changes as he enters an emotional state of perpetually anxious "expectation" that—when his tickets disappointingly are all revealed to be blanks—quickly turns to drinking, then to robbery (in an

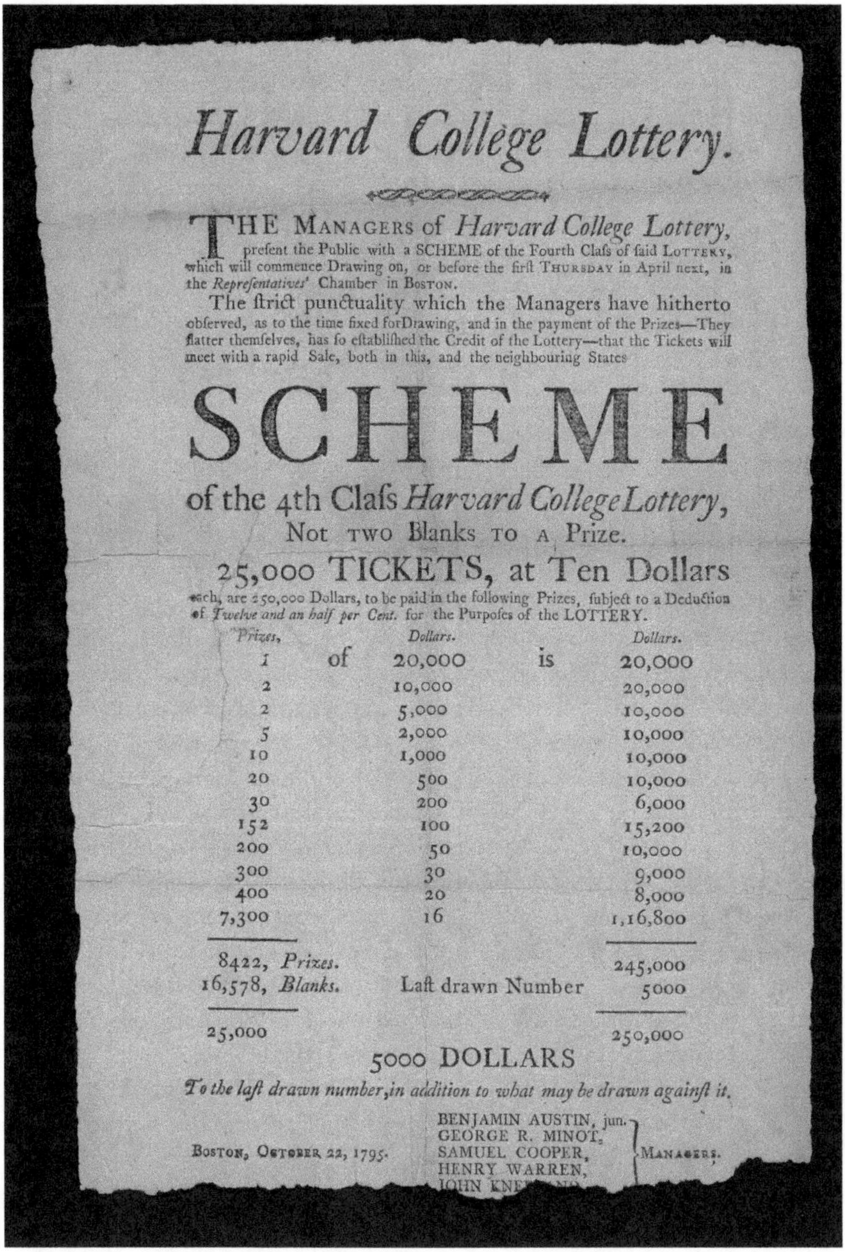

FIGURE 2.5. *Harvard College lottery [broadside], October 22, 1795. HUA 630 pf (1), olvwork178815. Harvard University Archives.*

attempt to gain back some of his lost money), and finally to murder (when the robbery goes awry). The story ends with his wife dead of grief, his son orphaned, and Brown himself *"hanged, drawn, and quartered"* for his crime. The judge proclaims that "I have never sat upon this bench after the drawing of the Lottery, but I had reason to think it had proved the ruin of many of the unhappy culprits who appeared before me."[47] The plot of this story offers an inverse morality to the lottery scheme's promised plot of growing rich quick, but in narrating the exponential growth of sin and destruction, it follows an absolutely equivalent temporality of suspense. This popular pamphlet appeared in ten editions between 1800 and 1820; one of its appearances was in a magazine that also contained an account of Alexander Selkirk whose fictional descendant Robinson Crusoe, as one recent critic notes, spends an inordinate amount of time on his deserted island calculating odds.[48] The Pacific connection here is not just happenstance. A Harvard professor as early as 1727 proposed in the Royal Society's *Philosophical Transactions* that surveys of wind and weather be conducted along trade routes in the world's oceans so that "the Probability of Voyages might then be calculated in the same Manner as that of other chances."[49] Every long transoceanic voyage was essentially a lottery ticket masquerading as a multiplication table.

Jesse Molesworth has argued that readers' experience with the new eighteenth-century genre of the novel informed their experience of the lottery, for the lottery provided a form of "speculation" that encouraged "the fantasy, however unlikely, of participating in a narrative of significant events, with plotlines frequently borrowed from novels." The lottery's appeal, then, was not only money but "plot—the momentary opportunity to imagine oneself as a fictional character."[50] Molesworth suggests that recent novel studies have missed the novel's continued engagement with a realm of magical enchantment because accounts of the genre's realism from Ian Watt onward have focused on character and setting "to the exclusion of plot." Turning to recent work in prospect theory, Molesworth maintains that believability at the level of plot depends not on particularity of detail or even on likelihood but rather on "the sense of mystery, causation, and temporality necessary for plot." And plot, he maintains, is "the lack of interest in blanks," those numerous tickets that would yield no prize whatsoever—like the 19,000 worthless tickets demoted to a footnote in the Harvard College lottery scheme. Jakob Bernoulli, the mathematician and early probability theorist, focused his interest on the "1,000 out of 1,001 trials yielding truthful information," but novelistic narrative, Molesworth insists, is interested in "the 1 out of 1,001 outlier."[51]

As I argued in Chapter 1 in relation to the commercial temporality of Pacific travel writing, however, narrative expectation actually depends on both. Narrative suspense emerges as a relationship between blanks and potentially winning tickets, between demonstrable truth and its absurd outlier, between patient tedium and sensational encounter. In narrative, blanks take the form of the prolonged delineation of minute and careful details. The accumulation of such details contributes precisely to the formal realism identified by Watt as the novel's central feature, just as it contributes a measure of truth as well to travel accounts about distant and exotic locations. As Cohen has explained, the descriptive details that populate novels like *Robinson Crusoe* "enrich the performance of craft" on the part of the mariner while also "helping to drive the action forward even as it brings to life a novel's imaginary world."[52] That forward-moving narrative action is driven by a dynamics of risk whose intersecting terms can be found in the kinds of numerical genres with which this chapter has engaged. Jonathan Levy has traced the movement of risk from the seaborne world of maritime insurance to its later life as a feature of land-based capitalism in the nineteenth-century U.S.[53] If we look to the world of fiction, however, we could argue that risk moved from the sea to land much earlier, and that it did so within the pages of the eighteenth-century novel.

Even if novelistic plot remains solely interested in that one potentially lucky ticket—the unlikely prospect of rescue or windfall or true love—there can be no sense of expectation and anticipation around that ticket unless it is spinning in a wheel that also contains 1000 (or 19,000) blanks. Novelistic plot requires the narrative equivalent of lottery blanks in order to provide a calculative context for its more engaging moments of anticipatory speculation. Suspense only gets created when there are enough blanks to provide a sufficient risk pool surrounding any ticket's chances of winning (or any heroine's chances of marrying up, any castaway's chances of rescue). A critical mass of carefully cautious and often utterly mundane details (the dull labor of calculation) is needed before generating the risky excitement of expectation (the heady flush of speculation).

Take the example of the 1823 children's book *The White Kitten*, in which the uncle of a young girl named Mary leaves Massachusetts on a commercial voyage to China, on a ship aptly named *Crusoe*. The uncle leaves his niece with a white cat and a golden locket, which she puts around the cat's neck. Meanwhile, the uncle takes with him its equally white kitten to hunt mice and rats on the ship. The *Crusoe* carries a cargo of cotton and iron goods as well as two Boston missionaries with the goal of converting to Christianity the Natives of O-wy-hee (Hawai'i), a frequent stopover location on transoceanic voyages. After a converted Hawai'ian delivers a sermon on the island, a cash box circulates to collect donations and Mary's uncle is surprised to find in that box the golden locket he recognizes as the one he gave Mary before his departure. He tracks down the locket's route through the sailor Tom Wilder, who arrived in Hawai'i on a separate ship that sailed from Salem. Tom explains that he took the locket from the neck of a white cat he saw running through the streets of Salem, but that before he was able to exchange the locket for cash he was hired on a ship heading for China. Upon undergoing a spiritual and moral conversion, Tom gives the locket to Mary's uncle, who—after exchanging in Canton for silks and teas the sandalwood he purchased in Hawai'i— returns to Boston to let his niece know that he found, 5,000 miles away, in a cash box on a tropical island in the middle of the Pacific, what she had lost on the busy streets of a port city in Massachusetts.[54]

This story provides a perfect example of Molesworth's point that what makes plot appealing to readers is to be found not in rational probability but in something more magically improbable. But I'd also like to draw attention to the series of purchases and profits made by members of the ship *Crusoe* as it makes its way across the Pacific, exchanges that depend on the knowledge and skills provided in books on mathematics, accounting, and navigation and that—as actual Pacific travel narratives repeatedly reveal—are subject to profound variability, uncertainty, and risk. Descriptions of these commercial activities make up precisely the mundane and realist backdrop (cotton, iron goods, sandalwood) that fills the pages of this novelistic fiction, much as precise geographical descriptions and tedious navigational details fill the pages of Pacific travel writing. The golden locket, on the other hand, is the lucky lottery ticket that miraculously shrinks the long distances of the global marketplace and dissipates the risk and uncertainty with which it is associated. Through all kinds of random uncertainty and chance experienced across astonishingly long distances, the object of novelistic sentiment wraps the risky improbability of this account within the soothing promise of security. The unrealistic resolution (a kind of magical lottery windfall) is only rendered believable by virtue of the quantity of realistic but mundane details (the blanks of formal realism) surrounding it.[55] The combination of bored detachment and expectant engagement serves as a critical resource for novelistic plot-spinning no less than for capitalist profit-making.

Gender and Disembodiment

Lottery players might have used the narratives of novels to plot out fantasized futures, but novels themselves embed improbable lottery logic within their narrative construction. Lottery schemes, like novels, banked on the imaginative substitutability made possible by the power of disembodiment. Catherine Gallagher aligns the parallel emergence of fiction and commercial logic in the eighteenth century with the feature of disembodiment that also correlated with the legal status of women, calling this the principle of "nobody's story" central to the literary genre. What differentiated novelistic fiction from earlier proto-novelistic writing was the presence of characters who were what Gallagher calls "nobodies." Unlike the readily identifiable characters found in romance, who were clearly allegorical or veiled representations of well-known figures of celebrity or scandal, the novel was populated by figures who were nobody in particular, and precisely by virtue of their not being somebody recognizable, it was possible for any reader imaginatively to substitute him or herself in the place of that character. When John Brown asks in *Wonderful Advantages of Adventuring in the Lottery!* "why may I not get it [the winning prize] as well as another?,"[56] he is essentially inserting himself into a plot about nobody (in this case, the hypothetical owner of the lucky winning ticket) that was peddled at once by lotteries, novels, and commercial investment schemes.

This capacity to identify with novelistic nobodies happens through an act of imaginative substitution that readers also practice in the exercises they encountered in the numerical genres popular during this period. Evidence of such imaginative substitution can be found, for example, in the mathematical copybooks produced by students at a female academy in Boston run by the novelist and playwright Susanna Rowson. In 1810, Eliza Houghton and Sarah Pollock, two students enrolled in Rowson's academy, created nearly identical manuscript folios entitled *Practical Arithmetic: Comprising all the Rules for Transacting Business.*[57] The instructional context in which the young women produced these copy books (which are essentially handwritten copies of math textbooks, produced in careful and sometimes ornate calligraphy) isn't entirely clear, but the two volumes are as interchangeable with each other as they are with the vast majority of published arithmetic books from the period. They begin with numeration, simple addition and subtraction, and the rules of three direct and inverse; they go on to discuss single and double fellowship, interest, loss and gain, tare and tret, and commission and brokerage; they then review insurance, discount, and buying and selling stocks; and they finally offer examples of such financial genres as bills of parcels, account books, and receipts before concluding with currency exchange tables. The volumes appear to have served simultaneously as penmanship exercises and math lessons, a pedagogy perhaps founded on the assumption that students could learn math by copying it: fan fiction with numbers.[58]

Houghton's and Pollock's manuscripts are identical to each other except in the minor details of the final section which illustrates various financial genres. There Houghton's sample bookkeeping entry shows facing debtor and creditor pages that identify the debtor as Sancho Panza and the corresponding creditor as Don Quixote. Her sample IOU, meanwhile, documents Jonathan Trusty's promise to pay $100 to Peregrine Pickle, signed by the witnesses Thomas Tinker and Robison [*sic*] Crusoe (see Figure 2.6).[59] Pollock's manuscript is the same as Houghton's except that the creditor to Sancho Panza is listed as one Walter Underwood, while in her note from Jonathan Trusty to Peregrine Pickle, the witness Robinson Crusoe's name is spelled correctly (see Figure 2.7).[60]

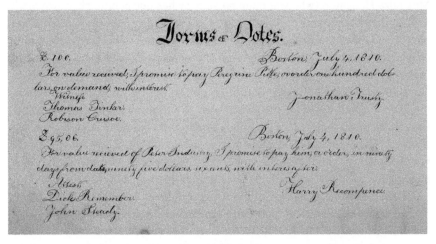

FIGURE 2.6. *Sample IOU showing Robison [sic] Crusoe as witness. Eliza Houghton,* Practical Arithmetic *manuscript copy book, created at Susanna Rowson's Female Academy (Boston, 1810). Courtesy, American Antiquarian Society.*

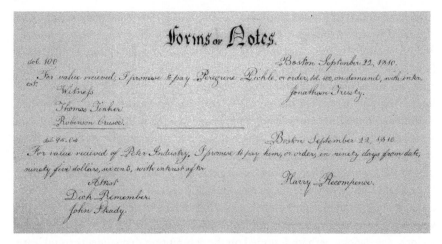

FIGURE 2.7. *Sample IOU showing Robinson Crusoe as witness. Sarah Pollock,* Practical Arithmetic *manuscript copy book, created at Susanna Rowson's Female Academy (Boston, 1810). Courtesy, American Antiquarian Society.*

The names of novelistic and otherwise invented characters are interspersed with the names of family members and acquaintances in both texts. The first of Houghton's examples for how to write "bills of parcels," for example, shows a Miss Susanna Price buying cloth goods from a William Rowson, Jr. (possibly a reference to the husband of headmistress and novelist Susanna Rowson) and the second shows an Abigail Phelps buying groceries of Jeffrey Houghton (likely a reference to a brother or father of Eliza). Meanwhile, the corresponding sample documents in Pollock's manuscript have a Mrs. Ann F. Trask purchasing cloth from an Allan Pollock (presumably a relation of Sarah's) while the second has her schoolmate Miss Eliza Houghton (who was quite possibly by her side penning her own math book at the time) buying groceries from a Josiah Bradlee.[61] This fascinating and unexpected substitution of names—drawn from a mixture of novel reading, family connections, and personal invention—illustrates precisely Gallagher's principle of "nobody's story." The financial genres illustrated in the manuscript books of Houghton and Pollock, and replicated in countless similar numerical genres from the period, clearly allow for the substitution of an infinite variety of real or fictional names into sample receipts or IOUs or account books, making it clear that math problems and financial templates were just as much "nobody's story" as were novels. Houghton's and Pollock's books offer only one piece of evidence that such numerical texts moreover reached female readers just as readily as novels did.

Caitlin Rosenthal explains that numeracy and literacy operated in tandem in the late eighteenth and early nineteenth centuries, when print and other material technologies made available tools for "democratizing access to calculation." Those tools included mathematical tables and algorithms that exposed an enormous proportion of the American population—including "women, wage laborers, farmers, and even slaves"—to the numerical skills needed in a marketplace that was part of an "increasingly global" economy.[62] Even though most books on the subjects of mathematics, accounting, or navigation seemed implicitly, if not explicitly, to address an audience of men (especially men who were—or boys who hoped to become—merchants and mariners), young women clearly participated in these forms of learning, and their experiences indicated that one needn't be on a ship to experience, or learn how to manage, the vicissitudes of its voyage.[63] Advertisements for schools that appeared in American periodicals during this time emphasized instruction—regardless of the students' gender—in the topics of writing, arithmetic, bookkeeping, and geography. All these topics appeared, for instance, in the notices for James Hardie's school (1797), the Bethesda Select Boarding School for female students in New Jersey (1799), and William Pirsson's academy for male and female students (1799).[64] At the same time, periodical articles such as "Improvements Suggested in Female Education" (1797) and "Outlines of a Plan of Instruction for the Young of Both Sexes" (1798) emphasized the importance of teaching young women as well as men the subjects of arithmetic, bookkeeping, calculation, and geography.

Benjamin Rush argued in his 1787 *Thoughts on Female Education* that women ought to be trained in bookkeeping for the explicit purpose of better managing the property of their present or future husband. It may have been with such goals in mind that David Kendal published his 1797 *Young Lady's Arithmetic*, but the description on its title page suggested that more purely intellectual pleasures were also being satisfied: the book has been "*published by request of several Young Ladies, desirous of adding to their other mental accomplishments the pleasing & useful science of figures.*"[65] Kendal's volume looks identical in content and arrangement to similar math textbooks, suggesting that methods of teaching these subjects were the same for young men and women. Moreover, women may well have been considered potential audiences for such books even if they were not explicitly identified as such in the text itself. Charles Hutton's *A Course of Book-keeping, According to the Method of Single Entry* (published in Philadelphia for the first time in 1788) begins by acknowledging that "almost every person who is intended for business, should learn a course of Book-keeping of this kind, because it is used in almost every shop." Merchants, however, regularly complain that "their boys, having learnt only the Italian form [double-entry bookkeeping]...are almost as ignorant in the management of their Books, as if they had never learnt any method." Hutton offers his single-entry course as an antidote to this problem and insists that it "is so easy, that it may also be taught, in a few weeks [*sic*] time to young Ladies, as well as to young Gentlemen."[66] Hutton was a renowned mathematician in England, and his claim here should be understood in the context of his role from 1774 to 1818 as editor of *The Ladies' Diary*, a British periodical that regularly published challenging mathematical problems explicitly for female readers who were encouraged not only to solve but to create new problems to appear in future publications.[67] The lag between issues of the magazine provided readers with time to solve these problems, but also created the suspense of waiting to find out if one's solution was in fact correct.

While the math problems in *The Ladies' Diary* were marketed as a kind of pleasurable leisure activity for elite women, such exercises in calculation may very well have helped women prepare themselves for financial uncertainties like debt or widowhood as well as for more mundane everyday practices like purchasing goods. This function is especially clear in the many questions in the Houghton and Pollock manuscripts that emphasize the risks, uncertainties, and mutual dependencies of commercial exchange: the "Merchant sailing in Trade, owes in all £3475, and has in money and effects but £2316, 13, 4: Now supposing his effects are delivered up; I Pray what will each creditor receive on pound?" or "Suppose I lend a friend £350 for 5 months, he promising the like kindness; but, when requested, can spare but £125; how long may I keep it to balance the favour?" or "Suppose I buy 47 yards of cloth for 141 dollars, and sell it 3 dollars, 75 cents per yard do I gain or lose, and how much per yard?"[68] Other problems address inheritance concerns that encouraged young women to calculate their financial value, such as the addition problem in *The Young Lady's Arithmetic* that asks if "A lady being heiress to her father's estate of twelve th. six hun. dols.—to an uncle's of nine th. fifty seven—and her aunt's of thirty eight hd. and forty; what is her whole fortune?"[69]

Other problems asked readers to calculate their exposure to financial risk, such as the following from the section on partnerships in Houghton's and Pollock's volumes: "A man dying left two sons and a daughter, to whom he bequeathed the following sums, viz. To the first son he gave 1200 dollars, to the second 1000 dollars, and to the daughter, 800 dollars; but it was found that his whole estate amounted only to 750 dollars; what must each child receive of the estate, in proportion to the legacies?"[70] The question asks students to solve through calculation a problem of proportionality, but a fundamental disproportionality based on gender (and birth order) is already written into its terms. These examples are also important reminders that one need not have traveled to distant oceans or invested in global commercial schemes to experience the risk that such travel or speculation entailed, because—for women in particular—the results of that risk-taking traveled home through a husband's or father's finances even if those husbands or fathers did not return home themselves.

We have seen that Gallagher distinguishes the novel from its fictional predecessors by the former's use of "nobodies"—characters who have no concrete referents in the real world—whereas pre-novelistic romance was populated by scarcely veiled characters who were clearly "someone" identifiable. While somebodies were possessed of actual bodies, nobodies literally had no body, and this crucial corporeal absence is key to the kind of believability and reader attachment long associated with novelistic narrative. Gallagher builds on Hume's discussion of the relationship between sympathy and property to explain that the novelistic "[n]obody was a more likely candidate for sympathy in this period than almost anybody else" because

[t]his proprietary barrier of the other's body is what fiction freely dispenses with; by representing feelings that belong to no other body, fiction actually facilitates the process of sympathy. It bypasses the stage at which the sentiments perceived in other bodies are mere matters of fact and gives us the illusion of immediately appropriable sentiments, free sentiments belonging to nobody and therefore identifiable with ourselves.[71]

Because fictional characters have no referential corporeality in the real world, their feelings do not belong to them and readers take possession of those feelings by substituting themselves for those disembodied figures, much like the infinitely replaceable debtors and creditors in the schoolbooks discussed above.[72] Novelistic sympathy, then, performs a kind of emotional robbery that isn't robbery only because the stolen feelings have no real owner. Through a substitution facilitated by disembodiment, readers take possession of the feelings of a lonely Robinson Crusoe, or an anxious Pamela Andrews (or Susanna Rowson's own bereft Charlotte Temple, for that matter). This powerful process allows readers to fall into the world of the novel, identify intensely with its characters, and believe in a story they know full well to be unreal.

This affective attachment to novelistic character, however, sustains (and may actually require) a diachronic dimension at the level of novelistic plot, where attachment gets temporally elongated into a future-oriented emotional investment otherwise known as suspense: that highly engaged interest in utterly fictional outcomes. Cohen has described *Robinson Crusoe* and the sea novel more generally as depicting a world in which sailors face "profoundly uncertain undertakings with a great chance of failure" and attempt to create "the best possibility for a positive outcome." In doing so, she explains, these novels bring the world of the sea and the stock market into experiential alignment by providing an exercise in "[h]ow to succeed in high-risk speculation." Although this feature may be especially identifiable in novels that happen to take place at sea, it isn't at all unique to that particular subgenre. Cohen suggests that a novel like Samuel Richardson's *Pamela*, for example, exemplifies a "feminine practical reason" that is parallel to the masculine version in *Crusoe*.[73] It might be said that all novels take up where insurance policies run out and take place where their terms do not reach—whether on deserted islands inhabited by an isolated castaway or in the house of an English aristocrat who wishes to possess the body of his virtuous maid. What a global transoceanic framework allows us to see is that these two very different kinds of locations, and the gendered subgenres of the adventure and domestic novel they represent, aren't so different from each other as they might seem.

Cohen describes the novel's narrative as having been linearized by Defoe, who produced a "well-oiled narrative chain of problem-solving" from what had been in earlier romance forms a much more disorganized and circuitous series of adventures. But I suspect that novelistic narrative acquires its seductively engaging momentum through more than the organization of scattered events into a "logic of cause and effect."[74] It does with words in long prose form what numbers did in the fraught context of long-distance transoceanic travel and commerce: it dangled promise about the future alongside the danger of getting there, offsetting speculative frenzy with calculative reassurance. Novels of all kinds offered readers regular practice in accommodating the sensations of expectation central to a world increasingly penetrated by global trade and its mechanisms of risk-taking and risk assessment. Novels provided a kind of affective and intellectual training ground for managing prediction and disappointment, for calculating probability and danger, and for responding to sudden and dramatic changes in fortune. Novels emerged, in other words, as numberless representations of an increasingly number-driven world. Gallagher compares novel readers to "merchants and insurers calculating risks" and insists that this practice of imaginatively investing in a probabilistic future characterized nearly every feature of an emergent modernity, such as the national sale of debt bonds to pay for "a vast military and imperial enterprise."[75] Like transoceanic travel narratives, novels were the textual companions to war capitalism; they encouraged calculating and speculating readers to subordinate the violent substrate of risk on which the exciting anticipation of reward fed and, as a result, to overlook its effects on real bodies.

It's not surprising that Crusoe and Cook were both associated with learning math, for the philosopher Enrique Dussel identifies mathematics as the central "language" through which the overwhelming size and enormous complexity of the world system was compressed and simplified by Europe and the West.[76] Indeed, one way of thinking about the numerical tables that filled books about mathematics, accounting, or navigation from this period is to see them as agents of such simplification. Tables, like algorithms, are shortcuts: they replace long, messy, and complicated calculative details with tight, neat, and orderly numerical schemas.[77] In this sense, they make it easier to navigate the globe and more efficient to exchange its incredibly diverse products across vast distances as well as differences of language, culture, and systems of exchange. But Dussel's point is that such calculative tools also made it possible to avoid confrontation with the gritty complexity and disturbing exploitation that invariably accompanied such movement and exchange, while also making profit from it possible. Anne Salmond points out that European tools of measurement, for example, reduced both islands and oceans "into space gridded by lines of latitude and longitude stripped of substance and emptied of people."[78] Mundane numerical calculation engaged in a similar disembodiment by obscuring the material losses and corporeal violence that buoyed fanciful speculation. Calculation underplayed by concealing the most devastating consequences of risk-taking (such as bankruptcy or shipwreck, death or incarceration) beneath the allure of risk's most desirable consequences (such as windfall or discovery, wealth or glory).

The tempered excitement of risk that novels require in their plots, however, always approaches re-embodiment, and this is perhaps nowhere more true than in the depiction of women.[79] Consider again the plot of *Pamela*—the novel whose engaging realism provided John Hawkesworth with the model for his version of

Cook's narrative of the Pacific—in which a serving maid's virtue wins out over aristocratic privilege. A satisfyingly romantic love story takes shape as Pamela's master, Mr B—, after a lengthy and tension-filled battle, finally relinquishes his prolonged efforts to possess her body through coercion or persuasion and asks for her hand in marriage instead. Pamela may be a nobody in whose place readers can substitute themselves, but what this satisfying and linearized plot summary stops us from seeing is that Richardson's novel is also a prolonged story about a woman whose body is repeatedly and relentlessly under threat; its propulsive linearity blurs the grueling cyclicality that buoys it up.

This chapter has argued that the combined temporalities demonstrated in the calculative mathematical table and the speculative lottery scheme produced a linear narrative of anticipatory promise that worked to conceal the unpredictable and cyclical dangers of risk and loss. This narrative dynamic developed within a transoceanic world of travel and trade that reached from the Atlantic to the Pacific and beyond, and it was fueled in part by numbers, which crucially assisted the expansion of that global market. As Dussel has reminded us, numbers simplified the movement of ships and goods while also hiding the often brutal effects on real bodies of war capitalism and expanding empire. The imaginative practice of disembodied substitution, learned through numbers and novels alike, facilitated global commerce to such far-away locations as the Pacific by redirecting the ever-present danger of risk into a future-oriented narrative of anticipated reward, dissuading both readers and investors from "believing the literal truth of a representation so that one can instead admire its likelihood and extend enough credit to buy into the genre."[80]

Pacific travel narratives told stories of commercial windfall, imperial triumph, and scientific discovery. But they also told stories of the violent and exploitative conflicts that helped make those achievements possible, and of the violent resistance of indigenous peoples who responded with rebellion and outrage. Those acts have never factored in dominant accounts about the age of revolutions, and in fact defy reigning definitions of revolution. Accommodating such evidence therefore requires new spatial and narrative models that make our histories and definitions of revolution more global and less linear. The next chapter pursues these possibilities by returning to the Pacific travel narratives introduced in Chapter 1, this time to focus on the political record of insurrectionary violence embedded in their accounts and left behind on bodies. Paying closer attention to bodies allows us to approach risk from below, from the cyclical underbelly of linearized narrative, where the actual experiences of indigenous peoples, sailors, and women in the eighteenth-century Pacific re-embody the consequences of risk obscured by otherwise disembodied scenes of calculation.

Politics

VIOLENCE AND GENDER IN THE
REVOLUTIONARY PACIFIC

Widespread protests erupted following the August 2011 police shooting of Mark Duggan, a 29-year-old black resident of Tottenham, one of London's poorest neighborhoods. The word repeatedly used by the media to describe the violent response—which quickly spread to other districts and cities—was riots. Two days later, the BBC interviewed Darcus Howe, a British journalist, civil rights activist, and resident of Brixton, a neighborhood which had seen some of the most dramatic violence during the uprisings. In the interview, Howe responds to broadcaster Fiona Armstrong's repeated use of the term "riot" by clarifying that "I don't call it rioting, I call it an insurrection of the masses of the people." Howe proceeded to place the London insurrection in global historical context by noting that "It is happening in Syria, it is happening in Clapham, it is happening in Liverpool, it is happening in Port-of-Spain, Trinidad, and that is the nature of the historical moment."

Armstrong nonetheless went on to ask Howe about his own involvement in earlier "riots" ("you are no stranger to riots…you have taken part in them yourself," she claimed).[1] Howe vehemently insists that he never took part "in a single riot." Rather, he has "taken part in demonstrations that ended up in a conflict," pressing against the media's chosen terminology and its implications for understanding the London events. While the BBC clearly expected Howe to share its own sense of "shock" at the violence, he instead places that violence within a prolonged history of police mistreatment of black and white youth in the city. "Have some respect for an old West Indian negro," claims Howe, "instead of accusing me of being a rioter."[2]

Riot, insurrection, revolt, uprising, rebellion, revolution: the vocabulary of political resistance is large, complicated, and inextricable from racial politics and history. But this vocabulary—the words we choose to describe acts of resistance— is also a function of narrative. Born in Trinidad before relocating to Britain (where he has lived and worked for over fifty years), Darcus Howe is the nephew of C. L. R. James, the writer and historian whose 1938 book *The Black Jacobins* offered a powerful, field-transforming history of the Haitian Revolution. Sarah Knott has recently pointed out that, before James, histories of Haiti "cast Saint Dominguan events as a bloody and barbarous race war that had no reason or rhyme—indeed, no narrative." Knott indicates that revolution has long been distinguished from resistance or reform because it dramatically transforms by rearranging the world, but she also acknowledges that this distinction rests on a "whole set of organizing terms and scripts." Thus James narratively transformed into revolution what had appeared to earlier generations of scholars a scene of riots in part by plotting a considerably lengthened timeline that, as Knott points out, begins not with eighteenth-century acts of plantation violence but with the violence of European colonialism stretching back to 1492.[3] His nephew similarly challenged spatial and temporal narrative conventions when he positioned the London events within a framework of global revolution and as a response to a history of racialized policing.

In this chapter, I bring the questions raised by the 2011 Darcus Howe interview to bear on the late eighteenth-century age of revolutions and the place of the Pacific in it. The Pacific is frankly absent from our histories of the American Revolution and of the larger revolutionary Atlantic, and the obvious explanation for this absence is spatial distance.[4] After all, one might ask, what did a Pacific population—made up, among others, of Russian settlers and traders, Aleut and Kodiak sea otter hunters, indigenous Hawai'ian royalty, Native northwest coast peoples, and Chinese merchants—have to do with the drama of colonial resistance to Britain carried out in seaboard cities such as Boston, New York, and Philadelphia, much less with subsequent upheavals in France and Haiti? More recently, scholars have begun to place these Atlantic events in more global context while expanding the spatial reach of the revolutionary era to sites across Asia and South America.[5] But the Pacific has been absent from these efforts as well, despite the fact that the arrival of Europeans there met with regular and considerable anti-colonial resistance by indigenous peoples—ranging from attacks by Aleuts on the Russians, uprisings by so-called Mission Indians against the Spanish, and violent confrontations between European explorers and sailors on numerous Pacific islands and coastlines, from Alaska and Hawai'i to New Zealand and Samoa. If these events are missing from more global accounts of the revolutionary age, the reason is less geographical location than political definition. Because these uprisings did not result in the formation of new nations or depend on new ideas about political rule and human rights, they have not "counted" as revolutions. Even if we acknowledge the history of violent resistance by Aleuts or Ohlones or Hawai'ians, can their acts qualify as revolution in the way those in British North America, France, and Haiti do? Whether calculating by geographic relevance or political import, the region of the Pacific doesn't measure up to the standards governing our narratives of the revolutionary age.

The problem with these perceptions is that they are already the product of powerful dominant narratives about America and revolution. In other words, we think the Pacific has nothing to do with early America or the revolutionary age because all of the stories we're told about early America and the revolutionary age have nothing to do with the Pacific. Early American studies have neglected the Pacific not because it's irrelevant but because its events and actors cannot be accommodated by the central story told by most narratives of American literary and cultural history. That central story is a linear one plotted around a particular notion of revolution that is inextricable from the nation that eventually took shape in its aftermath. Within the terms of this narrative plot, the eighteenth-century Pacific—to the extent that we see it in early American studies at all—looks more like a site of riots than of revolution.

It did not look that way, however, from the maritime perspective of contemporaneous European and American observers, whose travel narratives repeatedly describe the constant uprisings, rebellions, and acts of resistance occurring throughout the Pacific by reference precisely to the major revolutions of the Atlantic. This chapter finds in these late eighteenth- and early nineteenth-century texts a transoceanic spatial perspective that brings the Pacific and Atlantic worlds into greater dialogue within American literary and cultural history during the age of revolution. The widespread popularity and circulation of these narratives—often in abridged editions or collections, in translation, and in periodical excerpts—also meant that the distant and exotic locations they described did not always feel especially distant and exotic to readers in the early U.S. and elsewhere around the Atlantic. As Chapter 2 showed, even quotidian mathematical textbooks or household manuals brought Americans into regular contact with news and products from faraway locations around the globe. Caitlin Fitz has recently shown that in the fifty-year period from 1775 to 1825, North Americans regularly imagined their own anti-colonial revolution to be in hemispheric dialogue with movements throughout Latin America. But the transnational and multiracial terms of this revolutionary universalism began to curtail sharply in the decades following the 1820s; as Alan Taylor more bluntly puts it, in the U.S. "racism developed to protect inequality from the implications of revolution."[6] The resulting nineteenth-century exceptionalist narrative has stopped us from seeing an earlier emplotment for revolution that foregrounds empires rather than nation-states and depends on a cyclical rather than linear temporality. Travel narratives from the wider Pacific world that circulated during the revolutionary age provide evidence of this alternative narrative while also bringing into view the violence concealed by traditionally linear and nation-based narratives, a violence that scholars such as Sven Beckert and Lisa Lowe have identified as a central feature of the period's expanding global capitalism.

It can be challenging to recover the violent damage so expertly concealed by this dynamic because that narrative's prolonged sense of promise operates precisely by hiding it: it's the metaphorical oyster, as Neil Gaiman put it in the passage cited in Chapter 1, whose shiny pearl blinds us from thinking about the dirty nubs from which it was made. This book has argued that the hard truths of harm and loss provide the fuel, as it were, that narrative anticipation needs to run forward, but like fuel, those unpleasant truths tend to evaporate, get spent, along the way. One way to remember and recover them is to pay attention to those whose bodies (and not just whose pocketbooks) felt and endured that risk, whether on ships or on shore. These included, at different moments and in different ways, sailors, indigenous peoples, and women. Later in this chapter, I approach risk from below by focusing in particular on the bodies of women as one site where this concealed violence gets repeatedly exposed. When women appear in the scenarios of global commerce that fill late eighteenth- and early nineteenth-century Pacific voyage narratives, they almost invariably appear as nothing but body, and in the process expose the acts of violence on which the disembodying narrative work of numbers depend.

Revolutionary Narrative

Revolution's two definitions depend on competing temporalities: understood astronomically, revolution is the drone of circular repetition, like the rotational movement of planets; understood politically, revolution is the eruption of linear change, the arrival of a dramatically irreversible transformation. The latter understanding, however, as David Armitage and Sanjay Subrahmanyam observe, only emerges during the late eighteenth century as revolution begins to operate "less in the sphere of cyclical movement and more within a definite teleology, or sense of historical irreversibility."[7] Revolution is positioned within a history that Hayden White distinguishes from the chronicle precisely because it possesses plot.[8] In her study of the American and Haitian revolutions, Ashli White describes a tension between what she calls the "web" model that dominates accounts of the colonial period and the "chain" model that has defined historiography of the revolutionary period. The result, she argues, is that "the fluidity and contingency of the colonial era surrender, in most accounts, to the seemingly straightforward march of revolution and nation building." Ralph Bauer has made similar observations about American literary histories and anthologies that sacrifice the rich transnationalism and multilingualism of their colonial materials as soon as they arrive at the revolutionary and early national periods.[9] The Revolution, in other words, exerts what amounts to a gravitational pull in our stories of American history and literature, often yanking efforts at alternative perspectives back into more familiar temporal and spatial terms the closer one gets to 1776.[10]

This linearization of revolution does considerable ideological work: it constructs a triumphant narrative plot whose celebratory outcomes—such as democracy, freedom, and nation—retroactively hide, or at least cleanse, the acts of violent conflict that helped bring those supposed outcomes into being. By eliminating from view that retroactive curve and the cycles of violence within in, we flatten the rotational dynamics of revolution into a line; by losing sight of the justificatory work that flattening serves, we conveniently lose sight of what Robert A. Ferguson, in a review of Armitage's *The Declaration of Independence: A Global History*, calls "the blood of the Revolution."[11] Taylor observes as well that the American Revolution is routinely "miscast…as the polar opposite of even bloodier revolutions elsewhere," leading us to overlook the "cruelty, violence, and destruction" that characterized it. Our failure to recognize these features is the result, he observes, of historians who have told the Revolution's story "backwards" by importing a much later and more unified image of American nationalism into a period that was instead fraught with "divisions and uncertainties."[12] Revolutionary narrative is in this way constructed as anticipatory and expectant; like the commercial and novelistic forms of narrative examined in the two preceding chapters, its future-oriented momentum minimizes the uncertainties, risks, and losses necessary to reach its satisfying conclusion.

A number of historians have recently sought to undo the narrative deception produced by the linearized, nation-focused plotting of revolution by undertaking a spatial reorientation. Taylor's retelling, for example, nests the more familiar events of the eastern seaboard within a series of less familiar ones from around the continent in which "common people claimed the right to act violently when their supposed betters committed some glaring abuse or neglect."[13] These range from anti-impressment protests in 1747 Boston, and Tacky's 1760 slave rebellion in Jamaica, to a 1768 revolt in Louisiana that exiled the Spanish governor, and self-described "regulators" who rose up in defiance of corrupt land speculators across the eastern seaboard. Claudio Saunt's narrative decentering of the revolutionary age even more forcefully foregrounds the rest of the continent, demoting more familiar events and their northeast location to the narrative and geographical margins of his account. Fitz gives even larger, hemispheric shape to the Revolution's afterlife, tracking through newspapers evidence that the U.S. saw itself "as the anticolonial leader of an anticolonial hemisphere" that "emphasized solidarity in republican rebellion."[14] As noted in the preceding section of this chapter, however, by the end of the third decade of the nineteenth century, the American Revolution had become plotted around "a different storyline" that was "less about the spread of republicanism to all men in all nations than it was about the westward expansion and democratic equality for U.S. slaveholders."[15]

These recent historical accounts press against popular public assumptions about the American Revolution that persist, as Serena Zabin explains, in giving "only one explanation of the revolution's significance: the founding of the American nation." Taylor similarly concedes that the Revolution continues to be regularly romanticized and subject to "selective memory." Zabin suggests that one way to bridge the gap between "the popular narrative of democracy's heroic birth and the scholarly account of an imperialist and racist nation's origins" is to retell it by featuring the "lives of ordinary individuals of all races and genders."[16] Holger Hoock's unrelenting attention to the violence sustained by so many ordinary people on all sides of the Revolution begins to do just that, while also powerfully restoring the blood missing from our narratives of the event—even as his geographic focus remains on the more traditional battlegrounds of the continental northeast.[17] In this chapter I am interested in rethinking our dominant political narrative of revolution by extending Hoock's concern with the rotational revolutions of violence to a transoceanic spatial framework that reaches beyond the continent and the hemisphere.

Some of Fitz's evidence suggests that during the revolutionary age many Americans imagined their "solidarity in republican rebellion" in global terms. When, for example, in an 1818 letter to his brother, John Quincy Adams privately poked fun at the supporters of Henry Clay, he cast their imagined spread of revolution across the globe in transoceanic terms: "eighteen millions of virtuous Patriots!—Spanish tyranny and oppression!—Atlantic and Pacific Oceans!"[18] This kind of aquatic perspective has yet to be accounted for in transatlantic, continental, hemispheric, and global refigurations of the revolutionary era, which have remained almost exclusively terrestrial. Yet buried everywhere within the same popular travel narratives that describe efforts at scientific discovery and commercial profit in the Pacific are descriptions of political revolts and uprisings that European and American observers frequently understood to be commensurate with their better-known Atlantic counterparts, even if they look to us now very different.[19] This material offers an opportunity to circumvent the force field that shapes narratives of the Revolution. By expanding the period's spatial reach from the Atlantic to the Pacific, we are also able to reconfigure its linear terms.

Knott ends her taxonomy of the forms revolutionary history has taken with today's "situational" narratives that emphasize space rather than time, and that trade in linear teleology for a webbed network whose story helps to explain the "making of our transnational and globalized world." These webbed narratives also shun grand claims in favor of adopting a more tentative "stance, or a sensibility" whose political quietude, Knott argues, reflects the "neoliberal times" within which history is written today.[20] My inclusion of the Pacific might be seen as one more spatial reformulation of the revolutionary age, but the material I find there ultimately argues for a temporal reformulation of revolutionary narrative that is neither line nor web but instead circle or spiral. Those who carried Atlantic revolutionary experiences and reports with them as they traveled the globe were measuring the appearance or likelihood of revolution by how it starts, not by how it ends; indeed, an endpoint or outcome like the nation was so far beyond predictability as to be almost unthinkable at the time. As a result, Atlantic visitors repeatedly recognized revolutionary conditions in the Pacific when they saw the extreme inequality and bitter injustices of war capitalism, and anticipated anti-colonial violence in response to these. What they saw wasn't the glorious possibility of a future nation but the destructive effects of a present empire. To this extent, these texts allow us to apply some transoceanic pressure on dominant understandings about revolution and its role in American literary and cultural history, while restoring to our narratives of the revolutionary age some of the cyclicality the term has lost.

Pacific Revolts

One of the earliest publications of Pacific travel writing from this period was a collection edited by Alexander Dalrymple, a Scotsman who—reportedly inspired by reading in his youth Edward Kimber's 1750 novel *The Life and Adventures of Joe Thompson*—entered the British East India Company in 1752. He returned to England from Canton in 1765, after having spent many years as a clerk stationed in Madras, India where he was responsible for copying company correspondence and meeting notes.[21] During those years, Dalrymple combed through the company's Madras records for "expeditions and trade in Cochin-China, Borneo and the Sulu Islands."[22] He became committed to regaining and expanding England's "commerce to the Eastern Islands...after they were deprived thereof by the intrigues of the Dutch"[23] and became convinced of the existence of a great southern continent supposed to exceed America in size and resources. To further this project, Dalrymple published in 1770 and 1771 two volumes of early voyages to the South Sea, *An Historical Collection of Several Voyages and Discoveries in the South Pacific Ocean*. The first volume included English translations of Spanish narratives, from the 1537 voyage of Ferdinand Grijalva and Alvarado to the 1606 voyage of Pedro Fernandez de Quiros, while the second translated Dutch narratives, beginning with James Le Mair and William Shouten's 1616 voyage and ending with Jacob Roggewein's 1722 expedition.

The introduction to Dalrymple's two-volume work, however, is preoccupied with Britain's North American colonies, and it surprisingly reveals the central place of the Pacific in the eighteenth-century Atlantic revolutionary imagination. Noting the likelihood of American colonial rebellion, Dalrymple explains that "no colony would ever dispute the due authority of the mother-country, unless it thought the mother-country in great measure depended on that colony." The problem, as Dalrymple saw it, is that awareness of this dependence emboldened and empowered the colonies: "the American colonies know the trade from BRITAIN thither is so great a proportion of the commerce of this kingdom, that a stagnation in trade to AMERICA would reduce thousands to clamorous indigence." He insisted that it was to Britain's advantage to find new markets for English products, for once America becomes less commercially central to Britain, "the mother-country being less dependent would be less jealous."[24]

Interestingly, Dalrymple is far from opposed to the colonies' resistance; in fact, he explicitly supports colonial "struggles for independence" and adamantly objects to any plans to suppress those struggles. As he explains, "the common rights of humanity entitle them to represent their grievances, and whatever is *thought* unjust is a grievance; the *first* step of tyranny is to *shut* the *ear* against complaints: the *last* to *shut* the *mouth* of the complainant."[25] In a later 1778 volume titled *Considerations on the Present State of Affairs between England and America*, he argued that the "*sword* ought to be *sheathed*, and the olive branch presented to

America." He insists it is obvious that "the English Americans think they are fighting in a good cause" but also says he is "far from condemning their antagonists," whom he supposes "act equally from conviction, but I lament the *effusion* of *English blood*, on both sides, in this unhappy contest."[26]

Dalrymple's position was shared by many in Britain who opposed expansionism, the commitment to commerce it entailed, and the attachment to an extravagant luxury it seemed to fuel.[27] Far from being opposed to imperial expansion or its benefits for Britain, however, Dalrymple simply wants to replace its politically exhausted Atlantic version with one focused on the real or supposed resources of the Pacific. Rather than either repress or advocate for rebellion in the Atlantic, Dalrymple sought to avoid it through a strategic use of the Pacific: "if colonies are aiming at independence, and endeavouring to break off all connection with the mother-country, the only means of preventing these intentions, and of securing the power and prosperity of the mother-country, must be by extending its commerce to distant nations who can have no connexion with those discontented colonies." Discovery of and trade with the great southern continent Dalrymple believed to exist in the Pacific would relieve Britain's economic and political tensions with North America, maintain or even increase commercial profits, and avoid the prospect of a colonial revolution.[28] Dalrymple urges therefore a British imperial reorientation from the North American Atlantic to the Pacific and Asia. That shift remains a staple narrative feature of British histories that describe an imperial "swing to the east" in the second half of the eighteenth century.[29] As I explain in the Introduction, the narrative plots of European imperial and American national histories uncouple at precisely this moment, resulting in the occlusion of empire and the excision of the Pacific from our perception of eighteenth-century revolution in America and the Atlantic.

A close reading of Dalrymple's and other collections of Pacific travel narratives suggests, however, a way of recoupling these narratives in a transoceanic revolutionary framework that hinges on recognizing the role of empire in the global expansion of war capitalism. Dalrymple believed that Pacific commerce would help to regulate North American resistance to British empire, but the narratives he reprinted in his volumes reveal that resistance was in fact already a regular response to European arrival and contact in the Pacific. Nearly every location documented in Dalrymple's collection is marked by resistance, from the Native pearl divers of Sooloo who "rub off the outer coats of the pearl" to reduce them to a size that will allow them to keep them rather than turning them over to their masters, to the thirty tattooed men on Takapoto Island who greet the men sent ashore by Le Mair and Schouten with clubs.[30] These narratives chart a cyclical pattern repeated across the genre, in which Europeans arrive at a Pacific location, are met by curious Native men and alluring Native women, engage in violent skirmishes resulting from these encounters while seeking commodities for trade, and depart for a new location. The maps that chart these voyages depict them as lines moving across an aquatic globe, but if we were to insert into those transport lines the circular repetitions of these political shoreline encounters, we might end up instead with something more like a series of spirals that move across and around the Pacific.

Dalrymple's collection brought together early Spanish and Dutch narratives from the Pacific for late eighteenth-century English readers, but the many European and American accounts of travel in the Pacific produced in the decades following the publication of his volumes make it clear that uprisings, revolts, and rebellions continued to be a regular feature of their encounters with Pacific peoples. Together, these narratives suggest that the region operated less as a safety valve for an emerging Atlantic rebellion than as its own cauldron for insurrectionary violence. William Coxe's 1787 *Account of the Russian Discoveries between Asia and America*, for example, describes the quick and steady Native resistance to the early eighteenth-century Russian entry into the North Pacific. In 1741, Tlingit Indians attacked Aleksei Chirikov's two boats and their men. This event was followed by a series of Native uprisings against Russian fur hunters, from the "numerous body of…natives" who killed two Russians after the latter tried "to violate some girls upon the island Unyumga"[31] to the 1763–4 rebellion of the Aleuts that resulted in the deaths of 150 Russians. A 1764 trial in Russia of Ivan Bechevin concluded that his company of fur hunters "kidnapped, raped, and murdered a number of Aleut women."[32] That did not stop a 1766 retaliatory Russian massacre of the Aleuts, nor did it stop Native resistance to the Russians. Nearly thirty years later, George Vancouver recorded the murder of a Russian by a group of Natives along with the Russian murder of six Natives in response. When the fur hunter Ivan Solov'ev, who had been instrumental in killing hundreds and possibly thousands of Aleuts, returned to the islands in 1771, the Aleuts set up a winter-long siege of the Russian camp and killed one of his crewmembers because "he was just like you." When Solov'ev finally left in 1772 to carry his brutal methods to a different island, the Aleuts set his dwelling on fire.[33] William Coxe attributed an anti-imperialist imperative to such Native violence, for "all agree in hating the Russians, whom they consider as general invaders, and therefore kill them whenever they can."[34] These accounts register the rotational return of violence in the Pacific, as continued European commercial and imperial expansion—and the attendant appropriation and exploitation of Native labor, lands, goods, and women—trigger cycles of resistance and repression.

The Spanish presence in the Pacific met with similarly violent resistance, much of it located at missions. In his *Voyage Round the World*, the French explorer Louis-Antoine de Bougainville references the 1757 "revolt" by the Guarani Indians in Paraguay against the authority of the Spanish king, whose forces killed over 2,000 Indians in response. In fact, Bougainville's observations of Spanish America led him to revise utterly his formerly held romantic assumptions about the Spanish missions. News of the uprising and the "discontent of the Indians" is impossible for Bougainville to accord "with all I had read of the manner in which they are governed," and he concludes that "the theory is widely different from the execution of this plan of government." He reports that the Indians had in some manner no property, and that they were subject to a miserable, tedious uniformity of labour and repose. This tiresomeness, which may with great reason be called deadly or extreme, is sufficient to explain what has been told to us, that they quitted life without regret, and died without having ever lived or enjoyed life. When once they fell sick, it seldom happened that they recovered, and being then asked whether they were sorry to be obliged to die, they answered, no; and spoke it as people whose real sentiments coincide with their words. We can no longer be surprised, that when the Spaniards penetrated into the missions, this great people, which was governed like a convent, should shew an ardent desire of forcing the walls which confined them.

Bougainville concludes by referring to this event as "the revolution that happened in the missions."[35]

The 1757 Paraguayan uprising had numerous counterparts up and down the length of the Pacific Ocean's eastern coast. Twelve years later, in 1769, Kumeyaay Indians attacked the Spanish mission in San Diego, likely in response to the destruction of food sources and the abuse of Native women. In 1771 at Mission San Gabriel in southern California, a Native chief was shot and beheaded for attacking a soldier who had raped his wife.[36] In early 1776, while en route to Monterey, several members of the Anza expedition took a detour to San Diego to investigate a recent uprising at its mission. According to the expedition's chronicler, Pedro Font, approximately 400 Native Americans from forty different villages banded together and stole items from the church, "breaking in pieces with a stone the chest of the vestments" and "dispatching their women to the mountain with the plunder. Then taking some firebrands from the guardhouse, they began to set fire to the same guardhouse, to the church, and to the houses of the fathers which, being built of tule and logs, easily caught fire."[37] Others estimate that upwards of 1000 Kumeyaay Indians may have participated in the revolt. Among the Spaniards killed was a friar who had baptized many Natives; he was found disrobed and disemboweled, his head crushed and his body stabbed. Retribution against the Indians by the Spanish was swift and severe, and Anza traveled from Monterey to offer assistance to the southern mission. The day he arrived was two days after the publication of Thomas Paine's *Common Sense*.[38]

In 1775, the crew of a ship led by the creole Spanish explorer Juan Francisco de la Bodega y Quadra landed on the Pacific northwest coast, near what is now Washington State, and found themselves "ambushed by some three hundred Indians. Seven men—half of the *Sonora*'s crew—were killed while Bodega stood powerless to avenge his loss."[39] From its establishment in 1776 until the 1830s, resisting Indians at the mission in San Francisco were flogged,[40] while Natives at San Luis Obispo set fire to several mission buildings.[41] Plots to destroy the San Gabriel mission were discovered as well in the late 1770s and again in 1785.[42] Along the Pacific's western edges, similar indigenous uprisings in response to European violence took place. In the 1790s, violent conflicts erupted in Port Jackson, Australia between the Aboriginal peoples and settlers, set off as a result of "the practice of kidnapping, detaining, raping, and even murdering Aboriginal women and children." A subsequent bout of Aboriginal retaliation in 1800 was caused by the brutal murder of a woman and child by a soldier.[43]

Pacific Revolutions

These Pacific revolts do not readily fit into the political and narrative models of revolution developed out of contemporaneous Atlantic events—but this is because those events have since been measured, named, and narrated in relation to later outcomes that have shaped our perceptions. I don't wish to press these Pacific events into an Atlantic narrative framework, but I do want to allow these Pacific events to press against our current emplotment of Atlantic revolution, in part by shifting away from linear teleologies of nation toward the cycles of exploitation and resentment that fueled what Laura Doyle has called "anti-imperial collective action."[44] What Europeans and Americans saw when they entered the Pacific were conditions of inequality and injustice familiar to them from recent experience in the revolutionary Atlantic. British and French narratives in particular display an Enlightenment sensibility that, like Dalrymple, acknowledged the human right to rebel against tyranny and oppression. When the French explorer La Pérouse arrived on Marivelle Island in the Philippines' Manila Bay, he reported that the chief Indian—who possesses "the pompous title of alcalde" and practices "considerable authority over the Indians"—also enjoys

> the baneful monopoly of selling, on behalf of the government, the tobacco of which the Indians smoke a great deal and almost continually. This impost is fairly recent; the poorest members of the population can hardly bear this burden: it has already caused several rebellions, and I would not be surprised if one day it led to the same outcome as the tea and stamp duties had in North America.[45]

Such accounts make it clear that Atlantic revolutionary ideas were framing European and American responses to Pacific events. La Pérouse comes close to repeating this prediction on the other side of the Pacific, during his visit to the San Carlos mission near Monterey. He compares the huts of the Indians living under the rule of the Franciscans there to "a homestead in Sto Domingo or any other colony" and observes that "the similarity was even greater in that we saw men and women in irons, others were in the stocks and, finally, the sound of whipping could well have reached our ears." The sense that revolutionary response was imminent was renewed six years later when George Vancouver, visiting the same location, remarked that "should a conspiracy for their destruction take place, the mission would soon fall, and there would be little doubt of the conspirators being joined" by the approximately 600 additional "Indians of the village."[46]

Further south, the American David Porter arrived in the port city of Valparaíso in 1812 to learn that the Chileans had "shaken off their allegiance to Spain; that the ports of Chili [sic] were open to all nations; that they looked up to the United States of America for example and protection." The women at the dinners and balls there identify themselves as supporters of the patriot party, according to Porter, by "wearing their hair gracefully brushed over on the left side of the face: they seem to have entered into the spirit of the revolution, and perhaps not without cause, as most of the patriots are young, dashing native Chilians, and the adverse party are invariably crusty, old, formal Castilians."[47] For eighteenth-century observers from the Atlantic, the shared conditions of injustice and inequality bring together examples of revolutionary potential from both sides of the Pacific—in this case Chile, Marivelle Island, and the San Carlos Mission—that seem to us now sharply divided on the basis of their outcomes.

Such conditions were not limited in the Pacific to its indigenous and creole peoples. The sailor William Moulton's 1804 account of his six-year voyage from Connecticut to the Pacific on board the *Onico* indicts the tyrannical, abusive, and exploitative treatment of sailors by ship captains and merchants. Moreover, he repeatedly frames these complaints by reference to the American Revolution. Moulton observes that his service as a soldier during the Revolutionary War helped "*to extricate her* [his country] *from the shackles of tyranny*" and allowed him subsequently to "*enjoy all the blessings of a free subject of one of the best governments under heaven.*" He charges two men in particular with criminal conduct on board the *Onico*—George Howe and George Haley, both of whom coincidentally share the name of the British monarch against whom the North Americans had successfully rebelled. He compares shipboard conditions in the Pacific to those in the Atlantic colonies, remarking that he "thought the revolutionary war had exhibited in some instances what it was to suffer for want of food" but that he had never been "driven to the brink of perpetual suffering, not to say starvation, before this voyage."[48] He repeatedly positions his own attempt to resist such tyranny in the waters of the Pacific in terms of the American colonists' earlier resistance to British tyranny in the Atlantic.

Men like Dalrymple, La Pérouse, Vancouver, Porter, and Moulton clearly carried revolutionary thinking from the Atlantic as they traveled into the Pacific and recorded observations of its lands, peoples, and shipboard conditions. Some ships traveling to the Pacific also carried Atlantic revolutionary texts and activists with them.[49] A Boston sealing ship that left Australia's New South Wales for Alaska's Nootka Sound in 1796 carried Thomas Muir, a Scottish convict whose sedition conviction had included charges that he was "advocating the writings of Thomas Paine."[50] A New Englander engaged in the China trade distributed copies of the Declaration of Independence translated into Spanish when his ship stopped in Valparaíso, ten years before Porter remarked on the revolutionary spirit there.[51] And the Boston merchant and captain Samuel Hill reportedly "discarded his copies of Voltaire and Thomas Paine in favor of religious tracts" after he was converted by a missionary at the Cantonese trading factories in 1811—recalling in some ways the conversion experience in Hawai'i of Tom Wilder in the children's story *The White Kitten*, described in Chapter 2.[52]

Revolutionary writing and thinking from the Atlantic made their way into the Pacific, where they provided a framework for understanding indigenous, creole, and shipboard acts of rebellion against injustice, tyranny, and inequality. In 1804, a rebellion against colonial authority by Irish convicts in Australia's New South Wales was led by a man who had already been involved in a mutiny on a convict transport ship, and who was also a veteran of the 1798 Rebellion of the United Irishmen, an Atlantic uprising that was modeled on the American and French Revolutions. In fact, the Australian event was named the Second Battle of Vinegar Hill after its transoceanic predecessor.[53] Theobold Wolfe Tone, leader of the United Irishmen, published in 1788 his "Sandwich Islands Memorandum," outlining a plan for a republican military utopia located where Captain James Cook had been killed in Hawai'i.[54] Stories of revolution meanwhile moved the other way as well, carried in books and periodical articles about the Pacific that were published, reprinted, and translated around the Atlantic. As Greg Dening points out, for example, news of the mutiny on Bligh's *Bounty* arrived in the Atlantic at a moment when "American merchants were celebrating the new freedom of their revolution" and where recently the "French King had lost his freedom and was on his way to prison and death."[55]

Despite such evidence of transoceanic circulation, literary and historical narratives alike have been astonishingly resistant to recognizing Pacific–Atlantic connections from this earlier period. Bruce Cumings, for instance, has recently argued that America is "simultaneously an Atlantic and a Pacific nation" and that we must add a "Pacific dimension" to the overwhelmingly Atlanticist perspective that has dominated accounts of American international relations. But Cumings maintains that this Pacific dimension begins only in the mid-nineteenth century, stating that Americans met Pacific peoples as early as the gold rush but only "met them in economic exchange after 1960." These rather astonishing claims and dates depend on a terrestrial perspective quickly exposed by Cumings himself when he notes that the ship *Empress of China* departed from New York in 1784 with wild ginseng root from North America, and returned from Canton in 1785 "loaded with tea, silk, and porcelains, having made a whopping profit of $30,000, a net gain of 25 percent on the original investment."[56] Moreover, the voyage was financed by none other than Robert Morris, the figure often recognized as the American Revolution's primary financier.

For Cumings, these first three centuries of international activity in the Pacific seem a mere shadowy precursor or failed prelude to the "Pacific dimension" of American affairs that only takes hold in the nineteenth and finally consolidates in the twentieth century. But this narrative relies on a terrestrial and nationalist understanding of American identity which somehow discounts this earlier material from inclusion in a properly "American" narrative, presumably because the activities of its multinational participants did not necessarily originate from, return to, or remain grounded on space within the political outlines of what was or would become the United States. This same logic of terrestrial nationalism has made the Pacific appear irrelevant to American literary histories more or less until the mid-nineteenth-century novels of Herman Melville and the twentieth-century boom in Asian American writing, despite the warning by Paul Giles against "simply replacing nationalist essentialism predicated upon state autonomy with a geographical essentialism predicated on physical contiguity."[57]

From Nation to Empire

Reminders from both historians and literary scholars that the revolutionary period was not only one of nation-building but of empire, suggest a promising way out of this narrative dilemma. Armitage and Subrahmanyam insist that "the major political units of the era (and for long beyond) were not states, national or otherwise, but empires" and suggest that one of the challenges in understanding the revolutionary age is the need to "scrape away" the longstanding assumption that revolutions "had to be understood and analysed in a national (and nationalistic) framework."[58] Likewise, Jorge Cañizares-Esguerra points out that "for all the new emphasis on the global and the transnational, the teleological and the national have yet to loosen their grip on U.S. colonial historiography" and argues that these postnationalist approaches "may simply be a new response to the pedagogical and ideological demands of a nation that is, in fact, a global empire."[59] Ed Larkin, too, recognizes that the newer frameworks of postnationalism and Anglicization in American literary history together generate a narrative in which "the Revolution becomes a bottleneck interrupting the imperial story." Larkin exposes the ways in which the logic of empire was part of the national project from the very beginning, illustrating "how the politics and culture of the early US were shaped not by a national story, but by an ongoing effort to combine nation and empire."[60] Sven Beckert reminds us that nation and empire were already combined by the mechanics of global capitalism when he observes, "for most of capitalism's history the process of globalization and the needs of nation-states were not conflicting, as is often believed, but instead mutually reinforced one another," as nation-states worked to facilitate, protect, and ensure global expansion in the interest of capital.[61] We might combine this observation with Larkin's formulation as a way of moving from a continental to a transoceanic perspective that replaces a framework of geographically bounded nations with one of far-flung empires whose global reach was facilitated by the violent innovations of war capitalism.

The perspective of empire offers new narrative possibilities for the story of the American Revolution. Taylor positions the American Revolution as the political and economic result of British empire, as victories in the Seven Years War vastly expanded and stretched the resources needed to maintain its imperial commitments.[62] Kate Fullagar has pointed out that anti-expansionists in Britain saw the Sugar Act of 1764 and the Stamp Act of 1765 as the consequences of such excessive growth, the effects of a kind of addiction to imperial luxury that was fed by the exploited resources of the New World. Colonial resistance to and rebellion against those acts are, in such formulations, anti-imperialist rather than proto-nationalist responses. Indeed, Wim Klooster insists that the Atlantic Revolutions of the late eighteenth century—in British North America, France, and Haiti—did not aim at democracy and were contingent affairs whose outcomes were not predictable or determined.[63] It is precisely for this reason that Europeans and Americans traveling from the Atlantic in the late eighteenth century could so easily recognize the specter of revolution in the relatively indeterminate acts of rebellious violence they encountered in the Pacific. When these acts are understood not as attempts at democratic nation-building but as expressions of outrage against empires engaged in the violent expansion of global capitalism, Pacific and Atlantic revolts begin to look far more alike.

Michael McDonnell notes that the "American Revolution divided more than just the colonies from the metropole": it also divided the Pacific world and its indigenous peoples from those of the Atlantic.[64] Bringing the Pacific and Atlantic together in American studies during the revolutionary period compels us to recognize the force and reach of empire, as well as the alliance between nations and empires that Beckert describes as fundamental to the brutalities of war capitalism. The linear endpoint of the nation serves in many ways as an eraser of that violence. Indeed, the narrative intransigence that has beguiled reigning definitions of revolution might be traced directly to the problem of plotting violence, for in many ways it has always been the burden of revolutionary narrative to justify the violence of rebellion in relation to the outcome of freedom. Hannah Arendt, for example, differentiates "revolution" from other "rebellions," "uprisings," and "insurrections." Although all share the condition of violence, only in the case of revolution is violence used "to constitute an altogether different form of government, to bring about the formation of a new body politic," whereas revolts and rebellions, she insists, "never indicated liberation as the revolutions understood it, and even less did they point to the establishment of a new freedom."[65] While revolutions are differentiated here from lesser uprisings by what amount essentially to different narrative plots, the plots themselves are distinguished only according to future outcomes (a new form of government) that retroactively shape the political narrative—and that shape it in such a way as to buffer its violence, by converting that violence into a result whose value might be seen to outweigh its costs. This is revolutionary narrative's calculus of risk.

Embodiment and Commercial Violence

Many of the men who commanded Pacific voyages had significant prior naval experience in the Atlantic, at least some of it in the American Revolution. La Pérouse, for example, fought against the British during the American Revolutionary War in Atlantic locations ranging from Nova Scotia and Hudson's Bay to Saint

Domingue in the West Indies—an experience that made it possible for him to compare homesteads in the latter to living conditions at the San Carlos Mission in California. James Cook served in the Seven Years War during the siege of Quebec and mapped regions of Newfoundland and the St. Lawrence River prior to being selected to lead the Pacific voyages. Bougainville was also stationed at Quebec with the French and following his circumnavigation served for several years in a naval command during the American Revolutionary war. To these men, the Pacific seemed sometimes to reflect the political instability and upheaval of the Atlantic and at other times to offer a commercial solution to its problems. In the same year that saw La Pérouse's arrival in Monterey, Joseph Banks proposed to the British government that breadfruit trees be transplanted from Tahiti to the West Indies, where they might serve as an inexpensive and low-labor source of food for slaves. Banks was looking to the Pacific for a solution to conflict and difficulty in the Atlantic, much as Dalrymple had sixteen years earlier when he sought in the Pacific an alternative to the likely prospect of colonial rebellion in the Atlantic. In fact, Banks's proposal was designed to address fallout from the American Revolution, which put a stop to the North American food imports that had sustained slave populations in British West Indian sugar colonies.

But the fates of the two voyages by La Pérouse and Bligh suggest again that European presence in the Pacific replicated more often than it resolved the Atlantic problems that spurred such long-distance travel in the first place. Following his visit to Monterey, when La Pérouse's ships landed in Samoa, they were met by a Native uprising that left twelve of his men dead. And by the time Bligh was ready to leave Tahiti for the West Indies in 1789, his own crew rose up in rebellion against him, as if in minor Pacific echo to the French Revolution taking place in the Atlantic that same year. Amasa Delano was in Macao, China, where American ships were selling seal skins when he heard the news that "Louis XVI was beheaded; that France had declared herself a republic." This observation appears just after he tells the story of the insurrection on Bligh's *Bounty*, noting that the mutineers—who settled with kidnapped Tahitian women on Pitcairn's Island—would later become the victims of an uprising themselves when the Tahitians revolted against and killed all but one of the Englishmen.[66] The examples of Dalrymple, Banks, La Pérouse, and Bligh suggest how frequently and significantly conditions in the revolutionary Atlantic determined Europe's presence in, imagination of, and response to the Pacific. But they also demonstrate, over and over again, that accounts of revolution bend and rotate, that instead of moving forward in a line, they circle around into cycles and spirals.

Those political rotations were informed, of course, by economic circuits. Investment and return always linked the two oceans, and Pacific commerce contributed to financial empires in the Atlantic cities of Boston, New York, and Philadelphia, including those of the fur trade titan John Jacob Astor and the shipping merchant John Perkins Cushing who, after thirty years in Canton, returned to Boston with several Chinese servants and enough porcelain to construct a wall made out of the material to surround his Massachusetts mansion, which occupied an entire city block.[67] The practices that fostered such accumulation of wealth and its transport to the Atlantic left behind disruption and destruction in the Pacific. Explorers and travelers in the Pacific were not just reporting on acts of real or potential rebellion; they were directly contributing to its causes. While these travelers professed to have left behind the brutality practiced by older empires, their narratives reveal that they delivered it instead in new commercial forms, carrying out through a combination of physical force and economic manipulations the violence which helped state-sanctioned and private mercantile capital to join and expand. As agents of Atlantic empires eager to take advantage of Pacific lands, markets, goods, and people, the backers and leaders of these voyages provided the maritime battering rams of war capitalism, although they seldom saw themselves that way.

They most often saw themselves instead as scientific or commercial pioneers, in search of new knowledge and products. Dalrymple's collection of early Spanish and Dutch Pacific travel voyages provided in its narratives and maps some of the earliest textual and visual accounts of the region, and these two large volumes accompanied many of the ships that traversed the Pacific over subsequent decades, including Cook's. The information provided by these earlier accounts were used by later voyages to help guide them through an unfamiliar geography, and those later voyages in turn were committed to revising and improving the detailed understanding of that geography. It was as if European nations were participating in an effort to complete a map of the world by filling in blank spaces, correcting misinformation, and resolving contradictions that remained in the maps and accounts of their predecessors.

This effort was far more competitive than collaborative, however. The reputedly disinterested pursuit of scientific knowledge repeatedly intertwines with self-interested national boasting—and when it does, the activity of filling in the map often became an exercise in folding over the map by placing Atlantic names on top of Pacific ones. The American David Porter, for example, notes that some of the Washington Islands discovered by "a captain Roberts of Boston" were named "Adams, Jefferson, Hamilton, &c. &c." He goes on to explain, however, that the island called Adams by the Americans is called Rooahooga by the Natives, and the map that appears opposite the page offering this explanation labels each of the three Washington Islands with a succession of competing names. One island, for instance, is identified as "Novaheevah—Native; Madison—American; Isle Baux—French; Sir H. Martins—England."[68]

But names that proudly celebrate a nation's leaders and explorers also appear alongside names—like Murderers Bay, the Island of Traytors, Destruction River, and Massacre Bay—that document instead disaster, misery, and loss. The Dutchman Abel Tasman named Murderers Bay to memorialize the violent conflict with the Maori that erupted when his ship attempted to reach shore there in 1642. The Island of Traytors in the Tonga Islands was named by the Dutch explorers Le Mair and Shouten because "the greatest part of those who endeavoured to destroy us came from that island," and Traitor's Cove off present-day Alaska was christened by George Vancouver for the "number of Indians...which fell in the unprovoked attack upon our boats."[69] The Island of Sorrows (Isla de Dolores), located off of what is now the coast of Washington State, was named by Bodega after the Natives massacred a crew of seven men sent ashore there in 1775. When the English fur trader Charles William Barkley sent some men to the same fate on the same island in 1787, he called the nearby waterway Destruction River. Also in 1787, La Pérouse gave the name of Massacre Bay to the location in the Samoan Islands where twelve of his men were killed, by Natives who were likely responding to the French crew's aggressive pursuit of indigenous women.

These names speak to a deep history of conflict and bloodshed that their recorders otherwise disavow in a celebration of commerce positioned as an antidote to rather than trigger for violence. Dalrymple hoped that Europeans in the Pacific would "secure a patient abstinence from the use of fire-arms against the native Indians,"[70] and it was passages such as these that led his biographer Howard T. Fry to describe him as possessed of a "ready sympathy for the native peoples with whom he came in contact."[71] But Dalrymple's present sympathy is never divorced from future profit. Fry explains that for Dalrymple the "Spaniards were not the people to emulate, for they had subjected Columbus's new continent to pillage and conquest, whereas the humane policy of trading 'with the potent and populous empires of Mexico and Peru' would have brought them far greater wealth in the end." Like the repeated cautions in the period's mathematical school-books and manuals discussed in Chapter 2, Dalrymple's calculus of risk chooses patience over rapidity because it is ultimately more profitable; it depends on a prolonged and linearized temporality that conceals the cycles of violence that characterized the global expansion of war capitalism.

Acts of indigenous resistance persist as names on maps and as scattered anecdotes in the voluminous records of European explorers whose narratives often memorialized their own losses to Native violence without recognizing the longer cycles of commercial, colonial, and sexual exploitation to which that violence was most often a response. That cyclicality sometimes, however, emerged into clear view. After sailing from Monterey to the Hawai'ian island of Maui and back again to the far north coast of the American continent, Vancouver and his men are greeted with hostility by Indians who, he observes, "had been ill-treated in their traffic with white men," many of whom "have not only pursued a line of conduct, diametrically opposite to the true principles of justice in their commercial dealings, but have fomented discords, and stirred up contentions, between the different tribes, in order to increase the demand for these destructive engines [firearms]." After receiving defective commodities through practices of commercial fraud by European or American traders who "consider gain as the only object of pursuit," the Natives become themselves "tempted to trespass on the laws of honesty" and to "acquire by force" what they have failed to get through fair and honest trade. Vancouver repeats this complaint when he returns to the Hawai'ian

Islands later in the voyage, and worries that the islanders who had received poorly made firearms in trade might "resort to measures of revenge for the injuries thus sustained." Were they to do so, however, Vancouver recognizes that "they would be immediately stigmatized with the epithets of savages and barbarians, by the very people who had been the original cause of the violence they [the Natives] might think themselves justified in committing."[72] In this insightful political commentary, Vancouver recognizes revolutionaries in the Pacific as the very products of the exploitative practices of those they rise up against. In the process of doing so, he restores a cyclicality to narratives of Pacific violence, positioning such acts as anti-imperialist responses to the effects of an aggressively expanding war capitalism. Such rioters become would-be revolutionaries when their narratives are de-linearized and de-coupled from the nation.

Despite Vancouver's critical observations, he persists in subscribing to a fantasy of peaceable profit, insisting that the Spaniards' attempts to civilize the Indians will not succeed until their policy of keeping out foreigners is replaced by "an amicable commercial intercourse" whose newly introduced comforts would "stimulate them [the Indians] to industry" by cultivating their lands and trafficking in sea otter skins.[73] When indigenous violence is turned on his own crew, however, Vancouver finds himself at a narrative loss. In 1793 in what is now southern Alaska, Tlingit Indians "fell in the unprovoked attack upon our boats," he reports, and the incident "produce[d] in my mind much sorrow and regret, from which I could find no relief but in the consoling reflection, that nothing but the most urgent necessity, for our own preservation, would have compelled us to have adopted coercive measures."[74] Absent from this sentence—or rather concealed in its subjunctive tense, passive voice, and awkward syntax—is the violence with which Vancouver and his party responded. Revolution narratively dissolves into riot when the European explorer and his crew became the object of indigenous rebellion, leaving only the name of Traitor's Cove on a map.

But revolutionary narrative could be even more dramatically laid bare by ordinary seamen who sometimes recognized their own conditions reflected in those of the Natives. William Moulton, for instance, identified in the long-term financial relations of Pacific voyages a hidden exploitation and corruption. At one point he rather painstakingly calculates the economic arrangements by which men like him are hired to work on sealing ships, giving as an example the master of the ship *Jenney* that sailed from Boston to America's Pacific northwest coast. The terms offered to the nine hired men "were fifteen dollars a share per thousand to be paid after they return to America, allowing the head of the gang two shares and calculating the skins at one dollar and fifty cents each in Canton; this is allowing," Moulton notes, "just one tenth part to the sealers and nine tenth parts to the employer." He remarks that "there is no probability that they will complete the voyage short of three years from the time they entered on it, or that it will produce them enough to clothe themselves and fit out for a voyage of one year when they get home." Sailors are repeatedly tricked into joining voyages that go to different destinations for different purposes or under different terms than initially proposed, often putting the men on board at risk of capture or enslavement by the Spanish. Moulton recognizes that by prolonging the journey, captains and owners stretch profits while shrinking wages for laboring sailors. He asks whether "the enslaving or loosing [*sic*] one part of the natural born subjects of our country, to enhance the wealth of another part, or of foreigners who come among us" is really "preferable to the importation of slaves?" Moulton not only aligns the laborers on these ships with African slaves but aligns their plight with the indigenous peoples of the northwest coast, who are likewise tricked, treated unfairly, even "fired on and killed," only to be charged as hostile for rebelling against such mistreatment: "To have enquired what induced the natives to the hostile act they charge them with, would have brought into view a possibility of their having previously received some treatment which they had a right to resent; nothing however, could have been thought more ridiculous than such an enquiry."[75] Moulton is insisting that revolution is being misread as riot, and also suggesting that such re-scripting is made possible by limiting a narrative's focus to isolated incidents of violent conflict without accounting for the longer-range context in which they take place—which is very much the shift in scope that C. L. R. James made in his field-changing narrative treatment of the Haitian Revolution.

Gender and Risk from Below

If there is one thing most missing from the ships that traversed the Atlantic and Pacific oceans on long voyages of discovery and commerce, it would seem to be women. When Harriet Low left Salem for Macao in 1829 with her merchant uncle and aunt, she joined a small number of nineteenth-century women who accompanied their male relatives or husbands on commercial sea voyages. Earlier, there was the even more exceptional case of Jeanne Baret, the French herbwoman who traveled on Bougainville's 1766–9 circumnavigation of the globe by accompanying Philibert Commerson, the ship's botanist and her lover. Baret evaded restrictions on the presence of women on French Navy ships only by cross-dressing during the voyage—a feat so extraordinary that it seems only to prove the point that movement around the world was reserved for men.[76]

If women are absent from the European ships that ventured into and across the Pacific, however, they are everywhere present on shore, and in fact violent conflicts between Atlantic visitors and Pacific Natives are routinely marked by the sexualization of indigenous women's bodies. Patty O'Brien explains that "indigenous women were at the forefront of contact" throughout the Pacific, where they were often responsible for negotiating both commercial and sexual forms of exchange with visiting Europeans.[77] The French explorer La Pérouse, for example, noted that among the Natives of Castries Bay in Siberia, the "women seem to be fairly well respected among them; they never concluded a deal with us without their agreement."[78] Indigenous women were often directly involved with the activities of calculation and speculation in the context of trade between visiting Europeans and Native peoples, even when it was their own bodies being exchanged. On that same voyage much further south in the Pacific, older women reportedly "negotiated the transaction" between the French sailors and the "very small number of young and pretty island girls" whom they desired. La Pérouse explains that in one particular location, "an altar was set up in the most prominent hut, all the blinds were lowered, [and] inquisitive spectators were driven off."[79] Descriptions like these populate Pacific travel narratives, where the bodies of indigenous women were perceived by visiting European men as one resource among many. As O'Brien notes, "[a]ccess to the bodies of local women was an expectation of seafarers, and ports were graded according to the plenitude of available women as well as food, water, and alcohol."[80] La Pérouse, for example, describes the women of Lituya Bay (located in present-day Alaska) as "perhaps the most repugnant beings in the world," while the "very pretty" Samoan women, he claims, "offered with their fruit and poultry their favours to anyone who was prepared to give them beads."[81]

Because the experiences of women in the early Pacific were recorded and interpreted by European men—whose inadvertent and willful misunderstanding shaped their representations—they have been notoriously challenging to understand and reconstruct. In an early 1697 travel narrative, for example, William Dampier circulated the assumption that sexual access to Native women in the Pacific was used as a tool of diplomatic or commercial strategy by Native men. He also believed that Native women made themselves sexually available to visiting sailors to protect those British men, Pocahontas-like, from violent retribution by Native men. Dampier circulated these ideas a decade before rescuing Alexander Selkirk from the Pacific island then called Juan Fernandez. By 1722, the Dutch explorer Roggewein similarly interpreted the sexual invitations by women on Rapa Nui as a gesture of colonial submission on the part of the islanders.[82]

Explorers and merchants regularly consulted earlier Pacific narratives for information about navigation and geography and resources, but as they did so they would also have absorbed descriptions like these that teetered between ethnography and pornography as they integrated indigenous female sexuality into an ideology of imperialism and commerce. It was European encounters with Tahiti, however, that really consolidated an image of hyper-sexualized Pacific women, beginning with the arrival of Samuel Wallis's voyage on the *Dolphin* in 1767. The encounter began with a full week of violence that included Native stone-throwing met by British gunfire; only after several Natives were killed in this conflict did a robust exchange of sex for nails ensue. When Bougainville and his men arrived in Tahiti nine months after the *Dolphin*'s departure, they were unaware of what had transpired during Wallis's earlier visit and interpreted the local women's willingness to participate in sex as innate, rather than the direct result of what O'Brien describes as "recent violence and subsequent machinations of imperial commerce."[83] Although commerce and violence would remain complexly entangled with female sexuality in reports about Pacific encounters throughout the late eighteenth and early nineteenth centuries, it was the fantasy of the Pacific as a space of sexual freedom that dominated—especially in the later wake of the widely circulated sexual experiences of Joseph Banks in Tahiti during Cook's first voyage.

As O'Brien argues, this mythology conceals the fact that European sexual commerce on Tahiti was organized from the beginning through "the long-standing colonial practice of coercion" on shore, abetted by the collapse of discipline on the ship, as sailors routinely violated authority in the pursuit of sex with local women.[84] O'Brien's compelling analysis of what she calls the "gendered dynamics of imperialism," and the frequently harrowing history that accompanies it, is a reminder that when women appear in accounts of the Pacific, they are inescapably embodied. Paying attention to these accounts of gendered embodiment offers a way to counteract the disembodiment performed by numbers in transoceanic travel and commerce, to expose the violent substrate concealed by the calculus of risk. By the early nineteenth century, for example, in the Bass Strait area of southern Australia where the sealing trade thrived, Aboriginal girls as young as eight were living with seal hunters. The girls had been acquired through forcible abduction from other areas of the Pacific and transplanted for use as a source of labor as well as sex—a pattern that O'Brien identifies as consistent with British practices of colonization and settlement throughout the Pacific. Even Jeanne Baret herself, the unlikely female French circumnavigator on Bougainville's voyage, became the object of sexual violence as soon as her gender was openly exposed. After more than a year on the voyage, much of it spent scaling hillsides in Brazil and Patagonia in men's clothing to collect plants that her botanist lover Commerson, with an injured leg, could not reach, Baret was gang-raped by her own crewmembers on the Pacific island of New Ireland in Papua New Guinea.[85]

Even as violence against women in the Pacific became public knowledge in Europe by the 1830s, the relationship between sexual coercion and anti-colonial indigenous resistance was far less recognized.[86] When a minister forcibly abducted a chief's wife and daughter in Ra'iatea, the islanders responded with a violent uprising that was met, in turn, by a British war ship that arrived to kill more than sixty Natives. On the coral atoll of Ngatik in 1837, a ship engaged in the tortoiseshell trade ran into conflicts with the Natives, who refused to allow the crew on shore. The ship left, only to return to kill every man on the island and rape its women. O'Brien points out that even when it did not repeat the genocide of Ngatik, empire-building in the Pacific "increasingly featured violent retaliation by indigenes often sparked by sexual misunderstandings" that was in turn met with coercive practices of possessing and transplanting the bodies of women.[87] These repeated scenes of violent sexualized embodiment may seem a world away from the disembodied calculations and speculations, discussed in Chapter 2, that were performed on the profitable goods and products that these voyages carried around the globe. My point, however, is that they served as their critical counterpart, as these cycles of brutally embodied violence sustained a linear narrative of pleasurable disembodied profit. A similar logic operates in the popular emplotment of the American Revolution, where sexualized violence against women has been routinely given more metaphoric than material weight. In Holger Hoock's words, "the very ways in which Revolutionary Americans deployed rape as a political tool to discredit the British Empire have tended to obscure the actual practices of wartime rape." Hoock insists that our accounts of the American Revolution "need to write the abused women (and their abusers) back into the story," in order to recognize that rape was a consistent practice by both the British army and American soldiers.[88]

The Pacific uprisings documented in this chapter constitute a series of anti-imperialist revolts waged by various surprised or enraged indigenous inhabitants of the Pacific, from the western coasts of North and South America, the far eastern edges of Asia and Australia, and islands throughout the Pacific Ocean. But even if they represent a series of plots, it isn't possible to narrate these Pacific uprisings so as to constitute a single plot, nor can they individually be endowed with the narrative conventions typically required of current dominant definitions of revolution. These acts of resistance neither add up collectively to the kind of spatial self-containment represented by a continent nor move individually toward a temporal endpoint represented by a nation. On this basis, these might be rejected as not meeting the criteria of revolution at all. These acts of resistance, it might be argued, are too episodic, too isolated, too limited, and—perhaps most damagingly—insufficiently transformative (of political or cultural or economic forms) to qualify as revolutionary.

The very geography of the Pacific—where late eighteenth-century explorers found thousands of islands and circuitous coastlines instead of the great southern continent they had been led to expect—might offer one way to imagine these differences. These uprisings resemble less the geographical coherence and political magnitude of a continent or nation and more the scattered arrangement of islands and coastlines both connected to and separated from each other by various ties and distances around the Pacific. I have traded in a linear temporal narrative for a more cyclical spatial one that, on the one hand, brings the revolutionary Atlantic into transoceanic dialogue with its Pacific counterpart, and on the other, leaves exposed and unguarded the violence that attends revolutionary acts of anti-imperialism, regardless of their long-term traction or outcome. A transoceanic framework that registers the connections between the revolutionary Atlantic and its Pacific counterpart therefore also moves toward plotting revolution differently, within a more rotational model that restores to revolution some of its older cyclicality. The resulting narrative is more episodic and anti-colonialist than it is linear and nationalist—something more like a series of rotating spirals that undo the work of narrative flattening in order to lay bare both the costs of revolutionary violence (regardless of how we measure its results) and its emergence in contexts of inequality, injustice, and exploitation brought about by war capitalism. This new framework defamiliarizes standard accounts of early America, of the Atlantic world, and of the revolutionary age by exposing the narrative plot lines and devices that bind the concepts and categories of nation and revolution to each other. It admittedly diminishes the centrality of the American Revolution to our stories of American literature, culture, and history—not because it isn't important, but because its importance has been so magnified, mythologized, and multiplied that it has made it difficult to see late eighteenth-century America in a truly global, transnational context.

The result, however, may be that we are able to see other features of American literary and cultural history more clearly, both by recognizing new archives and by reading them in new ways. In Part II of *Transoceanic America*, I bring the transoceanic framework established in these first three chapters to bear on the reading of four novels, few of which are set at sea but all of which are about revolution. As noted in the Introduction, Margaret Cohen has identified the period covered in this book as one whose literary history curiously lacks sea novels. She speculates that writers and sellers of maritime fiction could not compete during these decades with the exciting non-fiction then being produced and circulated about the Pacific, although she also wonders whether such novels vanished during this period in favor of "the novel's pervasive association at this time with feminized sociability."[89] When the sea novel returns, she notes, with James Fenimore Cooper's renewal of the "maritime picaresque," it does so with a "maritime nationalism" that is "shaped by the political and ideological specificities of his position as an American writer." Here, in literary as well as political history, our narratives stumble during the revolutionary era over what amounts to a shift from empire to nation. What literary texts and formations are our dominant narratives of literary and cultural history preventing us from seeing during this especially fraught period? What if the gap identified by Cohen is the product of those narratives rather than the literary texts themselves? What if we bring to our literary histories of the novel the same questions about plotting that have been raised in this and the preceding chapters about the politics of revolution, the mathematics of capital, and the narratives of novels? The chapters in Part II engage with this possibility by reading novels within a global context that recognizes the commercial, textual, and political connections between the Pacific and Atlantic oceans in the age of revolutions.

PART II

Reading Novels across Oceans

Circles

SEDUCTION AND REVOLUTION IN
THE TRAVELS OF HILDEBRAND BOWMAN

Scott O'Dell's award-winning 1960 novel, *Island of the Blue Dolphins*, recounts the nineteenth-century story of an indigenous woman named Karana who lived alone for eighteen years on the Pacific island of San Nicolas off the coast of southern California. O'Dell's novel is based, of course, on the true story of the Nicoleño woman, later renamed Juana Maria by Catholic priests, and it begins with the brutal massacre of the island's Native population by Russian fur hunters. As the accounts described in Chapter 3 make clear, such acts of European brutality around the Pacific were often retributions for violent Native uprisings, which were themselves acts of protest against the exploitation and abuse—including the regular rape of Native women—they suffered at the hands of profit-seeking hunters and traders. Indeed, the Russians massacred in 1814 most of the island's population in response to the murder of one of their hunters by a Nicoleño man. When the island's remaining inhabitants were removed in 1835, Juana Maria was either left or stayed behind with her child. She was only discovered and brought to the mainland in 1853, by a fur hunter who found her wearing a skirt made of bird feathers.

As astonishing as her experience is, Juana Maria's survival may be even less exceptional than the survival of her story. Transoceanic traffic by European traders and explorers has for centuries left behind countless castaways—men and women abandoned or marooned on distant and deserted islands or coastlines—whose stories were lost forever, or never told or understood in full. Islands could be depopulated of an entire tribe, as San Nicolas was, or populated for the first time, as was the case of the tiny Indian Ocean islet, now named Tromelin Island, when the survivors of a wrecked French slave ship were cast ashore there in 1761. Fifteen years later, in 1776, all who remained of the ship's original 160 Madagascar slaves and 140 French crewmembers were seven Malagasy women, who were found with one eight-month-old boy when they were finally rescued. It wasn't the first rescue attempt, however; only a few months prior, a Frenchman sailed from the islet into the Indian Ocean with three men and three women and were never seen again. Their raft was powered by a sail made of woven feathers. Puzzlingly, archaeologists have found only two sets of human remains on the islet, despite having discovered at least 18,000 bird bones—material evidence of the diet of the castaways as well as, one supposes, the source of the feathers for the sail of the disappearing raft.[1]

Whether the trade was in sea animal pelts, as in the San Nicolas story, or the bodies of African slaves, as in the Tromelin Island case, the risk that attended transoceanic commerce regularly stranded or washed ashore bodies on remote islands and coastlines, the waste product of war capitalism's cyclical violence. This kind of residue from real stories of maritime disaster often cross-pollinated with the imaginary world of fiction, putting into circulation among the reading public of the Atlantic world stories of transoceanic disaster and survival in more distant oceans of the world. This chapter turns to one such fiction, an all-but-forgotten 1778 novel about an English sailor who leaves with Captain James Cook's second voyage around the globe and is mistakenly left behind on the south Pacific island of New Zealand. The eponymous (and fictional) narrator of *The Travels of Hildebrand Bowman* subsequently journeys through an imaginary south Pacific in his efforts to return home. Published when both the American Revolution and Cook's third and final voyage were under way, the novel explicitly links Atlantic politics with Pacific exploration. And despite being narrated by a man (like its more enduring counterparts *Robinson Crusoe* and *Gulliver's Travels*), *The Travels of Hildebrand Bowman* positions the bodies of women—especially ones covered in feathers—as central to understanding an eighteenth-century transoceanic world of global capitalism.

Hildebrand Bowman offers one of the earliest depictions of the American Revolution in the English novel, and the only one that explicitly situates the conflict as a product of the violent cycles of transoceanic commercial empire.[2] Britain's global maritime empire relied on more obvious forms of violence in the service of commerce, such as the enslavement of Africans and the exploitation of indigenous labor, but it also sustained, as part and parcel of that commerce, a regular sexual traffic in women's bodies that became especially associated with the Pacific. As Margaret Jolly points out, sexual exchanges in the Pacific between indigenous women and visiting Europeans "are saturated with the language of commerce and emergent capitalism." She furthermore observes that during the eighteenth century, the status of women served as a central indicator for Europeans of a society's stage of development, on a scale that ran from the depths of barbarity to the highest achievements of civilization.[3] *Hildebrand Bowman* inverts this scale and the assumptions on which it rests, for in the novel the feather-adorned bodies of women represent the barbarity within civilization itself, where acts of sexual seduction are one form of consumption among many fueled by transoceanic exchange and accumulation. Anna Neill has astutely observed that "the expansion of the world economy depended upon disciplining passions in the peripheral parts of the globe, even while commercial expansion required that appetites be stimulated in the metropolitan regions."[4] *The Travels of Hildebrand Bowman* encircles the Atlantic metropole and the Pacific periphery within a single global system in order to tell precisely such a story about the dangerous appetites of commercial expansion.

This anonymous novel was published only once, and although it is very briefly mentioned in several bibliographies and synthetic reviews of travel literature that focus on the South Seas or on the tradition of imaginary travel writing, no scholarly article or study has ever been devoted to it.[5] If literary critics have overlooked *Hildebrand Bowman*, it may be because the novel's transoceanic reach makes it resistant to inclusion in national and mono-oceanic literary histories. Yet it is precisely its global maritime compass that drives the book's rather remarkable anti-imperialist and anti-commercial argument. By acknowledging the connections between the Atlantic and the Pacific—and by paying attention as well to the role and presence of women in a transoceanic terrain often seen as the reserve of men—the novel positions political revolution as a consequence of the inequality and exploitation created by unchecked imperial expansion. *Hildebrand Bowman* insists on a rotational relationship between the Atlantic and Pacific oceans; its story might be thought of as a kind of subterranean Pacific plate pulled out from under the Atlantic to reveal, in fantastical form, its buried or repressed reality. The book implicitly links North America's Atlantic Revolution against England with indigenous anti-colonial Pacific uprisings against Europeans—not unlike the one that provoked the massacre which left Juana Maria the last of her tribe on San Nicolas Island. *Hildebrand Bowman* links Atlantic and Pacific rebellions, moreover, by transforming European stadial theory—then in vogue as a framework for understanding the long conjectural history of human development—from a linear into a cyclical narrative.[6] The resulting placement of anti-imperial revolt within the violent cycles of global commerce offers a compelling late eighteenth-century alternative to the heroic linearity of national politics that, since the nineteenth century, has provided the dominant narrative model through which to tell the story of the American Revolution.

Cannibalism and Dismemberment

The Travels of Hildebrand Bowman is set in an absurd eighteenth-century Pacific that pretends to be true. It begins, however, with a very true eighteenth-century Pacific event: the massacre in New Zealand of ten members of the crew of the *Adventure*, the ship that accompanied Captain James Cook's *Resolution* on his second global circumnavigation. The fictional travels narrated by Hildebrand Bowman supposedly supply missing pieces of the documentary record left behind by Cook and others. Bowman claims to have left England in 1772 as part of Cook's highly anticipated second voyage around the world, which planned to search for the long-fabled great southern continent. Often referred to as *Terra Australis Incognito*, this presumed super-continent was imagined to be massive, populated, and resource-rich—a prize to whichever European nation might first locate it in the unexplored southern reaches of the Pacific Ocean (see Figure 4.1). Alexander Dalrymple complained, in a seething response to England's multiple earlier discovery

FIGURE 4.1. *Map showing the massive continent imagined to occupy the southern hemisphere.* Abraham Ortelius, Typus Orbis Terrarum *(Antwerp, 1570?). MAP NK 10001. Courtesy, National Library of Australia.*

efforts, that even after four voyages "it was not yet determined whether or not there was a 'SOUTHERN CONTINENT,' " and insisted that had he been appointed to lead the expedition "*I* would *not have come back* in *Ignorance.*"[7] Cook's second voyage therefore went in explicit pursuit of this evasive continent. Along the way, the expedition hoped to locate new goods, materials, markets, and lands that might prove useful and profitable to Britain, while also introducing European live-stock and plants into the Pacific—thus providing sources of sustenance to them-selves on future visits while also taking steps to recreate the Pacific in the image of Europe.

Cook's *Resolution* was accompanied by a companion vessel, the *Adventure*, captained by Tobias Furneaux, and the two ships became the first to cross the Antarctic Circle as they made their way through often ice-strewn southern oceans. But they lost contact with each other several times over the course of the three-year voyage, and at these moments their stories diverged. In February 1773, for exam-ple, the two ships separated during a storm and remained unaware of each other's location before finally reuniting fourteen weeks later in Queen Charlotte Sound, New Zealand. There the combined crews spent several weeks gathering celery and grasses to help prevent scurvy, slaughtering animals, trading with Natives, engag-ing in sexual exchanges with Native women, and transplanting "several hundreds of Cabbages" to gardens they built among the island's many coves.[8]

The two ships then left New Zealand together for Polynesia, where in August 1773 the Ra'iatean man Mai (often mistakenly referred to as Omai) was taken aboard the *Adventure* for the remainder of its voyage.[9] After Mai joined the expedition, Cook and Furneaux again sailed south together toward New Zealand. When the much smaller and less sturdy *Adventure* went off course in another storm in late September, the two ships were once more separated. The *Resolution* arrived in Queen Charlotte Sound and waited three long weeks for the *Adventure*, which never appeared. Before leaving to continue his search for the elusive southern continent, Cook placed a note in a bottle buried beneath a tree stump on which the message "Look underneath" was carved. Six days after his departure, the storm-battered *Adventure* arrived. The two ships would never be reunited, but the story of what happened to the crew of the *Adventure* in New Zealand quickly made its way into print in Europe and was retold in several later published accounts of the voyage.

The fictional Hildebrand Bowman introduces himself as a "Midshipman on board the Adventure" and the novel told in his voice more or less begins in Queen Charlotte Sound, after "Furneaux found, by a letter Captain Cooke had left for him, in a corked bottle hid under ground, with directions to dig for it, that the Resolution had been there."[10] Bowman explains that after reading the note, Furneaux sends ten of his crewmembers, including "Mr. Rowe and Mr. Woodhouse, Midshipmen, with eight of his best hands, on shore, in the large cutter, to gather wild greens." Bowman, who describes himself as "a keen sportsman, begged leave to go with them, to try if I could meet with any game" (58). He therefore claims to be a forgotten eleventh member of the party that traveled ashore to Grass Cove, and wonders "by what mistake Captain Furneaux, in his letter to Captain Cooke, which he left for him at the Cape, makes no mention of my being in the cutter" (58–9).

Through this clever conceit, Bowman writes himself into this particular moment in the voyage's history. Bowman is hunting at a distance while the other ten men are gathering "wild greens, such as celery and scurvy-grass" (58). When he hears a shot, he runs toward his companions only to find the "horrid spectacle" of "all our men lying dead" and "surrounded by some hundreds of savages, of both sexes and of all ages" (59). Watching from a concealed "covert of the woods," he sees "the horrid feast which was prepared for that multitude" as "the mangled limbs of my poor countrymen and shipmates, were put on" the nearby fire "to broil for their unnatural repast; nay even some parts I saw devoured" (59). Bowman responds with horror to this scene as "my whole frame was in the most dreadful tremor! and scarcely able to support me in withdrawing into the woods: I staggered about without knowing what I did, or meant to do; excepting only the getting at a distance from those vile cannibals" (59). As Bowman wanders in shock and fear, the *Adventure* departs from New Zealand without ever realizing that he has been unaccounted for.

Upon recovering, and discovering that he has been abandoned in New Zealand—a land he describes as "divided into islands, lying contiguous to each other, and separated by narrow seas"—Bowman resolves to "explore some other part of it, where perhaps men of more humanity might be found, than those I so much feared and detested" (63). He soon escapes to the neighboring nation of Taupiniera, whose inhabitants live underground, eat raw food, and possess pig-like tails. Like the moles after whom they take their name, the Taupinierans are nearly blind and their fear of light renders them unable to defend or better themselves. Bowman's next stop is Olfactaria, whose inhabitants have developed an enhanced sense of smell that makes them exceptional hunters. In Olfactaria, Bowman marries before going on to mastermind that nation's strategic defeat of the invading Carnovirrians—described, by his Olfactarian benefactor Uncomia, as "those men-eaters who devoured your countrymen" (85). Leaving his pregnant wife Tewropa behind with the false promise of a future return, Bowman next arrives in the land of Auditante, where the people's overdeveloped sense of hearing leads them to spend too much time in idle entertainment. He finally leaves New Zealand altogether for the nearby island of Bonhommica, whose people have developed a sixth, moral, sense that renders them especially virtuous and resistant to excess. Bowman's south Pacific tour, then, is one through the various stages of human society as marked by their development of one of the five (or six, in the case of the exceptional Bonhommicans) senses. The Bonhommicans finally take him to the great southern continent his own expedition failed to find, where he visits the kingdom of Luxo-volupto and learns about the rebellion of its colony, Armoseria, before finally finding passage back to England by way of the Cape of Good Hope.

The novel's startling early depiction of the massacre of the *Adventure*'s crew draws on a number of contemporaneous sources—including documentary reports from multiple narratives of Cook's second expedition, writings about Joseph Banks and Tahiti from Cook's first voyage, and ongoing philosophical and proto-anthropological speculation about human history and development that emerged in response to these accounts and other literature about the Pacific. One of these was Cook's account of an event that took place in Queen Charlotte Sound near the end of the *Resolution*'s three-week wait for the arrival of the *Adventure*. Only a few days before they left, Cook reports that several members of his crew found on shore "the head and bowels of a youth who had lately been killed, the heart was stuck upon a forked stick and fixed to the head of their largest Canoe."[11] One of the crewmembers, named Pickersgill, "brought the head on board" the ship, where Cook decided to use the opportunity to test unconfirmed reports of cannibalism among the New Zealanders, about which some Europeans were skeptical. "Being desireous," he wrote, "of being an eye wittness to a fact which many people had their doubts about, I concealed my indignation and ordered a piece of the flesh to be broiled and brought on the quarter deck where one of these Canibals eat it with a seeming good relish before the whole ships Company."[12] Cook's strange experiment in indigenous cannibalism was conducted only a few days before he gave up waiting for the *Adventure*, and left New Zealand.

When Furneaux arrived in Queen Charlotte Sound less than a week later, he simply noted in his journal that they found the marked tree stump under which they discovered the "Bottle corked and waxed down, with a Letter in it from Captain Cook signifying their arrival on the 3ᵈ Instant and Departure on the 24ᵗʰ."[13] Hoping to catch up to the *Resolution*, Furneaux and his men sought quickly to ready the ship by taking on wood and water, making repairs, and exchanging nails for fish with the Natives. The midshipman James Burney made particular note in his private journal of Mai's fascinated response to watching the crew read Cook's note, and the failure of subsequent attempts to capitalize on the Polynesian's initial interest in literacy: "so many people gave him paper, pens etc and set him copies & tasks that in a weeks time the poor fellow's head was bothered—too many Cooks spoilt the Broth."[14] It was a suggestive metaphor, especially since—unbeknownst of course to any of the members of the *Adventure*—the Native head-boiling episode with Cook and his crew took place in this same location just over a week earlier. Moreover, that episode quite possibly set the stage for the violence that soon followed.

In preparation for a morning departure, Furneaux sent ten men from the ship in a boat, under the leadership of Mr. Rowe, with instructions "to gather wild greens for the Ship's Company with orders to return that evening." When the boat had not appeared by the next morning, a party went out to search for them and arrived the following evening with, in the later words of Furneaux,

> the melancholy news of her being cut off by the Indians in Grass Cove where they found the Relicks of several and the entrails of five men lying on the beach and in the Canoes they found several baskets of human flesh and five odd shoes new, as our people had been served [given] Shoes a day or two before; they brought onboard several hands, two of which we knew, one belonged to Thomas Hill being marked on the Back T.H. another to Mʳ Rowe who had a wound on his fore finger not quite whole [healed], and the Head, which was supposed was the head of my servant by the high forhead he being a Negroe.[15]

Burney was among those who had gone in search of the missing boat, and clarifies in his log that they identified the severed hand of Thomas Hill by the tattooed initials he had inscribed on it during their visit to Tahiti: "on further search we found more shoes & a hand which we immediately knew to have belong'd to Thoˢ Hill one of our Forecastlemen, it being marked T.H. which he had got done at Otaheite with a tattow [tattoo] instrument."[16] Burney explains that when they arrived the men opened fire on the large number of Natives they found gathered at Grass Cove, and discovered on the beach "2 bundles of Cellery which had been gather'd for loading" and a broken oar to which canoes were tied. In place of the boat they expected, they found instead "Such a shocking scene of Carnage & Barbarity as can never be mentiond or thought of, but with horror." In his grim accounting of the men lost ("10 in all—most of these were of our very best Seamen—the Stoutest & most healthy people in the Ship") and of body parts and possessions recovered, Burney notes that they found "none of their Arms [weapons] or Cloaths except part of a pair of Trowsers, a Frock & 6 shoes—no 2 of them being fellows."[17] These six shoes, forever separated from their "fellows," appear in this story rife with divided pairs: the *Adventure* from its companion ship the *Resolution*, the small boat from its host ship, and hands and heads from their bodies.

One way to think about the fictional version of this scene in *Hildebrand Bowman* is as a fascinating synthesis of the very different kinds of cannibalism and dismemberment experienced separately in Queen Charlotte Sound by the crews of both ships. By embedding a fictional character at the scene, the novel provides an imaginative version of what the documentary records lack: an eyewitness account of what happened on Grass Cove before Burney and others discovered the dismembered bodies and separated belongings of their fellow crewmembers. It moreover does so by bringing together Cook's shipboard eyewitness observation of cannibalistic consumption with Burney's second-hand and Furneaux's third-hand account of what would come to be called the Grass Cove massacre.[18] As dramatic as it is, however, the cannibalistic feast at Grass Cove soon proves to be among the novel's least remarkable episodes, as the synopsis of the novel's plot, described earlier in this section, begins to suggest. The abandoned Englishman proceeds to encounter a series of fantastical Pacific locations and civilizations in a narrative framework that led contemporary reviewers to compare the book to *Gulliver's Travels*. The review that appeared in *The London Review of English and Foreign Literature*, for example, describes it as possessing "some sense and some satire" but ultimately dismisses it as "a humble imitation" of "the travels of Lemuel Gulliver."[19] A notice of the novel that appeared in the *Monthly Review* similarly compares it to Swift, noting that Bowman, like Gulliver, travels to "unknown lands, for the purpose of astonishing, amusing, instructing, or reforming us who stay at home, by a relation of the marvelous and edifying events which befell him."[20]

But Bowman is less like Gulliver, I suggest, than he is an inverted, antipodean version of Mai, the Ra'iatean who journeyed on the *Adventure* from Polynesia to England, where he embarked on a grand tour and was widely feted and celebrated before returning to the Pacific two years later. Like Mai among the English, Bowman becomes an object of fascination to the Bonhommican elites he encounters near the end of his adventures and who respond with "great curiosity" once they learn that he "was of a nation on the other side of the world." In response to meeting him, the country's aristocrats wonder "what is he like? Is he a rational creature?" before discovering that "I was no monster, and could speak their language tolerably," whereupon they proceed to surround him in a "great circle" (145) and offer him "many invitations to dinners and suppers, from the principal nobility" (146). This describes almost precisely, in reverse geographical terms, Mai's reception by English aristocrats.

In the aftermath of his visit, Mai became a favorite subject of numerous poems and stage dramas, including the popular 1785 pantomime *Omai*, which Daniel O'Quinn has described as a performance that "shifts the specter of aristocratic dissipation onto racialized figures of the underclass." The play portrayed the British "metropole as a site of theft, avarice, corruption, and sexual vice" and characterized its aristocrats as beset by "sexual dissipation, disease, luxury, and racial degeneration."[21] *Hildebrand Bowman* makes a very similar argument about Britain through a mirrored move: it projects the specter of racialized cannibalism onto an English aristocracy dissipated by imperial gluttony. Written and published in a historical moment when debates about British empire were considerably more complex and unresolved than they would be a decade later, the novel suggests that to see England and the Atlantic world clearly, one must look to the other side of the globe. Indeed, by the book's end, the careful reader might well wonder whether those "vile cannibals" Bowman initially ran away from in Grass Cove were the New Zealand Natives or their British visitors.

The violence against the *Adventure* cannot be separated from the events that took place during the *Resolution*'s earlier sojourn, which included the murder of a Maori shot for stealing by one of Cook's crewmembers as well as the head-eating episode. In his book *Cannibals and Philosophers*, Daniel Cottom crucially positions cannibalism at the intersection of the Pacific and Atlantic worlds. He exposes the complicity of Enlightenment scientific practice with this act of New Zealand cannibalism when he points out that the "native's act of cannibalism . . . took place only after the head was brought on board the *Resolution*, broiled in the ship's galley, and offered to him." Cottom argues that "in the eighteenth century it became possible to see the fascination with cannibalism as a displacement and disavowal of the European consumption of human flesh that was most grievously carried out in the slave trade but also in myriad forms of exploitation, colonialism, enforced dependency, hierarchy, and, as William Blake would say, Christian mercy." Practices developed in the European Atlantic world are projected onto and played out within the indigenous Pacific world, and Cottom's careful reading indicates the ways in which the cannibal might be thought of not as "the cause but the effect of the European's endlessly mendacious and voracious desire."[22] In other words, Cook's cannibalistic experiment actually collapses rather than reaffirms the assumed distinction that underpins his actions: between the reputed advances of British civilization and the presumed savagery of indigenous peoples.

Hildebrand Bowman makes a surprisingly similar argument; by essentially folding a map of the world so as to place Atlantic society within Pacific space, it positions Britain as a cannibal empire that feeds on the bodies of others. Although concealed beneath its masquerade of civilizational luxury, British cannibalism is every bit as savage as its New Zealand counterpart. The novel moreover sexualizes this relation in ways that draw from European explorers' depictions of the Pacific, especially accounts of Tahiti. As Cottom explains, cannibalism inhabits a "nexus of desire" at scenes of exchange between Europeans and Natives in the Pacific, for "sex between Europeans and the peaceful Tahitians had taken place in the context of and as a part of commerce, and there was a growing recognition that the European encounter with the supposed cannibals of New Zealand and other lands was also a matter of trade. In fact, it had become clear that whatever else they might be, cannibals were being merchandised as objects of consumption."[23] *Bowman* brings cannibalism and consumption together in a critique of transoceanic war capitalism.

Human Senses and Stadial Theory

The narrative structure of *Hildebrand Bowman* relies on conjectural history, which emerged in mid-eighteenth century France and Scotland to establish progressive stages of human development. First outlined in a series of lectures by Adam Smith at Glasgow University in the 1750s (long before he published those ideas in his 1776 *Wealth of Nations*), stadial theory proposed that human development progressed in four stages, from savage hunters to pastoral shepherds to agricultural farmers and finally to commercial peoples. He furthermore insisted that the indigenous peoples of North America were the closest one might get in the modern era to those early hunters. As Ronald Meek points out, Smith shared with other thinkers in both Scotland and France at the time an almost obsessive fascination with Native Americans, as well as a belief that the superiority of European society at the time was the result of "certain important socio-economic institutions and phenomena which then as now were often coming under attack—notably inequality, property rights, and the accumulation of capital."[24] In this regard, stadial theory drew on John Locke's earlier ideas on the historical origins of property. Locke popularized the notion that the indigenous peoples of the Americas provided "a Pattern of the first Ages in *Asia* and *Europe*" because they represented, in his view, humankind at a stage of development that precedes the private possession of property; he famously remarked that "In the beginning all the World was *America*," since the American Indian "knows no Inclosure, and is still a Tenant in common."[25]

  Cook himself echoed these ideas in ways that complicated Smith's narrative of civilizational progress. In the journal he kept during the second voyage, Cook reflected on the 1773 visit to Queen Charlotte Sound in New Zealand. This "Second Visit of ours," he observed, "hath not mended the morals of the Natives of either Sex." He remarked that the region's once-virtuous "Indian Women" are now prostituted by the men "for a spike nail or any other thing they value," and makes it clear that this corruption has come at the hands of his own crew. According to Cook,

> such are the consequences of a commerce with Europeans and what is still more
> to our Shame civilized Christians, we debauch their Morals already too prone to
> vice and we interduce among them wants and perhaps diseases which they never
> before knew and which serves only to disturb that happy tranquility they and
> their fore Fathers had injoy'd. If any one denies the truth of this assertion let him
> tell me what the Natives of the whole extent of America have gained by the com-
> merce they have had with Europeans.[26]

These damning journal observations on the European corruption of Pacific Natives are left out of his 1777 published narrative of the second expedition,

A Voyage Towards the South Pole and Round the World, although the volume does include both his description of the shipboard cannibalism experiment and an appendix, titled *Captain Furneaux's Narrative of his Proceedings in the Adventure during the Separation of the Ships*, which describes the massacre at Grass Cove. Cook's published narrative, however, was preceded in print by another account of the expedition, titled *Voyage Round the World* and written by Georg (or George) Forster. Along with his father, Johann (or John) Forster, George served as botanist on the expedition—taking the place of Joseph Banks who served that role in the first voyage. Forster's volume therefore put into relatively wide circulation an account of the Grass Cove events that was based on the unpublished reports cited above by Furneaux and Burney of the search party's discovery of the body parts of the ten men. It is moreover almost certainly the more important of the two narratives for *Hildebrand Bowman*, for Forster's discussion of relations between the Natives and their European visitors suggests a source for the novel's fascination with the overdevelopment of human senses.

While Cook's published narrative explains that the killing of one of the Natives by a crewmember was the result of the theft by Natives of the Europeans' property, Forster lays much of the blame instead on English acts of theft, noting that the crew "seemed at New Zeeland to think they had a right to the property of the natives" and that some men "robbed the hut of a poor native of several tools, and forced upon him some nails, which they thought an equivalent." According to Forster, Cook prohibited his men from trading with the New Zealand Natives for any items other than "refreshments" because the sailors had developed such a "rage of collecting arms and utensils" from them that they would even forgo acquiring the food and drink necessary to their "own health." Most shocking of all to Forster are the "shipmates who readily took up with the same lodging, in order to receive the caresses of the filthy female inhabitants." He quickly discards the explanation that these were simply indulgences of sexual desire by the "brutish sailors," insisting instead that "when people habitually give full course to their unbounded desires, it is not surprising that they gratify one sense at the expence of all the rest." That claim perfectly describes the series of imaginary New Zealand nations visited by Bowman, who are precisely defined by their gratification of "one sense at the expence of all the rest."[27] For Forster, the sailors irrationally trade for weapons or utensils or sex rather than the food they need because they are in the habit of over-indulging particular desires. Forster's observation that an overindulged desire produces an overdeveloped sense might well serve as an epigraph to *The Travels of Hildebrand Bowman*, which amounts to a consolidated Pacific tour through the history of human progress based on a particular version of stadial theory informed by human sensory development then circulating in Scotland and England.[28]

Forster's distinction between human instincts on the one hand, and human habits misrecognized as instincts on the other, is almost certainly borrowed from the work of Lord Monboddo, or James Burnett, whose ideas are an explicit source for *Hildebrand Bowman*. Monboddo's theory on the role of the senses in human development posed a forgotten alternative to what would become, by the end of the eighteenth century, the dominant model of Scottish stadial theory.[29] In the first, 1773, volume of his six-volume work *Of the Origin and Progress of Language*, Monboddo advanced a four-stage narrative of the development of civil society that others have recognized as a version of Smith's.[30] But Monboddo's work did two things with stadial theory that distinguished it from the work of Smith and others: the first was to focus on the indigenous peoples of the Pacific rather than the Americas as models of earlier stages, and the second was to focus extensively on the role played by the senses in this development.

Monboddo's real interest, as his book's title suggests, is the origin of language out of sensory capabilities that humans share with other animals. Language, for Monboddo, required the development of ideas. Ideas themselves develop through a process of first preserving sensations by way of memory and imagination, and then subjecting those remembered sensations to reason, which allows for comparisons and, in turn, abstract thinking. Sense perceptions, in short, become remembered notions which then transform by way of reason into abstract ideas that enable language. But Monboddo insists that humans would not express ideas in language until they banded together in a society that made the communication of ideas necessary. Sophisticated animals like beavers or orangutans might have society without language, he argued, just as animals like dogs or horses might have memories of sensory perceptions without having the capacity for reason that enabled the abstract thinking necessary to develop ideas.[31]

As a result of this theory, the border between the realm of the human and that of the animal was, for Monboddo, surprisingly close. Details he gleaned from Pacific travel writings convinced him that humans had not simultaneously progressed all over the globe through these four stages of development, but that some creatures in other parts of the world still existed in one or more of the earlier stages—as proto-human animals, if you will. He was especially fascinated by reports of creatures who appeared to be in the long process of transition from an animal to a human stage of development. For better or worse, he found in Pacific travel narratives reports that confirmed this view, including such marvels as Ukrainian fox-like animals who live in caves (1.422), Siberian sea-cats who were organized socially and politically (1.424), tree-dwelling wood-eaters (1.242), tailed men from the Nicobar Islands (1.258), as well as the "brave and generous" (1.206–7) cannibalistic New Zealanders encountered and described by Joseph Banks and Daniel Solander during Cook's first voyage. His unskeptical reading of these materials inspired the embarrassing anecdote for which Monboddo remains best known. When Cook left on his second voyage around the world, his former shipboard botanist Joseph Banks undertook a voyage of discovery to Iceland, and stopped in Scotland on his return. In Edinburgh, he and fellow naturalist Daniel Solander had breakfast with Monboddo who—in a record of the meeting by James Boswell—asked Solander whether the inhabitants of New Holland (or Australia) had tails. The exchange provided comic material for Samuel Johnson, who saw the

FIGURE 4.2. *Four stages of human evolution, including tailed proto-human. Carl Linnaeus,* Amoenitates Academicae *(1749–90). Credit: Wellcome Collection.*

embrace of and appreciation for so-called primitive cultures as misguided and foolish, and took particular aim at Monboddo, unfavorably comparing his blinkered primitivism to Rousseau's.[32]

Monboddo's imagined creatures possessed of tails on the other side of the globe were inspired in part by Carl Linnaeus's 1764 *Amoenitates Academicae*, which included an illustration of a tailed proto-human presumed to represent one of the earlier four stages of human evolution (see Figure 4.2). These creatures appear in the Bowman novel, of course, as the Taupinerians, who live in caves and sport "a short tail, like that of a young pig" (75).[33] Worried that he will be (like Monboddo) disbelieved and mocked, Bowman goes on to express

> joy, to find that several travelers had seen men with such rear appendixes; which a learned judge in the northern part of this island has made a collection of, and, after a thorough examination, gives entire credit to. It is also very satisfactory to me, that this my account of the Taupinerians, will give a singular pleasure to this learned gentleman; who has been sneered at by some smatterers in knowledge, on this very account. (75)

Dror Wahrman has suggested that Monboddo is the central object of satire in *Hildebrand Bowman*, citing its print and visual depiction (see Figure 4.3) of the Taupinerians as a "Monboddian man-animal" and its title page epigraph declaring that "An Ape and Savage (cavil all you can), Differ not more, than Man compared with Man."[34] Wahrman makes the crucial point, however, that Monboddo was not collapsing the distinction between humans and animals so much as he was—like many of his contemporaries—marking the small gap between humans and an animal like the orangutan while simultaneously insisting on the impermeability of that gap (a gap sustained for Monboddo by the absence of language among

FIGURE 4.3. *Hildebrand Bowman with a tailed Taupinerian outside of his cave.* The Travels of Hildebrand Bowman *(London, 1778). Courtesy, Columbia University Library.*

animals). Wahrman explains that the position taken by Monboddo and others on the adjacency of the animal and the human fell quickly out of favor by the end of the century, when it became overwhelmed by the soon-dominant belief in the wide and absolute discrepancy between the categories of animal and human—and by the emergent racial categorizations that would support that belief.[35] As a result, texts such as Monboddo's and Bowman's produced in the transitional 1770s became subject to easy scorn in the short term and sustained oblivion in the long term.[36]

Monboddo believed that some animals could still develop the faculties needed to become human. He also believed that humans themselves had managed to corrupt their own process of sensory development. *Hildebrand Bowman* joins Johnson and others in scoffing at the first belief, but the novel actually deploys the second belief into a remarkable critique of British empire. Monboddo's first volume begins by declaring that some human powers are innate while others are acquired through habit, as "every faculty is the result of a previous habit or disposition, without which it cannot exist" (1.13). He explains that humans gradually lose innate instincts as they develop habits; these habits lead both to reason and to what he calls "that bastard kind of reason commonly called *opinion*" (1.23). Opinions are the result not of the "guidance of nature and instinct" but of "artificial habit," and have led humans to "become the artificial creatures we now are." Monboddo explains that our senses lead us by way of inferences toward reason, but as they do so we misperceive our developing opinions as natural: "Civilized man is so much more a creature of art than of nature, that his natural habits are almost lost in his artificial" (1.198). For Monboddo, human acts and desires are not the result of divine or natural inspiration but instead are man-made, the products of repeated practice. This is precisely the argument Forster is making in his observations of the irrational and abusive trade practices at Queen Charlotte Sound by Cook's crew. It's also the argument made in *Hildebrand Bowman* on a global, transoceanic scale.

Before we return to the novel, it's important to rescue one additional element of early stadial theory that animates *Bowman* but that fell out of favor not long after the book's publication. Adam Ferguson—whose 1767 *Essay on the History of Civil Society* popularized the ideas on which Smith had lectured at Glasgow—departed from Smith by questioning whether humans really had progressed morally as they progressed in time through these stages. Sounding very much like Rousseau, Ferguson asked whether the "refinements" of the civilized world were not rather corruptions from which savages remained free.[37] By contrast, Smith was convinced that the benefits of commercial society compensated for such losses. Over the following century, stadial theory began to naturalize what Meek calls the "machines" that drove historical as well as economic progress—namely "the division of labour, the growth of commodity exchange, and above all the accumulation of capital"—and that defined historical and economic progress alike in terms of a gradual but persistent increase in wealth.[38]

The result was to fix stadial theory within a linear and progressive narrative model whose dominance has since allowed us to forget that there were eighteenth-century versions of it that were cyclical instead. Monboddo offers one especially interesting version of this alternative that reshapes Smithian linearity into a circle specifically by way of empire. "It is by means of art," Monboddo claims, "that man has spread himself over the earth more than any other animal known" (1.413), and he notes that "the whole history of mankind is nothing but a narrative of the growth of families into nations, of small nations into great, and of great nations into mighty empires. These at last become too great, and fall by their own weight," as part of what he calls a "perpetual revolution and circle in human affairs" (1.366). Here progress is nothing more than the manufactured human habit of accumulation, abetted by sensory overindulgence, and doomed to collapse upon its own irrational excess. Monboddo's description of this circle as a "revolution" invokes, of course, the word's then-dominant astronomical meaning as repeated rotation. Given that *Hildebrand Bowman* explicitly positions the American colonial rebellion as the cyclical end result of a sensory-driven commercial empire, however, we can see the novel pressing Monboddo's thinking and meaning into more explicitly political terms.

Hildebrand Bowman suggestively opens with a dedication to Banks and Solander, the very naturalists who had only recently informed Monboddo that the Australians did not have tails. Bowman introduces them as "the best judges of the veracity" of his narrative, and even goes on cordially to invite them to accompany him when he is, in the future, made commander of one of the ships that will be sent to "cultivate *friendship* and *commerce* with the Nations I have discovered" (49). Monboddo's description of the "generous cannibals" found in New Zealand by Banks and Solander during Cook's first voyage would have certainly come under fire in the wake of Furneaux's news from Grass Cove, and this opening suggests that the novel's satire merely re-subjects the Scotsman to the kind of mockery he suffered at the hands of Johnson. But even if Monboddo is portrayed as a fool early on in the novel, by its end his ideas clearly drive the novel's portrayal of the foolishness of imperial Britain, where the destructive excesses of empire fuel a sensory overindulgence created by artificial human habits misunderstood as natural human needs. In Monboddo, stadial theory is reshaped from a line into a circle; in Bowman, that transoceanic circle closes where Maori cannibalism in the Pacific meets and mirrors British consumption in the Atlantic. In *Hildebrand Bowman*, men with tails soon give way to women with wings. Along the way, the novel reminds us of a historical moment in which political revolution marked the narrative end point of imperialism rather than the narrative starting point of nationalism.

Feathers and Luxury

Bowman begins to approach stadial theory's pinnacle of human society when his voyages take him to Seripante. This city serves as a factory for merchants on the coast of a large undeveloped country inhabited by a nomadic and idle people, the Auditantes, whose flocks of sheep produce enormous quantities of wool for which the visiting merchants come to trade.[39] In Seripante (whose residents, he is told, are actually from the island of Bonhommica) Bowman "began to think myself again in Europe" (91). At the request of his Bonhommican merchant host, Ouragow, he recounts the story of his travels and Ouragow is astounded to learn "that there are people on the other side of the globe, who have carried navigation to such a height, as to send ships all over the face of the earth, where seas will bear them, and ice not obstruct their passage; to discover new countries and new people!" (92). When pressed to explain the purpose of that expedition, Bowman describes their fruitless search for the supposed great southern continent, only to be informed by his host that "there certainly was one; and that the Bonhommicans carried on a considerable trade to one of its kingdoms" (98). Thrilled by this news, Bowman resolves to journey with his companion to Bonhommica, where he is promised passage to that continent and its kingdom.

Upon arrival in Bonhommica's capital city of Ludorow, he observes that he "was once again got into a civilised country" (106). A comprehensive tour of Bonhommica reveals it to be such an idealization of a perfect human society that the novel even supplements Monboddo's sensory-based ideas about human development by ascribing a "sixth sense" to its inhabitants: "the sense of conscience, or the moral sense; and they would much rather be without any of the others, even the sight or hearing, than destitute of it" (122). Signaling the imaginary country's alignment with Elizabethan England, the Bonhommican Queen is named Tudorina. She asks him for an account of his home country, and responds to Bowman's description by observing that "your nation is following exactly the steps of all rich and powerful kingdoms; luxury has got in among you, and will soon destroy you" (109). This warning accompanies Bowman as he departs for the kingdom of Luxo-volupto on the great southern continent, and its capital, Miro-volante—allegorical representations of Britain and London. His passage to Luxo-volupto is by way of a "convoy" of ships whose numbers are necessary, he is told, to protect them "from being insulted by the Armoserian privateers" (117)—the novel's first mention of the rebellious colony that allegorizes North America and about whose resistance Bowman will later learn more.

If Bonhommica represents the height of civilization within Adam Smith's linear stadial theory, Luxo-volupto represents the cyclical fate that Lord Monboddo warned would befall all such civilizations upon growing from nations into "mighty empires" that "become too great, and fall by their own weight." This fall is precipitated exactly by sensory overindulgence, for the Luxo-voluptans quickly turn out to be distinguished by the overdevelopment of the senses of taste and touch. Echoing George Forster's reflections on the English sailors who satisfy manufactured desires while neglecting their natural ones, Bowman immediately questions the Luxo-voluptans' own belief that this sensory development is natural and inherent rather than artificial and produced. The Bonhommicans report to Bowman that the Luxo-voluptans "pretended their sense of taste, or palate, was naturally formed more sensible of agreeable impressions than other nations." However, their visitors recognize that it was instead "a vitiated taste, become from long habit a kind of second nature" (135). Because of their empire's "extensive dominions in the southern hemisphere...and immense commerce, they had it in their power to indulge that vitiated taste, by ransacking half the globe for choice viands, the finest flavoured wines, and the most poignant sauces to gratify their appetite" (256–7).

This sentence emphasizes that sensory indulgence requires the paired violence of colonial conquest and commercial acquisition; through its imperial possessions abroad, the kingdom uses its "power" to "ransack" distant lands for desirable food and drink. The result is a city suffused with artificial desires. In Miro-volante, everyone feels the need to ride in a carriage, whether they can afford it or not, leading "all ranks and degrees of life...to be confounded" (137). Even the lowest servant-maid there "must breakfast on the infusion of an herb, that is brought ten thousand leagues from this country with the produce of a cane to sweeten it, which also comes from a great distance" (135). As Lance Bertelsen puts it, with Luxo-volupto the novel launches a "satirical simulacrum of mid-eighteenth-century Britain" (28) as Bowman describes London society's dependence on the global reach of Britain's commercial empire, where the sensory addiction to sweetened tea at home relies on continual imports from China and other Asian outposts in the Pacific as well as from Jamaica and other West Indian sugar plantation islands in the Atlantic.

Like the sailors on Cook's voyage who were so fixated on accumulating weapons that they forget to eat, the Luxo-voluptans suffer from their "luxurious way of life" (135). Their practice of overeating, for instance, "brings on the gout, and many other painful and lingering disorders, which make their lives miserable; but that neither deters others, nor (such is their propensity to these poisons) even the sufferers themselves from again indulging in them, as soon as the weakly and almost destroyed tone of their stomachs will permit" (135–6). And their suffering is moral as well as physical, for whether their "exquisite sense of taste was natural or acquired, there was scarcely a vestige of the moral sense left among the generality of them" (136). Bowman's extensive manners-and-customs portrait of Luxo-volupto goes on to describe its culture of continual litigation, political corruption, self-interested charity, excessive consumption, crushing debt, and fashions of dress and architecture which change so quickly that even expensive newly constructed buildings are almost immediately abandoned and left empty when a new building fad arrives to render the previous one out of style.[40] The Luxo-voluptans meanwhile take part in a continual round of clubs and balls, attend spas and horse races, and gamble continuously amidst runaway problems of personal and national debt. As one resident puts it, "we are all in debt, but the Nation owes two hundred millions, so it is the fashion you see" (150).

Perhaps the most fascinating feature of all to Bowman is the presence of "wings on the heads" of the women he sees on the streets of the city of Miro-volante (138)—a name that translates roughly to something like "flying wonder" (see Figure 4.4). His host explains to Bowman that these wings sprout on the heads of both women and men who engage in "dissipation, or violent passion for public places" (139), and increase in size according to the "strength" or repetition of "desire" (139). Those with especially "high" head wings will soon find wings also sprouting on their shoulders, where they are more easily concealed under coats. These shoulder wings appear on women "immediately after a failure of chastity"

FIGURE 4.4. *Winged women in Luxo-volupto.* The Travels of Hildebrand Bowman *(London, 1778). Courtesy, Columbia University Library.*

and they appear on every man "who has seduced a young maiden, or married woman" (139). Some women, called Alae-putas (more or less, "winged prostitutes"), shamelessly expose their wings publicly and use them to make further sexual commerce possible, for the wings allow them to fly to distant lovers faster. One woman whose wings were clipped by her jealous husband still managed to meet her lover, who used his wings to fly to her in the attic of her house. Bowman learns that those women whose virtuous behavior does not lead wings to grow from their heads nevertheless purchase and arrange feathers on their heads in order to look like those who have such wings, for they "are become so much the fashion; that all other women of any genteel station are obliged to imitate them, and wear false ones" (141).

Bertelsen astutely identifies these feathered wings as the novel's "most memorable and complex staging of luxury," since they evoke the eighteenth-century British fashion style known as "macaroni" (29). Patricia Fara describes macaroni as a term "coined to denigrate the aristocratic youths who had acquired continental manners during their Grand Tour to Italy, but it became a more general term of abuse for deriding foppish young gentlemen who adopted ridiculous extremes of stylish clothing."[41] Macaronis were largely young dandies who wore unnecessary swords and sported high wigs or hats, often topped with feathers—as in Philip Dawe's illustration of "The Macaroni" from 1773 (see Figure 4.5), or the fellow in the song "Yankee Doodle Dandy" who "put a feather in his cap, and called it macaroni." As Bertelsen notes, women too adopted the combination of high headdresses and feathers, which was associated with "upper-class luxury and profligacy" (233) but which was also mimicked by London prostitutes (30n.1).[42]

Macaroni style for both men and women was the object of considerable satire and critique in mid-eighteenth-century London, particularly in a series of cartoons

FIGURE 4.5. *Philip Dawe, "The Macaroni" (London, 1773). © Trustees of the British Museum.*

published by Matthew and Mary Darly. Two of these Darly cartoons, both of which appeared in 1772, use the figure of Joseph Banks to link macaroni excess to the Pacific and an expansionist empire. One of these labels Banks a "Botanic Macaroni," and depicts him carrying the traditional macaroni sword while fixated on the image of a plant (see Figure 4.6). Following Cook's first voyage to the Pacific, and

FIGURE 4.6. *Matthew Darly, "The Botanic Macaroni" (London, 1772). © Trustees of the British Museum.*

especially the narrative about that expedition written by John Hawksworth, Banks became known for witnessing, describing, and participating in sexual adventures with Tahitian women.[43] Fara observes that in this particular image, Banks is portrayed as a "botanical libertine whose excessive desire for women has been replaced by an obsessive preoccupation with plants."

Indeed, one popular poem about Banks that circulated after the first Cook voyage describes him presenting his erect penis to the Tahitian Queen in the form of a plant ("what a plant I did produce to thee") while another compared Tahitian women to prostitutes and referred to their genitalia as "the wonders of each cockle-shell" presented to "botanists."[44] A second illustration, titled "The Fly Catching Macaroni," depicts Banks straddling the Antarctic and Arctic poles of the globe trying to catch a butterfly (see Figure 4.7). This image, as Fara explains, attributes to Banks "imperial pretensions," mocking his effort to "catch a butterfly, symbol of triviality" as a grandiose attempt to capture and classify the world.[45] The out-of-place sword and the large feather in his hat align the ridiculous fashion pretensions of macaroni style with the ridiculous political and scientific pretensions of empire.

Other representations of macaroni style on both sides of the Atlantic indicated that the trend's surface luxury simply served to mask a barely hidden animality within. The satirical collection *Macaroni Jester* by John Cooke, published in London in 1764 and in Philadelphia in 1768, explicitly described those adopting macaroni style as apes that had been changed back into men, but only partially. As a result, their surface refinements ineffectually cover over their fundamentally primitive features. The poem titled "The Origin of Macaronies" that opens the book explains: "*Their hair in curls luxuriant now / Around their temples spread, / Their tails which then did hang below / Now dangle from their head.*" Despite efforts to transform or rearrange the crude physical features of the ape into those of a sophisticated human, the poem explains that the macaroni's face "*still retains a monkey's grin.*"[46] The poem concludes by noting that "*Men with contempt the brutes survey'd / Nor named the silly tonies / But women like the motley breed / And call them MACARONIES.*" The visual images of Banks and the textual descriptions by Monboddo therefore come together in *Hildebrand Bowman*, which pairs macaroni luxury in the European Atlantic with imperial expansion and sexual indulgence in the primitive Pacific, where tailed men and winged women might both be found.

Feathered heads also appear, however, at an especially significant moment in the documentary records of the *Adventure*, as the ship headed toward its expected rendezvous with Cook in Queen Charlotte Sound. More or less as Cook was ordering the severed head to be cooked in the galley of the *Resolution*, Furneaux and his crew encountered a severed head several hundred miles north in Tolaga Bay. When the ship made port there, Furneaux explains that the crew saw in one of the Natives' canoes "the head of a woman Lying in State adorned with Feathers and other ornaments." This feathered head, he notes, "had the appearance of being alive, but on examination found it dry and preserved with every feature perfect, and kept as the Relict of some deceased relation."[47] Nicholas Thomas explains that

17

V.3

Whipcord del.

The FLY CATCHING MACARONI.

I rove from Pole to Pole, you ask me why;
I tell you Truth, to catch a _____ Fly.

Pub. by Darly accor to Act July 12, 1772 (39) Strand.

FIGURE 4.7. *Matthew Darly, "The Fly-Catching Macaroni" (London, 1772).* © *Trustees of the British Museum.*

feathers "were highly valued across the Pacific"—not merely as decorations but as sacred and divine.[48] We might set this uncanny feathered head of a primitive New Zealand Native woman against the feathered heads of Bowman's elite aristocratic women who have developed artificial habits of sensory overindulgence. In the novel, the distinctions between the primitive and the civilized collapse in a transoceanic space where the achievements of imperial expansion are exposed as self-indulgent excesses that mask what is essentially a crude and cruel barbarism. The feathered head of the Tolaga woman might be thought of as a mirror to the feathered heads of the Luxo-voluptans—that point of self-reflection in the global circle where the bodies of women expose imperialist consumption as its own form of cannibalism. Bertelsen argues that in its Luxo-volupto segment, *Hildebrand Bowman* represents "the pessimistic endgame of stadial history," and indeed Bowman concludes that "if some convulsion did not happen to restore" the virtue they must once have had, Luxo-volupto appears headed for self-destruction "in anarchy and confusion" (143). But to the extent that the novel takes its cue from Monboddo, stadial history may not end so much as it rotates around to begin all over again.

The Luxo-voluptans, whom Bowman meets at the end of his Pacific travels, appear to occupy the opposite end of the stages of human society from that of the Carnovirrians, with whom Bowman's adventures began. But that's if stadial theory observes a linear and progressive pattern rather than a cyclical and rotational one. For all the supposed greater refinement of their tastes and manners, in the end the Luxo-voluptans' overdeveloped appetites and indulgent consumption practices ultimately align them with as much as they distinguish them from the bestial Carnovirrians who crudely chew on human carcasses. The Luxo-voluptans may not literally eat people, but their ungovernable desires to consume (whether expensive food and drink, lavish clothing and entertainment, or sexualized bodies) are both the effect and the cause of global practices of exploitation that do, in fact, harm and even kill people. The difference is merely one between "primitive and advanced cannibalism" (28), as Bertelsen aptly puts it. Elsewhere in his narrative of Cook's second voyage, Forster makes a direct connection between the indulgence of luxury and the violence of revolution. He warned that the "introduction of foreign luxuries" into Tahitian society would lead to social inequality, and predicted that while commoners would suffer, the elite would, "by indulging a voracious appetite, and living in absolute idleness," eventually produce the conditions that would "bring on a revolution. This is a natural cycle in human affairs," he warned.[49] Here Forster is grafting an explicitly political meaning onto what Monboddo described as a "perpetual revolution and circle in human affairs" (1.366). *Bowman* similarly positions political revolution at this critical point of dramatic inequality brought on by imperial excess.

Revolution and Consumption

In the world described by Hildebrand Bowman, global empire creates and then feeds ungovernable desires, manufacturing practices of excessive consumption that require compulsive and coercive acquisition. At the same time, however, imperial practices of violent oppression around the world create the conditions for revolution. The novel's central example of this phenomenon is Armoseria, a "large colony" of Luxo-volupto located "at a thousand leagues distance," which at the moment of Bowman's visit is engaged in a rebellion against its mother country (147). These Armoserians are the North Americans who, at the time the novel appeared in 1778, were engaged in the third year of a colonial war against Great Britain. *Hildebrand Bowman* offers a revealingly global analysis of this American uprising.

Some Luxo-voluptans find the rebellion by the Armoserians to be an act of "monstrous ingratitude" against a mother country who "nursed them up to maturity at so great an expence and entered a war solely on their account, by which the nation had incurred debt above sixty millions" (147). Others sympathize with the Armoserian rebels, whom they characterize as "the most oppressed and ill-used people under the sun," arguing that the "unconstitutional" practice of taxation without representation is the product of a selfish mother country who "gets enough by her exclusive trade with them" but now insists on "taxing her own children" (148). These recognizable dueling political positions are soon revealed, however, to have nothing whatsoever to do with the Armoserians, much less with the justice or injustice of their plight. Instead, their arguments represent the perpetual and vociferous disagreement between these two parties—a rhetorical battle so entrenched that if one party changed its position, the other would as well, simply in order to continue disagreeing (148). It is even suggested that the pro-Armoserian party in Luxo-volupto incited the rebellion by creating the false sense that they supported the rebels, and some worry that these strategies "will ruin millions of these people, and cost this country much blood and immense treasure" (149).

The images of a macaroni Banks in the Pacific world discussed in the previous section should be considered alongside macaroni images from the Atlantic world that explicitly connect the feathered fashion fad to political revolution in the American colonies. An image by Carington Bowles that circulated in London in 1774, for example, showed the tarred and feathered Loyalist John Malcolm forced to drink tea at the hands of American Patriots in Boston, Massachusetts. Curiously titled "A New Method of Macarony Making," the image casts the violence of colonial rebellion as the political counterpart to the fashion excess of London aristocrats (see Figure 4.8).[50] Another London cartoon—this one produced by the Darlys in 1776—helps to clarify the relationship between imperial consumption and colonial dissent. "Oh. Heigh. Oh. Or a View of the Back Settlements" depicts from behind a woman's enormous headdress topped with multiple large feathers (see Figure 4.9).[51] Its title aligns that view of feathered excess with North America's Ohio Territory, which marked the boundary between colonial American settlements and Indian country. The image and title together (including an implied reference to the feathered headwear of Native Americans) argue that colonial rebellion is the inevitable outcome of an empire driven by the accumulation and consumption of luxuries. Feathered excesses at home create and conceal insurrectionary violence abroad; behind the absurd hairstyles of the wealthy metropolitan

A New Method of MACARONY MAKING, as practifed at BOSTON.

FIGURE 4.8. *Colonial revolutionaries practice macaroni violence. Carrington Bowles, "A New Method of Macarony Making, as practiced at Boston in North America" (London, 1774). Courtesy of the Library of Congress, LC-USZ62-45386.*

English (and the violent practices of imperial accumulation that sustain those styles) is a backcountry uprising waiting to happen. Indeed, some print and visual depictions of the war represented British violence as cannibalism, such as the 1780 illustration "The Allies" that features King George feasting on the body parts of a dismembered colonist. Native Americans join him while his Archbishop arrives to bring him scalping knives and tomahawks (see Figure 4.10).[52] Just as these images do, *Hildebrand Bowman* positions the American Revolution within a global transoceanic framework of imperial consumption. But the novel's cyclical structure and transoceanic mirroring framework perhaps more daringly begin to pair Armoserian revolution with Carnovirrian riot, to offer ways of imagining North America's Atlantic Revolution and indigenous anti-colonial Pacific uprisings as part of the same rotating and destructive cycle of imperial expansion.

The eighteenth-century history of anti-luxury discourse, and the anti-expansionist position on which it tended to rely, has been unearthed by a number of literary critics and historians. John Sekora identifies a hostility in Britain toward commercial and imperial expansion that thrived in the first half of the eighteenth century. He explains that luxury in particular came under fire for "begetting new, false, and

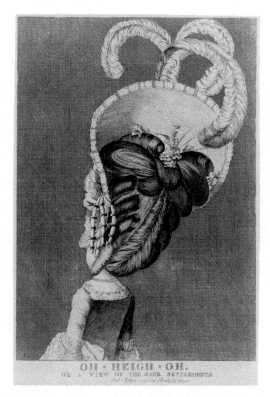

OH · HEIGH · OH.
OR A VIEW OF THE BACK SETTLEMENTS

FIGURE 4.9. *Backcountry insurrections brew behind elaborate metropolitan hairstyles. Matthew Darly, "Oh. Heigh. Oh. Or a View of the Back Settlements" (London, 1776). Courtesy of the Library of Congress, LC-USZ62-115004.*

artificial wealth, a new and noxious economic order, and a new and sinister breed of men whose sole office was to multiply by some nefarious means the new man-made values"—a description that echoes Monboddo's insistence on the human manufacture of artificial wants and needs. Sekora argues that these attitudes began to change after the 1763 Treaty of Paris, when frequent and intense earlier attacks on luxury diminished as support for British expansionism increased. Sekora identifies Scottish stadial theory—or at least the version of it that became aligned with Adam Smith—as one important source for "a more favorable view of commerce" that dovetailed with rising support for imperial expansion in the wake of British war victories. This pro-expansionist position achieved real dominance, Sekora claims, when Adam Smith's arguments in his 1776 *Wealth of Nations* about the favorability of commerce (which were themselves, of course, a product of stadial theory) found a political champion in Edmund Burke.[53]

Sekora's chronology would position *Bowman* as a belated entry into what he maintains was an already waning anti-luxury campaign by the date of its publication in 1778. Other scholars, however, convincingly argue that the decade of the 1770s actually saw the debate about expansion reinvigorated. As Kathleen Wilson

FIGURE 4.10. *King George engaging in a cannibalistic feast on dismembered body parts of colonial Patriots. John Almon (publ.), "The Allies—Par nobile Fratrum!" (London, 1780). Courtesy of the Library of Congress, LC-USZ62-34860.*

explains, the Paris Treaty "brought to the fore a long-suppressed unease at the enormity of British possessions, their racial and religious diversity, the domestic divisions they mirrored and reproduced, and the authoritarian techniques used to govern them." Such recognitions cast empire not as commercial triumph but rather as a source of corrupting luxury and polluting effeminacy that were sustained by unconscionable practices of violence. Wilson notes that news from the Pacific, especially via Cook's voyages, actually "mobilized sentiments against the use of force and conquest in the 'civilizing' process."[54] Kate Fullagar aligns these critical British responses with the return of the *Adventure* from its Pacific voyage, and more specifically to the public's fascination with the Oceanian Native Mai. Fullagar explains that Mai "provided a kind of catalyst for debate about British expansion." Because Mai was seen to represent "the precise opposite of everything Britain was moving toward," his visit prompted a critique of Britain's increased dependence on monied interests and luxury goods, as well as of the increased debt these new dependencies encouraged.[55]

The satirical Luxo-voluptan depiction of London expresses precisely these concerns, and as such the novel helps to bring this since-obscured debate into clearer view. Along the way, it also offers a compelling understanding of political rebellion or revolution as the product of expansionist violence. The novel's Armoserian rebellion is the result of a cycle of conquest undertaken in the name of trade, of the continued creation and circulation of the immense wealth that results from such commerce, and of the wanton spending and sensory indulgence that such wealth fosters. That cycle has created a world in which "wealth is become the only object which all men aim at to support that luxury, and all crimes of course are perpetrated to attain it" (315); it is a world where "a universal profligacy pervaded the whole" (317). To hammer home his point, Bowman observes that "it requires no nice investigation to discover, that the British manners at present resemble much more those of the Luxo-voluptans, than the Bonhommicans" (397–8).

The force and significance of this Mai-inspired debate in the 1770s have been obscured, Fullagar points out, first by the often fractured or contradictory ways in which anti-expansionist opinions were expressed, and then by what became in the ensuing decade the overwhelming dominance of a pro-expansionist position.[56] *Hildebrand Bowman* clearly emerges out of this forgotten 1770s debate, where the novel was in conversation with the volumes by Forster and Monboddo. These books were all prompted by events and encounters in the Pacific world to identify the senses as a crucial, if unwitting, driver of past human development and of present British imperial ambition. For all of these writers, the seductive and addictive fruits of empire engorge the senses to produce human artifice unable to recognize itself as such. A Britain committed to continued expansion was a Britain caught within a troublingly cyclical trajectory that heralded destruction.[57]

If Bowman circulates around the Pacific much like Mai, he returns to the Atlantic much like Columbus. When he finally manages to find a ship able to return him to England, it is 1777—three years after Furneaux's return on the *Adventure* in July 1774, and two years after the return of Cook's *Resolution* in August 1775. Bowman's fictional return brings with it his claim to have finally discovered the very landmass that Cook had conclusively announced upon his own return did not exist: Terra Australis Incognito, or the great southern continent, which Bowman immediately suggests naming Bowmania (if only because it is easier to say, he claims, than Hildebrandia). This claim to have discovered what does not exist registers at first as ridiculous fantasy, unless and until one realizes that what Bowman is really claiming to have found are the material global effects of Britain's destructive empire of commerce and consumption.

Transoceanic Literary History and the Novel

As Kathleen Wilson observes, "the period of the American war forced into the English national consciousness the contradictions, inequities, and atrocities perpetuated in the name of national identity and obscured by the fire and fury of imperial expansion."[58] This chapter has argued that *The Travels of Hildebrand Bowman* participated in such an anti-expansionist critique by asking its readers to see the colonial American war from the perspective of the Pacific, providing a global maritime view in which revolutionary violence around the globe is the result of British imperial atrocities. The novel joined a small but important chorus of voices and texts that expressed an anti-imperialist position that battled with and against rising British support for imperial expansion, and that never gained the kind of sustained traction needed to coalesce into a historical narrative of its own. I'd like to end this chapter by exploring the effects this now-recovered novel might have on our governing narratives about the genre of the novel and American literary and cultural history.

It may seem that such efforts would by hindered by the fact that *Hildebrand Bowman* was by any measure neither a popular novel (its first edition was also its only contemporary edition), nor an American novel (its sole contemporary edition appeared only in London), nor a novel by a recognized (or even clearly identifiable) author. However, I want to insist that as long as we maintain such criteria to identify texts that deserve archival recovery, scholarly attention, and inclusion in an American literary history, we will risk missing the context of the global marketplace and transoceanic political arena within which the late eighteenth- and early nineteenth-century novel was produced and to which it responded. A transoceanic American literary history that takes account of the Pacific furthermore allows us to see that stories about gender help us to understand stories about empire. "From the beginning," as Lee Wallace puts it, "imperial expansion in the Pacific has been imagined as sexual event."[59] In *Hildebrand Bowman*, women's bodies mediate global and economic anxieties, not just national or sexual ones, asking us to complicate some of the gendered assumptions that underpin our literary histories of the novel as a genre.

Amidst all the absurd content of its narrative, it's easy to forget that at one point in its plot, the protagonist Bowman impregnates and abandons an indigenous woman on an imaginary south Pacific island. The fact that he married her before doing so does little to distance him from the countless real European sailors whose sexual encounters with indigenous women left behind offspring—as well as venereal disease—throughout the greater Pacific world. When members of the overland Lewis and Clark expedition arrived at the mouth of the Columbia River in 1805, they found evidence of much earlier maritime contact among the region's indigenous inhabitants, who were seasoned traders, spoke some English, and displayed symptoms of venereal disease. One Native woman even had the name "J. Bowman" tattooed on her arm.[60] Although the name has nothing to do with the fictional H. Bowman, the anecdote is a reminder, at once concrete and ghostly, of the corporeal scars left by Europeans as they traveled across and around the Pacific in the willing or unwilling service of global empire. Like the tattooed and severed hand of Thomas Hill, found among its unmarked and unidentifiable partners in New Zealand's Grass Cove, transoceanic war capitalism left behind whole or dismembered bodies that carried evidence of violent acts of possession and dispossession.

As Chapter 3 suggested, indigenous sexual practices and beliefs from the Pacific have been so completely muddled and contorted by European assumptions that they are notoriously challenging to reconstruct. European men interpreted the lack of shame by indigenous women, for example, as an invitation, a temptation—as a form of seduction.[61] Whether under cover of such real or supposed misinterpretation or not, Europeans regularly raped indigenous women, and it would be hard to overestimate the extent and effect of sexual coercion and commerce throughout the Pacific. Those acts of sexual violence quickly shifted the indigenous culture of response to European arrival, as Cook himself acknowledges in the 1773 journal entry documenting his return visit to Queen Charlotte Sound discussed earlier in this chapter, where he identifies the corruption of its inhabitants as a direct result of their treatment by his own crewmembers. As Chapter 3 detailed more explicitly, sexual abuse of Native women is also frequently cited as the cause of indigenous acts of rebellion against visiting Europeans, triggering in turn often overwhelming violence against Native populations.

This cyclical violence, and the role of women in it, is a prominent feature of one of the better-known transoceanic predecessors to *Hildebrand Bowman*. Henry Neville's 1688 fictional *Isle of Pines* circulated as a true account of a shipwreck that left the Englishman George Pine stranded on a small island—previously populated only by birds—near the great southern continent of *Terra Australis Incognita*. Pine is cast ashore with four female survivors, all of whom he proceeds to serially rape and impregnate (the language of the text merely observes that he developed a "desire for enjoying the women") as he simultaneously constructs improvements to the barren island. When the isolated island is finally visited seventy-eight years later by a Dutch ship, it boasts a population of 1789 inhabitants, all descendants of Pine.[62] Although *The Isle of Pines* predates Defoe's novel by over a century, countless critics echo George Emery Littlefield's early description of it as "a book in the vein of Robinson Crusoe."[63] Aside from treating the four women as a kind of background feature to the narrative, a natural resource available to its central male protagonist, such a statement is evidence of the ways that critically privileged novels have overpoweringly shaped our narratives of literary history (much as the politically privileged event of the American Revolution has overwhelmingly shaped our narratives of national history). But it is also evidence of a persistence in dividing novels into gendered subgenres that distinguish between masculinist maritime content (represented by works like *Crusoe* and *Gulliver's Travels*) and feminized domestic content (associated with sentimental novels such as *Clarissa* and *Charlotte Temple*).

Titles like *The Isle of Pines* and *The Travels of Hildebrand Bowman* that can be difficult to assign to a particular oceanic, linguistic, or national tradition can be of value precisely because they demand a rethinking of standard literary histories and their generic divisions. *The Isle of Pines*, for example, sits at the awkward nexus of the maritime adventure and the domestic seduction novel, where Pine brings to the sexual assault of Richardson's Robert Lovelace all the economic enthusiasm of Defoe's Robinson Crusoe. To this day, however, *The Isle of Pines* is packaged and sold as a work of utopian literature, suggesting that its celebration of imperial reproductive energy continues utterly to obscure the sustained violence by which all that English offspring accumulated. Paying close attention to the bodies of women in the narrative exposes rape as a weapon of global empire.

The oceanic, national, and generic indeterminacy of *The Travels of Hildebrand Bowman* has no doubt contributed to its near-total obscurity within literary history. But it is also because of its unusually transoceanic eighteenth-century vision that the American Revolution appears as the end product of empire rather than the origin point of a nation—as one uprising in a continuing cycle of global commerce carried out by maritime empires. And the bodies of women in this imaginary Pacific world, whether they are abandoned and pregnant or indulgent and feathered, point toward the destructive effects of that cyclical violence. In *Bowman*, seduction is one form of consumption among many that characterize a transoceanic world of commercial exchange and accumulation, providing an enlarged spatial and political terrain on which to graph and track the period's obsession with seduction. Including texts such as this one in literary history foregrounds the context of the global marketplace and transoceanic political arena within which the late eighteenth- and early nineteenth-century novel was produced and to which it responded. More particularly, it recontextualizes seduction and rape in cyclical global and economic rather than only linear national and sexual terms. Finally, the uncanny geographical perspective it provides also offers a cyclical rather than linear narrative within which to understand political revolution in the age of war capitalism. Chapter 5 brings the global context of this transoceanic and revolutionary Pacific to bear on a more recognizably early American novel set in a more familiar early American location. I argue there that we need to know about the eighteenth-century Siberian Pacific to understand the depiction of Philadelphia in Charles Brockden Brown's surprisingly global novel *Ormond*; in this case, too, paying close attention to the bodies of women in the novel helps us to recover the transoceanic shape and force of revolutionary violence.

Coils

FINANCIAL SPECULATION AND GLOBAL REVOLUTION
IN CHARLES BROCKDEN BROWN'S *ORMOND*

The journals kept by the French navigator and commander La Pérouse were routinely ferried to trusted messengers at various landing points along the multi-year Pacific expedition. One of those landing points was the settlement of Petropavlovsk on the Kamchatka peninsula of Siberia on the western edge of the north Pacific. There the "dispatches" made up of the "commander's journals, officers' reports, scientific papers, artists' drawings, maps, letters" were entrusted to the voyage's interpreter Bartélemy de Lesseps, who was asked to carry them to the French ambassador in St. Petersburg after La Pérouse and his ships left to continue their voyage into the south Pacific.[1] Even today, there are no roads that connect Kamchatka to the rest of the world, and in 1787–8 the overland trek across Russia took Lesseps over a year, traveling alternately on foot, horse, sled, boat, and carriage. When Naomi J. Williams imagined that journey in *Landfalls*, her 2016 historical novel about the La Pérouse expedition, she emphasized the anxiety felt by Lesseps and his Russian companion Golikoff as they sought to keep the box of important manuscripts safe during their long and challenging trip across an unbearably cold and desolate landscape.

But Williams gives Lesseps another object that he carries with equal care across Siberia: the coat of a sable who had been captured by Natives on Kamchatka and given to Lessups in a cage to take with him to France. When the animal soon after dies in captivity, Golikoff skins it for Lessups and asks him to give its fur "to your queen as a gift." In Williams's novel, Lesseps took to wearing it around his neck like a cravat, where its sensation against his skin reminds him of his sexual intimacy with Daria, a part Kamchadal Native woman who was married to a Cossack in the town of Bolsheretsk. The circumstances of that sexual exchange are left unclear by Williams, although Lessups expresses surprise at her husband's apparent lack of jealousy and later in their trek, when Lessups and Golikoff are sexually serviced in one village by Native women, he wonders if someone was ensuring that "the women complied with the demands of Chukchi hospitality."[2] The dispatches are safely delivered to St. Petersburg, and from there to Paris. By that point Lessups' sable cravat is "too worn to serve as a gift for the queen."[3] But the worn sable fur enjoyed a far happier fate than La Pérouse and his crew, who never returned home. The eruption of the French Revolution made it difficult to organize a search effort once it became clear in Paris that the ships were missing, and it wasn't until 2005 that scientific methods definitively confirmed that suspected evidence of a wreck off the island of Vanikoro in the south Pacific belonged to the ships of La Pérouse.

In this chapter, I argue that news from and literary representations of the Siberian peninsula of Kamchatka, where Lessups's journey began, is one of several crucial sources for Charles Brocken Brown's 1799 *Ormond*—as improbable as that may sound. For understandable reasons, the novel's concerns with sexual and political seduction and its treatment of an emergent liberal economic order have repeatedly been positioned in a national or transatlantic postrevolutionary context, not a Pacific or global one.[4] Its plot unfolds so largely in the city of Philadelphia (and in surrounding areas of New York and New Jersey) that its connection to the Pacific or the eastern hemisphere, much less the isolated and remote Kamchatkan peninsula, would seem tenuous at best. Yet as the sometimes dizzying temporal and spatial windings of Brown's narrative play out, we are temporarily brought to distant locations in eastern Europe, the Middle East, and Asia—to the region of the Balkans, to the Russia of Catherine the Great, to the lands and conflicts of the Cossacks and Tartars. The sections of the novel referencing these sites and events are routinely passed over by critics, and by most readers as well, for whom they likely serve as especially distracting details in an already bewildering plot. But these obscure locations and events point to a global political and commercial geography that is crucial to understanding the temporality of seduction and speculation that sustains both the content and form of *Ormond*. Indeed, the city of Philadelphia developed a newly intimate commercial relationship with the East Indies during the final decades of the eighteenth century when the novel appeared. As a port city, Philadelphia had long been a central hub for American long-distance trade routes to Europe and the Caribbean, but it began also to serve as a hub for ships bound to and returning from Asia. As a longtime resident of Philadelphia familiar with its merchant community, Brown's own well-known interest in the Pacific and Asia almost certainly grew out of such developments.

Critics have routinely identified the novel's eponymous villain with the dangers of imported European ideas, particularly those associated with Illuminati conspiracies and perceived Jacobin threats to the nation.[5] In this chapter, however, I read *Ormond* in the context of the excess, deception, and inequality associated with an increasingly global business culture in which Philadelphia served an important role. Ormond, for example, embodies many of the features of the new merchant millionaires whose Philadelphia fortunes derived from transoceanic speculations in the East India trade. Such a transoceanic context furthermore aligns Ormond's revolutionary politics less exclusively with the obscure threats of Illuminati rationalism and more broadly with the dramatic logic of global finance capital. Brown's novel grapples with the implications of what Ian Baucom has identified as the violence of speculative finance in the Atlantic, most especially by exposing sexual seduction as a site within an economy of speculation where the violence of profit gets narratively managed. But Brown also suggests that the financial and political geographies of the Atlantic are embedded within a far wider global context that extends to Asia and the Pacific. In *Ormond* the Pacific and Atlantic worlds are, in fact, intimately if obscurely connected—just as they were for so many of the Philadelphia merchants newly interested and engaged in transoceanic trade to the East Indies. Indeed, the character of Ormond likely draws on accounts of the Pacific by such figures as Maurice Benyowsky, August von Kotzebue, and John Ledyard—contemporaries with whose work and lives Brown was almost certainly familiar. The rationalism of financial calculation emerges in this context as every bit as menacing and violent as political radicalism, and its effects are subtly embedded in everyday life—whether in the Atlantic port city of Philadelphia, the battlefields of the Cossacks, or prison camps on the Pacific peninsula of Kamchatka. The narrative of *Ormond* mimics the expectant temporalities of financial investment and revolutionary discourse to show how seductive spectacles of the future distract us from the present acts of violence necessary to arrive at them.

Philadelphia and China

Before turning to *Ormond*, I want to look more closely at the late eighteenth-century ties between the East Indies and North America. Philadelphians' interest in Asia and the Pacific began in the 1750s, when Benjamin Franklin and the wealthy merchant William Allen sponsored no fewer than three separate maritime expeditions to discover a Northwest Passage to Asia through the North American continent.[6] In 1776, Philadelphia sustained an especially keen interest in Cook's Pacific expedition, in spite of the local distractions of the Revolutionary war. As discussed in Chapter 1, it was during this third voyage that the crew on Cook's ships discovered the profits that could be made from the fur trade in the Pacific, offering the prospect of healthy returns on the considerable investments required to navigate the long distances between oceans. When the New Englander John Ledyard returned to America from his participation in Cook's final voyage, he went first to Philadelphia's merchant community to appeal for financial backing for his proposal to build an American trading presence in the Pacific.[7] Ledyard never found the investors he sought, but in the aftermath of his efforts, the Philadelphian Robert Morris collaborated with other merchants to finance the first U.S. ship to China. In a highly publicized voyage, the *Empress of China* left for Canton in 1784 and returned the following year with an impressive and inspiring 25 percent profit for its investors.[8] By the end of the century, this China trade had grown to the point where "floor carpets, window shades, draperies and other standard household decorations were imported in massive quantities" to America,[9] and products such as furniture, porcelain, and wallpaper from China could be found in the homes of wealthy Philadelphia citizens.

Stephen Shapiro has reminded us that the commercial revolution in late eighteenth-century America, which supplied the conditions for the first flourishing of the novel, relied on the Atlantic geography of the West Indian re-export trade.[10] It is indeed the case that most U.S. cargo-carrying ships during this period traveled back and forth to the Caribbean or Europe. But by the late 1780s, ships also began moving regularly between the Atlantic and Pacific oceans, engaging in trade with Canton and other sites in the East Indies. James Fichter notes that the period between 1783 and 1815 saw an extraordinary development in trade between the U.S. and Asia: East Indian commodities like Chinese tea, Indian textiles, and Sumatran pepper moved to Europe through the U.S., while Asia also became a source for many commodities—like cotton, sugar, indigo, or coffee—that had once been associated with the Caribbean. Goods from such distant ports as Manila, Batavia, Cape Town, and Mauritius overwhelmingly found their way onto U.S. ships as war in Europe "created a boom market for American-shipped goods, East Indian and otherwise." American merchants in particular developed a reputation for being "unconcerned with national boundaries; they bought what they could sell any-where, not just what they could sell in the United States."[11] John Turnbull confirms this reputation in the account of his 1799 voyage to China, during which he found that "the Americans carried on the most lucrative trade to the north-west of that vast continent." The first American edition of his Pacific travel narrative, *Voyage Round the World*—published in Philadelphia in 1810—explained that American commerce exceeds that of other nations, as "[s]carcely is there a part of the world, scarcely an inlet in these most unknown seas, in which this commercial hive has not penetrated. The East Indies is open to them, and their flags are displayed in the seas of China."[12] American ships made up over two-thirds of northwest coast fur trade during the years 1793–1815, a crucial node in triangular Pacific trade.[13]

Even if this Pacific commerce never reached the volume of Caribbean commerce, it nonetheless carried an especially high cultural profile—borne in part from its exotic and desirable cargo, and in part from the especially high financial stakes for merchants invested in that cargo and its movement. A commercial voyage to China took at least three times as long to complete as one to the Caribbean, and East India-bound ships were therefore expected to yield at least three times the profit of West India-bound ones. But as the prospect of profits multiplied, so did risk. The enormous distances of these transoceanic voyages multiplied risk many times over: not only did merchants have to raise consider-able capital to outfit ships for these long voyages, but they had to remain solvent while they waited, literally years, to see any return on those investments. As Carl Crossman notes, "[f]or the owners, the investors, the supercargos and the cap-tains, a good voyage under ideal conditions could return a considerable amount of money, and, in many instances a fortune, but it was a risky venture at best."[14] Even with Robert Morris's substantial wealth and the success of his first 1784 China voyage, he only narrowly escaped bankruptcy four years later as he impatiently awaited the return of his ship the *Alliance* from its prolonged trading voyage to Asia. Similarly, John Turnbull decided to invest "considerable shares" in a Pacific trade venture following his voyage to China—inspired by the profits he had seen American merchants make—only to learn that the "north-west speculation had wholly failed."[15]

While the especially high stakes of East Asian trade brought financial doom to many, they also brought extraordinary wealth to a few. As Fichter argues, it was the accumulation of financial capital through Asian trade that created those especially wealthy "financiers who would profoundly alter the shape of American business." Some of the most dramatic and astonishing fortunes in the early U.S. were made out of this high-risk, long-distance transoceanic trade—including such figures as Israel Thorndike, whose East Indian trade income helped start the Lowell iron mills, and John Jacob Astor, whose profits from the Pacific fur trade business helped establish the Second Bank of the United States.[16] Buoyed by the American East Indies trade, the number of banks in the U.S. exploded during this period.[17] Perhaps no figure exemplified these possibilities more than Philadelphia merchant Stephen Girard. As Girard's investments shifted from Atlantic to global commerce toward the end of the eighteenth century, he became "the most successful American in the China trade" and accumulated a stunning fortune.[18] That fortune made its way into the growing banking and insurance industries which, in turn, developed opportunities and strategies that helped to foster yet more transoceanic commerce. Beginning in 1792, for example, insurance companies began a new credit practice called "bottomry" designed to reduce the risk of transoceanic investments for merchants.[19] Bottomry essentially combined an insurance policy with a business loan, crediting money to merchants for long-distance ventures in exchange for interest-laden payments upon their return.[20]

Girard's wealth both created and was further fueled by such financial mechanisms: ships owned by him made 19 separate voyages to Canton between 1798 and 1826, the profits from which allowed him to help found several banks and insurance enterprises. He also took on risky political investments, using his resources to financially support global revolutionary efforts: he extended credit to rebels in Caracas and was seen as a potential source of funding for a rebellion in Buenos Aires.[21] He also purchased many blocks of real estate in Philadelphia as well as tracts of land and estates elsewhere in Pennsylvania. Another Philadelphia merchant, Thomas Fitzsimons, similarly used the money he generated through the China trade to invest in banking and speculate in lands.[22] Philadelphia fortunes like those of Girard and Fitzsimons accumulated from the movement of money, cargo, and ships—but that movement took place over such long durations and such remote distances that the detailed financial arrangements that facilitated them easily escaped notice by contemporary observers. The dangers of risk and loss became concealed, coiled within a seductive story about American entrepreneurial spirit and pleasurable expenditure.

Yet these dangers leaked out in the reputations for deception and excess of at least some of the Americans associated with the East Indies trade. Nathaniel Bowditch was a supercargo on an East Indian voyage who described an American ship captain who regularly bribed inspectors in Manila to value his indigo cargo at an inflated rate, and then spent his lavish income on a mistress. Bowditch similarly reports on a first mate who impersonated the dead captain of his ship in order to claim for himself the profits that would have gone to the captain. As Fichter points out, these varied transgressions—seduction and infidelity, indulgence and deception, excess and waste—are all intertwined for Bowditch, who critically observed this cycle of accumulation and expense.[23] And Bowditch himself fared better than many others; as Crossman notes, "[f]or every man who made a fortune" in the East Indies trade, "another hundred men slaved away on board the vessels for months and years at a time, suffering from disease and boredom, for a sailor's pay and no share in the voyage."[24] The inequality that characterized life in ports and on ships in the Pacific was also evident in cities like Philadelphia, where the great mansions of wealthy merchants—lavishly decorated with wallpaper, drapes, and furniture imported from China—were built not far from enormous prisons and poorhouses filled with debtors and the impoverished.[25] This is the late eighteenth-century port city of Philadelphia—formed out of the financial crucible of the East Indies trade—depicted in Charles Brockden Brown's *Ormond*.

Seduction and Speculation

The inequalities of late eighteenth-century Philadelphia are evident in the pages of *Ormond*, a novel which is also fascinated by the ways in which the coiled temporalities of speculation born under conditions of risk—in which one anxiously anticipates in the present outcomes yet to transpire in the future—create the conditions for seduction. Some critics have seen the novel's first half as an expendable prelude to the story of attempted sexual seduction that dominates its second half.[26] The opening account of the Dudleys' financial seduction at the hands of Thomas Craig, however, establishes concerns that persist as the novel later turns to its central figure of global mercantile and revolutionary speculation, Ormond. A close look at Brown's language throughout this opening section reveals a preoccupation with the ways in which speculation manipulates the experience of time by creating a sense of futurity so buoyed by distant expectations that it blurs the presence of suffering in the present.

The novel's opening introduces us to Stephen Dudley, who wishes to escape from the "drudgery" and "unvaried repetition" of running the apothecary shop he inherited from his father.[27] Impatient to arrive at a future of gentlemanly leisure in which he might "enjoy his darling ease" (7), Dudley outsources the daily grind of his business life to the English immigrant Craig, whose apparent virtue and hard work result in profitable business gains. Craig's assistance and the wealth it brings allow Dudley to enter the open-endedness of aristocratic time, where he "discarded all apprehensions respecting futurity" (9). Such futurity turns out, however, to have been a seductive fabrication wrought by Craig, who instead was borrowing off Dudley's credit and spending his money. Craig flees to Jamaica to enjoy the "spoils" he reaped from his con game, while Dudley's assets are seized to repay his debts, plunging himself and his daughter Constantia into dire poverty.[28] As the economic status of the Dudleys alternately grows and shrinks over the course of these events, the narrative takes careful account of their shifting experience of time, which opens out into a pleasurably expansive future only then to contract into an anxiously foreclosed present. Their transition between these temporal-economic states takes place at the hands of inscrutably seductive figures like Craig and Ormond, both of whom operate as transnational merchants whose investments and manipulations produce that peculiar sense of anticipatory time associated with financial speculation. Brown's *Ormond* formally experiments with such coiled temporality in its own narrative, as it goes on to expose the sexual and social forms of violence concealed within those coils—especially in the novel's second half, which reaches to the political and commercial geographies of the eastern hemisphere.

The Dudleys hit economic bottom when, in the wake of their betrayal by Craig, Stephen becomes blind and turns to drink, and Constantia is unable to pay their demanding landlord his overdue rent. Having exhausted all other options, she is on her way to resign herself to the city's "superintendents of the poor" when she sees Craig, now returned from Jamaica to Philadelphia, suggestively "passing into the marketplace" (69). Constantia meditates on the injustice of their relative situations when she realizes that "All that he had, according to the principles of social equity, was hers; yet he, to whom nothing belonged, rioted in superfluity, while she, the rightful claimant, was driven to the point of utmost need" (70). She trails Craig to a home where he awaits an appointment, and the subsequent standoff between them is characterized by a dramatic temporal tension between the impatient anxiety of Constantia's immediate need and the deliberative delay of Craig's calculative future. Her first demand to see him, for example, quickly escalates into a "more urgent summons" (73), as she "could not conveniently wait" for "her business was of the utmost moment" (73). Craig's repeated evasions of these appeals end when he finally opens his wallet, only to delay for several minutes more when he realizes that the smallest note in it is a $50 bill. Reluctant to part with such a large sum when he knows he could satisfy her with a smaller one, he eventually realizes that "[t]here was a method he conceived of procuring the repayment of it with interest" and thereupon sends the money to the waiting Constantia folded within "a blank piece of paper." Craig has secretly transformed what looks like a present act of generosity into a future-oriented investment, an interest-yielding loan masquerading as a gift.

Constantia, of course, remains oblivious to Craig's speculative coils and responds only with relief as she delivers the money to her landlord. Indeed, the future seems to have been restored to her: whereas before "never did futurity wear, to her fancy, so dark an hue" (28), she now finds herself luxuriating in the "sudden...transition from the verge of destruction to the summit of security" (74). This second prospect of futurity, delivered by Craig to Constantia, turns out to be every bit as false as the earlier one was for her father. Constantia discovers that Craig's $50 note was in fact counterfeit when her landlord—insisting that he "must be paid without delay" (77)—sends the authorities after her, throwing Constantia into a "gloomy interval" marked by hopelessness and suicidal despair (78).

Perhaps the strangest element in this scenario is Craig's bizarre hesitation to part with a counterfeit $50 bill. Why would he struggle to give away a fake piece of paper, a forged monetary note that he suggestively wraps inside a "blank piece of paper" when he delivers it to Constantia? What first looked like his reluctance to assent to an act of benevolence is revealed retrospectively to be instead a hesitation to give away a completely fictional piece of paper money. While it is possible that Craig doesn't realize the bill is counterfeit, the larger point seems to be that it does not matter whether he knows or not, because in the global revolutionary and commercial world of *Ormond* all speculation (whether financial or political, philosophical or sexual) possesses the danger of fictionality in its promise of futurity; speculation is always and everywhere an act of seduction. In fact, Craig himself might be thought to resemble the very contents of his own purse—a counterfeit bill wrapped in a blank sheet of paper.

Ian Baucom has described the eighteenth-century Atlantic world as haunted by the dual specters of finance capital and slavery, paired enterprises whose shared theory of value relied on "a mutual and system-wide determination to credit the existence of imaginary values." In that system, he explains, "such value exists not because a purchase has been made and goods exchanged but because two or more parties have agreed to believe in it. Exchange, here, does not create value, it retrospectively confirms it, offers belated evidence to what already exists."[29] As Baucom's description indicates, this system operates through a recursive temporality that prematurely represents uncertainty as certain—it coils time in order to counterfeit the future. Moreover, such speculation entails a violence easily obscured precisely by that twisted recursivity. While the violence of the revolutionary Atlantic is conventionally associated with its political instability, Baucom insists that violence also inheres in this logic of finance capital, and the modern subject is borne out of that intertwined crucible of "finance capital in partnership with the revolution."[30]

Ormond everywhere acknowledges this late eighteenth-century partnership between finance and revolution, and recognizes the shared violence so often concealed within both economic and political acts of speculation. By anticipating an expected future in an uncertain present, speculation subscribes to a political and economic temporality in which the unarrived future is absolved of its too-often violent past. Both of the Dudleys have been seduced by Craig into a future later exposed as false. In Constantia's effort to regain more "cheerful prospects" after this event, she returns to the merchant Mr. Melbourne, who explains that his wife will help her to "earn your subsistence by your own industry" and gives her money with instructions to "Place it to account. It is merely paying you beforehand, and discharging a debt at a time when it happens to be most useful to the creditor." This gesture generates yet another revolution of fortune and affect, "a transition from a state utterly destitute of hope, to a condition where all is serene and abundant" (81). But it is also yet another loan in the guise of charity. Constantia's attempt to climb out of the dead end of present poverty and into the prospect of an open futurity has really been a route into a series of debts to Philadelphia merchants: Craig, Ormond, and Melbourne have all advanced money to her, and all expect future returns on those investments. When Ormond later learns from Melbourne that Constantia possessed only a forged $50 bill rather than the authentic $100 he instructed Craig to give her, he wonders whether Constantia might have "mix[ed] a little imposture with her truth" (82), suspicious that she might be a forger and dissembler herself.

If Ormond suspects deception everywhere, it is because deception is for him, as it is for Craig, a way of life. Ormond is introduced as a skeptic and cynic who "was apt to impute deceit on occasions when others, of no inconsiderable sagacity, were abundantly disposed to confidence" (87). After secretly witnessing the virtue and good character of the Dudleys, Ormond takes up Craig's debt to them, pledging to pay it off at "uncertain" intervals in the "future" (102) while also helping Constantia to get seamstress work (103). But this act of apparent charity is very much like Craig's gesture of benevolence: an appearance of selfless good in the present that hides an opportunity for selfish gain in the future. Benevolence is repeatedly exposed not as a gift but as a risky yet potentially interest-bearing investment scheme. Whatever relief it might provide its recipients in the present becomes dependent upon a mortgage to the future that must ultimately be repaid.

Ormond is more typically associated with political than economic seductions. When the novel's narrator, Sophia, describes Ormond's "political projects" as "likely to possess an extensive influence on the future of this western world" (84), she identifies him with the subversive activities of what Robert Levine calls the "preposterous Illuminati fear of 1798–9" (17).[31] As Bryan Waterman suggests, Brown's novel is ultimately "less concerned with the existence of an actual order of the Illuminati than it is with the ways in which representations of such conspiracies in countersubversive discourse aimed to manipulate a gullible public."[32] But the manipulation of gullibility in *Ormond* is not just a threat by an obscure political and philosophical group; it's an everyday economic practice. Christopher Lukasik helps make this clear when he explains that *Ormond* departs from contemporaneous seduction novels by refusing to pretend that dissemblers and con men might be identified and exposed if readers and citizens would only become better judges of character. Such strategies don't work in *Ormond* because, Lukasik argues, for Brown "dissimulation seems less a threat to commerce than its very foundation."[33] Taking Lukasik's observation together with Levine's brief suggestion that "anti-Illuminati discourse also served to displace Americans' uneasiness about their own self-interested pursuit of money and power,"[34] we might even describe Illuminati thinking as an exaggerated projection of self-interested mercantile thinking.

Sophia explains that "the treachery of mankind compelled him to resort to" deception: for Ormond, the corruption of society makes the use of deceit necessary to achieve positive ends, and since others constantly used "stratagems and artifices, it was allowable, he thought, to wield the same arms" (87). But it's crucial to recognize that these presumed Illuminati strategies are precisely those associated with financial speculation. Ormond's refusal to believe anyone, his assumption that everyone is lying or misrepresenting themselves, is the product not only of his political identity but of his economic practice. Indeed, Illuminati-inspired rationalisms quickly take on the form of investment advice when Ormond reflects that

> the use of money was a science, like every other branch of benevolence, not reducible to any fixed principles. No man, in the disbursement of money, could say whether he was conferring a benefit or injury. The visible or immediate effects might be good, but evil was its ultimate and general tendency. To be governed by a view to the present rather than to the future was a human infirmity from which he did not pretend to be exempt. (100)

For Ormond as for Craig, money participates in a future-oriented temporality that is instrumental rather than sentimental. Money tends, in a corrupt world, to bend toward evil, even when it is committed to purposes of good—like a gift that turns out to be a loan from which only its lender will profit. Just as Craig's natural ability to inspire confidence in others makes it impossible to resist using that feature to exploit others, Ormond too possesses "a remarkable facility in imitating the voice and gestures of others" (86) that gives him extraordinary power over them. He is described as being simultaneously discernible and inscrutable, utterly legible and yet completely unreadable, a "man of speculation" (88). As Elizabeth Hinds observes, he "comes to function as an economic metaphor for free-market capital"—a representation of wealth akin to the "paper money, stocks, and credit" that are the " 'floating planks' of insecure investment."[35]

Ormond is repeatedly aligned with the financial speculation of merchants and with the rewards of such investments. He regularly and casually moves money about, sending Craig to Baltimore to transport "a considerable sum in English guineas" for him (76) and moving to New York where he "had some pecuniary concerns with a merchant of that place," with whose family he enjoyed "amusing speculation" (89). That speculation eventually resulted in his seduction of the merchant's daughter, Helena Cleves, who becomes his mistress.[36] Ormond speculates on property and bodies alike, combining financial with sexual predation. We learn later that he purchased the Dudleys' former New Jersey property from the creditors who claimed it in the wake of the business collapse engineered by Craig. Even the successful merchant Melbourne describes Ormond as a man "rioting in wealth" (82) whose "revenue was equal to the support of many household establishments" (99). Ormond lives in a "spacious and magnificent" home on Philadelphia's Arch

Street, where his parlor has relief-stuccoed walls, a Persian carpet-covered floor, a painted ceiling, and an array of "mirrors, tables and sofas" (72). By contrast, the Dudleys' Philadelphia home has plain white walls, a floor with loose boards and "gaping seams," and is decorated only with "pine tables, rush chairs, and uncurtained bed" (102).

Ormond's calculative rationalism extends even to matters of the heart, as he seeks a woman whose character "was squared, with a mathematical exactness, to his situation" (95). He responds to Constantia's proposal that he marry Helena as if it were an investment proposal or a math problem: "The evils of the present condition are known; those of marriage are future and contingent; Hellen cannot be the object of a genuine and lasting passion; another may ... This event, therefore, ought to be included in our calculation. There would be a material deficiency without it. What was the amount of the misery that would, in this case, ensue?" (116).[37] Ormond's language reduces human relations to an account book, a mathematical algorithm. Even if the novel ascribes such menace to the foreign politics of European Jacobins, it more often characterizes it in terms of the economic practices of American businessmen, especially those like Robert Morris or Stephen Girard whose risk- and promise-filled investments reached between oceans.

The Revolutionary and Commercial Pacific

Craig's movements in *Ormond* locate him in an Atlantic commercial network, but Ormond is explicitly situated within a far more global and transoceanic framework. As Philip Barnard and Stephen Shapiro remark in their edition of the novel, the "cosmopolitan, vaguely Eastern (Levantine or Ottoman) associations" (72n.3) of the furnishings in Ormond's Philadelphia home align him with an Asiatic commercial and political geography. As yet more of his past becomes revealed, Ormond, together with his sister Martinette, becomes linked to a global theater of empire and revolution. He is a man, for instance, half of whose life had been spent "at the head of a band of Cassacks, spreading devastation in the regions of the Danube, and supporting by flagitious intrigues, the tyranny of Catharine, and the other half in traversing inhospitable countries, and extinguishing what remained of clemency and justice, by intercourse with savages" (162). He has spent time in the Levant and in Russia, in eastern Europe and western Asia, in the American Midwest and the Siberian Far East, serving in capacities that seem to have combined the roles of soldier, explorer, and political operative as he secretly "engaged in schemes of an arduous and elevated nature" with colleagues "in different parts of the world" (130). Among those scholars to have explored Brown's interest in Pacific utopias, Nigel Leask observes that the voyages of Wallis, Bougainville, and Cook—and their descriptions of Tahiti, Hawai'i, and other Pacific island locations—would have been well known when Brown was writing.[38] Although no scholars have yet considered the role of the East in *Ormond*, the character of

Ormond should be understood in relation to two historical figures who—through a variety of commercial, political, and romantic forms of speculation—connected Philadelphia to the Pacific and Asia. The exploits of these figures circulated in popular American periodicals during the 1790s as well as in books authored by them.

The first of these was John Ledyard, a New Englander who visited China, the Siberian peninsula of Kamchatka (where he first heard reports of the American Revolution), and the northwest coast of America on that third Cook expedition that so interested Benjamin Franklin. When Ledyard's account of this voyage, *A Journal of Captain Cook's Last Voyage to the Pacific Ocean and in Quest of a North-West Passage*, was published in Hartford in 1783, it described how ordinary sailors who traded with northwest coast Natives later sold their furs at double to ten times their purchasing price in Canton or to the Russian fur traders living in Kamchatka. But the prospects for profit were painfully underrealized, in Ledyard's view, for they had failed to "purchase a quarter part of the beaver and other furr skins we might have done, and most certainly should have done had we known of meeting the opportunity of disposing of them to such an astonishing profit."[39] Ledyard spent the rest of his life trying to re-seize those imagined lost profits, and quickly followed up his book publication with a visit to Philadelphia's wealthy merchant community, where he hoped to convince financiers to invest in the transpacific fur trade.[40] After Robert Morris backed out of their initial agreement, Ledyard eventually attempted to reach Siberia on his own. The American periodical press circulated accounts of what became Ledyard's failed effort, including a piece in the February 1792 issue of *The Massachusetts Magazine* describing his plans to "travel over land to Kamschatka" before being arrested by the Empress Catherine, whose soldiers "left him at last on the frontiers of the Polish dominions."[41] An earlier report in the October 1788 issue of *The American Magazine* included excerpted observations from his journey into Siberia about the similarities between the "'Asiatic Indians, called *Tartars*, and... the American Tartar' (so he calls the natives)." Ledyard insisted that these Asian and American Natives were "of the same family: the most ancient and numerous people on earth, and what is very singular, the *most uniformly alike*."[42]

Ormond delivers a similar report to Constantia, who explains that his "narratives had carried her beyond the Mississippi, and into the deserts of Siberia. He had recounted the perils of a Russian war, and painted the manners of Mongals [Tartars] and Naudowessies [Sioux]" (157). Ormond's history moves him from service with the Cossacks in the Russo-Turkish war to Berlin, where he became involved with a branch of the Illuminati that "embraced an exploring and colonizing project" and "spent six years of his life, in journeys by sea and land, in tracts unfrequented, till then, by any European" (194). These tracts included such remote locations as "the shore of an *Austral* continent" or "the heart of desert America" (194), associating him with utopian projects in Australia (or the mythical great southern continent) and the American Midwest.

These travels and projects, together with his involvement in the Russian war, align Ormond even more closely with another late eighteenth-century figure who tied the Pacific to the Atlantic through a network of revolutionary, mercantile, and military associations. Maurice Benyowsky was a Hungarian (from a region in current-day Slovakia) who ventured to Poland in 1768 to fight in their revolt against Russia. He was captured by the Russians and sent into exile in Kamchatka, where he organized a prisoners' rebellion and escaped to lead a maritime expedition through the north Pacific that ended in Macao, China in 1771. The following year he befriended Benjamin Franklin in France, and traveled to America in 1779 to fight in the Revolutionary War. Benyowsky subsequently established an Anglo-American mercantile agreement with the help of Franklin, and departed on the ship *Intrepid* from the port of Baltimore for Madagascar in 1784,[43] the same year as Robert Morris's *Empress of China* left New York for Canton. Two years later, Benyowsky was killed in Madagascar by the French, in retaliation for usurping their colonial settlement for his own purposes.[44]

Late eighteenth-century audiences knew of Benyowsky primarily through two popular texts, in both of which he appears driven by an indistinguishable combination of revolutionary political commitments and self-aggrandizing personal interests. The first of these was the exaggerated self-portrait contained in his *Memoirs and Travels of Mauritius Augustus Count de Benyowsky*, where he evolves into a heroic and romantic adventurer who never makes a wrong decision and who is an object of irresistible attraction to men and women alike—including the daughter of the Kamchatka Governor, who becomes what he calls his "pretended future spouse." Whether despite or because of such hyperbole, the book enjoyed considerable international popularity and was translated from its original 1783 French edition into several languages, including an English edition that appeared in London and Dublin in 1790. The book's central episodes concern his experience in Siberia, where he imagines its large population of exiles and prisoners will someday ally with the "different hords of Tartars" in the region to "join the common cause to overthrow the Russian dominion" in a "revolution." But Benyowsky's Siberia is also a place of commercial profit where Russian merchants "usually gain 200 per cent. on the merchandizes of Europe, and on their arrival at China they again redouble their profit on the furs." Like Ledyard, Benyowsky aspires to cash in on these profits in transoceanic trade (as his later Baltimore–Madagascar commercial arrangement made clear). When he arrives in Japan after his escape, he describes merchants as driven solely by financial motives: "merchants had no religion, their only faith consisting in getting money," and explains that he himself "had no other respect for the Cross than what the value of its materials might demand."[45]

An abridged version of Benyowsky's story, focused on his exile in and escape from Kamchatka, appeared serially in *The New York Magazine, or Literary Repository* in March and April 1794. There were also clearly plans to publish a full American edition of his *Memoirs*, for a 1799 Boston broadside sought subscribers for the volume that would contain his "Military operations in Poland, his exile at Kamchatka, his escape and voyage from that Peninsula, through the Northern Pacific Ocean, touching at Japan and Formosa, to Canton in China, with an account of the French settlement he was appointed to form upon the island of Madagascar." This advertisement, which circulated well after Benyowsky's own sojourn in revolutionary America, reminded readers of his reputation as "a man of uncommon ability, possessed of a disposition singularly calculated for adventures, and brought up in a school of irregular warfare, in which the intrepidity of his mind, and the power he possessed of agitating and impelling the minds of others, were matured by a severe course of practice."[46] More than anything else, it is this practiced ability to "agitate and impel the minds of others" that links Benyowsky to Ormond.

These powers of seduction are foregrounded in another popular text about him, the play *Count Benyowsky; or, the Conspiracy of Kamtschatka*. Written by August von Kotzebue and first published in German in 1794, *Count Benyowsky* was translated into English in 1798 and frequently reprinted around the Atlantic, including an 1800 Boston edition.[47] Benyowsky is identified in the play as the leader of a group of conspirators, and the 1799 London edition is prefaced with recent reviews that establish his reputation both for an impressive "*intrepidity and genius*" and for a disturbing "*profligacy*."[48] Brown was clearly familiar with Kotzebue's work, which was reviewed favorably in the April 1799 issue of the Brown-edited *Monthly Magazine and American Review*, in an article titled "Anecdotes of distinguished Characters. KOTZEBUE."[49] Ormond shares with Benyowsky a series of global military and political adventures as well as his strangely powerful capacity for seduction, features highlighted in Kotzebue's portrayal of him.

Count Benyowsky begins with a chess game between the Governor of Kamchatka and the Captain of the Cossacks, while the Governor's daughter, Athanasia, looks on. As the men play, Athanasia and her attendant Theodora complain that men in Siberia are preoccupied with commercial calculation, spending their time "estimating the value of a sable's skin; computing the profit of a sea voyage; steering from hence to the Aleutian, and from the Aleutian to the Curilian Islands" (5). The arrival of the romantic Benyowsky into this tedious mercantile world enthralls Athanasia and impresses her father, especially after the new prisoner takes his place in the chess game and swiftly wins it for him. The Governor observes that he is "master at the chess board, as well as at sea: there you saved a ship that was on the brink of destruction, and here you have recovered a desperate game" (11). Benyowsky's impressive chess performance may have echoes in Ormond, for "Chess was his favorite amusement. This was the only game which he allowed himself to play. He had studied it with so much zeal and success, that there were few with whom he deigned to contend" (98). Elizabeth Hinds perceptively observes that Ormond's attraction to "the strategic game of chess" is visible in his investment strategies as well: he "hands out money and then watches to see what will happen" in what amounts to a rationalized benevolence that betrays his "cold, scientific amusement at the behavior of others."[50] Similarly, every one of Benyowsky's generous or heroic acts seems secretly determined by a calculative sensibility.[51] His participation in the chess game, for instance, is really a move in another unseen chess game—an apparent act of present benevolence that is really a self-interested loan designed for future payoff. Benyowsky proceeds to seduce both father and daughter, much as Craig and Ormond do Stephen and Constantia Dudley.

He also, along with the other Siberian prisoners, takes part in speculative schemes for planning revolutionary utopias that include fantasies of sexual and political mastery alongside radical political and sexual arrangements. These political speculations are paired with economic ones, and both have a transpacific, if not global, reach. The Governor of Kamchatka praises the merchant over the monarch, for instance, proclaiming that while the latter "surveys his dominions," it is "the merchant" who oversees "the world. With the right hand he touches Asia, and with the left America" (90). Benyowsky capitalizes on his fellow prisoners' expectant sense of political futurity in planning his escape. His Russian co-conspirator hands him a cherished copy of Anson's Pacific travel narrative and remarks that "Anson— Ah, Benyowsky!—[*Pointing to the book*] 'Twas Anson taught me hope" (37). The Russian summons Anson's description of the Pacific island of Tinian (see Figure 5.1) as a "terrestrial paradise! Free! free! a mild climate! a new created sun! harmless inhabitants, wholesome fruits—and liberty! tranquility!—Ah, Benyowsky! Liberate yourself and us!" (38). This vision of a Pacific island utopia leads Benyowsky to "fancy myself in China, Japan, the Indies; already do we sail round the Cape of Good Hope—Hope!" (65).[52] A Cossack exile similarly invites Benyowsky to join his plan to begin a colony in the Aleutian islands, promising that if their uprising is successful he can become "governor of Kamtschatka . . . and, before you are aware

FIGURE 5.1. *"View of the Watering Place at Tinian."* George Anson, A Voyage Round the World *(London, 1748). Courtesy of Archives & Special Collections, University Library, Santa Clara University.*

of it, conqueror of California" (85). These fantasies resemble Brown's description of Ormond participating in various plans for "an exploring and colonizing project" that sent him into the "*Austral* continent, or in the heart of desert America" (194).

The histories of Benyowsky and Ormond share other geographic similarities. The father of Ormond and Martinette, for example, is described as a "nautical vagrant" (145) who hails from Slavonia (or Sclavonia in the book's spelling), a historical region near the present-day border of Croatia and Hungary—not far from the Hungarian and Slovakian origins of Benyowsky.[53] Like Benyowsky, Ormond is linked not only with international political intrigue and mercantile investments, but with rationalism, sexual seduction, and radical ideas about marriage. Concealing the fact that he is already married, Benyowsky expresses a romantic attachment to Athanasia that strategically serves his plan for rebellion and escape. When Athanasia, taken by his "cool reason; he was so insensibly reasonable," asks her father for permission to marry him, he consents and agrees to free him on his daughter's behalf. After his liberation, he confesses to being married but professes still to love Athanasia. She immediately proposes a solution that will allow all three of them to live together in a domestic arrangement in which, she insists, "No base jealousy shall creep in amongst us—no officious neighbor shall disturb our mutual harmony" (135).[54] Ormond, too, is a sexual as well as political and economic speculator: he has seduced Helena, he continually defers the prospect of marriage and remains skeptical of it, and he persists in attempting to seduce Constantia. The intertwined practices and geographies of Ormond and Benyowsky call to mind Nathaniel Bowditch's portrait of the American captain of an East Indian merchant vessel whose lies and bribes brought him profits as he indulged an expensive mistress.

Athanasia also takes part in Benyowsky's rebellion in ways that echo the adventures of Ormond's sister, Martinette, who fought alongside her lover, Wentworth, in a series of revolutionary battles. Wentworth is described as a "political enthusiast, who esteemed nothing more graceful or glorious than to die for the liberties of mankind" (153). Martinette cross-dresses in order to accompany him into battle on behalf of the American colonies, traveling from Santo Domingo to Richmond to spend the next four years fighting alongside him, during which time she "more than once rescued him from death by the seasonable destruction of his adversary" (154). Athanasia similarly rushes to Benyowsky's rescue just as he is about to be captured by his betrayer, Stepanoff. Wearing the disguise of a Cossack and wielding a sword (183), she eventually disarms Stepanoff and saves Benyowsky's life, vowing to follow and fight next to him. As news of the uprising reaches him, the Governor reflects that "Rebellion is contagious as the pestilence. He who thinks to bind plebeian souls by benefits alone, reckons on the ocean's constancy" (190). Only moments later, as if to consolidate this reflection, he learns that Athanasia has "run away in man's clothes" (191). In the end, Benyowsky abandons both the Governor and his daughter as he heads into the Pacific Ocean with plans to return to his wife.

Expectation and Exploitation

Like Benyowsky, the initially benevolent figures of Craig and Ormond are revealed instead to be masters of deception and seduction, men who amass wealth and status by speculating on uncertain futures they pretend have already safely arrived. Such men appear hard to decipher because they conceal a menacing criminality behind an attractive exterior. But Brown's novel suggests that such figures exactly resembled everyday businessmen and their financial practices, celebrated and admired merchants like Robert Morris and Stephen Girard whose long-distance speculations coiled time into a sense of expectant promise underpinned by prolonged delay. Julia Ott has described the emergence of a new politics of time in late eighteenth-century business culture that "developed in tandem with new financial institutions, new public fiscal policies, and new systems of credit and methods of finance."[55] For investors and bankers engaged with commercial activity—but increasingly for other citizens as well—"time felt more pressing and seemed to elapse at a faster rate." In the face of this acceleration, merchants turned to punctuality and schedule-keeping as an expression of control in the face of what really amounted to an increased loss of control.

Ormond practices such time management in his first encounter with Constantia. She has requested an interview with him, ostensibly to inquire about the where-abouts of Craig but really to appeal to him on behalf of his unhappy mistress Helena. Constantia hopes to convince him to marry Helena, to bring certainty and security to the otherwise suspended and uncertain narrative of their relation-ship. Once Ormond realizes that she wishes to discuss a topic other than Craig, however, he asks that they "defer this conference six minutes, just while we eat our dinner" (112). Ormond's punctual specificity—he asks her to wait exactly "six minutes"—obscures what is really a strategic delay during which he can speculate on the content of her anticipated discussion and better control its out-come. This scene repeats the temporal encounter between urgency and deferral in Constantia's earlier appeal to Craig, who delayed responding to her anxious appeal for money until he could figure out a way to profit from it.

Ott locates a similar performance in Alexander Hamilton's act of donating one large clock to the Bank of New York in 1792 and another later that decade to the Philadelphia branch of the first Bank of the United States. The clocks' regular and synchronous chiming at the opening and closing of the markets each day belied the anxiety and indeterminacy of the risk culture that sustained these financial institutions. Beneath the apparent order of these redundantly ticking clocks seethed a "tension and temporal urgency" associated with a credit market that had "become an intangible abstraction—a hopelessly tangled web of interconnected and interdependent obligations and relationships that no single person or book-keeping system could possibly monitor." Moreover, because one's credit reputa-tion came to depend upon the external appearance of regularity or punctuality, it became almost compulsory to practice deceit and secrecy; as Ott points out, "lies and excuses played an acceptable part in commercial discourse" because the "*perception* of punctuality and character held greater import than intrinsic or 'true' attributes." The merchant's punctuality therefore performed reliability and certainty as if to compensate for and distract from the unreliable promises, uncertain delays, and acts of exploitation on which the seductive profit narrative of finance capitalism depended. Impatient uncertainty prematurely presents itself as steady certainty, through a process that coiled time. Craig practices precisely such tactics in his financial dealings with the Dudleys, while Ormond has gone so far as to adopt such principles as the very bedrock of his philosophy.

Sophia describes Ormond's "daily labour" as "[n]ot to reveal too much, and not to tire curiosity or over-task belief" (194). Like his strategic deferral by choosing to eat dinner while she waits, Ormond narratively manages his relations in order to keep others in suspense, expectantly waiting. His attempted seduction of Constantia follows this same strategy of narration: when he decides to let her into his secret schemes, he deliberately does so in a way that is "imperfect," by sharing details that at first seem "explicit" but later appear veiled by "obscurity," by always "inflame[ing]" rather than "appeasing" her "curiosity" (130). Thus by "piece-meal and imperfect disclosures, her curiosity was kept alive" (131). Ormond handles Constantia in the same way that his secret group aims to gain public opinion for their ideas: not through force but "in a way in which his subjects should be scarcely conscious" and in such a way as to leave his own "agency...least suspected" (131). These strategies of attempted sexual and political seduction replicate the practices of financial investment with which Ormond is associated, perhaps especially in his alignment with an East Indian commerce known both for its tempting promise and its dangerous risk.

Sophia insists to Constantia, however, that such seductive strategies can dangerously conceal violence, since "pillage and murder" may be "engrafted, on systems of all-embracing and self-oblivious benevolence" (194). When Sophia convinces her friend to abandon Ormond and accompany her instead to England, the terms of his speculative balance sheet are laid bare. He threatens to rape Constantia, promising her that "some mighty evil...awaited her" (200) that "will exterminate hope" (199), abolishing her sense of futurity once and for all. Matthew Garrett suggests that Ormond's attempted rape is an act of "insanity" resulting from his "political radicalism,"[56] but it looks more like a desperate final effort to ensure that his seduction investment will yield some sexual returns. If Constantia were a valuable cargo-filled ship on a prolonged transoceanic voyage (and my point is that, for Ormond, she may as well be), its investor is now panicking at the prospect of a loss that no bottomry arrangement can recoup. Ormond loses patience, and when he does the coils of temporality that sustained his performance of generosity and punctuality unravel to reveal a long trail of violence. While fighting with the Cossacks in Russia, for instance, Ormond committed both rape and murder. He killed his friend, Sarsefield, in order to claim for himself a captive Tartar girl, whom he subsequently raped and murdered: after he "exercised brutality of one kind, upon the hapless victim" he then "stabbed her to the heart." The following morning, he singlehandedly kills and beheads five "Turkish foragers" and leaves these as offerings on the grave of his murdered friend (202), as if in payment.

Ormond's acts of violence in Philadelphia operate with an even more pronounced business logic than those committed in Eurasia. Sophia suspects that Ormond's intimate knowledge about the murder of Mr. Dudley, Constantia's father, comes from "one who performed the act" (201)—but we learn that Ormond outsourced that task to his business agent, Craig, who also moves money for his employer around the Atlantic. Ormond explains that Craig's orders to kill Dudley "were stated and enforced by me" and "I stood beside him when it was done" (213). Ormond goes on to then kill Craig himself, depositing his body at Constantia's feet much as he delivered the bodies of murdered Turks to the site of his friend's grave. Indeed, Ormond understands this violence, too, as a kind of payment: he explains that he has killed Craig because the latter "has been a robber" to both of his employers (212), having defrauded the Dudleys of their business and Ormond of $100 in the earlier counterfeit note episode.

In explaining to Constantia the reasons for killing her father, Ormond reverts again to a language of financial exchange and the logic of investment. Constantia has not returned his philanthropic attentions with the kinds of returns such an investment should yield, for "To snatch you from poverty, to restore his sight to your father, were expected to operate as incentives to love" (213). He describes Dudley's death "as a due and disinterested offering," a necessary expense to secure his objective of possessing Constantia. In Ormond's world, violence can actually be construed as benevolence—much as it was by those Pacific explorers described in Chapter 1, who sought to explain violent encounters with resistant Natives as unfortunate but necessary episodes within a broader narrative of beneficial and civilizing commerce that also happened to enrich them: "My motive [for having Dudley killed] was benevolent. My deed conferred a benefit. I gave him sight and took away his life, from motives equally wise" (213). Ormond's coldly calculative reasoning here may seem an Illuminati-inspired rationalization, but more than that it is a hard-nosed business decision, made to minimize loss and maximize profit from a long-term investment. Only by uncoiling the seductive turns of investment time, do benevolent gifts (the cost to Ormond for the surgery that restored Stephen Dudley's sight, for example) get exposed as interest-bearing loans (Ormond's expectation to be repaid for this expense with Constantia's sexualized body—which he intends to take by force as his due when she refuses to "pay up").

Sophia may help to expose Ormond's violence and rescue Constantia from it, but it would be a mistake to imagine Sophia as somehow an alternative to the world of seduction and deception represented by him. Sophia—whose unreliable voice shapes and controls the narrative in ways that mislead readers as well as characters—remains every bit as secret, as difficult to decipher as Ormond. She may not be directly connected to maritime commerce like Craig or the transoceanic networks of revolution like Ormond, but Sophia is evidence that the effects of that global commerce ensnared everyone, that there was no escape from its seductive promises and the acts of exploitation such promise concealed. Brown experiments with this speculative temporality in his own narrative style, which repeatedly plays with the dynamics of advancement and retreat, anticipation and delay. Garrett perceptively remarks that Brown keeps his narrative "spring coiled" by a strategy of withholding that "takes shape through a language of deferral and dilation," and aligns such narrative hesitation with concerns about American national coherence.[57] Given the global geographic references within *Ormond* and the influence of Atlantic–Pacific commerce on Philadelphia at the time of its publication, however, the novel's form may say more about the global economics of finance capital than about the domestic politics of national identity. Revolutionary discourse and investment relations both promise an enticing future while sublimating the dangerous risks and often exploitative losses necessary to get there. Brown's novelistic narrative engages in a kind of exaggerated mimicry of these forms, drawing readers into an ever-renewed sense of anticipation, only to leave readers confronting the violence otherwise obscured within its temporal coils.

Stephen Shapiro observes that novels played a vital role in constructing the social framework for late eighteenth-century bourgeois consumer society by training the bodies of readers in the new manners and codes of sociability. Much like carefully calibrated clocks or punctual behavior, credibility and relations of trust were performances of dependability that distracted from the otherwise unstable mechanisms—the "time delays" and "waiting time"—of financial credit and exchange that characterized late eighteenth-century market society.[58] Brown's novels tend both to exaggerate and interrupt anxious expectation; readers follow one suspenseful narrative turn after another, only to be left feeling breathlessly exhausted, overtaken, and disappointed—repeatedly seduced into narrative promises that never quite pay off. In this sense, *Ormond* performs the anxious time-consciousness associated with new forms of finance, but not without exposing the ways in which political, financial, and narrative seductions all manage the violence they produce. *Ormond* may seem to be a novel about Philadelphia, but closer attention to the geographic range of Ormond's travels and adventures positions Philadelphia within a much larger, global and transoceanic, theater of speculation and seduction. The next chapter similarly argues that the Caribbean island of Jamaica in William Earle's 1800 novel *Obi; or, the History of Three-Fingered Jack* should be read in transoceanic dialogue with the Polynesian island of Tahiti, for the novel's treatment of plantation slavery and slave rebellion in the Atlantic is deeply engaged with the language and commerce of botanical transplantation that took place between oceans.

Cycles

ATLANTIC SLAVERY AND PACIFIC BOTANY
IN WILLIAM EARLE'S *OBI*

After months spent afloat in the emptiness of the vast Pacific in a lifeboat, the shipwrecked protagonist of Yann Martel's 2001 novel *Life of Pi* stumbles upon an island composed entirely of mysterious algae. Solid yet soilless, green and edible, the floating island presents Pi with a welcome oasis of firm land, vegetable sustenance, and fresh water amidst the brutally alienating saltwater expanse of the Pacific. The island's Edenic qualities, however, are soon eclipsed by Pi's dawning realization that the island is carnivorous—it literally eats human bodies. The island's utopian pastoral crosses into gothic menace when Pi discovers a human tooth embedded within each of the thirty-two fruit-like clusters of leaves on one of the island's trees, the only remaining evidence that the tree consumed the rest of the body to which the teeth once belonged. This episode in the novel's plot is disturbing in part because it inverts assumptions about the relationship between plant and animal bodies, animating the vegetable kingdom in uncanny ways. Here plants eat humans in order to sustain themselves and thrive, rather than the other way around. The episode has proved a conundrum for readers of Martel's novel searching for a predecessor or source of influence that might help to make sense of this unusual island. But that may be because readers have missed another, transoceanic, inversion: if you're looking for an island filled with tasty plants whose sustenance depends on the systematic abuse of human bodies, you need to look for a precedent not in the Pacific but in the Atlantic, and more particularly to West Indian sugar plantation islands like Jamaica, whose desirable products and seductive profits depended on the destructive system of slavery.

The preceding chapter on Charles Brockden Brown's *Ormond* argued for a Pacific extension to Ian Baucom's compelling insight about the violence of early modern finance capital in the Atlantic world. In this chapter, I bring that transoceanic framework back to the concern with Atlantic slavery that is at the center of Baucom's model by considering the overlapping languages of botanical transplantation and plantation slavery, especially as they intersect in William Earle's 1800 novel *Obi; or, the History of Three-Fingered Jack*. Set on the margins of Jamaica's sugar plantation society and published only a year after Brown's *Ormond, Obi* tells the story of Jack Mansong through a series of letters written by the Englishman George Stanford in Jamaica to his friend Charles in England. George is eager to share with Charles news of three-fingered Jack, a slave rebel who long eluded capture by Jamaican authorities by hiding out in the mountainous regions of the island before being killed and beheaded. Jack's prolonged success was reputedly fueled by the bag of protective obi worn about his neck. Obi (or obeah) was a syncretic Afro-Caribbean colonial practice in which various plant and animal part-objects were combined into a substance that possessed intertwined medical, religious, and political powers.[1] George is sympathetic to Jack's anti-slavery rebellion, a position that clearly separates him from the Jamaican planters, who view him as a dangerous menace and align themselves instead with Mr. Mornton, the slaveowner who purchased Jack from the former slave-trader, Henry Harrop.[2]

Obi therefore positions itself as an anti-slavery text that boldly defends a violent slave rebellion in the West Indies to an audience of English readers across the Atlantic. Like the popular pantomime on which it is based, the novel and its story trace out the contours of a transatlantic world, since the account of Jack's rebellion and his parents' enslavement tracks their forced movement westward from Africa to the Caribbean, while George's letters travel eastward from Jamaica to England.[3] In this chapter, however, I extend this geography by situating *Obi* within a network of texts—including histories, natural histories, poems, and travel narratives—that surface the novel's engagement with the profitable business of botanical transplantation which, at the turn into the nineteenth century, depended on connections between the Atlantic and Pacific oceans. Throughout his novel, Earle aligns human bodies with plants in order to represent the slave trade as a destructive form of transplantation and amputation. The intertwined treatment of slavery, horticulture, and revolution in *Obi* take place within a transoceanic marketplace of goods that connected the Atlantic and Pacific world throughout the revolutionary age.

The botanical practice of collecting plants and seeds from around the world rose to particular prominence with the figure of Joseph Banks, who returned from Cook's first transoceanic voyage with hundreds of new plants from such faraway locations as Brazil, Tahiti, New Zealand, and Australia. Banks, however, had a host of international counterparts.[4] Among these was John Reinhold Forster, who eventually traveled as botanist on Cook's second voyage, and who imagines, in the preface to his English translation of Bougainville's *Voyage Round the World*, the English East India Company sending on each voyage "a set of men properly acquainted with mathematics, natural history, physic, and other branches of literature" with the purpose of collecting specimens and observations from around the world.[5] Indeed, late eighteenth- and early nineteenth-century European expeditions to the Pacific Ocean regularly carried on board a small army of scientists and naturalists—astronomers, geographers, hydrographers, and, perhaps especially, botanists—assigned to gather new scientific knowledge. As Alan Frost remarks, the "movement of plants" along these transpacific navigational routes functioned "as a fundamental aspect of British imperialism."[6] Even for the naturalist Forster, this disinterested pursuit of knowledge was quite explicitly paired with commercial interests in "discovering many new branches of trade and commerce; and there is likewise the highest probability, that some unsearched island, with which the Eastern Seas abound, might produce the various spices, which would greatly add to the rich returns of Indian cargoes, and amply repay the expenses caused by such an expedition."[7] Forster's sentence—with its "highest probability" and "amply repay"—embeds a calculus of risk that subtracts the present costs of such global expeditions from the imagined future prospect of profitable new products. In this case, those products just happen to be plants.

We have seen, in Chapter 2, the detailed alphabetic survey of the sources and uses of popularly traded items in the 1805 *Dictionary of Merchandise*, produced for European and American merchants interested in global trade. Its entries provide substantial evidence of the number and value of Pacific-derived plant products in Atlantic marketplaces. The entry on aloe, for instance, explains that the purest aloe is on "the island of Socotora in the Indian Ocean" and that it is used as a "stomachic purge"; the nutmegs entry identifies the spice's source in "several islands of the eastern ocean"; the opium entry describes the East Indian methods of preparing from the heads of poppy flowers "one of the most valuable of all the simple medicines"; and the pepper entry locates this popular "seasoning" in the "islands of Java, Sumatra, and Ceylon."[8] Plants such as pepper, nutmeg, and clove were sought after and fought over for their value in adding flavor to dishes; plants such as ginseng, aloe, and cassia (a powerful laxative) were destined for physicians and apothecaries; plants such as bougainvillea, fuchsia, and the pagoda tree were highly prized for the exotic beauty or novelty they could add to botanic gardens in Europe and the Americas.[9] Whether used as foods, spices, medicines, or luxury items, plants were an extraordinary source of eighteenth-century profits—a practice Londa Schiebinger calls "economic botany."[10]

International competition over plants often produced peculiar kinds of botanical warfare. The Dutch, for example, jealously held on to their control of markets for spices, while the crewmen of one French ship traveling from Mauritius to the West Indies tossed overboard its entire cargo of breadfruit trees after being captured by a British ship, to prevent the trees from falling into the hands of their enemies.[11] Competition for plants could also spur rebellion: Bougainville remarks that the "Dutch are now at war with the inhabitants of Ceram; an island that is very rich in cloves. Its inhabitants would not suffer their plants to be extirpated, and have driven the company from the principal stations which they occupied on their ground."[12] Plants (as well as animals, such as sea otters or whales) were, for Europeans traveling to or speculating in the Pacific, objects of economic calculation whose movement across and between oceans often seemed to result in forms of violent rebellion.

The botanically rich and exotic Pacific was often imagined during this period as a kind of pharmacy for Atlantic ailments, as Pacific products were offered up as potential antidotes to a wide range of Atlantic infections—including not only physiological diseases of various kinds but intractable political and economic difficulties like revolution or slavery. Although explicitly situated in a transatlantic world, William Earle's *Obi* relies on a variety of textual sources that are acutely aware of these wider global circuits of botanical movement. In this sense, the novel returns Jack's story to the genre of natural history in which it first circulated in print form—in 1799, it appeared in Benjamin Moseley's *Treatise on Sugar*, a book described as "a study of natural history, tropical medicine, and colonial plantation management."[13] Whereas Moseley explicitly condemns Jack's rebellion in that book, however, Earle supports it in his novel. That shift owes a great deal, I argue, to the influence on Earle of Erasmus Darwin's popular two-volume 1791 poem *The Botanic Garden*. In contrast to the profit-oriented "economic botany" that charac- terized this period, Darwin advanced a "vegetable economy" that saw revolution as a natural, botanical response to the violent transplantation project of the Atlantic slave trade. The surprisingly transoceanic and political life of plants during this period therefore forms the backdrop for the novel's anti-slavery argument, which aligns human bodies with the bodies of plants and understands plantation slavery in terms of botanical transplantation. In fact, the world's boldest transplan- tation project was completed only seven years before the publication of Earle's novel, when Captain William Bligh left the south Pacific island of Tahiti with 2,126 breadfruit seedlings stuffed into pots and tubs on the deck and in the nursery of his ship, the *Providence*. Several thousand saltwater miles later, Bligh delivered sixty-six of these plants to the West Indian island of Jamaica, where they were car- ried a final 6 miles overland to the botanical garden established by Hinton East, which boasted a wide variety of plants from Asia and other parts of the world. Elizabeth DeLoughrey has argued that the movement of this breadfruit marked "an attempt to displace a growing abolitionist revolution with a scientific one derived from the new knowledges of tropical botany."[14] Earle's novel reverses that displacement, exposing how the violence so often exacted by these profit-seeking acts of transplantation was obscured, falsely naturalized by the expectationist lan- guage of commercial empire. The novel's intertwined representations of slavery, horticulture, and revolution expose that violence by confronting the commercial economy of the human world with the vegetable economy of the botanical world, by challenging a plantation economy with a plant economy.

Plants and Bodies

About halfway through *Obi*, a sudden and lengthy footnote appears from Earle explaining to readers the difference between the plantain and the banana tree. The note is inserted at a point in the narrative when the slave rebel Jack—who is hiding out in a mountain cave in which he has built "a couch of grass which he covered with plantain leaves" (122)—is spotted "cutting Plantains" near his hideout (123) by his pursuer, the slave Quashee. The extensive note (which takes up a full page of small-sized font in the book's most recent edition, and is several times over the longest note in the entire edition) informs readers that the plantain should not be mistaken for the banana and carefully explains their differences. What may be most interesting about the note, however, is its description of the plantain in surprisingly corporeal terms: the tree rises "with a soft stalk, fifteen or twenty feet high; the lower part of the stalk is often as thick as a man's thigh" and it possesses leaves that have a "strong fleshy midrib and a great number of transverse veins, running from the midrib to the borders." The plantain tree's substantial supporting structure is ironically counterbalanced, however, by its rather frail extremities, for its "leaves are thin and tender, so that, when they are exposed to the open air, they are generally torn by the wind; for, as they are long, the wind has great power against them" (124).

This description presents the plantain tree as a human body characterized by enormous strength and size despite its surprisingly fragile extremities. In doing so, the text rather obviously aligns the plant with Jack himself, who is first described in the novel as being "of the most manly growth, nearly seven feet in height, and amazingly robust; bred up to hardihood, his limbs were well shapen and athletic; he could endure the most laborious toil, and would with ease perform the office of any two negroes within the plantation" (72). This otherwise admirable specimen of muscular manhood, however, will have two of his fingers cut off—just after the interruption of the footnote mentioned above—by Quashee, who is hunting him for the bounty offered by the planters. Jack's body thus comes to resemble even more closely the strong and sturdy plantain tree with its finely shredded leaves/fingers. As if his identity needed any further to be associated with this plant, Jack responds to the loss of his fingers by wrapping "his wound with a Plantain leaf" (125).

The exchangeability between the plant and the human here is much more than metaphorical. Indeed, the physical world of Jamaica described in *Obi* conforms to what Monique Allewaert has called the ecology of the plantation zone, a space whose knotty entanglements "disabled taxonomies distinguishing the human from the animal from the vegetable from the atmospheric" and in which "animals, persons, plants, artifacts and their histories, and even land were penetrating, fusing with, transforming one another."[15] These entanglements run throughout Earle's text but as they do so, they explicitly position a vegetable economy against a plantation economy, using the former to expose the illegitimate violence of the latter.[16] George's defense of Jack's violent rebellion and celebration of it as heroic actually draws on these naturalist ideas, for *Obi* ultimately positions slave rebellion as a natural response to a world set dangerously off course by the unnatural commerce of an Atlantic slave system. Earle's long footnote takes elaborate care to differentiate plantain from banana, but we might think about his novel as more radically, if far more implicitly, differentiating plantain and its cultivation in the provision ground from sugarcane and its cultivation on the plantation.

The description of a plant-like Jack wrapping his wounds with plantain leaf is not the first time in *Obi* that plants and bodies are aligned with each other.

The story of Jack's rebellion is preceded by two framing narratives, both told to Jack by his mother, Amri (transcribed and retold in the text by George to Charles).[17] The cultivation of plants is central to the first of these, which recounts the life of Amri and her husband, Makro, in Africa. (The second framing narrative, to which I turn later in this chapter, tells the story of Amri and Makro's forced transportation in a slave ship across the Atlantic.) Amri's first "African Tale" (73) describes her homeland as a pastoral place of vegetable abundance, where "our herbage grew beneath our eye." This Edenic scene of lush fecundity is interrupted, however, by the arrival of a violent storm that at once "blighted the fruits of the earth" (74) and delivered the floating wreck of an English slave ship to the beach. Despite the fact that the two Englishmen who wash ashore aboard a "fragment of the wreck" are "my country's foes," Amri explains, "they claimed my pity." She takes in Captain Henry Harrop and his servant boy (who we later learn is Harrop's young cousin, William Sebald). Amri develops a strong sense of attachment to Harrop as she helps nurse him back to health, and Harrop's first act upon recovery from his fever was to "walk out and view our herbage. 'Nature! nature!' would he cry, as he inspected our fertile fields, 'how profuse art thou, how lavish of thy bounty!'" (77). The African village appears as a space of horticultural bounty, a place where plants or "herbage" grow successfully, profusely, and nearly effortlessly.

But as Harrop begins to introduce Amri and Makro to both Christianity and Enlightenment scientific rationality, he introduces the Christian God as a mediator between the newly separated natural and spiritual worlds. Harrop explains that the sun is not a god who disappears "into the sea" each night (78), but that the earth rotates around the sun at the hand of God. This scientific and religious instruction "rendered" the two Africans "more rational" and enabled them, Amri reports, to find "beauties in nature which our countrymen could not discover" (79). Harrop explains that the sun "cheers the herbage of the field, when drooping; it sheds its enlivening rays, expands the opening leaf, which soon revels in prosperity." For him, a Christian God motivates both the sun's enlivening energy and the human charity it symbolizes, for "So the charitable man spreads his kindly rays around, revives the depressed, becomes a father to the orphan, a husband to the widow" (77). Amri finds herself shaken in her own beliefs, and entranced by Harrop's apparent knowledge and virtue.

During one of these strolls, he stops before a tree with a severed branch, and asks Amri and Makro to observe "this tree flourishing, while an arm that was lopped from its side now withers on the ground." Harrop explains that "this arm, divested of nourishment, withers; the falling dew cannot revive it, nor the sun cheer it. Compare it to a limb torn from you or me; it needs must die, receiving no succour from the body, to which it once belonged. The blood that flows in our veins would no longer enliven that limb, and the place from whence it was torn would soon be covered by a growing skin" (83). Embedded in this early exchange of knowledge about plants is, of course, the foreshadowed specter of Jack's severed fingers: like the "torn limb" of the tree, the "lopped" fingers become "divested of nourishment" from the body's circulatory systems and "needs must die." But embedded here also is the specter of the bodies of Africans torn from Africa itself, violently uprooted in order to be transplanted an ocean away.

Harrop demonstrates not only that the tree is a body (since it "has its veins as we have ours") but that human bodies depend on plants to sustain and reproduce themselves (as we "renovate life with a sustenance we gather from the earth"). Plants and humans sometimes seem to blend into one another in the novel, but there is also a necessary and symbiotic reciprocity between them, demonstrated by the cycle of nature as one in which "we eat, and are eaten by creatures of the earth" (83).[18] The economy of nature as it is described in *Obi* everywhere depends on circulation: of the sun around the earth, of the sun's energy through the veins of plants and animals alike, of the sustenance of creatures by consuming other plants and animals. Harrop's vision may look like a benignly rational as well as Christian system, but it turns out instead to be a seductive cover for profit and economic speculation, a system in which circulation generates inequality rather than balance. The cyclicality of the natural world is governed by an economy of balance that is violently disrupted by the commerce of the slave trade, only to be violently restored by revolution.

Jamaica and Tahiti

In 1804, the American sailor William Moulton published a narrative about his five years spent on board the *Onico*, a commercial vessel that left Connecticut to gather seal furs in Staten-Land (or New Zealand) and sell them in Canton, China. Moulton introduces himself as a veteran of the Revolutionary War who had proudly fought "*to extricate*" America "*from the shackles of tyranny.*" Once at sea, however, he finds the tyrannical conditions of government on board the ship so insupportable and oppressive that he is led to document its injustices and to defend efforts at resistance by those "*who knew how to use their liberty, after having got the power in their own hands. They were driven by desperate oppression and sufferings, to a desperate alternative, which produced indeed desperate resolutions.*" Moulton does more than parallel the rebellion of sailors against the tyranny of officers with that of colonial Americans against Great Britain; he compares their abominable treatment with that of African slaves and even of those northwest coast Natives who traded furs with men on the ship. These Indians, he notes, were often "fired on and killed ... in their canoes" and "if they were dilatory in bartering or cavilled at the prices the captain set on his articles," they might face the ship's cannon. His remarks about a recent uprising of Native peoples against the Russians in the region, noted in the brief discussion of Moulton in Chapter 3, bear remembering in this context: "to have enquired what induced the natives to the hostile act they charge them with, would have brought into view a possibility of their having previously received some treatment which they had a right to resent." As Moulton succinctly puts it, "the Indians did not go into Russia to annoy them."[19]

Rebellion appears throughout Moulton's narrative—as it did in so many contemporary accounts of the Pacific—as a right and necessary way to correct the unnatural and unjust imbalances of tyranny, slavery, and colonialism, whether those occur in the Atlantic or the Pacific worlds. At one point, Moulton quotes Captain Cook's observation, in the narrative of his second voyage, that the animals of New Zealand live in such peaceable mutuality with each other that even the birds of prey feed first off dead animals before killing weak animals as a food source.[20] Moulton remarks that this example is "worthy the imitation of rational beings, and is a striking admonition to men of inflammatory, rancorous spirits." For Moulton, the tyrannical behavior of the American men leading his voyage falls far short of the mutually sustaining behavior exemplified by New Zealand birds, and it is the pursuit of commercial profits that drives these men so far from their natural counterparts. When, shortly after this, Moulton is kicked off of the ship, he aligns himself with the many "deserters from American and English ships" found on islands around the Pacific who "gave the whole of their voyages to get out of the clutches of their tyrants. The oppression of these tyrants was insufferable the moment their voyages were obtained, and the shares of their men more coveted than their services."[21] Moulton even launches what amounts to an early nineteenth-century critique of offshore outsourcing when he remarks that sailors are frequently discarded at foreign ports without pay and replaced with other crew members who "can be obtained for wages a little less per month than is given in America." When he praises New Zealand's animal economy reported by Cook, therefore, he is using the natural world as a model from which to critique the violence and exploitation practiced by a commercially driven human world.[22]

The rebellion on the *Onico* is also described in the much better-known Pacific travel narrative of Amasa Delano, which has long been recognized as a source for Herman Melville's story "Benito Cereno." In contrast to Moulton's sympathy for the rebellious sailors, Delano sympathizes with the challenged ship's captain. But both Delano's anti-revolutionary account and Moulton's pro-revolutionary one illustrate that Pacific uprisings were perceived as participating in the political logic and language of the revolutionary Atlantic. Delano places the *Onico* uprising in company with several other transoceanic and transnational acts of resistance, including the slave rebellion on the Spanish ship the *Tryal*, the mutiny on the English *Bounty*, and the French Revolution, which he explicitly condemns for its example of "very low men, without talents or integrity, in possession of power" who use "it for the worst purposes, under the name of liberty."[23] As we saw in Chapter 3, Delano's report of the Atlantic beheading of the French king is followed by his account of the Pacific mutiny against Bligh, creating a transoceanic pairing of these two 1789 revolts.

The mutiny on the *Bounty*, of course, interrupted what was to have been a botanical transplantation project of unprecedented proportion, a Pacific project driven by political consequences in the revolutionary Atlantic. The British West Indian sugar islands had long depended on food imported from the North American colonies to feed its large slave populations. When these North American food imports were cut off after the American War of Independence, Joseph Banks turned to the Pacific. *The Bounty* was specially outfitted to transport thousands of breadfruit seedlings from the south Pacific island of Tahiti across thousands of miles of transoceanic waterways to be replanted on several Atlantic islands in the British West Indies, including Jamaica. As a sailor familiar with both the Atlantic and the Pacific, Bligh was in many ways ideal for the project: he had traveled on Cook's third voyage to the Pacific, and had earlier worked for an uncle in Jamaica carrying rum and sugar on merchant ships across the Atlantic from the island colony to the island empire, a trip he completed no fewer than ten times over a four-year period.[24] Bligh therefore transitioned from running the products of slave-driven sugarcane plants across one ocean, to running breadfruit plants intended to feed those slaves between one ocean and another.

The logic of Banks's breadfruit transplantation scheme depended on both the profitability of transoceanic plant movement and fantasies about the south Pacific. Polynesia represented for eighteenth-century Europeans an alternative Caribbean, in which Tahiti seemed a kind of antipodean Jamaica free of slavery and revolution, even of labor and jealousy. Breadfruit trees were central to this fantasy because the presumed ease with which the fruit could be grown and gathered contributed to the image of Tahitian society as utopic and leisurely, a land where readily available fruit fed its inhabitants year-round—not unlike the spontaneous and bountiful "herbage" of Amri's African village.[25] As Greg Dening explains, the *Bounty* was "transporting the breadfruit tree, the very symbol of a free and unencumbered life, from the island of freedom, Tahiti, to the islands of bondage, the West Indies and their slave plantations." Jill Casid reminds us that our visual images of the Atlantic tropics are literally formed out of the organic matter of the Pacific since "plant transfers to the Caribbean from Europe, Asia, Africa, and the South Pacific so radically transformed the landscapes of the Caribbean islands that those species of flora most symbolically associated with the 'tropics' were precisely those plants by which the British grafted one idea of island paradise onto another."[26] Banks and Bligh were among those who turned to the Pacific and its plant life as a kind of medicine cabinet whose contents might cure the infections that plagued the Atlantic.

But Jamaica hadn't always needed to import Tahiti to maintain an image of health. Earlier, the island had seemed to contain the elements of its own utopia; Richard Dunn notes that early English colonists saw Jamaica as "the most fruitful, the most lushly tropical, in every way the most promising land for settlement" while also acknowledging that it was "hot, wet, stormy, steamy, craggy, jungled, infested with insects and vermin."[27] Edward Long's popular *History of Jamaica*, originally published in three volumes in London in 1774, counteracts reports of the island's unattractive environment by evoking a portrait of a landscape so lush and luxurious that its "lands in pasture, as well as in culture, require an unremitted attention to free them from weeds and young trees, which would otherwise infallibly spring up, and multiply in all parts like the hydra's heads"—a description that masks the need for labor within an image of organic super-fertility. He notes the example of one large cotton tree on the island's South shore that was "felled...and left to rot on the ground," recalling the scene from *Obi* when Captain Harrop explains to Amri and Makro the inevitable death of any tree's severed limb. But this Jamaican amputated tree doesn't wither; its "limbs had been all cut away; but there remained a very small twig, of two or three inches length, growing on the middle of the trunk; this, as the under part of the trunk next the earth decayed more and more, seemed to be recruited with a copious supply of nutriment, and in three years time grew up into a fine young tree, several feet in height; rising like a phoenix from the parent-dust, it became an absolute re-production."[28] Long evokes a natural world in Jamaica so fecund that even dead plants magically reproduce themselves.

Although entangled and potentially threatening (the "hydra's head" of the cotton tree calls to mind images of revolutionary unrest), the natural world of Jamaica as described by Long avoids Allaewaert's "swamp sublime" by romanticizing it into what amounts to a sugar plantation pastoral. Long describes fields of sugarcane "which spread through the vales, and climb the hills till they blend with the deep-green forests." As the cane first grows it "assumes a delicately light verdure" which gradually darkens to a "stronger green" until a "sweet mixture of white and yellow" indicates its maturity. Into this scene "appear the busy slaves, like reapers, armed with bills instead of sickles to cut the ripened items; and teams of oxen in the field to bring the treasure home." Finally, the sun's "majestic orb" graces this "pleasing and picturesque" scene at sunset, "leaving a trail of splendor aloft, which streaks the clouds, according to their different positions and distances, with the most lovely and variegated tints that the happiest fancy can imagine."[29] Long claims to have found in Jamaica "the idea realized" of a poet's "romantic" vision of "some Utopian island, blessed with perennial verdure and unfading spring." Like Harrop, Long celebrates a natural fecundity by eliminating the labor of human slaves. Interestingly, Long turns to Asia to remark on the only improvement Jamaica might make on its natural bounty: it could imitate "the Chinese method of forming terraces" since leveling the hillier terrain would make it "as fertile and commodious almost as plains."[30] It was those hillier regions, of course, that sheltered Jamaica's runaway slaves and rebels like three-fingered Jack, sites that were home to maroon communities as well as to sustainable provision grounds or plantain walks.

Bryan Edwards explicitly compares Jamaica with Tahiti in his later *History, Civil and Commercial, of the British Colonies in the West Indies*. He draws from

John Hawkesworth's collection of British Pacific voyages to detail, over the course of nearly five pages, "the wonderful familiarity observable in many respects, between our ill-fated West Indians" and the "native of the South-sea Islands." Edwards takes particular interest in comparing plants on the two islands, noting that among the native crops of Jamaica are "plantains, bananas, yams of several varieties, calalue...eddoes, cassava, and sweet potatoes" while the Tahitians are supported by "the bread-fruit and the plantain; both of which flourish there spontaneously."[31] A later edition of Edwards' history concludes its section devoted to Jamaica with a 34-page catalog titled "Hortus Eastensis," which lists the 1792 contents of Hinton East's botanical garden. This catalog was moved, in a third 1801 edition of the book, to the end of a newly added third volume which recounted the history of the Haitian revolution as a cautionary tale of "the danger to which every island in the West Indies would be exposed."[32] The botanical catalog is arranged by Linnaean classes and includes plants such as Guinea pepper, common ginger, and turmerick from the East Indies; sweet-scented olive, spotted ixia, and starry gardenia from China; aloe from Ceylon, honeysuckle from Russia, and lilac from Persia. But this catalog follows a table that outlines, by county, the proportion of "Negro Slaves" to "Sugar Plantations in the Island of Jamaica" in 1789—as if the order of the exotic Asian plant catalog provides an antidote to the unruly dangers represented by the African population table. The botanical garden, in other words, operates here as a kind of veil for the sugar plantation, much as Harrop's aesthetic appreciation of African botanical bounty hides the greed and violence of the slave trade.[33] When Edwards notes that Jamaica's botanical garden did not thrive until the British captured a French ship in 1782 which happened "to have on board some plants of the genuine cinnamon, the mango and other oriental productions," he begins to indicate the ways in which these botanical gardens were themselves populated through plunder and fertilized from the mulch of empire. Richard Drayton notes that Bligh's missions to the Pacific "and the botanic gardens to which they were connected, were...very public gestures of solidarity with the West India interest," and points out that Edwards' *History* supported this effort by turning "the botanic initiatives of his fellow planters into an emblem for the enlightened cast of their administration."[34]

Seeds and Transplantation

The understanding of the natural world depicted in Earle's *Obi* relies on multiple sources of botanical knowledge, one of which was likely Sir Hans Sloane's "Natural History of Jamaica." Published in a two-volume edition in London in 1707 under the title *A Voyage to the Islands Madera, Barbados, Nieves, S. Christophers and Jamaica*, Sloane's book offered a particularly rich documentation of Jamaica's botanical resources, recording in an extensive and detailed catalog the island's varieties of corals, mosses, ferns, grasses, and herbs. Kay Dian Kris points out that despite its clear generic identity as a scientific catalog, Sloane's text remains focused "on the interaction between plants and people," and observes that its claims to scientific neutrality are everywhere marked both by the repressed violence of the Atlantic slave trade and by "individual and collective acts of resistance" to it.[35] We might think of the novel *Obi* as offering a slightly inverted version of this dynamic between natural history and Atlantic slavery. Whereas in Sloane's text the violence of slavery erupts into the visual and textual representation of the island's plants and animals, in Earle's novel the tropical ecosystem of plants and animals erupts into the island's conditions of plantation slavery, almost as if in a kind of organic rebellion.

As a physician, part of Sloane's interest was clearly in the medicinal uses for plants. Thus the "long-pepper" has leaves and fruit that are "thought good against the Belly-ach," while the ginger found on the island can cure "Stoppages in Women after Childbirth" as well as soothe stomach ailments, and the leaves of horse-eye-beans can "keep Women with Child from Vertigo." Sloane goes on to note a curious feature of the beans themselves, which "are very often to be gathered on the Sea Shore, cast up by the Waves, being dropt into some Rivers, or the Sea its self, whence they are again thrown up." Horse-eye beans, in other words, are naturally transplanted by being carried across the ocean; the Jamaican seeds are sometimes "thrown by the Currents of the Sea on the North-West parts of *Scotland*" where they then grow, an ocean away, into plants. This figure of a natural cross-oceanic transplantation is central to *Obi*'s critique of the slave trade.[36]

By the time *Obi* was published in 1800, however, it had been nearly a century since the 1707 publication of Sloane's book. By then, the extraordinary botanical discoveries by Banks on Cook's South Sea voyages, together with the development of the Linnaean sexual system of classifying plants, had helped to build what Alan Bewell describes as "a wide analogical thoroughfare…between plants and humans."[37] The best-known source for such an understanding at the time Earle composed his novel would have been Erasmus Darwin, a physician like Sloane whose book *The Botanic Garden* reveals that Sloane's natural history of Jamaica was one of its many sources.[38] Darwin's two-volume poem, published in London in 1791, describes the earth's natural resources and plant varieties, supplemented by scientific footnotes so extensive they virtually make up their own companion prose text to the poem. Throughout the book, plants are characterized as bodies, and Darwin confesses that he has sought to "restore" to trees and flowers "their original animality." He accordingly aligns the "leaves of plants" with the "lungs or gills of animals," describes the "pulmonary circulation of their juices," and identifies in the "approaches" of males and females to each other the "sensibility" of plants. He locates evidence for the "voluntary power" of plants in their practice of contracting their petals during the cold or dark and suggests that a plant's "muscles" are connected to "a *sensitive* sensorium, or brain, existing in each individual bud or flower" (II.x, I.101 I.205, I.148–9).

Clearly, Earle's description of the plantain's veins, muscles, and limbs participates in the kind of corporealized botanical understanding popularized by Darwin's book, which analogically made "plants into people."[39] *Obi* adopts this botanical analogy from Darwin in order to frame its political argument against slavery, using the figure of transplantation to critique the plantation economy. In particular, Earle borrows from Darwin a circulatory model of nature that the slave trader Harrop corrupts when he turns the natural economy of botany into an unnatural economic botany.[40] There is no doubt of Earle's familiarity with Darwin, for one of the two epigraphs on the original title page of *Obi* is from *The Botanic Garden*. Darwin's lines "*Hear him!* ye Senates! hear this truth sublime, / HE WHO ALLOWS OPPRESSION SHARES THE CRIME" appear along with several lines from Robert Southey's well-known sonnet from *Poems Concerning the Slave Trade*, which chastise those who "Sip the blood-sweetened beverage!" without thinking about the "sable brother [who] writhes in silent woe" (67). Both passages announce the novel's anti-slavery agenda, just as both also summon images of the slave labor that cultivated sugarcane on plantations in the British West Indies, where Jamaica was the English empire's dominant source of sugar products and profits. In a sense, Earle's novel gives voice to one of Southey's "sable brothers" through the figure of the slave rebel Jack.[41]

The Darwin passage quoted by Earle directs a clear anti-slavery argument at political leaders, but it also appears in a section of *The Botanic Garden* that details a fascinating example of cross-oceanic transplantation. Darwin introduces the cassia plant as "one of the American fruits" whose seeds are often found on such faraway coasts as Norway where they appear to arrive by means of "under currents in the depths of the ocean" (II.128–9). Darwin turns to Sloane in his scientific notes to document the transportation of such "emigrant seed" across the Atlantic by means of the "gulf-stream" (I.129), referring to such examples as the horse-eye bean. In his poetic account, however, Darwin humanizes this unusual botanical phenomenon by imagining the plant's seeds as children sent by their mother into the vast waters of the ocean. The yellow-blossomed cassia plant has black seeds, so that Darwin describes "Fair CASSIA" as a mother who "trusts her tawny children to the floods" (II.128) whose waters "bear to Norway's coasts her infant-loves" (II.130). Darwin furthermore aligns this plant and its errant seeds with the biblical story of Moses when he imagines "the sad mother at the noon of night" placing her "dear babe" into "a floating cradle." She "hides the smiling boy in Lotus-leaves" and "trusts the scaly monsters of the Nile" for his safe passage (II.130). Moses, this dark-hued seed-child, would of course go on to lead his people out of slavery after killing the Egyptian masters who hold them captive. As Darwin describes it, the seedling sent away by Cassia would "Wrench the red Scourge from proud Oppression's hands, / And broke, curst Slavery! thy iron bands" (II.131). Darwin's observation that "E'en now in Afric's groves with hideous yell / Fierce SLAVERY stalks, and slips the dogs of hell," begins a long anti-slavery passage which concludes with the couplet that appears on *Obi*'s title page: "*Hear him*, ye Senates! hear this truth sublime, / 'HE, WHO ALLOWS OPPRESSION, SHARES THE CRIME'" (II.131). If Jack is figured as a plantain elsewhere in the novel, he is also intertextually figured here as the cassia plant borne from a diasporic Mosaic seed that has survived a cross-oceanic transplantation.

Plants and Revolutions

Most scholarship on *The Botanic Garden* focuses on its second volume, "The Loves of Plants," which was published first. This volume poetically catalogs and describes plants from around the world according to the Linnaean sexual system, including such examples as the plant *Adonis* whose "many males and many females live together in the same flower" (II.182)—an arrangement that Darwin associates with the polygamous "marriage customs of the people of Tahiti."[42] The quotation from Darwin that appears on Earle's title page comes from "The Loves of Plants," but its content corresponds closely to an argument outlined in more detail in the book's first and often overlooked volume, "The Economy of Vegetation," which presents the vegetable world as a model to reflect on and critique contemporary politics and economics. Fredrike Teute is one of the few to draw attention to this volume's celebration of revolution as a correction to the exploitative inequities of tyranny and slavery. In fact, Darwin's account of the natural world locates revolution as the inevitable result of the mismanagement of plant life.

Obi first introduces the disjunction between a natural and commercial economy through Harrop, who uses the language of nature to describe the world of empire and commerce. When he explains to Amri, for instance, that Europeans "barter our commodities more extensively than you do here, and the great exchange is diffusing round the world, like the generating sun, the rays of prosperity and affluence" (81), his language naturalizes as well as celebrates European commerce by equating it with the sun. What had seemed the apparently disinterested acquisition of knowledge for its own sake suddenly appears instead to be in the service of self-interested profit; the vision of Christian charity turns into one of commercial profit. As she hears Harrop celebrate global commerce, Amri witnesses on the plain below their vantage point the Slatees (African merchants who trade in slaves) selling their products "like cattle" to be "dispersed over the world" (84). And shortly thereafter, Harrop, a man "who has gained no inconsiderable fortune by this Man-traffic" (126) and to whom "trade was his idol" (128), will take possession of both Amri and Makro as his property and transport them on a slave ship to Jamaica, where the former will be sold to the planter Mr. Mornton.

Harrop will later resort to the self-justifying logic of the civilizing mission when he explains to Jack why he transported Amri from her African home to Jamaica. But his explanation also interestingly depends on the language of botanical transplantation. "She was a wild untutored being," he explains,

> bred up in native simplicity, in the bosom of Africa; she was ignorant, and I matured her understanding; her good heart was incircled by weeds of a savage growth; I plucked them by the roots and implanted in their stead seeds of a more

refined nature; by my daily perseverance, and the susceptibility of a heart that owned all tender feelings from her birth, they soon expanded and ripened into blossom. I felt a pleasure in the culture of her mind, such as you must feel, when raising from the ground a nutriment to life.   (107)

Harrop describes himself here as a gardener attending to the plant Amri, clearing the soil in which she lives of "weeds" and replacing those with more "refined" plants in order to allow her to "blossom." He compares his cultivation of Amri to Jack's cultivation of plants that provide "a nutriment to life." On the one hand, this analogy reinvokes the cyclical co-dependence of human and vegetable life that Harrop outlined earlier, but on the other it positions the human slave Amri as another "nutriment to life," cultivated explicitly to be consumed. For Harrop, both humans and plants are commodities. He explains that "in return for her saving my life, I have brought her to happier climes, accompanied by the partner of her heart; to climes, where the virtues born in our bosom are more refined than in the savage bowels of Africa" (107). This account makes clear that Amri has not simply been cultivated; she has been prepared for transplantation from the plains of Africa to the plantations of Jamaica. If she is a plant, then she, along with her husband Makro, has been wrenched from her native soil in order to work on New World plantations that grow plants—sugarcane in particular—precisely for consumption. Amri's enslavement and transportation is presented as a kind of forcible transplantation of a body to a different continent and environment.

The story of her husband Makro—the second of the novel's two framing narratives—exposes the violence of such transplantation. Amri tells how Makro rejected his enslavement and commodification: he refuses to become a "nutriment to life" whose body and labor will feed other bodies and creatures, and he does so by refusing himself to ingest any such nutriments. When the men working the slave vessel "poured the loathsome beverage down his feverish throat," he "spit it back, accompanied by blood; for, in forcing their spoon into his mouth, they tore his throat in a most inhuman manner" (87). Makro becomes a body refusing nourishment, rejecting its participation in the cycle of sustenance that Harrop had earlier taught him, and rejecting too Harrop's naturalization of that paradigm. Makro may even be seen to model here the rejection of the "blood-sweetened beverage" that Southey encourages British citizens to perform. Makro appears in this scene as a body that has been forcibly torn from the tree, like the damaged limb whose fate was earlier described by Harrop. In refusing to be unnaturally and forcibly grafted onto another tree, he becomes instead a body whose "limbs forget their use" in the end (92)—or a body who, like one of Darwin's sensate plants, voluntarily contracts its petals.

Once Makro determines that he will "no longer take aught to nourish life," he asks his wife to raise their unborn child "to hate the European race," identifying revenge as "the seeds" she will "sow" in their son and which will "ripen as he grows in years, and expand into a flame" (90). As Makro dies, continuing to refuse "thy beverage" which is "encompassed round with slavery," he passes on a different lesson about the politics of cultivation and transplantation to his unborn child, Jack. When Amri imagines upon Jack's birth that he will "be the saviour of our country! the abolisher of the slave trade!" (95), she is imagining Jack precisely as Darwin's dark cassia seed, carried over the waters of the Atlantic to lead his people, Moses-like, to resist their oppressive New World enslavement.

There are competing models of horticulture at work in this novel: one that is commercial and one that is organic. The vegetable economy does not work like the slave economy for, as Jack explains to an audience of slaves, in the latter the "fruits of my labor and yours go to pamper the sordid appetites of the rich and proud, and not to relieve the distresses of the poor and needy, either of this country or ours" (110). In other words, sugar is no "nutriment to life" and Jack's speech exposes the ways in which Harrop's speech to Amri attempts to conjoin the incompatible realms of nature and commerce. In the commercial economy of the sugar planta- tion run by slave labor, it is not "dew" or a "cooling stream" that feeds the earth but instead "the sweat of our brow [that] drops upon the land in streams." Unlike water, the effect of this human sweat is not to nourish but to "clog the earth" (110). Drawing on a revolutionary language of "rights" (109) and "liberty" (110) that oppose "tyrannical power" (110) and the "chains that incircle ye" (109), Jack calls on his fellow slaves to "rise into a firm body, cemented by the ties that bind us to each other" (110). Jack's language encourages the revolutionary re-grafting of a col- lective body of resistance that has been otherwise torn to pieces by the violence of slavery. When the slave Mahali, one of Jack's African countrymen, responds to Jack's appeal, he invokes images that recall Harrop's description of the African village where Amri and Makro lived; Mahali observes that "Nine annual suns have cheered the herbage of the field, since Mahali was dragged from his native clime" and calls for the "reverberation of Liberty [to] ascend to heaven, and reach on earth the gaudy dwellings of our tyrant masters" (111).

Jack and Mahali's opposition of liberty to tyranny conforms to a revolutionary language that saturated the Atlantic world in the late eighteenth century, and that was transported into the Pacific as well. It is a language that also appears in Darwin's *Botanic Garden*, particularly in the book's first volume. There Darwin celebrates the recent American and French revolutions while lambasting Spain's crimes against the Native population of the Americas and Britain's against Africans through the slave trade. The "flame" that Jack's revenge embodies has its counter- part in Darwin's account of Benjamin Franklin's simultaneously scientific and political encounter with lightning. Franklin's bold experiments with electricity, wherein the "Immortal FRANKLIN sought the fiery bed," precisely match his revolutionary spirit:

> Immortal FRANKLIN watch'd the callow crew
> And stabb'd the struggling Vampires, ere they flew.
> —The patriot-flame with quick contagion ran,

> Hill lighted hill, and man electrified man;
> Her heroes slain awhile COLUMBIA mourn'd,
> And crown'd with laurels LIBERTY return'd.   (I.91)

Franklin's electrical currents of liberty turn against the tyrant-vampires here, but those electrical currents also have a natural source. Darwin earlier described the nervous system of animals as driven by an electricity that "Starts the quick Ether through the fibre-trains / Of dancing arteries, and of tingling veins" (I.35), and then proceeds similarly to characterize the circulatory system of plants as animated by "electric torrents [that] pour" nourishment into the "dull root, relax its fibre-trains / Thaw the thick blood, which lingers in its veins" (I.46). In both animal and vegetable realm alike, nourishment travels along electrical "fibre-trains" to animate bodies. But this system applies equally to the globe as a whole, as he explains in his account of the origin of the world:

> Through all his realms the kindling Ether runs,
> And the mass starts into a million suns;
> Earths round each sun with quick explosions burst,
> And second planets issue from the first;
> Bend, as they journey with projectile force,
> In bright ellipses their reluctant course;
> Orbs wheel in orbs, round centres centres roll,
> And form, self-balanced, one revolving Whole.   (I.9–10)

Darwin moves from this account of the cyclical, self-balanced order of the natural world in his first canto to the problem of slavery, tyranny, and oppression in the second canto, which focuses on the element of earth and its mineral wealth.[43]

The American Revolution is imagined by Darwin as fueled by the electrical forces of the earth seeking to restore its lost revolving balance, returning an organic equilibrium to a system into which an unnatural commerce introduced an upsetting inequality. Events in revolutionary France are similarly described as the response of an enchained liberty to cruel tyranny. The people of France are imagined as a "Giant-form" that "slept, unconscious of his chains" wound around "his large limbs." Those chains were imposed "By the weak hands of Confessors and Kings" who covered the people's eyes with a "triple veil" and with "steely rivets lock'd him to the ground" (I.92). The image of a "stern Bastile with iron cage [that] inthralls / His folded limbs, and hems in marble walls" (I.92) might be seen to parallel Earle's description of the conditions in the hold of the slave ship, where Amri is held with an "iron ring, which bound me by a chain to the wall [and] galled my ankles" and where the slaves are "miserable wretches, deprived of liberty, confined within the narrow limits of a loathsome dungeon" (86). Darwin's footnote to the Bastille passage explains that the prison contained dungeons in which "skeletons were found…with irons still fastened to their decayed bones" (I.92). Like the colonial Americans before them, the French giant is awakened once he is "Touch'd by the patriot-flame, [and] he rent amazed / The flimsy bonds, and round and round him gazed" (I.92).

The repetition of the same phrase "patriot-flame" used in the account of Franklin explicitly links the two revolutions to each other, and ties both to the similarly repeated term "fibre-trains" describing the vessels that carry electrical fluid through the bodies of plants, animals, and now nations, alike. Moreover, the description of an awakened, postrevolutionary France looking "round and round" matches Darwin's frequent doubling of circular words to describe the universe as a scene of perpetual rotation, with orbs and orbs turning, centers and centers rolling, suns sinking on suns, and systems crushing systems (I.191). These images insist on the literal meaning of revolution as regularized rotation; such large-scale cyclicality is also micro-replicated by the tiny seeds of each plant, each of which "grain within grain" turns "in endless circles" to recycle and reproduce itself. Darwin's imagery of revolutionary cyclicality informs Earle's understanding of what amounts to a political ecology of the earth.

The imagery of electricity and revolution binds together Darwin's discussions of the American and French revolutions, but that imagery suggests connections to the West Indian context as well, in ways that may be especially relevant to Earle's use of Darwin. In colonial Saint Domingue, for instance, there was a, well-established elite scientific community and, as James McClellan has shown, electrical demonstrations were often held there in the years before the Haitian Revolution erupted.[44] Moreover, Christopher Iannini has made it clear that debates about the Haitian Revolution were carried out "around the Atlantic rim" precisely through the scientific community's "exchange of specimens, seeds, and texts from the West Indies and through their rhetorical appeals to nature as the new secular ground of revolutionary authority." These botanical exchanges and the political discussions they engendered stretched, of course, beyond the Atlantic and into the Pacific, as natural history societies began to cooperate with imperial officials on projects of economic botany designed to support West Indian planter interests. This included "the introduction of Asian plants into the West Indies, and their acclimatization in well-funded botanical gardens, as a potential solution to chronic food shortages."[45] Earle's novel challenges such efforts, directly linking transplantation schemes (including the slave trade itself) to the plantation regime, and draws on Darwin to imagine a revolutionary response to resulting violence and inequality.

For Darwin, the imbalance of tyranny is righted by the earth itself, represented by its caretakers the gnomes: "When Heaven's dread justice smites in crimes o'ergrown / The blood-nurs'd Tyrant on his purple throne / GNOMES! YOUR bold forms unnumber'd arms outstretch, / And urge the vengeance o'er the guilty wretch" (I.96). The poem's treatment of these Atlantic revolutions is bracketed by the problem of the Atlantic slave trade, first introduced through the Englishman Josiah Wedgwood's manufacture of a cameo depicting "The poor fetter'd SLAVE on bended knee / From Britain's sons imploring to be free" (I.87). While the cameo may have served largely sentimental purposes for Wedgwood, Darwin invests it with more radical potential, and the fact that it was crafted from the earth's clays provides for him a perfect example of the soil providing the natural materials for revolutionary action. Darwin similarly celebrates the discovery of gunpowder from materials provided by the earth because it "weakens the tyranny of the few over the many" (I.25), allowing "Fear's feeble hand [to] direct the fiery darts, / And Strength and Courage yield to chemic arts; / Guilt with pale brow the mimic thunder owns, / And Tyrants tremble on their blood-stain'd thrones" (I.26). Here human ingenuity transforms natural substances into political replicas of lightning and thunder, which work to displace tyrants and restore the world's natural cyclicality and balance. In this sense, Darwin's text participates in what Allawaert describes as an "awareness that those who could manipulate ecology possessed a transformative power associated then and now with revolution" or what DeLoughrey describes as an awareness that "cataclysmic change might also arise from environmental agents."[46]

The footnote accompanying Darwin's passage on Wedgwood's cameos explains that these lines are "alluding to two cameos of Mr. Wedgwood's manufacture; one of a Slave in chains, of which he distributed many hundreds, to excite the humane to attend to and to assist in the abolition of the detestable traffic in human creatures."[47] Darwin returns to Wedgwood's cameo following his account of the American and French revolutions, reminding readers of its image of "The SLAVE, in chains, on supplicating knee" asking "ARE WE NOT BRETHREN?" He concludes with an appeal to "EARTH! cover not their blood!" (I.96). That appeal links this passage in "The Vegetable Economy" with the anti-slavery passage discussed earlier in "The Loves of Plants" which—after the description of the cassia plant as a Moses figure—represents a distressed and weeping Goddess of Botany: "For human guilt awhile the Goddess sighs, / And human sorrows dim celestial eyes" (II.132). Throughout *The Botanic Garden*, slavery and tyranny are exposed and resisted by the natural world. Revolutionary action becomes, in Darwin, a political version of the rotations that already characterize the natural world, a violent uprising that acts to restore to the world its natural and self-balancing forces against the corrupting ones of tyrannical inequity. Slavery as Harrop imagines it positions humans as cash crops transplanted for purposes of profit. Earle's novel holds out instead for a kind of collective grafting among these violently transplanted humans, whose disfigured bodies sprout new revolutionary outgrowths nurtured by the soil not of the plantation, but of the provision grounds.

Provisions and Infections

In 1787—the same year as the failed *Bounty* voyage to transplant breadfruit— provision grounds for slaves were mandated in Jamaica as a means to reduce the reliance on imported food sources.[48] These provision grounds quickly became a food source for slave families as well as for planter families, who came to depend on the excess harvest from these gardens sold, often quite profitably, in local markets.[49] Provision grounds therefore served as powerful alternatives both to the colonial plantation's profitable sugar monoculture and to the botanical garden's aestheticized imperial exotics.[50] Earle is clearly familiar with provision grounds for he informs readers in an earlier footnote that slaves "are allowed a small por-tion of ground, which they cultivate for their support, after the labor of the day is completed for their masters" (n.101). Plantain dominated the provision economy of Jamaica much as the cash crop of sugarcane dominated the plantation economy, and the description of Jack's hideout in Earle's novel discussed at the beginning of the chapter—where the products of the plantain tree make up Jack's furniture, food, and medicine—suggests that it is located precisely at or near such a provision ground.[51] In his longer footnote on the plantain tree, Earle suggests the wide range of ways in which plantain provides for human and animal bodies, explaining that it

> is cultivated on a very extensive scale in Jamaica, without the fruit of which, Dr. Wright says, the Island would scarcely be habitable, as no species of provision could supply their place. Even flour, or bread itself, would be less agreeable, and less adapted to the support of the laborious negroes, so as to enable them to do their business or keep in health. Plantains also fatten horses, cattle, swine, dogs, fowls, and other domestic animals. The leaves being smooth and soft, are used as dressings after blisters. The water from the soft trunk is astringent. Every other part of the tree is useful in different parts of the rural economy. The leaves are also used for napkins and table-cloths, and are good food for dogs.   (n.124)

The favorable comparison of the fruit to "bread itself" here may even be positioning local Jamaican plantain trees as explicit alternatives to recently imported Tahitian breadfruit trees—as well as to the sugarcane whose cultivation harms and destroys rather than nourishes and heals bodies.[52]

Jack's rebellion is therefore located at a site traditionally associated with slave agency, self-sufficiency, and sustainability. Provision grounds were at once com-munity gardens, medicine cabinets, and vegetable armories, for the plants grown there could provide nurturing food, healing medicines, and poisonous weapons. Early accounts of Jamaica by Barham, Sloane, Long, and Edwards include descrip-tions of poisonous plants being used to kill, and Payne-Jackson and Alleyne note that "African slaves and obeah-men used plants as weapons of resistance against whites."[53] Darwin's volume on "The Economy of Vegetation" contains a section devoted to the powerful poisonous properties of some plants, from deadly night-shade to the hyppomane tree whose "milky juice" is used by Indians to "poison their arrows" (II.111). Many flowers, he notes, "possess narcotic quality" whose purpose in "the vegetable oeconomy" is to "protect them from the depredations of their voracious enemies" (II.110). One especially notorious "poison-tree in the island of Java" even emitted "malignant exhalations" so toxic that it reportedly "depopulated the country for 12 or 14 miles round the place of its growth" (II.115).[54] The practice of obi which gives Earle's book its name yokes Jack's slave rebellion to the political, medicinal, and military power of the earth's vegetable economy, but it also quite explicitly ties this power to Jamaican provision grounds, which often housed obi practitioners as well as fugitive slaves.

Benjamin Moseley suggests that obi-men and women were sometimes slaves formerly afflicted by the highly infectious disease of yaws; it was customary "when a negro was attacked with it, to separate him from the rest, and send him to some lonely place by the sea side, to bathe; or into the mountains, to some Provision Ground, or Plantain Walk; where he could act as a watchman, and maintain himself, without any expence to the estate, until he was well; then he was brought back to the Sugar-Work."[55] Moseley goes on, however, to note that such a return to the plantation "rarely happened" for many of these infected slaves died of the disease in the remote locations to which they had retreated, while those who survived did so with "a general mutation of their muscles, ligaments, and osteology; became hideously white in their woolly hair and skin; with their limbs and bodies twisted and turned, by the force of the distemper, into shocking grotesque figures resembling woody excrescences, or stumps of trees, or old Egyptian figures, that seem as if they had been made of the ends of the human, and beginnings of the brutal form." Diseased slave bodies are here described, among other things, as the stunted remains of—or the contorted outgrowths from—chopped trees; as Moseley notes, "the most wrinkled, and most deformed *Obian* magicians, are most venerated."[56]

This description gives a kind of uncanny life to the severed limbs that, according to Harrop, withered and died after being cut from the tree—bringing these discarded human stumps into closer alignment with Edward Long's self-reproducing and hydra-headed cotton tree, or to the collection of slave rebels Jack calls on to "rise into a firm body, cemented by the ties that bind us to each other" (110). These deformed yaws survivors became physician-magicians able both to afflict and to heal bodies through incantations and the use of "some potent roots, weeds, and bushes, of which Europeans are at this time ignorant." These plant ingredients were often mixed together with other part-objects from the natural world—such as egg shells, feathers, blood, hair, and parts of animals such as a pig's tail, a bird's heart, a cat's foot, or a human's fat—to produce medicines to protect the political as well as biological health of slaves.[57]

William Earle's 1800 novel and William Moulton's 1804 narrative both turned to the politics of nature to understand acts of rebellion—mutinies, revolts, uprisings, and revolutions—as justifiable responses to an unnaturally exploitative economy of transoceanic capital.[58] While Earle's concern was the Atlantic plantation and Moulton's was the Pacific ship, the experiences of oppression and rebellion were accompanied in both locations by disease—and descriptions of sailors' bodies often matched those of slaves. The abolitionist William Clarkson, for example, described high death rates experienced by sailors aboard Atlantic slave ships and the abandonment of infected sailors left to die in Caribbean ports. Clarkson describes these men lying about the wharves of Kingston, Jamaica with ulcers on their legs and bodies that became "covered with mosquitoes."[59] The discarded bodies of infected sailors echo here the discarded bodies of infected slaves on the island of Jamaica.[60] Similar plights affected crews in the Pacific, where upwards of 40 percent of the crew on Bligh's *Bounty* were afflicted with venereal disease and required as a result to pay a fee to the ship's surgeon of 15 shillings, the equivalent of over half a month's pay. Because both gonorrhea and syphilis were incurable, infected sailors were moreover compelled to pay this fee over and over again. These exploited cargos of expendable human bodies provide a sharp contrast to the ship's nurtured cargos of indispensable plant specimens. Even as food for the sailors was sparingly rationed out, for example, enormous amounts of space in the *Bounty's* great cabin and on its deck were reserved for the pots of breadfruit, in order to protect the plants' health and ensure their survival. When the crew decided "to throw overboard the breadfruit plants" as one of the first acts in their mutiny, they were no doubt responding to the disproportionate treatment of seamen and seedlings.[61]

Plants and seeds were carried into as well as out of the Pacific, as the narratives of many transoceanic voyages remind us. George Vancouver, for example, reports the disappointment of his expedition's botanist to find that the Native Hawai'ians had failed to cultivate the plants and seeds left there by members of Cook's earlier expedition.[62] But the men who went on these voyages also left other kinds of seed behind, for if the islanders aren't caring for the plants sowed by European crew-members, they clearly are caring for the children sired by them. These men moreover left behind disease as well as children: Vancouver comments that many of the women have contracted "lamentable diseases introduced by European visitors." Earlier in the century, Bougainville discovered that many on board his French ship contracted venereal disease from women in Tahiti, who had earlier been infected by the men on Wallis's English expedition.[63] Disease and desire accompanied the movement of people and plants between oceans, often leaving infected, exploited, and rebellious human bodies behind.

Despite the highly publicized mutiny that doomed Bligh's 1789 voyage, concerns with food supply in the Atlantic slave system sent him to the Pacific again in 1791. After two transoceanic voyages, one mutiny, six years, and tens of thousands of saltwater miles, Bligh finally delivered Pacific breadfruit to the Atlantic, arriving at his last West Indian destination of Kingston, Jamaica in 1793. The success of the voyage was not without considerable losses, however, since fewer than 700 of the over 2,000 plants taken from Tahiti survived—a kind of transoceanic botanical survival statistic that recalls those of the transatlantic slave trade's middle passage. Still, the treatment and fate of the bodies of sailors and slaves—as well as the bodies of transported felons and indigenous men and women—must be imagined alongside the care and protection with which Bligh's breadfruit trees were carefully carried, when they finally arrived in Jamaica, for miles overland from the port in Kingston to Hinton East's botanic garden, where they would be successfully transplanted and where they still grow.[64] Bligh was really transplanting an imagined Pacific herbal remedy representing a sexualized and laborless freedom—the fantasy of a pleasurably painless cycle of reproduction—into an Atlantic otherwise characterized by a slave labor regimen so back-breaking that it continually spawned violent resistance and depended on continual replacements of bodies through the slave trade.[65] But the goal of his project was never really reached, for West Indian slaves roundly rejected the breadfruit and continued to consume plantain instead—much in the way that the subsistence economy of the provision ground in Earle's novel challenges the profit economy of the sugar plantation.[66]

J. R. McNeill describes the plantation system as "a short-term strategy for turning sunlight and soil nutrients into money as fast as possible,"[67] and early efforts like Edward Long's to ascribe a natural fertility and abundance to Jamaica were designed to counteract knowledge about the notorious difficulties of cultivating and securing steady profits from sugarcane. Despite insisting on the island's spontaneous natural growth, for instance, Long recounts the commercial struggles of Jamaican sugar plantations, which "can hardly be expected to arrive at any tolerable state of perfection in less than seven years…for, the first years, the produce will do little more than subsist the owner, his labourers, and stock, and pay the taxes and contingent charges of the year; while the merchant's advancement for purchasing labourers, stock, and utensils, and erecting works, must remain a debt until the gradual increase of produce may enable the planter to pay for these articles."[68] Prospective planters who expect or have been promised quick, substantial, and certain sugar profits are here asked to decelerate this appealing narrative and imagine instead uncertain profits after enduring prolonged financial patience.

The narrative of *Obi* might be thought to translate the temporality of the sugar business into the temporality of revolution. The novel never specifies the precise terms of the relationship between its letter writer George and his addressee Charles, but it seems likely that Charles is one of the many absentee English owners of Jamaican sugar plantations, while George is probably the agent or factor who represents and reports on his interests on the island.[69] The letters from George recounting Jack's story clearly interrupt a more routine kind of correspondence between the two men. George notes in his first letter that Charles will be wrong to assume that he has been "wholly and exclusively engrossed by your business" because he has instead become entirely preoccupied by "Jack!!! and his cursed three fingers!!!"[70] Those business concerns to which George was supposed to attend are summarily cast aside at the outset; he explains that although he has just reread Charles' letter, he "cannot see that the business it is about is of such great importance" and responds to his friend's "queries" by instead telling him the story of three-fingered Jack (69). The novel thus cleverly and immediately replaces the expectant business of sugar plantation management with the suspenseful politics of slave rebellion. As such, the novel's opening might be seen to perform in miniature the work of the whole, for the compelling story of three-fingered Jack counters commercial exploitation with revolutionary expectation, turning to the ecology of plant life to summon a natural form of political justice to resist the pull of profit.

The epistolary form of Earle's novel may well resemble the therapeutic bundles for which it is named—a textual version, perhaps, of an obi bag that collects fragments into a simultaneously botanical and political medicine with the power to counteract the destructive forces of Atlantic plantation slavery.

The next chapter turns from a novel set on the island of British-controlled Jamaica to one on the French-controlled colony of Saint Domingue, but remains focused on the transoceanic dimensions of plantation slavery in the Caribbean. By the turn to the nineteenth century, Saint Domingue—the island Columbus had named Hispaniola when he arrived there 300 years earlier—had become a kind of western hemispheric replacement for the bountiful East Indies he mistakenly thought he had reached. In this case, the extraordinary wealth so many European voyagers sought by transoceanic travel came not from the Asian spice trade but instead from American sugar plantations. By acknowledging the considerable extension of global commerce into the Pacific taking place at the time of the Haitian Revolution, and by paying attention to the bodies of women in transoceanic context, the next chapter examines the dynamics of capitalist drive that fuel war capitalism's calculus of risk while hiding its violent costs.

Circuits

FEMALE BODIES AND CAPITALIST DRIVE IN LEONORA SANSAY'S *SECRET HISTORY*

Junot Díaz prefaces his 2007 novel *The Brief Wondrous Life of Oscar Wao* with a condensed history of the Caribbean island that is now home to the two nations of Haiti and the Dominican Republic, the island named Hispaniola by Christopher Columbus and later called Santo Domingo. The "Admiral" of Díaz's passage below is Columbus, whose 1492 landing in the Caribbean marked the first moment when Europeans set sight and foot on what would be called the New World. Díaz describes the haunting legacy of Santo Domingo's difficult history, ignited by this arrival:

> They say it came first from Africa, carried in the screams of the enslaved; that it was the death bane of the Tainos, uttered just as one world perished and another began; that it was a demon drawn into Creation through the nightmare door that was cracked open in the Antilles. *Fukú americanus*, or more colloquially, fukú—generally a curse or a doom of some kind; specifically the Curse and the Doom of the New World. Also called the fukú of the Admiral because the Admiral was both its midwife and one of its great European victims...
>
> No matter what its name or provenance, it is believed that the arrival of Europeans on Hispaniola unleashed the fukú on the world, and we've all been in the shit ever since. Santo Domingo might be fukú's Kilometer Zero, its port of entry, but we are all of us its children, whether we know it or not.[1]

This passage describes the Columbian arrival as a kind of "big bang" moment marking the origin of the modern/colonial world-system, that uneven network of global capitalist relations facilitated by the discovery of the New World's resources.[2] Díaz locates the epicenter of the world-system's emergence at the "ground zero" of Santo Domingo, in a suggestively gendered scene where the "midwife" Columbus assists at the colonial birth of a child whose destructive power is launched by the terrifying violence of its own conception.

In this chapter, I turn to another novel set on this same island, a novel which until recently languished in near obscurity since its publication almost exactly 200 years before Díaz's Pulitzer Prize-winning novel. Written by Leonora Sansay and published in 1808, *Secret History; or the Horrors of St. Domingo* is an epistolary novel set in the French colony of Saint Domingue following the slave revolution that erupted there in 1791. Saint Domingue was a spectacularly profitable French sugar colony that occupied the western portion of the island; following its independence from France in 1804, Saint Domingue was once again given its indigenous name, Haiti. The eastern portion of the island—now the Dominican Republic—was in Sansay's time the Spanish colony whose name, Santo Domingo, was then used also to designate the entire island.[3] The novel takes place in the years 1802 and 1803, when the slave revolution in Saint Domingue transitioned into a war for independence from France. I begin this consideration of Sansay's novel with Díaz's brief history because *Secret History* recognizes and plays out precisely the violent spin and repeating whirl of colonial violence described in his passage above. The charges of sexual abuse recently made by many women against Díaz, alongside Díaz's own confession that he was raped as a child, give new weight to the circuits of violent harm described in his passage about Santo Domingo and remind us of the vulnerable bodies that suffer at the violent nexus of personal desire and global greed.[4] Sansay's *Secret History* plots precisely this axis where the intimate domestic dynamics of sexual desire meet the transcontinental economic relations of capitalist drive, and it does so by superimposing erotic and economic triangles.[5]

We might recall Sven Beckert's reminder, cited in the Introduction, that the western voyage of Columbus and the eastern one of Vasco de Gama "fed on one another" by funneling gold and silver from the Americas into Asian trade. This global maritime network established at the beginning of the sixteenth century—and the dynamics of war capitalism that kept it running—persisted in expanded form at the turn into the nineteenth century. Indeed, as Beckert points out, sugarcane was only one of the plants that by the late eighteenth century made Saint Domingue so immensely profitable. In 1791, the island had nearly as many cotton as sugar plantations, and exported well over 50 percent more cotton by then than it had eight years earlier. In 1770, the island was already the source of 36 percent of the Caribbean's total cotton exports. Those exports were made possible, of course, by the import of human bodies. Beckert notes that as the price of cotton rose "by 113 percent over 1770 levels, nearly thirty thousand slaves were shipped to Saint-Domingue annually. That elasticity of the labor supply, a hallmark of war capitalism, was unmatched by any other region of the world."[6] Those slaves were often exchanged for cotton cloth imported by Europeans to west Africa from India, in a global series of transfers of human and non-human commodities along maritime trade routes that fueled "a regime of violent supervision and virtually ceaseless exploitation."[7]

Scholarship on *Secret History* has understandably read the novel in the context of the Atlantic world, but the novel was written during a period when Atlantic trade routes were being aggressively extended through exploration and commerce into the Pacific, in part as a result of changing Atlantic commercial relations in the wake of the American Revolution. The many narratives of these Pacific voyages that circulated throughout Europe and the United States during this period, as described at length in Chapter 1, presented an image of an exotic and lucrative Pacific world that recalls the frequent pairing of wealth and sexuality in some of the earliest accounts of the Americas. Patty O'Brien points out that American colonization efforts had long operated in tandem with African slavery, beginning in 1501 in what was then the Spanish colony of Santo Domingo, where stereotypes of female promiscuity helped both to justify enslavement and to excuse sexual violence against women. O'Brien points out that in the wake of European voyages to Tahiti in the 1760s and 1770s, these stereotypes were extended to the Pacific, a region that—following Balboa's naming of the South Sea—was often associated with the American tropical and slave-holding South.[8] I situate *Secret History* in this transoceanic commercial and literary context and argue that the vulnerable bodies of women repeatedly function in this novel as a kind of switch that exposes the dynamic interrelation between individual desire and capitalist drive.

The psychoanalytic category of desire has been central to postcolonial theory and colonial studies, from Frantz Fanon and Albert Memmi to Homi Bhabha and Robert Young.[9] Even the model of triangulated desire—while largely developed by narrative and queer theory to describe the detouring of desire to accommodate social restrictions—has been applied to the contexts of colonialism and race relations.[10] The companion concept of drive, however, has been strikingly absent from this work, despite the fact that psychoanalysis regularly describes the two together, typically by distinguishing them from each other. Whereas desire is determined by the subject's relation to lack, by its ceaseless striving for partial objects that ultimately fail to satisfy, drive describes the systemic circulation around a void or hole where failure itself is a source of satisfaction. As Slavoj Žižek puts it, "desire desperately strives to achieve *jouissance*, its ultimate object which forever eludes it; while drive, on the contrary, involves the opposite impossibility—not the impossibility of attaining *jouissance*, but the impossibility of getting *rid of it*." The difference is one between, on the one hand, wanting and pursuing a series of particular objects that never fulfill and, on the other hand, being unwittingly caught up in an impersonal system of perpetual pursuit and unavoidable fullness.

Drive, in other words, reveals the way in which a triangle can also function as something more like a circuit. Žižek locates drive at the very heart of "the whole capitalist machinery" where, he explains, "it is the impersonal compulsion to engage in the endless circular movement of expanded self-reproduction."[11] Drive is continuing to acquire or ingest or possess long after becoming sated and satisfied. It is precisely this exhausted and repetitive sensation of drive, I suggest, that characterizes both the content and the form of *Secret History*, a novel in which sexual alliances offer not so much a geometry of desire as a kinetics of drive, in which triangles always reveal themselves also to be circuits around which goods and bodies ceaselessly and compulsively turn. Repeatedly, the bodies of women serve as a kind of pivot point that exposes local and individual desire as implicated in an impersonal global system of capitalist drive whose circuits generate violence and inequality. In Sansay's Saint Domingue, moreover, this drive of endless circular revolutions generates another kind of revolution, one defined less by a kinetics of rotation than by a politics of resistance. Revolutionaries and coquettes emerge in *Secret History* as unexpected products of the sexual-economic circuits of drive, risk-taking figures whose actions threaten to turn against those "midwives" who, like Columbus at the birth of the New World, helped bring them into being.

The Colony and the Wife

Secret History was originally published anonymously under the full title of *Secret History; or, the Horrors of St. Domingo, in a Series of Letters, written by a Lady at Cape Francois. To Colonel Burr, late Vice-President of the United States, Principally During the Command of General Rochambeau.* The novel consists of thirty-two letters written by two sisters, Mary and Clara. The first twenty-six and the final one of these letters are written by Mary from the Caribbean to Aaron Burr in the United States. Mary's letters originate from three island sites that mark out a Caribbean geographical triangle: first Santo Domingo, then Cuba, and finally Jamaica (see Figure 7.1). The intervening five letters (letters 27 through 31) represent an epistolary exchange back and forth between Mary and Clara after both have fled Saint Domingue, when Mary is in Kingston, Jamaica and Clara is in Bayam, Cuba.[12] Three of those five letters (numbered 28, 29, and 31) are penned by Clara, marking the only direct representations of her voice in the novel. As this enumeration suggests, the story of Clara's plight is told almost entirely through the voice of her concerned but distracted sister Mary.[13] Burr himself—the addressee of all but two of Mary's twenty-nine letters—never participates in this letter exchange and

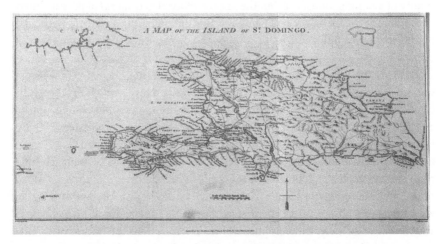

FIGURE 7.1. *"A Map of the Island of St. Domingo," showing St. Domingo, and the eastern portions of Cuba and Jamaica. Marcus Rainsford,* An Historical Account of the Black Empire of Hayti *(London, 1805). RB 353144. The Huntington Library, San Marino, California.*

never appears as a character in the novel, except to serve as the final destination for both Clara and Mary as they leave the Caribbean for the United States, where Mary hopes her sister will find in Burr "a friend and a protector" (154).[14]

What little biographical evidence there is of Leonora Sansay indicates that she was born and raised in Philadelphia, where her widowed mother eventually remarried a tavern-keeper. Scholars disagree about whether she later met Aaron Burr at this tavern or elsewhere, and about whether he merely served as a "mentor" figure for her or whether she became his "sometime mistress, confidante, and, perhaps, a political operative as well."[15] In any case, in 1800—perhaps at the suggestion of Burr—Leonora married Louis Sansay, a French planter who had sold his Saint Dominguan plantation to the revolutionary black leader Toussaint Louverture before fleeing to New York in an effort to "escape the retribution meted out against the former slave holders of the revolted French colony."[16] By 1802, some degree of order seemed to have been restored in Saint Domingue and numerous French planters and their families returned to the island hoping to recover their lost estates and income, among them Louis Sansay and his wife Leonora. Their arrival, however, coincided with that of the French General Leclerc who had been sent by Napoleon Bonaparte to restore white control over the island and, it was feared, to restore slavery as well. In response to such threats, blacks once again revolted, setting numerous plantations and portions of the city on fire. Leclerc, who died from the yellow fever epidemic that ravaged the island shortly after his arrival, was replaced by General Rochambeau, a military commander known equally for his excessive acts of violence against blacks and for his excessive indulgence in opulent luxury and sexual conquest.

Secret History is generally recognized as a fictionalized transformation of Sansay's actual letters to Burr, written while she was trapped in the small portion of the city of Le Cap (also known as Cape François, or Cap Français) that remained in French control before it finally fell to the black army. Although these historical events frame the novel and these historical figures populate its pages, the slave revolution itself is relegated to the very margins of this novel, where it only occasionally interrupts the story of sexual scandal that otherwise dominates the book. As Michael Drexler puts it, Haiti itself often seems "lost in the shuttling of the novel's gaze back and forth between ballroom and battlefield."[17] Recent scholarship on *Secret History* has recognized its interwoven dynamics of gender relations and racial revolution, often by emphasizing how the politics of colonialism plays itself out in the domestic spaces and intimate relations within the book.[18] But the violence of both marital and plantation intimacies in the novel are situated within the turning circuit of sexual-economic drive and its production of disproportion and inequality. Powerful generals and plantation owners become midwives at the violent births of the very coquettes and revolutionaries who later violently seek to gain power over them. If this novel is able to tell that story so easily through its narrative of private sexual intrigue, it is because the bodies of women in it pivot between economic and sexual circuits, exposing the pursuits of desire as inseparable from the motions of drive.

Throughout the book, colonial relations are described as marriage relations and vice versa. The novel's subtitle, for example, "The Horrors of St. Domingo," refers at once to the violent slave uprising and to Clara's personal "horror" of "breaking" the "life-long tie" that bound her to her husband. These intersections are in place from the novel's first pages, which essentially alternate between updates on the uncertain status of the colony and updates on the uncertain status of Clara, who "repents every day having so precipitately chosen a husband…and I foresee," her sister Mary acknowledges, "that she will be wretched." The "wretched" Clara inhabits an equally wretched colony, which has become "a heap of ruins" with "streets choked with rubbish."[19] The New World colony, like the American wife, is suffering the destructive effects of an ill-considered marriage to a possessive and violent French husband.

Likewise, the book's language of military conquest is sexualized, and its language of sexual conquest militarized. When Clara's flirtation with the French General Rochambeau leads him to call her a "charming creature," she is at first "delighted with a *conquest* she now considered assured" (75, emphasis added) until she learns to regret her overtures and the frightening desires they inspire. The General later combines military with sexual tactics when he asks St. Louis to lead a dangerous battle against the revolutionaries, hoping in the process to remove the husband as an obstacle to pursuing his wife. When St. Louis, who survives the battle, learns that Clara has been in the General's company against his express demands, he "seizes [her] by the arm, and dragging her into a little dressing-room at the end of the gallery," locks her up (84). The General, who subsequently tries to prevent St. Louis from sending Clara away from the island and himself, in turn "laid an embargo on all the vessels in the port" (86) to prevent her departure. Later, St. Louis arrives to find Clara "surrounded" by Rochambeau declaring his love, and moves "to defend her." Only a sudden reminder about the "situation of the colony" made "him forget the dangerous one in which he had found his wife" (102). The very language of these passages indicates that the battle for possession of Clara and for possession of the colony are inseparable. But it also indicates the oscillation of each figure—the wife and the colony, Clara St. Louis and Saint Domingue—between the positions of agent and victim, sometimes appearing as powerful coquettes and sometimes as overpowered bodies.

As these descriptions suggest, a triangulated relationship between Clara, St. Louis, and Rochambeau occupies the heart of this novel, and that triangle plays out a dynamics of desire, consumption, and subjection.[20] The very dynamics that define this relationship, however, also characterize the material conditions that enable it, for this novel's central sexual triangle mimics the Atlantic trade triangle in which French Europeans and French creoles battle for possession of the desirable sugar colony, including its profits, its pleasures, and its population of African slaves. These interlocking economic and sexual triangles are sustained by vectors of jealousy (by creoles of Europeans, by husbands of seducers, by wives of mistresses), of desire (by Europeans for black slaves, by seducers for women, by coquettes for attention), and of subjection (black slaves to creoles, creoles to the French, and wives to husbands). They trace out relations of competition, seduction, and oppression that stretch between continents and oceans, and that get performed in colonial dining rooms, bedrooms, and parlors. These are relations of appetite, force, and waste that are at once sexual and economic. In one of the many anecdotes that circulate through the story, for example, we learn of one French general who "is enriching himself by all possible means," and has "taken possession of a plantation on which he makes charcoal, and which he sells to the amount of a hundred dollars a day. A caricature has appeared in which he is represented tying up sacks of coal. Madame A—, his mistress, standing near him, holds up his embroidered coat and says, 'Don't soil yourself, General'" (78). Like the cartoon, the novel recognizes that it's all a dirty business: private scandals are shot through with the obscenity and violence of colonialist and capitalist relations, and the endless rotations of drive verge on the pornographic.

Atlantic Triangles and Pacific Circuits

In his book *The French Atlantic Triangle*, Christopher L. Miller explains that the Atlantic triangle "was driven partly by cravings in Europe—for sweetness and the energy of caffeine but also more generally for wealth." These cravings were produced and satisfied through intercontinental strategies that generated radical disproportion, as Miller observes: the Atlantic triangle was sustained along one of its sides by "[t]he enslavement of subaltern Africans" which in turn "raised the living standard of elites in Europe, in Africa, and in the islands" along another side. Miller's account of the French Atlantic triangle emphasizes the ceaseless rotation that Žižek associates with the psychoanalytic concept of drive and the circuits of capitalism. But Miller notes as well that this rotation both produced and was fueled by an "imbalance of values" that "kept the triangle turning, as Europeans continually sought to increase their wealth by turning, spinning, and sweeping around the Atlantic."[21] As relations of force and exploitation redistributed goods, bodies, and products around the triangle, both accumulation and disproportion increased until Saint Domingue could be called "the richest single colony on Earth" in the same year, 1791, that the colony's half-million black slaves "launch[ed] a massive, coordinated, and sustained rebellion against the plantation regime."[22] As Doris Garraway puts it, "if French profits soared during this time, it is because of the extraordinarily violent disciplinary regime, which extracted on average ten to fifteen years of labor from captive men and women before they were driven to death."[23] *Secret History* moves toward recognizing that these two phenomena of profitability and violence are products of the same circuit, and it often does so through the female bodies that repeatedly appear at the transition point from one side of this circuit to the other.

Antonio Benítez-Rojo offers a suggestive description of the Atlantic triangle's dynamic that brings together the languages of economic and sexual reproduction and that also brings together the Atlantic with the Pacific. The enormous accumulation of Western capital before the nineteenth century depended, he explains, on "deliveries from the Caribbean womb." But these deliveries (of physiological and visual stimulants including sugar, rum, coffee, and indigo) arrived only with the help of violent force, for the Atlantic as we know it, he explains, is "the painfully delivered child of the Caribbean, whose vagina was stretched between continental clamps...; all Europe pulling on the forceps to help at the birth of the Atlantic." Echoing Díaz's image of Columbus as brutal midwife, Benítez-Rojo describes the machine that suctioned resources, bodies, and products out of the feminized Caribbean Sea as something "like a medieval vacuum cleaner" that was "coupled to the Atlantic and the Pacific."[24]

Benítez-Rojo's inclusion of the Pacific in this description acknowledges the often overlooked fact that the Caribbean at the start of the nineteenth century was part of a global and transoceanic system of exchange, contact, and exploitation that extended well beyond the Atlantic. For all the wealth generated by its Saint Domingue colony and its Atlantic triangle, France was simultaneously engaged in significant Pacific exploration aimed primarily at entering into the lucrative China trade. State-sponsored voyages led by Louis Antoine de Bougainville in the 1760s and by Jean-François de Galaup de La Pérouse in the 1780s brought back tantalizing accounts of scientific discovery, commercial promise, and sexual freedom. In fact, the same year the slave revolution erupted in Saint Domingue, France sent an expedition into the Pacific to search for the lost ships of La Pérouse, whose expedition had failed to return to France when it was expected several years earlier.[25]

The numerous narratives of international Pacific exploration and commerce that circulated in Europe and the United States during the late eighteenth and early nineteenth centuries, discussed in detail in Chapters 1 and 3, formed part of the print and cultural context for a novel like Sansay's. Many of these circumnavigations of the globe left in search of a supposed southern continent whose size and resources might rival the Columbian "discovery" of the Americas, and the Pacific travel narratives describing these voyages included scenes of contact with indigenous peoples, and encounters with products (like furs or sandalwood or bêche du mer) that had the potential to become the Pacific equivalent of sugar (or tobacco or indigo)—a highly desirable resource that made the Atlantic triangle so prosperous for so much of Europe. These Pacific travel accounts, in other words, recalled in many ways those produced about the Caribbean and the island of Santo Domingo (Hispaniola) three centuries earlier.

The ostensible purpose of La Pérouse's global expedition was to rival the geographical and botanical discoveries of the Englishman James Cook, but its ulterior purpose was to gain for France some of the commercial profits and trade advantages enjoyed by other European nations who had ventured into the Pacific. In addition to the official royal instructions outlining hopes for new scientific knowledge, La Pérouse also received a special set of private and "secret" instructions which reportedly included details and advice about identifying commodities for trade and locating potential sites for trading posts that might allow France to compete in the Pacific's highly lucrative fur trade.[26] News of extraordinary profits through Pacific trade circulated widely throughout the Atlantic world at the turn of the nineteenth century, especially with the publication in 1784 of Cook's last voyage. As Chapter 1 explains, that narrative included the account of one sailor who "disposed of his stock" of sea otter furs "for eight hundred dollars" and even sold "a few of the best skins...[for] a hundred and twenty dollars each," an exchange that amounted to a profit of 1800 percent.[27] This passage from Cook's widely printed and translated narrative sent numerous men and ships into the Pacific—including the two ships that left under La Pérouse's leadership in 1786, two years after Cook's narrative was published. Such numerical anecdotes—which recall Sansay's description of the filthy rich dealer in charcoal who made as much as a "hundred dollars a day"—indicated that Pacific commerce might supplement or outstrip France's Atlantic numbers.

These Pacific voyages, however, became associated with the pursuit of sexual as well as economic desire. On the one hand, they were known for "lucrative profits," since the return on investment for these voyages could be anywhere from 200 to over 2000 percent.[28] On the other, they were known for "exotic stopovers" such as Hawai'i, where one European voyager explained that "[w]omen can be considered one of the commodities that these islands abundantly furnish to visiting ships."[29] The alluring bodies of Native women were often packaged with the allure of financial profits, and stories of these paired delights circulated through numerous Pacific travel accounts published during this period.[30] The discussion in Chapter 3 also makes clear that those female bodies regularly appeared at sites of anti-colonial resistance around the Pacific, at moments when the pursuit of sexual-economic desire suddenly transformed into an encounter with rebellious violence. Such moments expose the imbalances produced by the revolving circuit of drive.

When La Pérouse reflects on the Spanish mission he visited at Monterey in California, for instance, he simultaneously notes the disciplinary and sexual abuse of Native women and the likelihood of Native rebellion. Not only is "corporal punishment administered to Indians of both sexes who fail in their religious duties," but "several sins which in Europe are reserved to divine retribution are punished by being placed in irons or in the stocks." Indians who do not return an adequate amount of flour from the wheat they are sent to grind every morning are "punished with the whip," although "[w]omen are never whipped in the public square, but in an enclosed space, fairly distant, maybe so that their cries do not arouse too much compassion, which might cause the men to rebel." La Pérouse describes the government of the Franciscans as "reprehensible," and he expresses a wish "that the truths of Christianity had been backed by a legislation that would gradually transform into citizens men whose present condition is not different from that of blacks in our colonial settlements that are ruled with gentleness and humanity."[31] Here La Pérouse imagines refashioning the Spanish Pacific in the image of the French Atlantic, even though his prediction of rebellion at Monterey could easily have described the French Atlantic colony of Saint Domingue, where revolution erupted only a few years after his disappearance at sea.

Indeed, La Pérouse's critique of Spanish colonialism in the Pacific never extended to the French, even when he found himself the object of rebellion later in his voyage, when in 1787 twelve of his crew were killed in an attack by islanders at Mahouna (or Massacre) Bay in Samoa. One interpretation of the Samoan uprising suggests that it was likely in response to the Frenchmen's overtures toward Native women, "some of whom," La Pérouse reports, "were very pretty, [and] offered with their fruit and poultry their favours to anyone who was prepared to give them beads." These included, he notes, "a certain number of women and very young girls who made advances to us in the most indecent fashion, of which several people took advantage."[32] Although La Pérouse has absolutely none of the sympathy for these rebelling Samoans that he had for the oppressed Indians at Monterey, the bodies of Native women similarly appear here—as they frequently do in contemporaneous accounts of the Pacific—at the site of anti-colonial resistance where the individual pursuits of desire suddenly appear implicated in the impersonal compulsions of drive. Indeed, Pacific voyages like La Pérouse's helped put into place much of the machinery of that enormous "vacuum cleaner" Benítez-Rojo describes as "coupled to the Atlantic and the Pacific" and which suctioned both bodies and commodities into a series of spinning circuits that increasingly connected the Pacific to the Atlantic and the Caribbean (as well as to the Indian Ocean).

Even as the French Atlantic triangle described by Christopher Miller continued to spin—generating enormous wealth through enormous exploitation—encounters and events in the transnational Pacific (news of which circulated in books and periodicals in both America and Europe throughout this period) were laying bare the unequal terms and coercive relations that underpinned such triangles and the circuits that spun around them. Sansay's novel foregrounds those terms and relations through the anecdotes of sexual-economic pursuit and accumulation that spin around, and provide an ongoing context for, her story's central triangulated relationship.

Until Clara departs from Saint Domingue for Cuba, she and her sister circulate through a world of obscene luxury and startling prosperity; as C.L.R. James remarks, "on no portion of the globe did its surface in proportion to its dimensions yield so much wealth as the colony of San Domingo."[33] It is easy to read this novel and nearly forget that a revolution is taking place at all since the vast majority of *Secret History*, narrated by Mary, focuses on the lavish entertainments, scandalous intrigues, and parlor gossip engaged in by members of the French military, their families, and the French creoles. When news of the slave uprising does enter the text, Mary represents it largely as an irritating interruption to this round of entertainment. She wishes, for instance, that "the negroes... were reduced to order that I might see the so much vaunted habitations where I should repose beneath the shade of orange groves" and "be fanned to sleep by silent slaves, or have my feet tickled into extacy by the soft hand of a female attendant." For "[s]uch were the pleasures of the Creole ladies whose time was divided between the bath, the table, the toilette and the lover" (73). These expressions of desire for the safety in which indulgence could once be experienced in the city of Le Cap represent what one critic calls "racialized melancholy" and another calls "creole fantasy."[34] Although Sansay does recognize how the French Europeans exploit French creoles as they satisfy their addiction to ease, luxury, and excess, she generally attributes the same cravings to the creoles.[35] Mary mentions one creole man whose "annual income before the revolution was fifty thousand dollars [the equivalent of over $1 million in today's currency], which he always exceeded in his expenses." He "now lives in a miserable hut" and indulges in "gaiety" with the "young girls of the neighbourhood" while hoping "for better days" (74). At one point Mary recounts prerevolutionary descriptions of the island from "some Creole ladies," who describe it as "a garden" in which "[e]very inhabitant lived on his estate like a Sovereign ruling his slaves with despotic sway, enjoying all that luxury could invent, or fortune procure" (70).

But the novel more subtly recognizes that the "pleasure and luxurious ease" (70) of Saint Domingue are invariably accompanied by, because they are literally created by, violence. For instance, one creole wife becomes so jealous of the way her husband looks at the "beautiful negro girl" who accompanied her that "[s]he ordered one of her slaves to cut off the head of the unfortunate victim." When her husband insists at the dinner table later that night that he is not hungry, she promises him "something that will excite your appetite; [since] it has at least had that effect before" (70), and presents him with the severed "head of Coomba." This scene recalls the cannibalism reported by James Cook in his visit to Pacific; during that voyage, as Chapter 4 described, a Native New Zealander delivered a severed head to the English ship where it was boiled in the galley and then offered by Cook to the Natives. As Daniel Cottom has explained of this scene, "cannibalism finds its source here in the context of institutionalized trade between New Zealanders and Europeans, and the act itself figures in this setting as another item of trade."[36] This blurring of acts of extreme corporeal violence with acts of routine consumption (whether commercial, sexual, or culinary) perfectly describes the tone and content of Sansay's *Secret History*, which might be said to be composed of vignettes of capitalist pornography. The novel's form—whose central romantic triangle represents a rather thin central plotline around which constantly circulate countless disconnected anecdotes like those cited in this section—emphasizes the implication of individual desires in the impersonal circuits of capitalist drive, and repeatedly suggests that an obscene violence underpins the appetite for colonial food, clothing, fine tableware, and flesh.

Coquettes and Revolutionaries

In 1805, three years before *Secret History* was published, the Englishman Marcus Rainsford published *An Historical Account of the Black Empire of Hayti*, a book that shares with Sansay's novel the recognition that the bodies of women have played a central role in the repeating history of this Caribbean island. Rainsford's history begins in 1492, and it begins with the body of a woman. Christopher Columbus, he explains, "first had access to [the island's] inhabitants, through the means of a female whom his people overtook, and prepossessed in their favor, by the usual means of trifling presents and gentle behavior." According to Rainsford, the conquest of the island proceeded through seduction, and his account acknowledges that this seduction is accompanied by a violence whose effects reappear in a cycle of accumulation, exploitation, and resistance. When Columbus leaves the settlement to return to Spain, the Spaniards he left behind proceeded to "gratify their avaricious and licentious desires at the expence of the natives, making a wasteful prey of their gold, their women, and their provisions." These acts of violent possession lead some of the Natives to flee the plantations on which they are forced to labor and to hide out in the mountains. They later descend from these mountains—much like the slave revolutionaries nearly two centuries later—to carry out their revolt. But the Natives' unfamiliarity with European warfare only leads them, Rainsford remarks, to produce "in themselves the effects [of destruction] they vainly hoped to produce in their usurpers."[37]

This early Spanish history on the island is replicated later by the French in Rainsford's account. Indeed, his history resembles nothing so much as a repeating narrative whose accompanying spinning commercial triangle had produced by the 1770s a colony that he describes as "[l]ike a rich beauty, surrounded with every delight" and all "the politicians of Europe, sighed for her possession."[38] In Rainsford's history as much as in Sansay's novel, the island is portrayed as a seductive coquette, caught within a triangle of jealous and competing admirers. Rainsford's book recounts the ways in which this coercive courting resulted in both the island's enormous wealth and its violent revolutions, such that the history of the island plays out the imbalances and velocities of the spinning Atlantic triangle described by Miller or the circuits of fukù described by Díaz. But *Secret History* furthermore suggests that coquettes are not just passive figures whose alluring qualities activate triangles of desire but are themselves *created by* the circuits of drive.[39]

As Mary considers the case of her sister Clara, for instance, she remarks that women who do not have the "rare fortune of becoming early in life attached to a man equal or superior to themselves" and who are "surrounded by seductive objects...will become entangled" and, like her sister, "be borne away by the rapidity of her own sensations, happy if she can stop short on the brink of destruction" (153). Clara is portrayed here as a figure entangled in the relentless circuits of drive—much like the anecdotal parade of generals, plantation owners, and creole wives that continually interrupt her story. Mary recognizes that Clara's coquettish flirtation with Rochambeau arises from her unhappiness, that her sister "sighs for conquest because she is a stranger to content, and will enter into every scheme of dissipation with eagerness to forget for a moment her internal wretchedness" (72).

It is because St. Louis is possessed of an "irascible temper" that inflicts "torments" on "his wife" that his wife is in turn forced "to seek relief in the paths of pleasure" (80). Meanwhile, Mary reports that her sister has "often...assured me that she would prefer the most extreme poverty to her present existence, but to abandon her husband was not to be thought of" (88). It does not take long, however, before what seemed like a harmless and empty game of coquetry erupts into violence as Clara finds herself trapped between a ruthless French military general used to getting what he wants and a jealous creole husband who wants sole possession of his wife. Clara ultimately becomes filled with "regret" when "contemplating the splendor which has been so dearly purchased" (80). The coquette emerges as a *product* of the accumulated violence of colonialism's sexual-economic drive, a figure who oscillates between a potential agent and victim of power. In these respects, coquettes are not unlike revolutionaries.

As it moves linearly from the 1490s to the 1790s, Rainsford's history ends up telling a revolving or cyclical story (what Junot Díaz might identify as the returning orbit of the fukù) whose narrative contours resemble that of the spinning Atlantic economic triangle traced out by Christopher Miller and replicated in its Pacific extensions. Even the engravings in Rainsford's text seem to mirror this cyclical movement. One set of paired images from his account of the Haitian Revolution, for instance, shows acts of French violence against the black revolutionaries followed by retaliatory black violence against the French (see Figures 7.2 and 7.3). These two images, whose actions repeat and fuel each other, constitute a circular as much as a linear visual narrative. Both images even contain triangular shapes—the ship's sail and the reinforced hanging posts—that form a backdrop to and support for the violence carried out before them. Rainsford describes the resulting horror of revolutionary violence as a delayed effort at rebalancing, an inevitable auditing in which the white victims of the slave uprising "paid for the luxurious ease in which they revelled at the expense of these oppressed creatures."[40] The Haitian uprising therefore emerges in these texts and images as a revolution in both the political and temporal senses of the world: a singular dramatic uprising aimed at radical change and a repeated rotation in the circuits of transcontinental and transoceanic capital.

Bloodhounds and Land Crabs

Rainsford's book devotes special attention to one sort of violence in revolutionary Saint Domingue: the use of bloodhounds imported from Cuba and trained by Rochambeau's army to hunt down and literally consume black bodies (Figure 7.4). His book includes an appendix devoted to describing the ways in which Rochambeau and his men trained these dogs on the bodies of black women, and includes one engraving showing how the dogs are caged and starved before being tempted with the exposed flesh of black women in order to whet and train their

FIGURE 7.2. *"The Mode of exterminating the Black Army as practised by the French." From Rainsford. RB 353144. The Huntington Library, San Marino, California.*

violent appetites (Figure 7.5).[41] This image emphasizes the ways in which desires are produced, and its representation of the literal consumption of flesh brings to mind the anecdote in which the creole wife presents her husband with the severed head of his attractive slave on a platter for dinner, as well as conjuring the accounts that circulated in contemporaneous narratives of the Pacific of seductive female bodies and violent acts of cannibalism.

The bloodhounds may furthermore correspond to an especially compelling scene that takes place near the end of *Secret History*, in one of the few episodes narrated entirely by Clara, which occurs after she has fled Santo Domingo for Cuba. In Cuba, Clara seeks "asylum" with a Frenchwoman named Madame V—who owns a plantation near the town of Cobre (139). In their efforts to evade pursuit by

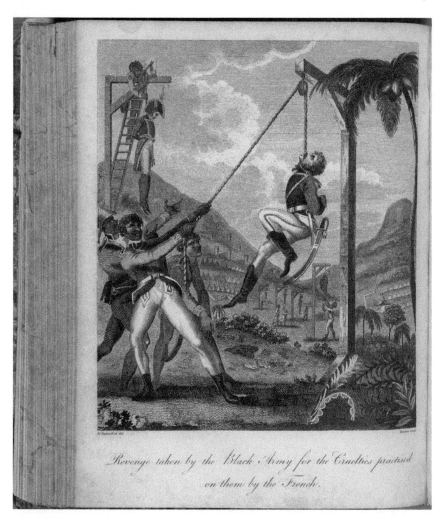

FIGURE 7.3. *"Revenge taken by the Black Army for the Cruelties practised on them by the French." From Rainsford. RB 353144. The Huntington Library, San Marino, California.*

Clara's jealous husband, Clara and Madame V—spend the night sleeping on "a hide laid on the ground" (145) of "a little hut" (143) in a village Clara characterizes as beset by "wretchedness" and "poverty" (144). Clara finds herself, in other words, in the very condition of economic deprivation that she earlier welcomed as an alternative to her marriage. Clara describes being awakened during the night by "the most unaccountable noise, which seemed to issue from all parts of the room, not unlike the clashing of swords; and, as I listened to discover what it was, a shriek from Madame V—increased my terror. In sounds scarcely articulate, she said a large cold animal had crept into her bosom, and in getting it out, it had seized her hand" (145). Their local guide, who slept instead in a hammock hanging from a tree, laughs when he informs them that "it was nothing but land crabs, which, at

Blood Hounds attacking a Black Family in the Woods.

FIGURE 7.4. *"Blood Hounds attacking a Black Family in the Woods." From Rainsford. RB 353144. The Huntington Library, San Marino, California.*

this season, descend in countless multitudes from the mountain, in order to lay their eggs on the sea shore." These crabs, he explains, "strike their claws together as they move with a strange noise, and no obstacle turns them from their course" (145). Despite subsequently moving into a hammock herself, Clara finds herself unable to sleep due to the continued noise of the crabs which, she notes, "appeared like a brown stream rolling over the surface of the earth" (146).

The metaphor here appears rather obvious, considering that *Secret History* is set during the uprising of Saint Domingue's nearly 500,000 black slaves against their approximately 40,000 white French slavemasters.[42] As Michael Drexler has noted, Clara's description of this multitude of crabs "rolling over the surface of the earth" "like a brown stream" while making the martial sounds of "clashing swords" clearly

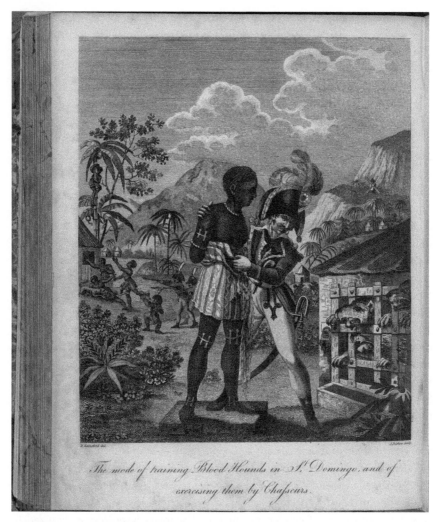

FIGURE 7.5. *"The mode of training Blood Hounds in St. Domingo, and of exercising them by Chasseurs." From Rainsford. RB 353144. The Huntington Library, San Marino, California.*

conjures images of the black revolutionary masses that initially descended from the mountains to attack the city of Le Cap in their pursuit of freedom.[43] But despite the easy alignment of this crab invasion with the violence of racial revolution, it's important to remember that the attack is initially misinterpreted in the novel as a violation of the female body—a "cold animal" slipping uninvited into a Frenchwoman's "bosom" and proceeding to "seize her hand." Adding these gender details to the racial relations embedded in this scene might suggest that the image emphasizes the threat of black sexual violence against white women, a threat described in several print and visual depictions of the slave revolution.[44] Such a reading would position Clara against the crabs, as the white female object of black male violence.

But further details complicate these gender and racial associations and threaten to disable this particular reading. Clara, for example, is in flight not from black revolutionary violence but rather from the violence of her abusive and jealous white husband whose recent actions included locking her up, raping her, and threatening to pour disfiguring acid on her face. The Cuban crabs recall the Cuban bloodhounds imported by General Rochambeau, who trained them to desire and hunt black slaves once "possessed" by French creoles, just as he himself desires and hunts Clara who has escaped her "possession" by the French creole St. Louis. This reading might be enriched even further if we consider some carcinological details (or facts about crabs) that were not likely available to most of her readers, but that, as a sometime Caribbean resident, may well have been known to Sansay herself. These crabs, for instance, would have all been female, since each spring millions of them migrate several miles from the forested interior of the island to the sea, the only environment in which the eggs they are carrying will hatch.[45] In fact, following this scene, Clara more or less follows the route of the crabs by going to the shore herself in order to board a boat that will take her to join her sister Mary in Jamaica, where the two women will finally sail together to the United States. In this reading, Clara's gender and route align her with rather than against the brown crabs, and the regularity of their seasonal migration might even imply that the descent of the revolutionaries was as natural and instinctive an act as that of the crabs making their way toward the island's beaches. Furthermore, the guide informs Clara that the crabs are very nearly a patron saint of Cuba, because a Spaniard once convinced a group of invading Englishmen who "had always wished to possess" (145) the island that the sound of the crabs was in fact the sound of Spanish forces preparing to resist their invasion. In response, the terrified English abandoned their plans for conquest. The imagery of domestic and revolutionary violence is hopelessly entangled in this crab scene, and the symbolic meaning of the crabs oscillates between their status as heroic liberators and dangerous terrorists.

On the one hand, the difficulty of this scene would seem to be a reflection of the complex contortions of gender and race that scholars have long recognized in revolutionary Saint Domingue.[46] But situating this novel within a larger framework of global commerce and capitalist drive suggests that the complexities of domestic and revolutionary violence in Saint Domingue participate in the turning triangles and spinning circuits of the transoceanic and transcontinental trade networks that make up the modern/colonial world-system. Domestic and economic triangles transect each other through and through, and the rotations of drive that keep these circuits in motion produce pleasures and profits but also despair and abuse, coquettes as well as revolutionaries. The contradictions embedded in this Cuban land crab scene reflect the multilayered effects of the modern world-system's foundational violence and reveal that agents and victims of power often rapidly trade places as these circuits continue to turn.[47]

Whether or not Leonora Sansay read Rainsford's book, her novel on the "horrors of St. Domingo" is indebted to the history Rainsford tells of colonial exploitation of Natives, resources, and women that begins with Columbus, and to the continuation of that history in the early nineteenth century, especially in sites around the Pacific. Read together, these texts provide evidence of the disproportion that results from the spinning drive of capitalist accumulation and that fuels repeating cycles of revolution, just as they record the foundational acts of violence and seduction that create such disproportion in the first place. In such a system (much as in the novel's land crab scene), revolutionary and domestic violence are easily grafted onto and misrecognized for each other: they hold hands, as it were, across the obscene terrain of capitalist appetite. By presenting French European and French creole desire in terms of a sexualized colonialism and a pornographic capitalism, *Secret History* exposes the rotations of capitalist drive as a violent obscenity, and revolution as its violent offspring.

Epilogue

TOWARDS A TRANSOCEANIC AMERICAN
LITERARY HISTORY

Wave-piloting is an indigenous form of oceanic navigation whose only instrument is the human body reading the movement of waves, wind, stars, and the sun. Until recently, wave-piloting was at threat of extinction from the combination of environmental crisis, population diaspora, and new technologies brought to the Pacific by way of U.S. empire. In her 2016 *New York Times Magazine* article "The Secrets of the Wave Pilots," Kim Tingley describes the efforts of Alson Kelen, a Marshall Islander and the last wave pilot apprentice, to pass the test of finding land on the vast open waters of the Pacific using the knowledge handed down to him through what remained of indigenous training networks. Kelen was followed on his journey by a small group of scientists interested in identifying a particular wave, unknown to Western science, that serves as the foundation of wave-piloting because, by connecting atolls to each other, it directs mariners to otherwise unseen land. The scientists who accompanied Kelen hoped to be able to plot the wave—called *di lep* or "backbone"—with data they collected on his voyage.[1]

After successfully navigating to land, Kelen was awarded wave pilot status, but the scientists struggled to identify in their computerized data the presence of a wave where there appeared to be none. Only once they shifted the way they were looking at their combined information did they realize that the "backbone" wasn't the visible line they were expecting to see, but instead a curve that resulted from repeatedly orienting the vessel perpendicularly to what at any given time was the largest swell between bodies of land. Tingley describes these liquid routes as "invisible roads that no one was seeing because they didn't know how to look." Indeed, the answer in some ways was not to look, for the *di lep* took its shape not by sight but by way of the sensations it produced in the human body, characterized most of all by a bowel-distressing rockiness. Tingley observes that "storytelling, the way we structure and make meaning from the events of our lives, arose from navigating."[2] The lesson provided by the search for *di lep* may then be that new ways of navigating ultimately lead to new methods for telling stories, even if they also cause discomfort along the way.

I began this book with the Bengal elephant that, in 1796, sailed on a ship named *America* with Nathaniel Hathorne Sr. from Calcutta to Salem, and asked then how recognizing this kind of regular transoceanic, global movement might change the way we narrate stories about America and American literature. In this Epilogue, I want to venture some tentative answers to that question by nominating water as a material in which to replot and retell American literary and cultural history in global context. I suggested in my Introduction that one way to imagine such an aquatic approach to American studies is as the cartographic equivalent to a photographic negative, a visual inversion of the usual markers by which we indicate, and give relative prominence to, land and water on maps. But this perspectival shift sounds a lot easier to achieve than it is, because regardless of how we differentiate water from land, our eyes and brain are trained to privilege the latter. No matter how we mark or distinguish it so as to diminish its presence in relation to water on maps, it's always the land we see first (see Figure B.1).

Yet if we think of the sea instead as offering an alternative dimensionality— what Hester Blum, drawing on the work of Philip E. Steinberg, has described as a "methodological model for nonlinear or nonplanar thought"[3]—it has the capacity to reorient in more fundamental ways both the maps and the narratives we use to study, teach, and understand American literary history. What kind of literary history do we get when we follow scholars such as Epeli Hau'ofa, Damon Salesa, and Matt Matsuda in treating oceans not as rimlands, or as empty space surrounded by land, but as multidimensional space? I'm not suggesting there is one *di lep* that will allow us to curve a single new way through American literary history, but by positioning ourselves, like wave pilots, across rather than along the overpowering swells of our current narratives, we are bound to find new routes and ways of understanding that have been invisible only because we haven't known how to look.

Narrative plotting. In his book on the pre-history of fiction, Nicholas Paige recognizes that narratives of literary history, and the works and authors we choose to include in them, are governed by plot—and plot is organized around a predetermined endpoint. "This is the way much literary history is done," he explains. "Individual works are important insofar as they are signs of something else [such as fiction, or the novel, or modernity] that is otherwise out of sight but nonetheless on the rise." Paige offers a suggestive visual image (see Figure B.2) to accompany this observation, and identifies points "A, B, and C" as those "great authors who over time were coming to see that their works could be fictional," who "sighted the conceptual territory of fiction (D) that would soon emerge for all to colonize. D had always been there, pushing up, but aside from these islands, it remained under water."[4]

This description works just as well for a national literary history as it does for a genre like the novel. Instead of the islands, for example, of Behn, Defoe, and Richardson that lead us toward the continent of the novel, we have those, say, of

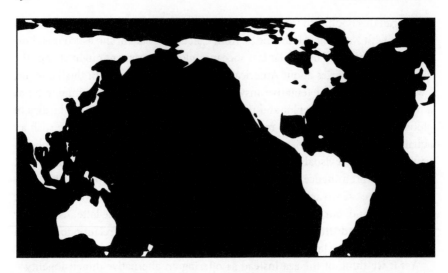

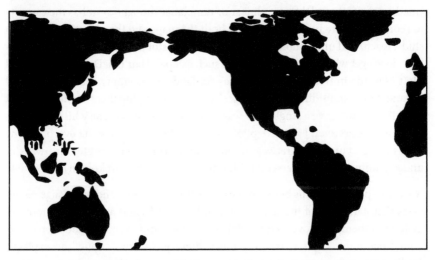

FIGURE B.1. *Positive and negative global maps: it's always the land we see first. Drawing by Tanya Chiykowski-Rathke.*

Winthrop, Mather, and Edwards ushering us toward the future landmass of American literature. It goes without saying that the more scholarship we produce on these figures, the larger and more prominent their literary islands become, and the more overpoweringly definitive the line that narratively connects them to the shore ahead. Our selection of anticipatory islands moreover depends on how we characterize their continental endpoint to begin with, as a shift in interest from American exceptionalism to American cross-cultural contact might nominate instead the atolls of Christopher Columbus, Mary Rowlandson, and Phillis Wheatley, and while doing so, encourage us to notice other features, perhaps, of the islands

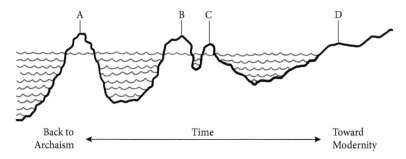

FIGURE B.2. *The history of fiction. From Nicholas D. Paige,* Before Fiction: The Ancien Régime of the Novel *(University of Pennsylvania Press, 2011). Reprinted with permission of the University of Pennsylvania Press.*

of Winthrop, Mather, and Edwards. Shifts of emphasis like this one have been crucially important to changing the landscape of American literary history. But even when such changes lead us to reposition that narrative line, it still keeps aiming at the nation.[5] Can we do more than repeat variations of this same, fundamentally linear, narrative? How might we do so, and what difference would it make?

The most intriguing feature of Paige's illustration in this respect is his inclusion of water, because its presence compels us, first, to recognize that vast territory below the waterline and second, to acknowledge the deceptive partiality of the view from above. Paige asks,

> What if nothing below the waterline links these islands to each other or to the mainland in the distance? Sicily lies smack up against the boot of Italy. But despite appearances, it was never part of the boot; geologically speaking, it's part of North Africa. We see our canonical novels of the past as an archipelago connected to the mainland of now, whereas they may be only a series of data points acting as hosts for our perception of patterns—patterns we perceive based on our knowledge of what is to come.[6]

In other words, we retroactively construct a literary history whose raised points we connect in order to neatly and speedily deliver us, as if via zipline, to our own comfortable and recognizable present, the "mainland of now." In our curricula, we call this trip the Survey of American Literature, and its chronological linearity offers in many ways a pleasurable and satisfying narrative as it moves through a colonial archipelago of texts toward what feels (to most undergraduate students at least) like the more dependable and recognizable solidity of antebellum American literature. If we horizontally split and separate Paige's image directly across the waterline, we can see more clearly the neat linearity of the literary historical narrative formed by connecting the visible literary peaks that dominate its top portion (see Figure B.3).

Transoceanic America has repeatedly argued that linear narratives like this— including those that emerge in the late eighteenth century to drive our experiences

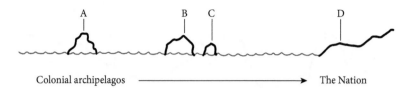

FIGURE B.3. *The terrain of the American literature survey course. Modified detail from Paige. Reprinted with permission of the University of Pennsylvania Press.*

of capitalism, revolution, and the novel—actually depend on repressed cycles of episodic violence, that they hide the negative consequences of risk beneath the forward drive impelled by its potentially positive outcomes. In this book, I have often veered more than a bit off course from what most might identify as the recognizable terrain of American literature in order to begin to explore what lies beneath the surface of our more familiar narratives. I have done so because, by allowing maritime transportation and linguistic translation in the context of global empire to shape these histories instead, we are better able to see and expose the accumulated risks, costs, and losses otherwise calculated away by the satisfactions of linear narrative—whether its endpoint be identified as American freedom or American multiculturalism. The result might well lead us toward that balance between "misery and redemption" Jorge Cañizares-Esguerra calls for in narrative histories of the Americas.[7]

We can add another dimension to this effort by asking not just what allows narrative to be linear, but whether the line needs to be straight. In his anthropological history of the line, Tim Ingold identifies the "straight line" as the "virtual icon of modernity, an index of the triumph of rational, purposeful design over the vicissitudes of the natural world." Ingold positions modernity's straight line—created by joining together a series of points, so that the destination from any one point is always known in advance—against the premodern line, whose destination remains unknown until the moment at which it has been reached. Unlike its modern counterpart, this line is not in a hurry; instead, it "goes out for a walk" and as a result is possessed of breadth and width as much as length, as well as potentially unexpected and inconsistent curls and curves. This comparison extends to travel, where modern transport is destination-oriented and plotted along grids and coordinates, while premodern wayfaring is characterized by a meshwork of entangled lines with no predetermined endpoint.[8]

Ingold reinforces this difference by turning to design theorist David Pye's distinction between risk and certainty in workmanship. Pye associates the "workmanship of risk" with writing by pen and the "workmanship of certainty" with modern printing, whose mechanisms are designed to minimize the kinds of uncertainty, error, unevenness, and difference penmanship entails.[9] Of course, anyone familiar with modern printing knows that it hardly avoids risk or error, and the same might be said, for that matter, about modern travel. Indeed, Ingold's opposition often feels overdrawn, and his distinction might be better understood less as one between a curved and a straight line, between risk and certainty, and more as one between a curve and the illusion of straightness, between all-out risk and the fantasy of its avoidance. What would a narrative look like whose line coiled to accommodate both violence and promise?

Elsewhere, Ingold distinguishes between plotlines and guidelines: guidelines are the grid of lines on a sheet of graph paper, or the parallel lines on a sheet of notebook paper; plotlines are the particular points drawn and connected on the graph paper, or the lines penned on the binder paper. Another example moves this distinction to the world of the early printing press, where "the line of assembled type is a plotline" and the "raised edges of the composing stick and the galley, against which the type rests, are guidelines."[10] Ingold points out that both of these become more or less invisible once the page is printed (much less bound into a book), but their effects silently shape the way a story is composed and read. New plotlines (drawn across different textual archipelagos of A, B, and C) may make little impact, in other words, if the guidelines (our terrestrial-national destination of D) remain firmly and invisibly in place. Taking to the oceans may therefore introduce a greater wayfaring sensibility into our plots of American literary history by leaving familiar guidelines behind, allowing us to restore lost dimensions of breadth and depth to our narratives of American literary history as we wave pilot our way toward some undetermined new shorelines. I offer a few preliminary reflections and examples below of how such literary historical wayfaring might proceed.

Transoceanic drifting. One strategy is simply to drift far enough away from D that its magnetizing force on the plot of American literary history is weakened enough to open up new narrative possibilities that are less straight, less sure about where they're headed. *Transoceanic America* has focused on a relatively brief period of history when, on the one hand, projects of nation-building characterized much political life on land around the Atlantic while, on the other hand, aquatic news from the Pacific really began to saturate its print world. I have pursued a transoceanic refiguration of this period and its literature by bringing the distant and relatively unfamiliar Pacific world into greater proximity with the very familiar Atlantic one—heading out in what may have seemed the wrong direction to find a new way to shore. Similar acts of transoceanic drifting might enable alternative ways to plot other periods of American literary history, both earlier and later.

There is plenty of writing from or about the Pacific for centuries prior to the eighteenth century, for instance. But because its geographical and linguistic distance from D has always seemed so great, none of it has ever been considered and read in the context of American literary history. As American literature anthologies currently have it, the Pacific only arrives and begins to matter about 350 years after the Columbian Atlantic, when definitively American writers like Charles Henry Dana, Jr. and Herman Melville described it or set their fiction in it. Yet as my Introduction notes, it was 1513, barely two decades after Columbus's Caribbean landing, when Balboa became the first European to see and remark on the body of water we now call the Pacific Ocean. Later that century, desirable spices and fabrics began arriving from the East by galleon to the bustling annual Acapulco Fair, which drew visiting merchants from Peru and Mexico City. Those goods then made their way overland by mule to the port of Veracruz in the Gulf of Mexico for transport on the Spanish treasure fleet across the Atlantic to Europe. This West Indies fleet joined the Manila galleons as, respectively, the first permanent transatlantic and transpacific trade routes, fueled as much by the silver and gold transported in both directions from American mines as they were by wind and water currents. But the point I wish to make is that these two oceanic routes were commercially, politically, and textually connected; what this history and its archives tell us is that the Pacific and Atlantic were for Europe in conceptual and material dialogue from the very beginning, materially joined in a kind of elongated figure eight that met at the transfer station of the Americas.

Illustrations marking the route of Pacific galleons from the East Indies to the Americas abound, and it's not much harder to find visual depictions of the Atlantic treasure fleet routes from the West Indies to Europe. It's far more difficult, however, to find an illustration representing both routes in transoceanic linkage. The image showing these connected routes (see Figure B.4) is adapted from a report on the global dispersion of tropical fire ants, which were carried on these ships in the soil they used as ballast and which entered the ecologies of faraway ports when that soil was dumped to make room for new cargo. Scientists have recently learned that fire ants in the Philippines, for example, actually originated in southwest

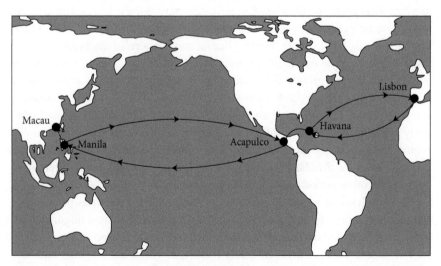

FIGURE B.4. *Pacific (East Indian Manila Galleon Routes) + Atlantic (West Indian Spanish Treasure Fleet Routes) = Transoceanic Materiality for American Studies. Drawing by Tanya Chiykowski-Rathke.*

Mexico, and that the species' spread across the globe followed the timeline and route of Spanish trade.[11] Of course, people, goods, plants, animals, and diseases moved along those routes as well as insects—but so did stories, manuscripts, logs, records, diaries, and books. The ships that carried sought-after goods from the East (along with undesirable by-products like Mexican fire ants in the other direction) also carried Chinese, Filipino, and Indian sailors and slaves, some of whom ended up in Mexico or Louisiana or California—not to mention Philadelphia or Salem or London. This Spanish transoceanic trade alone generated two centuries of histories and writing that have hardly begun to be recovered, much less read together with literatures of the Spanish Americas, of the British and Dutch Atlantic slave trades, and writing in Dutch, English, French, and Russian from and about the Pacific and Indian Oceans.[12]

An aquatic global framework that acknowledges the intercontinental and transoceanic context for American literature and culture would emphasize that sea travel has materially connected continents, peoples, and products from the colonial period to the present day; that the Atlantic, Pacific, and Indian oceans (as well as the Caribbean and Mediterranean seas) were tied to each other through exploration, empire, and commerce; and that indigenous peoples both participated in and vigorously resisted all three. The texts that document this often violent movement of bodies, goods, and ships represent a centuries-long transnational archive of waterlogged writing that remains excluded from a simultaneously terrestrialized and nationalized American literary history. If we haven't read these texts, it's because—like Hathorne Sr. and his Bengal elephant—they don't conform to the narrative plots that govern most American literary and cultural histories. A more specifically oceanic orientation compels us to think not only about the transportation of commodities, bodies, and raw materials—and the residues of that movement left behind in character, form, setting, plot, and theme—but about the material movement and circulation of texts. As soon as we think about the world's oceans less in isolation from each other and more in connection to each other, as soon as we approach American literature in a materialist transoceanic context that interweaves literary with book history, the texts and figures we include in our narratives of American literature change. Those unfamiliar texts will also compel us to see more familiar writing—texts that we have in many cases been looking at for a long time—in entirely new ways.[13]

Archival diving. The kind of transoceanic drifting at the waterline outlined in the section above must also be accompanied by diving below it. If we return to the lower portion of Paige's diagram (see Figure B.5), for example, we see that it constitutes nothing less than a massive repository of neglected texts whose contents have never been considered as material around which to construct a literary history. Caroline Levander has observed that transnational, hemispheric, multilingual, and global approaches to American literary studies have broken open the field's boundaries to produce a flood of content that, as she puts it, sometimes feels

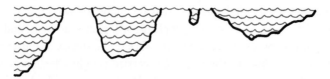

FIGURE B.5. *The terrain of archival diving. Detail from Paige. Reprinted with permission of the University of Pennsylvania Press.*

less like an archive and more like "junk, a mélange of incomprehensible detritus accreted through the failed endeavor that is the development of a coherent Americas tradition."[14] Yet it is exactly down here amidst the accreted layers of discarded textual junk that literary historical equivalents to the geological plate that connects the island of Sicily to north Africa might be found—formations that are invisible from the surface and that seem narratively unthinkable from the proximities of its overland terrain.

We can take as one example an island peak such as *Robinson Crusoe*, and ask what its prominence prevents us from seeing. What texts lie scattered in the waters around it? What formations and connections are buried on the sea floor below? The Englishman Alexander Selkirk's story has always been given pride of place as a predecessor to Defoe's novel, but in fact that story was itself preceded by that of a Mosquito Indian who, before Selkirk, was also abandoned on and rescued from Juan Fernandez Island. When these two Pacific castaway stories circulated in the Atlantic print world, they were almost certainly linked to a well-known twelfth-century Arabic story set on a deserted island in the Indian Ocean. Ibn Tufayl's *Hayy Ibn Yaqzan* had already been translated into Latin and Dutch before appearing in several English translations in the late seventeenth and early eighteenth centuries, and it quickly generated an extraordinary number of revisions and adaptations that relocated this deserted island many times over, in the Atlantic and Pacific and Indian oceans. Some scholars have insisted that *Robinson Crusoe* is one of those adaptations, even though for others that claim sits at an angle of distress within the dominant swells of our histories of the novel—in part because it threatens to lower or shift its island peak and to upset the line of narrative that moves through it to the land of the English novel.[15] But it's exactly this submerged plate and its transoceanic, transnational, and multilingual literary history that the towering offshore peak of *Robinson Crusoe* prevents us from seeing.[16]

Oceans are spaces with little regard for the coherence of national languages or claims to textual originality, and a more oceanic, or at least more amphibian, orientation to literary history demands our engagement with underexplored archives, including such historically undervalued print forms as translations, reprints, adaptations, and periodical excerpts. Meredith McGill has taught us to recognize a reprint culture in which "authorship is not the dominant mode of organizing literary culture" and in which "texts with authors' names attached take their place alongside anonymous, pseudonymous, and unauthorized texts." Reprint culture recovers those texts that inhabit the submerged underside of the "author-centered literary nationalisms" with which literary history has traditionally been preoccupied;[17] they litter the ocean floor of Paige's diagram. Among these reprints are translations, which perhaps deserve a special word here because scholars, for good reasons, have generally distrusted and avoided them, ceding their study to those with sufficient linguistic competence to read them in the original.[18] Under such conditions, it would be a multilingual near-impossibility to adopt a global transoceanic scope that might include texts not only in Spanish and French (the more traditional hemispheric or transatlantic partners to English), but in Russian and Chinese and Dutch, not to mention accounting for an astounding diversity of oral cultures and Native peoples—from the Kamchatka peninsula in Siberia to Cavite in the Philippines, from the Hawai'ian islands and the Pacific northwest coast to Acapulco, Chile, Polynesia, New Zealand, Macao, and Goa. McGill's argument about the "author-centered literary nationalisms" that exclude reprints can be extended, however, to translations as well. Rather than allow the stumbling blocks of linguistic facility or geographical expertise to prevent a global approach to American literature, we might turn to transoceanic practices of translation and transportation as productive responses to them.

Like reprints, or abridged editions and unacknowledged borrowings, translations often have a remarkable disregard for the "original" to whose language and meaning they can be quite egregiously unfaithful; translations say as much if not more about the culture of the translator than they do about the text or culture translated.[19] Rather than invite immediate skepticism and avoidance, this indeterminacy should encourage us to study these texts in the way James Clifford has taught us to think about cultures—not just fixed in place like continental land but moving about like the unstable multi-dimensionalities of water, possessing at once the regularity of tides and the unpredictability of waves. Clifford argues that anthropology has privileged the village as the authentic site of a culture, ignoring the often far-flung reaches of a culture's own travels.[20] If we think of a textual original as an equivalent to Clifford's "authentic" anthropological village, then that text's many translations, reprints, and rogue editions are the equivalent of his hotel lobbies and airport terminals (or, in oceanic terms, ship decks, holds, and ports) around the globe, through which texts (like cultures) travel and in response to which they change in selective ways. And of course, it bears remembering that our current American literature anthologies already traffic considerably in translation, particularly in their colonial selections.[21]

Along with reprints and adaptations, translations occupy the indeterminate regions outside of definitive authorship, beyond the certainties of geographical location and national identity which authorship so often confers. The assortment of castaway texts briefly described earlier in this section, for example, dissolves usual categories of belonging like nation or language within an oceanic logic of shift and flux. Reading these texts together in a transnational, multilingual, and transoceanic literary history creates a sense not so much that their shared island setting is moved from one ocean to another, but rather that the island stays in place while the globe is turned around it to situate its story in a new body of water. The difference between these two orientations is the latter's emphasis on the mobile water around the island more than the stability of the island itself, a reorientation that rejects what Elizabeth DeLoughrey calls the "myth of island isolation" to find islands in dialogue with one another as they engage in a shared disregard of continents.[22] How might thick networks of transoceanic contacts, exchanges, and movements provide new contexts in which to narrate our stories of literary history, genre, linguistic style, prose aesthetics, and book form?

America in the world. Paige's reference to canonical texts as "data points" gestures toward the possibilities of using digital tools and methods to gather this lost archival cargo and begin to analyze it as the enormous cache of "big data" that it is. Doing so constitutes a significant alternative to current methods of literary history that select individual texts and connect them through a linear, chronological narrative. New and emerging digital humanities methods offer in this respect an enormously promising resource for a future literary history that takes into account the archival vastness (rather than the canonical selectivity) of literary production. While these prospects are exciting indeed, more circumscribed (and less methodologically ambitious) diving expeditions are also crucial to shaping new narrative forms, and to knowing what questions to ask while doing so.

While the prospect of scraping the ocean floor of print history to capture its entire contents for data analysis is tempting, we also ought to resist the assumption that expanding the scope of American literary history necessarily means covering, including, and accumulating more.[23] It might also mean simply heading in unexpected directions and finding new texts, or new approaches to old texts, along the way. Whether we ultimately maintain or abandon literary surveys and anthologies as we integrate the resources of digital archives and collections, we could productively replace a terrestrial model of textual stockpiling with an oceanic one of textual exploration. Thomas Bender has insisted that a global approach within the field of history, for example, "is not in any way a brief for writing global histories. The point is not to displace the monograph, only to thicken the layers of context it incorporates."[24] Similarly, a global transoceanic approach to literary studies does not mean that we must now write histories of world literature, or that we need to understand the entire world before we can understand a single text. Instead, we should read a text or collection of texts so that we are able to locate the world, the intersections of intercontinental and transoceanic connection and circulation, within it. Doing so means heading into the dimensions and depths of oceans, and recognizing the routes both across and between them. America and its literature is and always has been connected to the world—commercially, politically, and textually—and is bound in surprisingly intimate ways with places and peoples at great distances away. These material connections are recorded in the content, publication, and circulation of texts, and in the other bodies, materials, and goods that circulate with them.

A transoceanic American literary studies does not claim that there is anything particularly or uniquely American about the texts it studies, regardless of where they were published or what language they were written in; but it does claim that this larger archive and context must be taken into account in any attempt to rewrite American literary history in relation to the globe. Like the strangely liquid map reproduced in the Introduction, it asks us to imagine America as both there and not there, at once central to and yet profoundly decentered from the globe and its connections, part of both Atlantic and Pacific waterworlds that are in turn linked to the Caribbean Sea, the Indian Ocean, and polar seas. That map is centered where it is only by virtue of being an American literary history. A literary history with a different geographical emphasis (English, or Middle Eastern, or Chinese) would, much like the alternative versions of the island castaway stories described above, turn the globe to focus on a different location and its aquatic contexts. These literary histories would moreover invariably overlap, blend, and mix.

Monique Alleweart has suggested that the image of a continentally coherent North America has dominated conceptions of American literary history, and offers in its place the image of a dissolving continent, a landmass that is instead fragmented by "a liquefying natural world."[25] Similarly, Brian Russell Roberts and Michelle Ann Stephens call for an archipelagic American studies that takes into account the "island-ocean-continent relations which have exceeded US-Americanism and have been affiliated with and indeed constitutive of competing notions of the Americas since at least 1492."[26] If a global, transoceanic literary history threatens at times to decenter the continent of America from its own narrative, we might ask whether this effect is altogether a bad thing. Even as this model may leave America as a nation at times strangely displaced from its own narrative, it also ties America and its literature to the world through its materialist relations with the globe's often overwhelming and far-flung network of routes and relations. Recognizing transoceanic textual and material dimensionalities within a globalized American literary history is not to assign to all texts some kind of American identity, nor is it to claim some kind of American possession of them. What these texts and the connections between them reveal instead is the complex and multifaceted ways in which America has been connected to the world.

That story and the way we tell it matters because the tools we use to navigate through the world determine the way we interact with the humans and non-humans who live in it. Tingley's exploration of wave-piloting arrives at the intersection of anthropology and neuroscience when she observes that memory and orientation are located in the same part of the human brain. The neuroscientist Edward Tolman argued that "broad cognitive maps," for instance, lead to empathy, while narrow ones lead to "dangerous hates of outsiders" that range from "discrimination against minorities to world conflagrations." Anthropologists similarly insist that the cognitive maps we produce of our environment are both spatial and social, determining the way we see and respond to others; as Tingley summarizes it, "people's physical environment—and how they habitually move through it—may shape their social relationships and how those ties may in turn influence their orienteering."[27] Our task should be to locate and analyze the multidimensional materialities of historical, cultural, and literary networks so that we might tell a story about what the connections between America and the rest of the world have been, what they are now, and what they might be in the future.

{ ENDNOTES }

Introduction

1. For a concise account of the elephant, see George G. Goodwin, "The Crowninshield Elephant," *Natural History* (Oct. 1951), www.naturalhistorymag.com. Goodwin, however, confuses this first elephant with another elephant named Old Bet, who was purchased by Hachaliah Bailey of eventual Barnum and Bailey fame. See John and Alice Durant, *Pictorial History of the American Circus* (New York: A. S. Barnes, 1957), 24–5, who note that the first elephant (the "Crowninshield" elephant who arrived on the *America*) was sold to a "Philadelphian named Owen" for $10,000 (24). See Luther S. Luedtke, *Nathaniel Hawthorne and the Romance of the Orient* (Bloomington: Indiana Univ. Press, 1989) for an account of Hawthorne's reading of his father's logbooks (5–12). This and other Hathorne logbooks are held at the Essex Institute. While several historical and Salem-focused websites repeat the beer-drinking story, I have otherwise been unable to substantiate it.

2. Kendall A. Johnson, *The New Middle Kingdom: China and the Early American Romance of Free Trade* (Baltimore: Johns Hopkins Univ. Press, 2017), 14.

3. Wai Chee Dimock, *Through Other Continents: American Literature across Deep Time* (Princeton: Princeton Univ. Press, 2009); Dimock and Lawrence Buell, eds. *Shades of the Planet: American Literature as World Literature* (Princeton: Princeton Univ. Press, 2007); Lisa Lowe, *The Intimacies of Four Continents* (Durham: Duke Univ. Press, 2015); Paul Giles, *Antipodean American: Australasia and the Constitution of U.S. Literature* (New York: Oxford Univ. Press, 2013); Stephen Shapiro, *The Culture and Commerce of the Early American Novel: Reading the Atlantic World-System* (University Park: Pennsylvania State Univ. Press, 2008); Caroline F. Levander, *Where is American Literature?* (Malden, MA: Wiley Blackwell, 2013). Although it is not specifically focused on American literature, see also Sahar Amer and Laura Doyle's "Introduction" to the forum "Reframing Postcolonial and Global Studies in the Longer *Durée*," *PMLA* 130.2 (Mar. 2015), 331–5. For a recent discussion of these concerns within the field of early American history, see Joshua Piker's post on Karin Wulf's electronic project of tracking #VastEarlyAmerica and a defense of the field's geographic breadth; "Getting Lost," *Uncommon Sense—The Blog*, Omohundro Institute for Early American History and Culture, blog.oieach.wm.edu/getting-lost/

4. For Pacific studies, see David Igler, *The Great Ocean: Pacific Worlds from Captain Cook to the Gold Rush* (New York: Oxford Univ. Press, 2013); Matt K. Matsuda, *Pacific Worlds: A History of Seas, Peoples, and Cultures* (Cambridge: Cambridge Univ. Press, 2012); David Armitage and Alison Bashford, eds., *Pacific Histories: Ocean, Land, People* (Houndmills: Palgrave Macmillan, 2014); Epeli Hau'ofa, *We Are the Ocean* (Honolulu: Univ. of Hawai'i Press, 2008); Gary K. Okihiro, "Toward a Pacific Civilization," *The Japanese Journal of American Studies* 18 (2007), 73–85; O. H. K. Spate, *The Spanish Lake* (Minneapolis: Univ. of Minnesota Press, 1979) and *Monopolists and Freebooters* (Minneapolis: Univ. of Minnesota Press, 1983); Bernard Smith, *Imagining the Pacific: In the Wake of the Cook Voyages* (New Haven:

Yale Univ. Press, 1992) and *European Vision and the South Pacific* 2nd ed. (New Haven: Yale Univ. Press, 1989); Patty O'Brien, *The Pacific Muse: Exotic Femininity and the Colonial Pacific* (Seattle: Univ. of Washington Press, 2006); and Lee Wallace, *Sexual Encounters: Pacific Texts Modern Sexualities* (Ithaca: Cornell Univ. Press, 2003). For oceanic studies, see Philip E. Steinberg, *The Social Construction of the Ocean* (Cambridge: Cambridge Univ. Press, 2001) and "Of Other Seas: Metaphors and Materialities in Maritime Regions," *Atlantic Studies* 10.2 (2013), 156–69; Hester Blum, "Introduction: Oceanic Studies," *Atlantic Studies* 10.2 (2013), 151–5 and *The View from the Mast-Head: Maritime Imagination and Antebellum American Sea Narratives* (Chapel Hill: Univ. of North Carolina Press, 2008). Crucial recent transoceanic work includes Elizabeth DeLoughrey, *Routes and Roots: Navigating Caribbean and Pacific Island Literatures* (Honolulu: Univ. of Hawai'i Press, 2007); Kate Fullagar, ed., *The Atlantic World in the Antipodes: Effects and Transformations since the Eighteenth Century* (Newcastle upon Tyne: Cambridge Scholars, 2012); Christine Skwiot, *The Purposes of Paradise: U.S. Tourism and Empire in Cuba and Hawai'i* (Philadelphia: Univ. of Pennsylvania Press, 2010); Joyce Chaplin, *Round About the Earth: Circumnavigation from Magellan to Orbit* (New York: Simon and Schuster, 2012); Matthew Guterl and Christine Skwiot, "Atlantic and Pacific Crossings: Race, Empire, and the 'Labor Problem' in the Late Nineteenth Century," *Radical History Review* 91 (Winter 2005), 40–61; Jerry H. Bentley, Renate Bridenthal, Kären Wigen, eds., *Seascapes: Maritime Histories, Littoral Cultures, and Transoceanic Exchanges* (Honolulu: Univ. of Hawai'i Press, 2007); and Brian Russell Roberts and Michelle Ann Stephens, eds., *Archipelagic American Studies* (Durham: Duke Univ. Press, 2017). Useful histories of early U.S.–Asia trade include James R. Fichter, *So Great a Proffit: How the East Indies Trade Transformed Anglo-American Capitalism* (Cambridge: Harvard Univ. Press, 2010); Jonathan Goldstein, *Philadelphia and the China Trade 1682–1846: Commercial, Cultural, and Attitudinal Effects* (University Park: Pennsylvania State Univ. Press, 1978); Caroline Frank, *Objectifying China, Imagining America: Chinese Commodities in Early America* (Chicago: Univ. of Chicago Press, 2011). Jorge Cañizares-Esguerra and Antonio Benítez-Rojo have begun to point transoceanically by recognizing the ways in which the administrative coordinates and material networks of early modern empires linked multiple oceans—as Spain, for example, moved resources extracted from both the Atlantic and the Pacific through Mexico and the Caribbean. Jorge Cañizares-Esguerra, *How to Write the History of the New World: Histories, Epistemologies, and Identities in the Eighteenth-Century Atlantic World* (Stanford: Stanford Univ. Press, 2001), 219, and Antonio Benítez-Rojo, *The Repeating Island: The Caribbean and the Postmodern Perspective*, trans. James E. Maraniss (Durham: Duke Univ. Press, 1992), 7. Paul Van Dyke offers an excellent transnational history of Chinese trade during this period in *The Canton Trade: Life and Enterprise on the China Coast, 1700–1845* (Hong Kong: Hong Kong Univ. Press, 2005). For transpacific studies, see Janet Hoskins and Viet Thanh Nguyen, eds., *Transpacific Studies: Framing an Emerging Field* (Honolulu: Univ. of Hawai'i Press, 2014); Yunte Huang, *Transpacific Displacement: Ethnography, Translation and Intertextual Travel in 20th Century American Literature* (Berkeley: Univ. of California Press, 2002) and *Transpacific Imaginations: History, Literature, Counterpoetics* (2008); and Yuan Shu and Donald E. Pease, eds., *American Studies as Transnational Practice: Turning Toward the Transpacific* (Lebanon, NH: Dartmouth College Press, 2015). Although my focus throughout this book is dominated by English North America, this transoceanic framework can be configured to accommodate more or other languages and hemispheric locations, a possibility I discuss in more detail in the Epilogue.

5. Roberts and Stephens, "Introduction: Archipelagic American Studies: Decontinentalizing the Study of American Culture," in Roberts and Stephens, eds., 9–10.

6. Levander, 18.

7. Bartholomew's image represents only the northernmost portion of South America, but it is worth imagining this map in a way that sustains its strange Pacific–Atlantic interchange across both the northern and southern hemispheres. J. G. Bartholomew, *A Literary and Historical Atlas of North and South America* (1911; London: J. M. Dent & Sons, 1930). I thank Gretchen Woertendyke for first bringing this map to my attention.

8. See Peter Hulme, "Columbus and the Cannibals," in *Colonial Encounters: Europe and the Native Caribbean, 1492–1797* (New York: Routledge, 1992), especially 20–33.

9. James Belich, "Race," in Armitage and Bashford, eds., 263. Nicholas Thomas, *Islanders: The Pacific in the Age of Empire* (New Haven: Yale Univ. Press, 2010), 9–10. Mary Louise Pratt, "Language and the Afterlives of Empire," *PMLA* 130.2 (Mar. 2015), 348.

10. John E. Wills, Jr., "A Very Long Early Modern?: Asia and Its Oceans, 1000–1850," *Pacific Historical Review* 83.2 (2014), 190.

11. Gary Y. Okihiro, *Common Ground: Reimagining American History* (Princeton: Princeton Univ. Press, 2001), 26–7.

12. For literary and cultural scholarship on the early Pacific, see Greg Dening, *Islands and Beaches: Discourses on a Silent Land: Marquesas, 1774–1880* (Honolulu: Univ. Press of Hawai'i, 1980); Jonathan Lamb, *Preserving the Self in the South Seas, 1680–1840* (Chicago: Univ. of Chicago Press, 2001); Vanessa Smith, *Intimate Strangers: Friendship, Exchange, and Pacific Encounters* (Cambridge: Cambridge Univ. Press, 2010); Nicholas Thomas, *Entangled Objects: Exchange, Material Culture, and Colonialism in the Pacific* (Cambridge: Harvard Univ. Press, 1991). None of these works, however, engages with American literary history. For scholarship that incorporates the Pacific into early American literary and cultural contexts, see Paul Giles, *Antipodean America*; as well as Geoffrey Sanborn, *Whipscars and Tattoos: The Last of the Mohicans, Moby-Dick, and the Maori* (New York: Oxford Univ. Press, 2011).

13. Kariann Akemi Yokota, *Unbecoming British: How Revolutionary America Became a Postcolonial Nation* (New York: Oxford Univ. Press, 2014), 205; Rosemarie Zagarri, "The Significance of the 'Global Turn' for the Early American Republic: Globalization in the Age of Nation-Building." *Journal of the Early Republic* 31.1 (2011), 4–5.

14. See, for example, recent historical studies by Paul W. Mapp, *The Elusive West and the Contest for Empire* (Chapel Hill: Univ. of North Carolina Press, 2011); Claudio Saunt, *West of the Revolution: An Uncommon History of 1776* (New York: W.W. Norton, 2014); and Igler, *The Great Ocean*.

15. Jim Egan, for example, has identified a profound engagement with the East in the texts of such colonial writers as John Smith and Anne Bradstreet, while Geoffrey Sanborn has brought to light the Pacific influences on and context for James Fenimore Cooper's otherwise landlocked novel *Last of the Mohicans*. See Jim Egan, *Oriental Shadows: The Presence of the East in Early American Literature* (Columbus: Ohio State Univ. Press, 2011); Sanborn, *Whipscars and Tattoos*.

16. Michael A. McDonnell, "Facing Empire: Indigenous Histories in Comparative Perspective," in Fullagar, ed., 220.

17. Kathleen Wilson, *The Island Race: Englishness, Empire, and Gender in the Eighteenth Century* (New York: Routledge, 2003), 51, 56. C. A. Bayly, *Imperial Meridian: The British Empire and the World, 1780–1830* (London: Longman, 1989), 8.

18. Philip E. Steinberg, "Of Other Seas: Metaphors and Materialities in Maritime Regions," *Atlantic Studies* 10.2 (2013), 157, 158; Kären Wigen, "Introduction" to Forum on "Oceans of History," *American Historical Review* 111.3 (June 2006), 721. See also Alison Games, who remarks that the "land-based" or even "landlocked" character of "Atlantic history that many historians produce is rarely centered around the ocean, and the ocean is rarely relevant to the project"; "Atlantic History: Definitions, Challenges, and Opportunities," *American Historical Review* 111.3 (2006), 745. This Atlantic model limitation might be extended to its Pacific and Indian Ocean counterparts, each of which likewise positions a major ocean at the liquid center of a transnational, transcultural, and multilingual world, rimmed and held together by a container of land. For Pacific studies see, for example, Arif Dirlik, *What Is In a Rim? Critical Perspectives on the Pacific Region Idea* (Lanham, MD: Rowan and Littlefield, 1998) and Huang, *Transpacific*. For Indian Ocean studies, see Shanti Moorthy and Ashraf Jamal, *Indian Ocean Studies: Cultural, Social, and Political Perspectives* (New York: Routledge, 2009).

19. Felipe Fernández-Armesto uses this term to describe those great modern European maritime empires that, as he observes, really occupy the western edges of Europe at the Atlantic's shore, though the term might also be usefully extended to describe the models of study for other oceanic worlds; see "Empires in Their Global Context, ca. 1500 to ca. 1800," in *The Atlantic in Global History, 1500–2000*, eds. Jorge Cañizares-Esguerra and Erik R. Seeman (Upper Saddle River, NJ: Pearson, 2007), 97. For another critique of land-based global perspectives, see Martin W. Lewis and Kären Wigen, *The Myth of Continents: A Critique of Metageography* (Berkeley: University of California Press, 1997). Steinberg refers to the "complex, four-dimensional materiality" of oceanic space ("Of Other Seas," 156).

20. Adam McKeown, "Movement," in Armitage and Bashford, eds., 143.

21. Games, 746. Damon Ieremia Salesa accurately notes that "histories of empire and colonialism entwined the Antipodes and the Atlantic from the beginning and ever since." But while "[t]he Antipodes and the Atlantic share some deep histories...they have only a shallow shared historiography." "Afterword: Opposite Footers," in Kate Fullagar, ed., 283, 284.

22. Okihiro, *Common Ground*, 16.

23. Paul Gilroy's *The Black Atlantic: Modernity and Double-Consciousness* (Cambridge: Harvard Univ. Press, 1995) and Ian Baucom's *Specters of the Atlantic: Finance Capital, Slavery, and the Philosophy of History* (Durham: Duke Univ. Press, 2005) might be said to engage with a more aquatic Atlantic. For scholarship focused on slavery in the West and the Pacific, see Stacey Smith's *Freedom's Frontier: California and the Struggle over Unfree Labor, Emancipation, and Reconstruction* (Chapel Hill: Univ. of North Carolina Press, 2013), Jean Pfaelzer's forthcoming *Of Human Bondage: The History of Slavery in California* (Berkeley: Univ. of California Press), and Greg Grandin's *The Empire of Necessity: Slavery, Freedom, and Deception in the New World* (New York: Metropolitan Books, 2014), which more implicitly points to the Atlantic slave trade's transoceanic as well as hemispheric reach. Lisa Lowe's *Intimacies of Four Continents* more explicitly situates slavery in global terms.

24. Etsuko Taketani, *The Black Pacific Narrative: Geographic Imaginings of Race and Empire between the World Wars* (Hanover: Dartmouth College Press, 2014).

25. Salesa, "The Pacific in Indigenous Time," in Armitage and Bashford, eds., 32. Hau'ofa, *We Are the Ocean*, 28.

26. Salesa, "The Pacific," 32, 45.

27. Matsuda, 3, 2.

28. McKeown, 144.

29. DeLoughrey, *Roots and Routes*, 2.

30. See Goodwin. See also Jennifer L. Mosier, "The Big Attraction: The Circus Elephant and American Culture," *Journal of American Culture* 22.2 (Summer 1999), Humanities Full Text.

31. Margaret Cohen, *The Novel and the Sea* (Princeton: Princeton Univ. Press, 2010).

32. Sven Beckert, *Empire of Cotton: A Global History* (New York: Knopf, 2015), 33, 35, 37, 53. We might add to this list Magellan's 1519–22 circumnavigation of the globe and crossing of the Pacific, which finally yoked together the planet's oceans. While Beckert's focus of course is the Indian cloth trade and its role in the emerging empire of cotton, his global model works equally well to frame the development of global commercial relations and inter-imperial rivalries over a host of Asian products (spices, furniture, porcelain, and tea as well as fabrics that include silks and cotton) in the later eighteenth century.

33. Bernard Smith, *Imagining the Pacific: In the Wake of the Cook Voyages* (New Haven: Yale Univ. Press, 1992), 208, 209.

34. Lowe, 6, 102.

35. Beckert, 30; Lowe, 109. Beckert points out that many of the coercive rules and accounting systems associated with modern industry were developed in colonies and on slave plantations (as well as, I would add, on ships and in the merchant companies that owned them), 44–5. See also Ian Baucom's *Specters of the Atlantic* on the entanglements of slavery and finance capital.

36. Cohen, 3, 14.

37. O'Brien, 10.

38. See, for example, the North American-focused work of Jennifer Baker, *Securing the Commonwealth: Debt, Speculation, and Writing in the Making of Early America* (Baltimore: Johns Hopkins Univ. Press, 2005); Karen Weyler, *Intricate Relations: Sexual and Economic Desire in American Fiction, 1789–1814* (Iowa City: Univ. of Iowa Press, 2004); and Shapiro; see as well the British-, French- and/or Atlantic-focused studies of Mary Poovey, *Genres of the Credit Economy: Mediating Value in Eighteenth and Nineteenth-Century Britain* (Chicago: Univ. of Chicago Press, 2008) and *A History of the Modern Fact: Problems of Knowledge in the Sciences of Wealth and Society* (Chicago: Univ. of Chicago Press, 1998); Catherine Gallagher, *The Body Economic: Life, Death, and Sensation in Political Economy and the Victorian Novel* (Princeton: Princeton Univ. Press, 2008); Christopher L. Miller, *The French Atlantic Triangle: Literature and Culture of the Slave Trade* (Durham: Duke Univ. Press, 2007); and Baucom.

39. See the 1774 New York Rivingon edition of Hawkesworth, including the excellent version of the image online from the John Carter Brown Library via Luna Imaging: jcb. lunaimaging.com/luna/servlet/detail/JCB~1~1~2914~4690002:Dramatic-Interlude-&-Dance-given-by

40. Fichter, 220, 221.

41. Joyce Chaplin, "The Pacific Before Empire, c.150-1800," in *Pacific Histories: Ocean, Land, People*, eds. David Armitage and Alison Bashford (Basingstoke: Palgrave Macmillan, 2014), 57. Kathleen Donegan, *Seasons of Misery: Catastrophe and Colonial Settlement in Early America* (Philadelphia: Univ. of Pennsylvania Press, 2014).

42. Andy Martin has suggested how intertwined violence and pleasure were during the revolutionary age, and how much that imagination depended on Pacific–Atlantic exchanges.

As Martin reminds us, the Marquis de Sade, who read Pacific travel narratives while imprisoned in the Bastille amidst revolutionary uprisings, always insisted that "without violence there is no pleasure" (142). "Introduction: Surfing the Revolution: The Fatal Impact of the Pacific on Europe," *Eighteenth-Century Studies* 41.2 (Winter 2008), 141–7.

43. Jorge Cañizares-Esguerra, *Puritan Conquistadors: Iberianizing the Atlantic, 1550–1700* (Stanford: Stanford Univ. Press, 2006), 232, 233.

44. Matsuda, 5; Salesa, 49; Hauʻofa, *We Are the Ocean*, 66–7.

45. Lon Kurashige, Madeline Y. Hsu, and Yujin Yaguchi, "Introduction: Conversations on Transpacific History," *Pacific Historical Review* 83.2 (May 2014), 184, 187. Matsuda has elsewhere pointed out the connections between new modes of narrating history and new geographic understandings of the Pacific as a "'civilization without a center,' an Oceanic space of movement, transit, and migration in a *longue durée* of local peoples and broad interactions, what Rob Wilson and Arif Dirlik call 'heteroglossic spatiality'" ("The Pacific" 769). The essay collection *Pacific Histories*, edited by Armitage and Bashford, resists the terrestrializing effect of a rimlands approach to Pacific studies while also countering narrative anxiety about coherence by shifting between an assembled "wealth of historiographies and the particularities of experiences and practices" (Matsuda, "Afterword," 327). The collection *Remembrance of Pacific Pasts* likewise responds to the narrative as well as geographic challenges of Pacific history, acknowledging the confrontation of multiple voices and perspectives with the compulsion for coherent and progressive narrative histories; see Robert Borofsky, "An Invitation," in *Remembrance of Pacific Pasts: An Invitation to Remake History*, Robert Borofsky, ed. (Honolulu: Univ. of Hawaiʻi Press, 2000), 1–30.

46. Paul Carter, *The Road to Botany Bay: An Exploration of Landscape and History* (Chicago: Univ. of Chicago Press, 1987), xvi, xxii–xxiii.

47. Geraldine Heng, "Reinventing Race, Colonization, and Globalisms across Deep Time: Lessons from the Longer *Durée*" *PMLA* 130.2 (Mar. 2015), 360.

48. Mary Poovey has expertly explored the Enlightenment split between literary and scientific writing that aligned economic genres with the latter. The long-term effects of this division blind us to the literary features of financial forms and genres as well as to the economic features of literary texts. See *A History of the Modern Fact*.

49. Peter Coclanis, "ReOrienting Atlantic History: The Global Dimensions of the 'Western' Rice Trade," in Jorge Cañizares-Esguerra and Erik R. Seeman, eds., 117. Martine Van Ittersum and Jaap Jacobs, "Are We All Global Historians Now? An Interview with David Armitage," *Itinerario* 36.2 (Aug. 2012), 25.

50. Okihiro, *Common Ground*, 17.

Chapter 1

1. Neil Gaiman, *American Gods* (New York: William Morrow, 2011), 285. I am citing the 10th anniversary edition of this novel, which presents the author's preferred text.

2. David Igler, "Diseased Goods: Global Exchanges in the Eastern Pacific Basin, 1770–1850," *The American Historical Review* 109.3 (2004), 695. Igler is here extending to the Pacific Karen Kupperman's argument that the Atlantic "was international before it was national"; see Karen Ordahl Kupperman, "International at the Creation: Early Modern American History," in *Rethinking American History in a Global Age*, ed. Thomas Bender (Berkeley: Univ. of California Press, 2002), 105.

3. Margaret Cohen, *The Novel and the Sea* (Princeton: Princeton Univ. Press, 2010), 14. Cohen is referring here to an observation by Hegel.

4. See Joyce Chaplin, *Round About the Earth: Circumnavigation from Magellan to Orbit* (New York: Simon and Schuster, 2012) for the history of efforts, early and late, to round the earth. Chaplin notes that Balboa was likely preceded in seeing the Pacific by other Europeans on the António de Abreu expedition to the Spice Islands in 1511, but in the absence of any written description, Balboa has received credit (14).

5. Juan De Fuca was a Greek mariner who sailed for Spain in 1592, and whose narrative was published in 1625; Bartholomew de Fonte's Spanish expedition sailed in 1640, and his account appeared in 1708. For more on these figures and a history of efforts to locate the Northwest Passage, see Glyn Williams, *Voyages of Delusion: The Quest for the Northwest Passage* (New Haven: Yale Univ. Press, 2003).

6. Many of these narratives have, however, been studied in the context of various European national traditions (on the English, French, Spanish, or Russian Pacific, for example). Despite the fact that the texts themselves were in transnational dialogue with each other when they were initially published and translated, there has as yet been little work done to integrate these texts into a transnational literary history of the period. Recent scholarship on eighteenth-century British travel narratives to the Pacific place that writing thoughtfully in the context of global commerce without, however, considering its production and circulation in a global literary context; see, for example, Jonathan Lamb, *Preserving the Self in the South Seas, 1680–1840* (Chicago: Univ. of Chicago Press, 2001) and Anna Neill, *British Discovery Literature and the Rise of Global Commerce* (London: Palgrave, 2002). Paul Giles considers some of these narratives in his globalized approach to American literature; *Antipodean America: Australasia and the Constitution of U.S. Literature* (New York: Oxford Univ. Press, 2014). Neil Rennie places British literature on the Pacific in dialogue with some French texts in *Far-Fetched Facts: The Literature of Travel and the Idea of the South Seas* (Oxford: Clarendon Press, 1995). Hester Blum discusses several in her work on sea narratives in *The View from the Mast-Head: Maritime Imagination and Antebellum American Sea Narratives* (Chapel Hill: Univ. of North Carolina Press, 2008). Cynthia Kleker assembles interdisciplinary approaches to eighteenth-century Pacific material in Kleker, ed. "Reconstructing History: Literature, History, and Anthropology in the Pacific," Spec. issue of *Eighteenth Century* 49.3 (2008), 193–6. J. Kommers reads these narratives in relation to the history of travel writing as a genre in "The Significance of 18th-Century Literature about the Pacific for the Development of Travel Literature," *Bijdrage tot de Tall-, Land- en Volkenkunde* 144.4 (1988), 478–93.

7. Among recent hemispheric approaches to early American literature, Cañizares-Esguerra alone points toward the possibility of a transoceanic extension when he notes that "even a wide Atlantic perspective could be distorting, for most of the early modern European empires were in fact global ones. There is indeed no reason not to fold the Spanish American Pacific into the geographies of the Spanish American Atlantic, since the colonization of the Philippines was directed from and through Mexico, not Madrid"; *Puritan Conquistadors: Iberianizing the Atlantic, 1550–1700* (Stanford: Stanford Univ. Press, 2006), 219.

8. Matt K. Matsuda, *Pacific Worlds: A History of Seas, Peoples, and Cultures* (Cambridge: Cambridge Univ. Press, 2012), 116.

9. John Gascoigne's recent history counteracts this nationalizing impulse by ably interweaving the stories of British, French, Spanish, Dutch, and Russian voyages to the

Pacific. *Encountering the Pacific in the Age of Enlightenment* (Cambridge: Cambridge Univ. Press, 2014). See also O. H. K. Spate, *Paradise Lost and Found* (Minneapolis: Univ. of Minnesota Press, 1988) and *Monopolists and Freebooters* (Minneapolis: Univ. of Minnesota Press, 1983).

10. Gwenn A. Miller, *Kodiak Kreol: Communities of Empire in Early Russian America* (Ithaca: Cornell Univ. Press, 2010), 22–4. Miller points out that although the indigenous peoples of the Kodiak and Aleutian islands are often referred to collectively as Aleuts, they are distinct peoples. Kodiak islanders are the Alutiiq and those of the Aleutian chain are Unangan (1).

11. Other land routes to the Pacific at this period included the Scot Alexander Mackenzie, who achieved the first transcontinental crossing to the Pacific in 1793, and Lewis and Clark, who would arrive overland at the Pacific in 1805. For an account of the American West during this period, see Claudio Saunt, *West of the Revolution: An Uncommon History of 1776* (New York: Norton, 2014).

12. Iris H. W. Engstrand, "Spain's Role in Pacific Exploration during the Age of Enlightenment," in *Enlightenment and Exploration in the North Pacific, 1741–1805*, eds. Stephen Haycox, James Barnett, and Caedmon Liburd (Seattle: Univ. of Washington Press, 1997), 30.

13. [John Callander, ed.], *Terra Australis Cognita: or, Voyages to the Terra Australis, or Southern Hemisphere, during the Sixteenth, Seventeenth, and Eighteenth Centuries*, 3 vols., (Edinburgh, 1766), 1, n.p.

14. Gillian Russell, "An 'entertainment of oddities': Fashionable Sociability and the Pacific in the 1770s," in *A New Imperial History: Culture, Identity and Modernity in Britain and the Empire, 1770–1840*, ed. Kathleen Wilson (Cambridge: Cambridge Univ. Press, 2004), 48.

15. More extensive and more specialized archival work than I have been able to accomplish for this project may well bring a much more detailed reception history to light.

16. James Rivington, "Whosoever would purchase the English edition of *The Late Voyage Round the World*," Mar. 16, 1774. *America's Historical Imprints*, Readex.

17. James Kirker, *Adventures to China: Americans in the Southern Oceans, 1792–1812* (New York: Oxford Univ. Press, 1970), 25.

18. William Fordyce Mavor, *An Historical Collection of the Most Celebrated Voyages, Travels, and Discoveries*, 14 vols. (Philadelphia, 1802), vii, viii.

19. Anthony Payne, "The Publication and Readership of Voyage Journals in the Age of Vancouver, 1730–1830," in Haycox, Barnett, and Liburd, eds., 180.

20. "Epitome of Captain Wallis's Voyage Around the World," *The Royal American Magazine, or Universal Repository of Instruction and Amusement* (Jan.–Feb., Apr. 1774), *American Periodicals Series Online*, ProQuest; "An account of the new Northern Archipelago, lately discovered by the Russians," *The Pennsylvania Magazine; or, American Monthly Museum* (Jan. 1776), *American Periodicals Series Online*, ProQuest; "On the Impracticability of a Passage into the Pacific Ocean Round the N.W. Part of America," *The New-Haven Gazette, and the Connecticut Magazine* (Aug. 17, 1786), *American Periodicals Series Online*, ProQuest; "Circumnavigator," *The Massachusetts Magazine: or, Monthly Museum of Knowledge and Rational Entertainment* (Mar. 1789), *American Periodicals Series Online*, ProQuest. Many similar (and in some cases identical) articles appeared as well in British periodicals at the time.

21. France's plan for the journey of La Pérouse, for example, may have deliberately emphasized the scientific elements in order to hide from Britain France's interest in fur trade possibilities along North America's northwest coast and in China:see John Dunmore, "Introduction," in *The Journal of Jean-François de Galaup de la Pérouse, 1785–1788*, 2 vols., trans. and ed. John Dunmore (London: The Hakluyt Society, 1994), I.xxv.

22. John Mack, *The Sea: A Cultural History* (London: Reaktion Books, 2011), 15.

23. Saunt, 44.

24. James Cook, *Captain Cook's Three Voyages to the Pacific Ocean. The first performed in the years 1768, 1769, 1770 and 1771: the second in 1772, 1773, 1774 and 1775: the third and last in 1776, 1777, 1778 1779 and 1780.* 2 vols., abridged (Boston, 1797), II.319.

25. James R. Gibson, *Otter Skins, Boston Ships, and China Goods: The Maritime Fur Trade of the Northwest Coast 1785–1841* (Seattle: Univ. of Washington Press, 1992), 22–3.

26. Cook, *Captain Cook's Three Voyages*, II.343.

27. Cook, *Captain Cook's Three Voyages*, II.319–20.

28. Gibson, 57, 49. This description was made by Louis Choris, the artist who accompanied the Russian-sponsored voyage led by the German navigator Otto von Kotzebue into the Pacific from 1815 to 1818. Otto was the son of playwright August von Kotzebue, whose play *Count Benyowsky* figures centrally in my reading of Charles Brocken Brown's *Ormond* in Chapter 5, and who wrote several plays about adventures in the Pacific.

29. George Vancouver, *A Voyage of Discovery to the North Pacific Ocean, and Round the World*, 3 vols. (London, 1798), I.408, I.348, I.375. As Gibson's history makes clear, a trade glut and a decrease in furs led to a rapid dwindling of profits beginning in the 1820s and by the 1840s the fur trade was depleted and abandoned; see Gibson, 66, 82.

30. This temporal duration is of course matched with a spatial expansiveness, and the middle portions that are elided in the already long titles mentioned here typically offered a brief list of the most important or interesting regions visited during the course of the voyage.

31. J. Kommers discusses the tension between narration and description in Pacific travel texts, but leaves out of consideration the element of time that I am associating with each of these modes (488–90).

32. Gérard Genette, *Narrative Discourse: An Essay in Method*, trans. Jane E. Lewin (Ithaca: Cornell Univ. Press, 1980), 87–8.

33. Peter Brooks, *Reading for the Plot: Design and Intention in Narrative* (New York: Knopf, 1984), 10, 44.

34. Anne M. Thell, *Minds in Motion: Imagining Empiricism in Eighteenth-Century British Travel Literature* (Lewisburg: Bucknell Univ. Press, 2017), 88; see Genette, 166.

35. Thell, 22, citing Daniel Defoe, *A New Voyage Round the World* (London: A. Bettesworth, 1724), 3.

36. Callander, vii; Vancouver, I.xxix; James Burney, *A Chronological History of the Discoveries in the South Sea or Pacific Ocean*, 4 vols. (London, 1803), IV.506; John Turnbull, *A Voyage Round the World, in the Years 1800, 1801, 1802, 1803, and 1804* (Philadelphia, 1810), 6.

37. Neil Rennie, "The Point Venus 'Scene,'" in *Science and Exploration in the Pacific: European Voyages to Southern Oceans in the Eighteenth Century*, ed. Margarette Lincoln (Suffolk: Boydell Press, 1998), 137. For more on Hawkesworth's version of Cook's narrative, see Rennie, *Far-Fetched Facts*, 94–108 and Carol E. Percy, "In the Margins: Dr. Hawkesworth's Editorial Emendations to the Language of Captain Cook's Voyages," *English Studies* 77.6 (1996), 549–78.

38. John Hawkesworth, *An Account of the Voyages Undertaken by the Order of His Present Majesty for Making Discoveries in the Southern Hemisphere*, 3 vols. (London, 1773), I.vii.

39. Travel narratives have long been seen as an important early source for novelistic narrative. My interest here is in these two genres' participation in a protracted and expectant narrative temporality that is shared by contemporaneous developments in mathematical and numerical thinking. For other considerations of the novel in relation to political economy, see James Thompson, *Models of Value: Eighteenth-Century Political Economy and the Novel*, (Durham: Duke Univ. Press, 1996) and Mary Poovey, *Genres of the Credit Economy: Mediating Value in Eighteenth- and Nineteenth-Century Britain* (Chicago: Univ. of Chicago Press, 2008).

40. Thell, 155, 177.

41. Alan Taylor, *American Colonies* (New York: Penguin, 2001), 451.

42. Callander, 11, 12, 7. *Terra Australis Cognita* represents what Jorge Cañizares-Esguerra calls "philosophical travel writing" which, unlike earlier travel writing, established its authenticity through its internal coherence rather than through the social status of eyewitnesses. Brosses's collection also made a philosophical argument on behalf of a commercial colonialism that would be "based on trade and commercial exchange and committed to the scientific study of exotic places, rather than their destruction"; *How to Write the History of the New World: Histories, Epistemologies, and Identities in the Eighteenth-Century Atlantic World* (Stanford: Stanford Univ. Press, 2001), 26.

43. James Colnett, *A Voyage to the South Atlantic and Round Cape Horn into the Pacific Ocean* (London, 1798), xv, 24.

44. Turnbull, 5.

45. Vancouver, I.i, I.v.

46. Hawksworth, n.p.

47. Dalrymple, *An Historical Collection of the Several Voyages and Discoveries in the South Pacific Ocean*, 2 vols. (London, 1770), I.xvii, I.v–vi, I.xxi.

48. Howard T. Fry, *Alexander Dalrymple (1737–1808) and the Expansion of British Trade* (London: Frank Cass & Co., 1970), 123.

49. Dalrymple, I.xxvi, I.xxvii.

50. Vancouver, II.498, II.502–3, II.498.

51. Fry, 124.

52. Hawkesworth, xvii.

53. Lorraine Daston, *Classical Probability in the Enlightenment* (Princeton: Princeton Univ. Press, 1988), 115.

54. Hawkesworth, vii.

55. Jonathan Lamb, "Minute Particulars and the Representation of South Pacific Discovery," *Eighteenth-Century Studies* 29.3 (1995), 291.

56. Daston, 115.

57. Jonathan Lamb, Vanessa Smith, and Nicholas Thomas, eds., "Introduction," to Part One: Adventurers and Explorers, in *Exploration and Exchange: A South Seas Anthology, 1680–1900* (Chicago: Univ. of Chicago Press, 2000), xvi, xx.

58. Cohen, 68.

59. Cohen, 58.

60. Lisa Lowe, *The Intimacies of Four Continents* (Durham: Duke Univ. Press, 2015), 14.

Chapter 2

1. William Moulton, *A Concise Extract, from the Sea Journal of William Moulton* (Utica, 1804), 101. See Greg Grandin, *The Empire of Necessity: Slavery, Freedom, and Deception in the New World* (New York: Metropolitan Books, 2014), 133–4, for a description of Masafuera, the seal trade, and Delano's role in it. It should also be noted that although the English Selkirk is often privileged as Crusoe's prototype, his was only one of many earlier castaway stories—set in the Indian, Pacific, and Atlantic oceans—on which Defoe's story is likely based. See Srinivas Aravamudan, "East-West Fiction as World Literature: The *Hayy* Problem Reconsidered," *Eighteenth-Century Studies* 47.2 (Winter 2014), 195–231; and Michelle Burnham, "Introduction" to *The Female American*, by Anonymous, 2nd ed., Burnham and James Freitas, eds. (Peterborough, ON: Broadview Press, 2014), 14–16.

2. Jonathan Franzen, "Farther Away: 'Robinson Crusoe,' David Foster Wallace, and the Island of Solitude," *New Yorker* (Apr. 18, 2011), 94.

3. Franzen, 87. Franzen draws this summary from Gallagher's "The Rise of Fictionality," in *The Novel*, Vol. 1, ed. Franco Moretti (Princeton: Princeton Univ. Press, 2006), 336–63.

4. See especially Catherine Gallagher, *Nobody's Story: The Vanishing Acts of Women Writers in the Marketplace* (Berkeley: Univ. of California Press, 1995) and *The Body Economic: Life, Death, and Sensation in the Victorian Novel* (Princeton: Princeton Univ. Press, 2008). See also Catherine Ingrassia, *Authorship, Commerce, and Gender in Early Eighteenth-Century England: A Culture of Paper Credit* (Cambridge: Cambridge Univ. Press, 1998) and Mary Poovey, *Genres of the Credit Economy: Mediating Value in Eighteenth- and Nineteenth-Century Britain* (Chicago: Univ. of Chicago Press, 2008). To be clear, I'm interested here not in numbers as novelistic content but in numerical calculation as a narratological component. On the more specific appearance of numbers in novels, consider the economist Thomas Piketty's recent attention to the citation of money amounts in novels, which he uses as an index to measure the growing instability of wealth from the nineteenth to the twentieth centuries; Piketty, *Capital in the 21st Century* (Cambridge: Harvard Univ. Press, 2014). See also Ted Underwood, Hoyt Long, and Richard Jean So, who use digital tools to count money references in a large corpus of novels to disprove Piketty's conclusions; "Cents and Sensibility," *Slate* (Dec. 14, 2014), www.slate.com. As Mary Poovey has reminded us, literature and economics shared eighteenth-century origins that became obscured as these were later pried apart into separate disciplinary domains whose division bred defamiliarization (1–7, 417–19). It is also likely the case that the boundary between these disciplines became intensified through the nineteenth-century gendering of public and private space, which would have retroactively obscured even further the reach of numerical knowledge and calculative thinking during this earlier period.

5. Elizabeth Maddock Dillon, "The Original American Novel, or, The American Origin of the Novel," in *A Companion to the Eighteenth-Century Novel and Culture*, eds. Paula R. Backscheider and Catherine Ingrassia (Malden, MA: Blackwell, 2005), 245.

6. Grandin, 132.

7. Daniel Defoe, *The Life and Strange Surprising Adventures of Robinson Crusoe of York, Mariner* (1719; New York: W. W. Norton, 1994), 14. James Cook, *Captain Cook's Three Voyages to the Pacific Ocean*, 2 vols. (Boston, 1797), I.v.

8. On novelistic sympathy and reader identification, see Gallagher (*Nobody's*, 165–74). Mary Poovey discusses reader engagement using the example of Defoe's *Roxana*, describing

the novel's "situation of undecidability" as one in which readers' "evaluation had to take the form of *deliberation*—a self-conscious consideration of evidence, probability, and generalization" that was very much like the process that "made the credit economy work" (120).

9. George Fisher, *The American Instructor: or, Young Man's Best Companion.* 15th ed. (Philadelphia, 1770). Fisher first gained success as the author of a spelling book and co-author of a popular arithmetic book, *Cocker's Arithmetic*, before becoming sole author of *Arithmetick in the Plainest and Most Concise Methods*.

10. Fisher, iii, 379, 380.

11. Michael Walsh, *A New System of Mercantile Arithmetic* (Newburyport, MA, 1801), v, ii, ix.

12. Erastus Root, *An Introduction to Arithmetic for the use of Common Schools* (Norwich, CT, 1795), v. Nicolas Pike, *A New and Complete System of Arithmetic, composed for the use of the citizens of the United States* (Newburyport, MA, 1788), 7. By 1823, James Maginess would proclaim that he "did not undertake the work, because there was an apparent dearth of Arithmetical books in being; no, there appears to be no scarcity of such works; and, indeed, it may by some be considered vanity in him, to suppose, that by adding another Arithmetical work to the already full swelled list, he has contributed much to the advantage or benefit of society; or added any thing material, which can be called new." *A New, Copious, and Complete System of Arithmetic, for the Use of Schools and Counting-Houses, in the United States of America* (Harrisburg [PA], 1821), 3.

13. Walsh, 2nd ed. (1803), vii. Walsh, 3rd. ed. (1804), vii. In subsequent years, Walsh's book changed little in content, but its circulation expanded significantly, with republications in Charleston, South Carolina; Northampton and Salem, Massachusetts; and Pittsburgh and Harrisburg, Pennsylvania.

14. Root, 5.

15. Maginess, 6; Walsh, 3rd ed. (1804), viii; both emphases added.

16. Pike, 58; Root, 11, 66. Compare these problems with the following from Fisher's *American Instructor*, which was preceded by an English edition called simply *The Instructor*, first published in London as early as 1727: "admit a Nobleman hath 30,000 *l. per Annum*, what is his daily Income?" (98).

17. Walsh (1801), 65, 66, 71.

18. Walsh (1801), 196.

19. Walsh (1801), 130.

20. [C. H. Kaufmann], *The Dictionary of Merchandise, and Nomenclature in all Languages; for the Use of Counting-Houses: Containing, the History, Places of Growth, Culture, Use, and Marks of Excellency, of such Natural Productions, as Form Articles of Commerce; with their names in all European languages* (Philadelphia, 1805), 9, 10, 11, 14, 86.

21. [Kaufmann], 171, 11, 318, 232.

22. George William Anderson, *A New, Authentic, and Complete Collection of Voyages Round the World* (1784), 243.

23. The solution to this enticing equation is provided by the fur trade historian James R. Gibson, who explains that the sale of these "best skins" amounted to a return of £90 on an investment of 1 shilling, or a profit of 1800 percent; see Gibson, *Otter Skins, Boston Ships, and China Goods: The Maritime Fur Trade of the Northwest Coast 1785–1841*, (Seattle: Univ. of Washington Press, 1992), 22–3.

24. Jean-François de Galaup de Lapérouse, *The Journal of Jean-François de Galaup de la Pérouse, 1785–1788*, 2 vols., trans. and ed. John Dunmore (London: The Hakluyt Society, 1994), I.225. I have retained the appearance of the author's name as it is printed in each publication title, but have regularized its appearance to the more common La Pérouse throughout this book.

25. See Lorraine Daston, *Classical Probability in the Enlightenment* (Princeton: Princeton Univ. Press, 1988) and Theodore M. Porter, *The Rise of Statistical Thinking, 1820–1900* (Princeton: Princeton Univ. Press, 1986).

26. James Allen Park, *System of the Law of Marine Insurances* (Boston, 1799), 178.

27. Park, iii; Samuel Marshall, *Treatise on the Law of Insurance*, 2 vols. (Philadelphia, 1810), I.4. The opening of Marshall's two-volume tome could easily be mistaken for one of the multivolume collections of Pacific travel writing examined in the previous chapter. Like the volumes of Alexander Dalrymple discussed in the following chapter, Marshall begins by celebrating the navigational achievements of Columbus and Vasco de Gama, but emphasizes their commercial effects on expanding global trade over their nautical feats.

28. Dillon, 246. Dillon aligns the earlier world of romance with a kinship model that was in contrast to the newer logic of contract associated with the novel as well as with an expanding global market facilitated by transoceanic travel and trade. Lorraine Daston explains that the category of the aleatory contract includes "any formal agreement in which chance might figure," including "inheritance expectations and even risky business investments" (19).

29. *Universal Magazine of Knowledge & Pleasure* (June 1, 1748), 285. American Antiquarian Society Historical Periodicals Collection.

30. *Universal Magazine of Knowledge & Pleasure* (June 1, 1748), 286, 287.

31. Walsh (1801), 53.

32. Walsh (1801), 64. In his slightly later, 1821 text, Maginess refers to this not as the rule of three but as the "rule of proportion." For a fuller discussion of the rule of three as an algorithm whose understanding gave Americans a tool for economic independence, see Caitlin Rosenthal, "Numbers for the Innumerate: Everyday Arithmetic and Atlantic Capitalism," *Technology and Culture* 58.2 (Apr. 2017), 531–5.

33. Walsh (1801), 71.

34. There are some exceptions to this general rule, as in this question from the geometrical proportion section of Pike's book that positions the reader-student as the victim of potential fraud: "A Merchant wanting to purchase a cargo of horses for the West-Indies, a Jockey told him he would take all the trouble and expence [*sic*], upon himself, of collecting and purchasing 30 horses for the voyage, if he would give him what the last horse would come to by doubling the whole number by a half-penny, that is, two farthings for the first, four for the second, eight for the third, &c. to which the merchant, thinking he had made a very good bargain, readily agreed: Pray, what did the last horse come to, and what did the horses, one with another, cost the Merchant?" The answer is over £111 million, with the average price per horse over £37,000. Pike, 237.

35. "The Ways to Raise a Fortune; or, the Art of Growing Rich," *Universal Magazine of Knowledge & Pleasure* (June 1, 1748), 250.

36. "Ways to Raise a Fortune," 252.

37. Jackson, 18.

38. John Hamilton Moore, *The New Practical Navigator* (Newburyport, 1799), 166.

39. Thomas Haselden, *The Seaman's Daily Assistant* (Philadelphia, 1777), 126.

40. Haselden, 130.

41. Joseph Huddert, *The Oriental Navigator, or New Directions for Sailing to and from the East Indies* (Philadelphia, 1801), 23, 24.

42. Thomas Dilworth, *The Schoolmasters Assistant: Being a Compendium of Arithmetic, both Practical and Theoretical, In Five Parts*, 17th ed. (Philadelphia, 1773), v.

43. Marshall, 118.

44. Jackson, 75.

45. "Scheme of a Lottery." Handbill for Hartford Woollen Manufactory Lottery (Hartford, 1791), *Early American Imprints*. July 25, 2011.

46. *Wonderful Advantages of Adventuring in the Lottery!* (Boston, 1802), 156. This practice of insuring lottery tickets would later be controlled. In his 1810 insurance manual, Marshall notes that among the insurance frauds formerly practiced, "the most mischievous" was "that upon *lottery chances*, which, long after the passing of the above act, sprung from that spirit of gaming which public lotteries are but too well calculated to excite in the people"; Marshall, 2.

47. *Wonderful*, 170.

48. See Paul K. Alkon, "The Odds against Friday: Defoe, Bayes, and Inverse Probability," in *Probability, Time, and Space in Eighteenth-Century Literature*, ed. Paula R. Backscheider (New York: AMS Press, 1979), 29–61; see also Paul Newsom, *A Likely Story: Probability and Play in Fiction* (New Brunswick: Rutgers Univ. Press, 1988), 83.

49. Isaac Greenwood, "A New Method for Composing a Natural History of Meteors," *Philosophical Transactions of the Royal Society of London* 35 (1727), 397. Cited also in Simon Schaffer, "In Transit: European Cosmologies in the Pacific," in *The Atlantic World in the Antipodes: Effects and Transformations since the Eighteenth Century*, ed. Kate Fullagar (Newcastle upon Tyne: Cambridge Scholars Publishing, 2012), 73.

50. Jesse Molesworth, *Chance and the Eighteenth-Century Novel: Realism, Probability, Magic* (Cambridge: Cambridge Univ. Press, 2010), 9, 28. Scholarship on issues of belief and believability in the novel—especially on what distinguishes the novel's realism from its fictional predecessors and allies—is vast, from Ian Watt's *The Rise of the Novel* (Berkeley: Univ. of California Press, 1957) to Lennard Davis's *Factual Fictions: The Origins of the English Novel* (Philadelphia: Univ. of Pennsylvania Press, 1997), from Nicholas D. Paige's *Before Fiction: The Ancien Régime of the Novel* (Philadelphia: Univ. of Pennsylvania Press, 2011) to Srinivas Aravamudan's *Enlightenment Orientalism: Resisting the Rise of the Novel* (Chicago: Univ. of Chicago Press, 2012), from Michael McKeon's *The Origins of the English Novel, 1600–1740* (Baltimore: Johns Hopkins Univ. Press, 1987) and Barbara Foley's *Telling the Truth: The Theory and Practice of Documentary Fiction* (Ithaca: Cornell Univ. Press, 1986) to Sarah Tindal Kareem's *Eighteenth-Century Fiction and the Reinvention of Wonder* (Oxford: Oxford Univ. Press, 2014). The relationship between calculation and speculation I develop here bears some resemblance to McKeon's dialectic between credulity and skepticism or to Kareem's focus on the coincidence of "marvel and doubt," but both tend to treat these novelistic features as static rather than mobile. I am drawn to Molesworth's study precisely for his attention to the temporal dynamics of plot. The use of numbers in the world of an emerging global capitalism helps us to understand, I'm suggesting, the novel's unique narrative temporality of expectation.

51. Molesworth, 2, 8, 39, 128.

52. Cohen, 75–6.

53. See Jonathan Levy, *Freaks of Fortune: The Emerging World of Capitalism and Risk in America* (Cambridge: Harvard Univ. Press, 2012).

54. E. Fenwick, *The White Kitten* (Boston, 1823). For a discussion of another children's story that connects the Atlantic and Pacific worlds, see Melissa Gniadek, "*Mary Howard's Mark*: Children's Literature and the Scales of Reading the Pacific," *Early American Literature* 50.3 (2015), 797–826.

55. The missionaries who brought Christianity to Hawai'i also brought math. In 1837, William Fowler published in Honolulu a math textbook for use in the island's missionary school. The book's back cover featured both an addition and a multiplication table, and inside its covers was a fascinating numerical table that translated numbers into Hawai'ian words. This mathematics textbook produced for a Hawai'ian missionary school might be thought of as an example of imperialist and commercial pedagogy designed to discipline young Native islanders into the calculative mentality that organized Europe's and America's commercial relations with the rest of the world, helping to produce for them pliable trading partners. William Fowler, *He Helu Kamalii, oia ka mea eao aku aii na keiki, ma na ui ao mua o ke aritemetika* (Honolulu: Mea Pai Palapala na na Misionari, 1837).

56. *Wonderful*, 26.

57. Eliza Houghton, *Practical Arithmetic: Comprising all the Rules for Transacting Business* (Boston, 1810?); Sarah Pollock, *Practical Arithmetic: Comprising all the Rules for Transacting Business* (Boston, 1810?). Manuscript, Mss. Folio Vols. H. American Antiquarian Society. The title pages of each specify that these manuscripts were "*Executed at Mrs. Rowson's Academy*." The page numbers of both texts are identical.

58. It's unclear whether the students might be copying classroom lessons or the contents of existing textbooks. For discussion of a similar 1788 volume by Rebeckah Salisbury, see Caitlin Rosenthal's "Storybook-keepers: Narratives and Numbers in Nineteenth-Century America," *Common-place* 12.3 (Apr. 2012), www.common-place-archives.org

59. Houghton, 79, 78.

60. Pollock, 78.

61. Houghton, 77; Pollock, 77.

62. Rosenthal, "Numbers," 531, 540.

63. Games, tools, and posters designed to help families teach and learn their multiplication tables begin to appear in popular material culture in the nineteenth century. These included sets of flashcards that used rhymes as a mnemonic device, multiplication tables set to music, and rotary multiplication tables that entailed turning a wheel so that the answers appeared in a series of circles. In this sense, mathematical literacy suffused everyday life in the early republic much in the way that Martin Brückner has demonstrated geographical literacy did through the use of maps; see *The Geographic Revolution in Early America: Maps, Literacy, and National Identity* (Chapel Hill: Univ. of North Carolina Press, 2006).

64. The only difference here is that Hardie's school, presumably for male students, also included instruction in navigation. For the Hardie advertisement, see Advertisement in *Weekly Museum* (Oct. 21, 1797); for Bethesda and Pirsson ads, see Advertisement in *Weekly Museum* (May 4, 1799).

65. David Kendal, *The Young Lady's Arithmetic* (Leominster, MA, 1797).

66. Charles Hutton, *A Course of Book-keeping, According to the Method of Single Entry* (Philadelphia, 1801), 4.

67. Joe Albree and Scott H. Brown, "A Valuable Monument of Mathematical Genius: *The Ladies' Diary* (1704–1840)," *Historia Mathematica* 36 (2009), 11. Albree and Brown explain that the periodical began in 1708 and published mathematical material addressed to women from the very beginning, but the sophistication of its mathematical content increased over time.

68. Houghton, 31, 33, 65; Pollock, 31, 33, 65.

69. Kendal, 7.

70. Houghton, 56; Pollock, 56.

71. Gallagher, *Nobody's Story*, 167, 171.

72. Gallagher turns to Hume in order to demonstrate that the hidden feature linking fiction with sympathy is property. As she notes, sympathy for Hume "is complete when it dispenses with its original 'object,' the original sufferer. I sympathize with the sentiments of others by making them mine; and the conditions for such an appropriation must be there at the outset: the person who originally feels them must somehow 'belong' to me. Otherwise my senses will not travel the pathway to sentiment" (*Nobody's Story*, 171).

73. Margaret Cohen, *The Novel and the Sea* (Princeton: Princeton Univ. Press, 2010), 63, 13. Cohen suggests that such heroines are the domestic analogues of Crusoe or other shipwrecked sailors; they simply use a different set of tools—what she calls "a kind of feminine practical reason"—to craftily navigate the treacherous waters of an aristocratic estate or a patriarchal marriage market in the way that Crusoe and other sailors used practical craft to solve the kinds of problems entailed by maritime risk.

74. Cohen, 8, 70–1.

75. Gallagher, "Rise," 347, 346.

76. Dussel maintains that the "*simplification* of complexity" was the primary means by which a European center managed the overwhelming size of the world system that took shape in the long aftermath of Columbus's arrival in the Americas. "Beyond Eurocentrism: The World-System and the Limits of Modernity," in *The Cultures of Globalization*, eds. Fredric Jameson and Masao Miyoshi (Durham: Duke Univ. Press, 1998), 13.

77. I thank my colleague Michael Malone for helping me to recognize this function of tables, particularly in a period without any technological instruments (such as a slide rule) to make computation quicker.

78. Anne Salmond, "'Their Body is Different, Our Body is Different': European and Tahitian Navigators in the 18th Century," *History and Anthropology* 16.2 (June 2005), 169.

79. Gallagher aligns the novel's fictional nobodies with real women because, like the characters in novels, they were legally not in possession of themselves, and served as mechanisms for property transfers between men just as novelistic nobodies permitted the transfer of sympathy between text and reader (194–6). But those men continued to possess themselves in ways that women did not; "the commercial man is imagined to undergo spells of suppositional self-suspension in order to invest profitably and increase his property, but representations of property exchange involving women frequently stress that they lose whatever property they had previously owned" (*Nobody's Story*, 194). Men associated with the world of financial speculation were themselves feminized (and also linked to novel reading) during this period; see Ingrassia, *Authorship, Commerce, and Gender*.

80. Gallagher, "Rise," 347.

Chapter 3

1. Armstrong is presumably referring to Howe's 1970 participation in a Notting Hill march to protest police raids on the Caribbean restaurant, The Mangrove, and to his 1981 role in organizing the 20,000-strong "Black People's March" to protest the tepid police response to a house fire that killed thirteen black youths in New Cross.

2. Footage of the interview can be seen at "Darcus Howe BBC Interview on Riots," youtube.com, uploaded Aug. 9, 2011. Throughout the interview, the "Breaking News" banner on the bottom of the screen reads "UK RIOTS."

3. Sarah Knott, "Narrating the Age of Revolution," *William and Mary Quarterly* 73.1 (Jan. 2016), 3rd ser., 15, 3. For a seminal study of narrative emplotment in history writing, see Hayden White, *The Content of the Form: Narrative Discourse and Historical Representation* (Baltimore: Johns Hopkins Univ. Press, 1987). Similar narrative choices inform the diction of mainstream media, whose use of the term "riot" implied the senselessness of the London uprisings while their description of contemporaneous Syrian uprisings as a revolution cast those events in a heroic mode.

4. The applause Alan Taylor's history of colonial America has received for including a chapter on the Pacific indicates just how unusual it is for this material to be accounted for in historical or literary studies of this period. See Taylor, *American Colonies: The Settling of North America* (New York: Viking, 2001), 444–77, and his subsequent volume, *American Revolutions: A Continental History, 1750–1804* (Ney York: W. W. Norton & Co., 2016). Claudio Saunt's *West of the Revolution: An Uncommon History of 1776* (New York: W. W. Norton & Co., 2015) offers another continental view of the revolutionary period that focuses on the West, but does not venture into the Pacific. The recent joint issue on the American Revolution of the *William and Mary Quarterly*, 3rd ser. 74.4 (Oct. 2017) and the *Journal of the Early Republic* 37.4 (Winter 2017) emphasizes the increasing variety of approaches to and a widening geographical framework for scholarship on the revolution, but similarly never approaches the Pacific.

5. For recent works that put multiple Atlantic revolutions into dialogue with each other, see Wim Klooster, *Revolutions in the Atlantic World: A Comparative History* (New York: New York Univ. Press, 2009); Ashli White, *Encountering Revolution: Haiti and the Making of the Early Republic* (Baltimore: Johns Hopkins Univ. Press, 2010); and Caitlin Fitz, *Our Sister Republics: The United States in an Age of American Revolutions* (New York: Liveright Publishing, 2016). For global approaches to the American Revolution, see David Armitage, *Declaration of Independence: A Global History* (Cambridge: Harvard Univ. Press, 2007); and Steven Pincus, "Placing the American Revolution in Global Context," *Age of Revolutions* (June 20, 2016), ageofrevolutions.com. For a global approach to the revolutionary age writ large, see Armitage and Sanjay Subrahmanyam, eds., *The Age of Revolutions in Global Context, c.1760–1840* (New York: Palgrave Macmillan, 2010).

6. Taylor, *American Revolutions*, 478. Fitz observes that by the 1820s, many North Americans "were openly starting to question their own Declaration's soaring universalist implications" and began to "define a narrower kind of nationalism, one that proclaimed the nation's uniqueness rather than its universality" (11).

7. Armitage and Subrahmanyam, eds., xvi.

8. Hayden White, 172. White insists that although history and fiction are not the same, they both reference "the human experience of time" (175).

9. Ashli White, 6. The "chain" model, White notes, emphasizes linear connections between revolutions (and, one might add, also retroactively yokes colony to nation through the selection of particular texts, events, and figures in order to sustain attention to such themes as democracy or freedom). Ralph Bauer, "Hemispheric Studies," *PMLA* 124.1 (2009), 234–50.

10. Jessica Choppin Roney observes that this focus on 1776 naturalizes both an independence that had yet to be won and a unified nation that did not yet exist; "1776, Viewed from the West," *Journal of the Early Republic* 37.4 (Winter 2017), 656.

11. Robert A. Ferguson, "Still Not Global," *William and Mary Quarterly* 65.2 (Apr. 2008), 365.

12. Taylor, *American Revolutions*, 3, 4, 8.

13. Taylor, *American Revolutions*, 46, 48, 37–8.

14. Fitz, 135, 247. Fitz acknowledges that the U.S. was both anti-colonial in its rhetoric and imperialistic in its actions.

15. Fitz, 244.

16. Serena R. Zabin, "Writing To and From the Revolution," *William and Mary Quarterly* 3rd ser. 74.4 (Oct. 2017), 761. Taylor, *American Revolutions*, 434.

17. Holger Hoock, *Scars of Independence: America's Violent Birth* (New York: Crown, 2017), 12. Hoock insists that in order to understand the Revolution, "we must write the violence, in all its forms, back into the story" we tell of it. The result of this focus is a narrative that, although still fundamentally chronological, manages quite successfully to circumvent narrative triumphalism through means other than spatial enlargement.

18. Fitz, 181. Quoting letter from John Quincy Adams to Thomas Boylston Adams, Apr. 14, 1818, Founders Online, National Archives (founders.archives.gov)

19. This approach also shares an interest in intertwining economics and commerce with politics and conquest as critical contexts for the Revolution; see, for example, C. Dallett Hemphill, "Manners and Class in the Revolutionary Era: A Transatlantic Comparison," *William and Mary Quarterly*, 3rd ser. 63.2 (Apr. 2006), 345–72; and Paul A. Gilje, "Commerce and Conquest in Early American Foreign Relations, 1750–1850," *Journal of the Early Republic* 37.4 (Winter 2017), 735–70.

20. Knott, 21–4.

21. See Howard T. Fry, *Alexander Dalrymple (1737–1808) and the Expansion of British Trade* (London: Frank Cass & Co., 1970), 2–5.

22. Andrew S. Cook, "Alexander Dalrymple: Research, Writing and Publication of the Account," in Alexander Dalrymple, *An Account of the Discoveries made in the South Pacifick Ocean* (1767; repr. Sydney: Hordern House, 1996), 17.

23. Dalrymple, *An Account*, v.

24. Dalrymple, *An Historical Collection of the Several Voyages and Discoveries in the South Pacific Ocean*, 2 vols. (London, 1770), I.xxvi, I.xxvii.

25. Dalrymple, *Historical Collection*, I.xxviii.

26. Dalrymple, *Considerations on the Present State of Affairs between England and America* (London, 1778), 2, 4–5.

27. On British anti-expansionism during this period, see Kate Fullagar, *The Savage Visit: New World People and Popular Culture in Britain, 1710–1795* (Berkeley: Univ. of California Press, 2012); on anti-luxury discourse, see John Sekora, *Luxury: The Concept in Western Thought, Eden to Smollett* (Baltimore: Johns Hopkins Univ. Press, 1977).

28. Dalrymple, *Historical Collection*, I.x.

29. See Michael A. McDonnell, "Facing Empire: Indigenous Histories in Comparative Perspective," in Fullagar, ed., *The Atlantic World in the Antipodes: Effects and Transformations since the Eighteenth Century* (Newcastle upon Tyne: Cambridge Scholars Publishing, 2012), 220.

30. Dalrymple, *Historical Collection*, I.11, II.10.

31. William Coxe, *Account of the Russian Discoveries between Asia and America. To which are added, the Conquest of Siberia, and the History of the Transactions and Commerce between Russia and China* (London, 1780), 73.

32. Saunt, 49.

33. Saunt, 41–4, 50–1. Claim by Aleut is quoted by Saunt from "Report of Ivan Solov'ev to T.I. Schmalev," in *Russian Discoveries in the Pacific Ocean and North America in the 18th Century*, ed. A. I. Andreev (Moscow: cosudarstvennoe izdatel-stovo geographfischeskoi literatury, 1948), 238r–39v.

34. George Vancouver, *A Voyage of Discovery to the North Pacific Ocean, and Round the World*, 3 vols. (London, 1804), III.225; Coxe, 216.

35. Lewis de Bougainville, *A Voyage Round the World*, trans. John Reinhold Forster (London, 1772), 99, 100, 101, 102, 106, 119–20.

36. Robert H. Jackson and Edward Castillo, *Indians, Franciscans, and Spanish Colonization* (Albuquerque: Univ. of New Mexico Press, 1995), 74, 73.

37. Jackson and Castillo, 199.

38. Saunt, 64, 69. Saunt notes that the murder of the friar happened on the same day that George Washington called for a "defense of the general Liberty of America" by those who insulted the Catholic religion.

39. Iris H. W. Engstrand, "Seekers of the 'Northern Mystery': European Exploration of California and the Pacific," in *Contested Eden: California Before the Gold Rush*, eds. Ramón A. Gutiérrez and Richard J. Orsi (Berkeley: Univ. of California Press, 1998), 95.

40. Steven W. Hackel, *Children of Coyote, Missionaries of St. Francis: Indian-Spanish Relations in Colonial California, 1769–1850* (Chapel Hill: Univ. of North Carolina Press, 2005), 330–2.

41. James A. Sandos, *Converting California: Indians and Franciscans in the Missions* (New Haven: Yale Univ. Press, 2004), 163.

42. Hackel, 263; Sandos, 4. As numerous scholars note, the number and variety of acts of Indian resistance to the mission system far exceeded what is recorded in print. See esp. Hackel; Sandos; and Virginia Marie Bouvier, *Women and the Conquest of California, 1542–1840* (Tucson: Univ. of Arizona Press, 2001). For a chronological summary of these events, see Ojibwa, "Indian Resistance to the California Missions." Native American Netroots. May 28, 2010. Web. Aug. 12, 2013.

43. Patty O'Brien, *The Pacific Muse: Exotic Femininity and the Colonial Pacific* (Seattle: Univ. of Washington Press, 2006), 135, 136.

44. I borrow this phrase from Laura Doyle, "Inter-imperiality and Literary Studies in the Longer *Durée*," *PMLA* 130.2 (2015), 340. It should be noted that the European and American travelers describing these Pacific events were, of course, reading them through an Atlantic lens that very likely results in poor, inaccurate, or misleading portrayals of Pacific peoples and relations.

45. Jean-François de Galaup de La Pérouse, *The Journal of Jean-François de Galaup de la Pérouse, 1785–1788*, trans. and ed. John Dunmore. 2 vols. (London: The Hakluyt Society, 1994), I.230–1.

46. La Pérouse, I.180; Vancouver, II.12.

47. David Porter, *Journal of a Cruise made to the Pacific Ocean*, 2 vols. (Philadelphia, 1815), I.102, I. 115–16.

48. William Moulton, *A Concise Extract, from the Sea Journal of William Moulton; written on board of the Onico* (Utica, 1804), iii, 21.

49. As Hester Blum has recently demonstrated, voyages during this period regularly carried highly literate crews as well as sometimes extensive shipboard libraries. Details from several voyages of the period suggest that these libraries may have included revolutionary literature as well as travel narratives and navigation manuals. See Blum, *The View from the Masthead: Maritime Imagination and Antebellum American Sea Narratives* (Chapel Hill: Univ. of North Carolina Press, 2008), 5, 30–3.

50. James Kirker, *Adventures to China: Americans in the Southern Oceans, 1792–1812* (New York: Oxford Univ. Press, 1970), 105.

51. Richard J. Cleveland, *A Narrative of Voyages and Commercial Enterprises* (Boston, 1850), 174; Kirker, 86. Muir was a global revolutionary figure whose French Revolution-inspired activities with the United Irishmen led to his arrest, incarceration, trial and transportation to Botany Bay in 1794. He escaped from there on a Boston ship in 1796 and arrived in Monterey, California via Nootka Sound in 1796, before an attempted journey through Mexico and transportation to Cuba.

52. Kirker, 174.

53. See Lynette Ramsay Silver, *The Battle of Vinegar Hill: Australia's Irish Rebellion, 1804* (Sydney: Doubleday, 1989).

54. See Nigel Leask, "Irish Republicans and Gothic Eleutherarchs: Pacific Utopias in the Writings of Theobold Wolfe Tone and Charles Brockden Brown," *Huntington Library Quarterly* 63.3 (2000), 347–67.

55. Greg Dening, *Mr. Bligh's Bad Language: Passion, Power and Theatre on the Bounty* (Cambridge: Cambridge Univ. Press, 1992), 253.

56. Bruce Cumings, *Dominion from Sea to Sea: Pacific Ascendancy and American Power* (New Haven: Yale Univ. Press, 2009), x, xiv, ix, 5, 8. Cumings makes the point that scholars whose work may be focused "on a village in colonial New England" are often perceived as writing more important or more central histories with a national scope than their colleagues whose work on the West is positioned as regional.

57. Paul Giles, "Commentary: Hemispheric Partiality," *American Literary History* 18.3 (2006), 649–50; see also Bauer.

58. Armitage and Subrahmanyam, eds., xxii, xxxii.

59. Cañizares-Esguerra, *Puritan Conquistadors*, 215.

60. Ed Larkin, "Nation and Empire in the Early U.S.," *American Literary History* 22.3 (Fall 2010), 502, 503.

61. Sven Beckert, *Empire of Cotton: A Global History* (New York: Knopf, 2015), xxi.

62. Taylor, *American Revolutions*, 50.

63. Klooster, 2, 158–62.

64. McDonnell, 223.

65. Hannah Arendt, *On Revolution* (repr.; New York: Penguin, 1963), 199.

66. Amasa Delano, *A Narrative of the Voyages and Travels*, 2nd ed. (Boston, 1818), 200.

67. On Cushing's Belmont home, see Jacques M. Downes, *The Golden Ghetto: The American Commercial Community at Canton and the Shaping of American China Policy, 1784–1844* (Hong Kong: Hong Kong Univ. Press, 2015), 246.

68. Porter, *Journal*, II.9. Of course, this linguistically and nationally layered map implicitly calls into question the claim of discovery given to the Boston captain. Porter makes frequent reference to the maps and charts of Colnet, which he is clearly using as a guide and as an incomplete template that his own voyage is filling in more fully (see I.167).

69. Dalrymple, *Historical Collection*, II.30; Vancouver, III.488.

70. Dalrymple, *Historical Collection*, I.xxv.

71. Fry, xxi.

72. Vancouver, II.364, II.365, III.30.

73. Vancouver, II.498.

74. Vancouver, III.488.

75. Moulton, *A Concise Extract*, 103–4, 128–9. It's worth considering the implications of Moulton's critique for an understanding of sympathy, which doesn't appear in this example as an independent emotion so much as the affective remainder of a rational economic calculation.

76. For more on Low, see Dane A. Morrison, *True Yankees: The South Seas and the Discovery of American Identity* (Baltimore: Johns Hopkins Univ. Press, 2014), 151–83. For a wonderful account of Baret's life and experience on Bougainville's voyage, see Glynis Ridley, *The Discovery of Jeanne Baret: A Story of Science, the High Seas, and the First Woman to Circumnavigate the Globe* (New York: Crown, 2010).

77. O'Brien, 10.

78. La Pérouse, II.311. Some of these narratives also describe creole women, usually members of a local elite in such places as Concepción, Chile.

79. La Pérouse, II.419. A footnote to the edition suggests that this ritual may have been perceived by the Natives as a marriage ritual, although La Pérouse clearly interprets it as prostitution and as evidence of the lack of sexual virtue among indigenous women.

80. O'Brien, 25.

81. La Pérouse, I.125, II.393.

82. O'Brien, 25–6. See William Dampier, *A Collection of Voyages in Four Volumes* (London, 1729), 394–5.

83. O'Brien, 71.

84. O'Brien, 68, 71.

85. O'Brien, 9, 160. In Bougainville's version of events, Baret's gender was exposed in Tahiti by the Natives, from whom she had to be protected from sexual assault. Ridley argues instead that Bougainville hid his knowledge that Baret was a woman until confronted by the Tahitians.

86. O'Brien, 157, 69.

87. O'Brien, 158, 159, 160, 69.

88. Hoock, 166, 170–4.

89. Cohen, 8–9, 103.

Chapter 4

1. For an account of this remarkable story, see Samir S. Patel, "Castaways," *Archaeology* (Sept. 15, 2014), www.archaeology.org

2. The first novelistic reference to the American Revolution appears in Samuel Jackson Pratt (writing as Courtney Melmoth), *The Pupil of Pleasure*, 2 vols. (London, 1776). Two other novels in which the conflict appears were published in the same year as *Hildebrand Bowman*: Lady Mary Hamilton, *Munster Village*, 2 vols. (London, 1778) and [Phebe Gibbes], *Friendship in a Nunnery; or, The American Fugitive*, 2 vols. (London, 1778). See Barbara Frances Tarling, "Representations of the American War of Independence in the Late Eighteenth-Century English Novel," PhD diss. (Open University, 2010), 45. See also Christopher Flynn, *Americans in British Literature 1770–1832* (Aldershot: Ashgate, 2008) and R. B. Heilman, *America in English Fiction 1760–1800: The Influences of the American Revolution* (Baton Rouge: Louisiana State University Press, 1937; repr. New York: Octagon Books, 1968). Heilman briefly mentions the reference to the American Revolution in *The Travels of Hildebrand Bowman* (90–1) and goes on to consider its treatment neutral, as it presents (and ridicules) both sides in the debate (140).

3. Margaret Jolly, "Women of the East, Women of the West: Region and Race, Gender and Sexuality on Cook's Voyages," in *The Atlantic World in the Antipodes: Effects and Transformations since the Eighteenth Century*, ed. Kate Fullagar (Newcastle upon Tyne: Cambridge Scholars Publishing, 2012), 8, 21. Jolly attributes these gendered views on stadial

theory to Johann Forster, the botanist who accompanied Cook's second voyage along with his son George Forster, who wrote the first published account of the voyage. Kathleen Wilson observes that both Forsters "used women to assess the levels of savagery and progress towards civilization within Pacific societies"; *The Island Empire: Englishness, Empire and Gender in the Eighteenth Century* (London: Routledge, 2003), 74.

4. Anna Neill, *British Discovery Literature and the Rise of Global Commerce* (London: Palgrave, 2002), 29.

5. See, for example, *Bibliography of Captain James Cook*, 2nd ed. (Sydney: Library of New South Wales, 1970), 781; George Watson, ed., *New Cambridge Bibliography of English Literature, Vol. II: 1660–1800* (Cambridge: Cambridge Univ. Press, 1971), 1005; Philip Babcock Grove, *The Imaginary Voyage in Prose Fiction: A History of Its Criticism and a Guide for Its Study, with an Annotated Check List of 215 Imaginary Voyages from 1700 to 1800* (New York: Octagon Books, 1975), 369–70. See also Marina Warner, *Stranger Magic: Charmed States and the Arabian Nights* (Cambridge: Harvard Univ. Press, 2011), 349–50; Paul Longley Arthur, *Virtual Voyages: Travel Writing and the Antipodes, 1605–1837* (London: Anthem Press, 2010), 166n.21. Dror Wahrman offers perhaps the most substantial treatment of the novel in *The Making of the Modern Self: Identity and Culture in Eighteenth-Century England* (New Haven: Yale Univ. Press, 2004). The novel's recent reissue in a wonderfully informed edition by Lance Bertelsen may change this fate; see Bertelsen, ed., *The Travels of Hildebrand Bowman* by Anonymous (Peterborough, ON: Broadview Press, 2017). Although the novel remains anonymously authored, for ease of reference I refer to its author throughout this chapter using the pseudonym Bowman, including any references to or citations of notes in the Broadview edition.

6. See Bertelsen, "Introduction" (17–26) to Bowman, for an informative discussion of stadial theory in the context of the novel.

7. Alexander Dalrymple, *A Letter from Mr. Dalrymple to Dr. Hawkesworth* (London, 1773), 26, 32. Hawkesworth responded to Dalrymple's critique in the second edition of his narrative by writing that he "most sincerely wish[ed] that a southern continent may be found" for the "good Gentleman," since he was convinced that "nothing else can make him happy and good-humoured." John Hawkesworth, *An Account of the Voyages...in the Southern Hemisphere*, 2nd ed., 3 vols. (London, 1773), I.1; qtd. in E. H. McCormick, *Omai: Pacific Envoy* (Auckland, NZ: Auckland Univ. Press, 1977), 88.

8. Tobias Furneaux, "Furneaux's Narrative," in James Cook, *The Voyage of the Resolution and Adventure, 1772–1775*, Vol. II of *The Journals of Captain James Cook on his Voyages of Discovery*, ed. J. C. Beaglehole, 4 vols. (Cambridge: The Hakluyt Society, Cambridge Univ. Press, 1961), 741.

9. The scholarship on Mai is extensive. His 1774 arrival in Britain was followed by a well-publicized visit and tour that ended when he departed in 1776 on Cook's third (and final) Pacific expedition, which returned Mai to Polynesia. See especially Kate Fullagar, *The Savage Visit: New World People and Popular Culture in Britain, 1710–1795* (Berkeley: Univ. of California Press, 2012) and McCormick.

10. Bowman [Anonymous], *The Travels of Hildebrand Bowman*, ed. Lance Bertelsen (Peterborough, ON: Broadview Press, 2017), 57, 58. All future references to this text will be cited parenthetically. References to the text of the novel use Bowman; references to the "Introduction" are cited as Bertelsen. For a detailed discussion of the novel's authorship, see Bertelsen (35–40), as well as Cliff Thornton's four-part "The Hunt for Hildebrand Bowman," *Cook's Log* 33.4 (2010), 1–2; 34.1 (2011), 1–3; 34.2 (2011), 1–2; 34.3 (2011), 6–9.

11. Cook, *The Voyage of the Resolution and Adventure*, 292.

12. Cook, *The Voyage of the Resolution and Adventure*, 293.

13. Furneaux, 743.

14. James Burney, *With Captain James Cook in the Antarctic and Pacific: The Private Journal of James Burney*, ed. Beverley Hooper (Canberra: National Library of Australia, 1975), 89. See discussion as well in McCormick, 67, 68, 67. The brother of novelist Frances Burney, James Burney began the voyage as midshipman on the *Resolution* and was promoted, partway through the voyage in November 1772, to a position as second lieutenant on the *Adventure*. See McCormick, 40.

15. Furneaux, 743, 744. Wilson identifies this victim of the Grass Cove Massacre as the black Briton James Swiley, a seaman on the *Adventure* (174).

16. James Burney, "Burney's Log," in Cook, *The Voyage of the Resolution and Adventure*, 750.

17. Burney, 751, 752.

18. The novel does not include, of course, any details from the *Resolution*'s voyage, but Bowman does direct readers "to receive further information, from the well wrote and candid relation of it, given to the Public by Captain Cooke" (57).

19. Review in *The London Review of English and Foreign Literature* 7 (June 1778), 499–500.

20. Review in *The Monthly Review* 59 (1778), 409. The review concludes by evaluating Bowman as an inferior Gulliver, in large part because his satire is too blunt and lacking in subtlety: "the author depicts, as plainly as he can—indeed too plainly and tritely—the present manners of our own dear country, under the semblance of this part [Luxo-Volupto] of *Terra Australis*" (410).

21. Daniel O'Quinn, *Staging Governance: Theatrical Imperialism in London, 1770–1800* (Baltimore: Johns Hopkins Univ. Press, 2005), 75, 76, 82.

22. Daniel Cottom, *Cannibals and Philosophers: Bodies of Enlightenment* (Baltimore: Johns Hopkins Univ. Press, 2001), 154, 149, 152. Cottom also notes that Pickersgill's motivation in bringing the head on board in the first place was "for the express purpose of preserving it in spirits so that it might be placed in the anatomical collection of Dr. John Hunter, the eminent London surgeon" (155).

23. Cottom, 153.

24. Ronald L. Meek, *Social Science and the Ignoble Savage* (Cambridge: Cambridge Univ. Press, 1976), 99, 129.

25. John Locke, *Two Treatises on Government*, ed. Peter Laslett (New York: New American Library, 1965), 383, 343, 328. Quoted and discussed in Meek, 22.

26. Cook, *The Voyage of the Resolution and Adventure*, 174, 175.

27. George Forster, *A Voyage Round the World. 1777*, eds. Nicholas Thomas and Oliver Berghof, 2 vols. (Honolulu: Univ. of Hawai'i Press, 2000), II.611, II.612.

28. This structure of the novel aligns it less with Swift perhaps than with Bishop Joseph Hall's 1605 *Mundus Alter et Idem*, a satire whose description of the great southern continent divided it into four regions distinguished by practices of overindulgence, feminism, folly, and crime. For a discussion of Hall's book in the context of other early Pacific fiction, see David Fausett, *Writing the New World: Imaginary Voyages and Utopias of the Great Southern Land* (Syracuse: Syracuse Univ. Press, 1993), 44–51. Fausett more explicitly argues, however, that *The Travels of Hildebrand Bowman* draws from a travel report attributed to Henry Shooten, titled *The hairy-giants, or, A description of two islands in the South Sea*, an undated publication that likely appeared in 1671 (91–6).

29. Bernard Smith is almost certainly the first to have noted Monboddo's influence on *Hildebrand Bowman*; see *European Vision and the South Pacific*, 2nd ed. (New Haven: Yale Univ. Press, 1989), 102.

30. For discussions of Monboddo and Smith, see Wilson, 77, and Meek, 240–3.

31. See James Burnett, *Lord Monboddo's Of the Origin and Progress of Language*, vol. 1 (New York: AMS Press, 1973), 6 vols. Future references to this text will be cited parenthetically. See also E. L. Cloyd, *James Burnett, Lord Monboddo* (Oxford: Clarendon Press, 1972), esp. 64–72.

32. James Boswell, *Boswell for the Defence, 1769–1774*, eds. W. K. Wimsatt and F. A. Pottle (New Haven: Yale Univ. Press, 1960), 146; *Boswell's Life of Johnson*, ed. G. B. Hill (Oxford, 1887), 2.73–4. McCormick points out that it was during this visit that Banks may have acquired a copy of a book, *An Account of a Savage Girl, Caught Wild in the Woods of Champagne*, that Monboddo had a hand in preparing for publication (73–4). For an analysis of Monboddo's views in relation to Rousseau's, see Arthur O. Lovejoy, "Monboddo and Rousseau," *Modern Philology* 30.3 (1933), 275–96. For a comparison of Monboddo to Kames, see Robert Workler, "Apes and Races in the Scottish Enlightenment: Monboddo and Kames on the Nature of Man," *Philosophy and Science in the Scottish Enlightenment* (1998), 145–68. On Johnson and Mai, see Pat Rogers, "The Noblest Savage of Them All: Johnson, Omai, and Other Primitives," *The Age of Johnson* 5 (1992), 281–301.

33. See Patricia Fara, *Sex, Botany, and Empire: The Story of Carl Linnaeus and Joseph Banks* (New York: Columbia Univ. Press, 2003), 102–8 for a discussion of Linnaeus's four-stage theory, which included both humans with tails and humans who lived in caves.

34. Wahrman, 137.

35. See Wahrman's extended discussion of this transition in British thinking about the relationship of animals to humans (127–45). Interestingly, Johann Forster is one of those who characterized a belief in the bridgeable proximity of animals and humans as ridiculous (see Wahrman 136, citing Johann Reinhold Forster, *Observations Made during a Voyage round the World* [London, 1778], 254–6).

36. These British texts can be seen as counterparts to the anti-imperialist political philosophy of Diderot, Kant, and Herder in the late eighteenth century, which Sankar Muthu identifies as a "historically anomalous and understudied episode of political thinking" in the Enlightenment; see *Enlightenment Against Empire* (Princeton: Princeton Univ. Press, 2003), 1.

37. Fullagar, *Savage Visit*, 123–4. Cook seems to be echoing this perspective when, in the more private journal entry quoted above, he perceives indigenous peoples in New Zealand as the virtuous victims of European greed.

38. Meek, 220, 222.

39. Bertelsen remarks on Seripante's similarity to Canton, China, where the British had a "substantial factory," as well as its similarity to the slave factories on the west coast of Africa (93n.2).

40. See Fausett for an account of the 1605 "Description of the Isle of Hermaphrodites recently discovered," which describes the island's inhabitants as having a sartorial obsession that compels them to change fashion every month and to ban the renewal of old fashions (51).

41. Fara, 9.

42. See the discussion by Bertelsen in his Introduction (29–32) and Appendix F (233–41).

43. See McCormick for a discussion of the role played in Hawkesworth's version of the expedition by the personal journal of Banks, which included a description of a "public act

of copulation" by Tahitians witnessed by Banks and others, another episode in which Banks "shed his clothes and blackened his person," and others in which he "enjoyed the favours of island women" (82–3).

44. For a discussion of these depictions of Banks, see Patty O'Brien, *The Pacific Muse: Exotic Femininity and the Colonial Pacific* (Seattle: Univ. of Washington Press, 2006), 64. The first quotation is from the anonymous poem *An Epistle from Mr. Banks, Voyager; Monster-Hunter and Amoroso to Oberea, Queen of Otaheite* (1773) and the second from the poem *Transmigration* (1778).

45. Fara, 11, 15. Kathleen Wilson, too, observes that calling Banks a "butterfly catcher" was a way to mock him as an "aristocratic sensualist" (172). The wings of the Luxo-voluptans bring together the sexual license and consumer excess of the British macaroni with earlier literary associations between wings and female sexuality in the fantastical south Pacific. Robert Paltock's 1750 *Peter Wilkins* tells the story of a shipwrecked British commoner who finds a winged woman somewhere near the South Pole, whom he marries and fathers several children with before joining her nation to help them secure a military victory against their enemies. Some of the details of this earlier story appear in the Olfactaria segment of *Bowman*. These eighteenth-century texts carry on a far older tradition, however, that include the mutual appearance of giant birds and sexual communism in Iambulus's *Heliopolis* (a lost narrative that lives on in a retelling by Lucian). Gabriel de Foigny's 1676 *La Terre Australe connue* (1676) also features giant birds, and giant birds are shot and eaten by El-ho, the Dutch castaway figure in Hendrik Smeets's 1708 *Kingdom of Krinke Kesmes*, likewise set in the southern Pacific. See Fausett, 30, 131, 147.

46. John Cooke, *The Macaroni Jester* (Philadelphia, 1768), 6.

47. Furneaux, 742.

48. Nicholas Thomas, *Islanders: The Pacific in the Age of Empire* (New Haven: Yale Univ. Press, 2010), 74.

49. Forster, I.367. See Bertelsen for a discussion of this passage, 16.

50. For a discussion of this image in the context of the American Revolution's violence, see Holger Hoock, *Scars of Independence: America's Violent Birth* (New York: Crown, 2017), 57. Although he does not mention it in the context of this image, the "45" on the rebel's hat associates him with the Jacobite uprising of 1745, which Hoock elsewhere identifies as "the most pertinent example of insurgency in living memory" (78). The number 45 would have resonated at the time much more explicitly, however, as a reference to supporters of John Wilkes on both sides of the Atlantic. See John Brewer, "Commercialization and Politics," in Neil McKendrick, John Brewer and J. H. Plumb, *The Birth of a Consumer Society: The Commercialization of Eighteenth-Century England* (Bloomington: Indiana Univ. Press, 1982), 197–262. Wilkes defended the American colonies before and during the Revolutionary War, and his tactics of resistance were adopted by many in the colonies, especially Boston. Thanks to Lance Bertelsen for pointing this connection out to me.

51. Bertelsen's edition of Bowman has brought this image to my attention (238).

52. Hoock observes that during the war, American "prints and broadsides routinely depicted the latter [British and American Loyalists] in the acts of scalping and cannibalizing Patriots," and argues that these depictions were effective because they invoked actual battles, such as the Wyoming Massacre in Pennsylvania and the Cherry Valley conflict in eastern New York (279). Both of those battles took place in 1778, the year *Hildebrand Bowman* was published.

53. See John Sekora, *Luxury: The Concept in Western Thought, Eden to Smollett* (Baltimore: Johns Hopkins Univ. Press, 1977), 68, 104, 104–9. It should be noted that Burke, who spoke out in support of the American colonies' grievances against the king, occupied a more complicated position in these debates.

54. Wilson, 50, 51. Wilson also notes that the abolitionist movement was born out of this period, an argument developed fully by Christopher Leslie Brown, *Moral Capital: Foundations of British Abolitionism* (Chapel Hill: Univ. of North Carolina Press, 2006).

55. Fullagar, *Savage Visit*, 3, 191.

56. Fullagar, *Savage Visit*, 11, 190–1.

57. To this extent, we might add this network of texts to that late eighteenth-century body of political philosophy that Sankar Muthu has recovered and identified as Enlightenment anti-imperialism. Like the debate about expansion recovered by Fullagar, this tradition has been long forgotten, drowned out by the pro-imperialist sentiment that surrounded or followed it, and which has since become identified with Europe during this period. As a result, Muthu observes, "Enlightenment anti-imperialism remains a historical curiosity" but one that is important to rescue from obscurity (278).

58. Wilson, 51.

59. Lee Wallace, *Sexual Encounters: Pacific Texts, Modern Sexualities* (Ithaca: Cornell Univ. Press, 2003), 1.

60. James R. Fichter, *So Great a Proffit: How the East Indies Trade Transformed Anglo-American Capitalism* (Cambridge: Harvard Univ. Press, 2010), 213.

61. See O'Brien, 184, 188.

62. Henry Neville, *The Isle of Pines, in Three Early Modern Utopias*, ed. Susan Bruce (Oxford: Oxford Univ. Press, 1999), 197. See Karen A. Weyler and Michelle Burnham, "Reanimating Ghost Editions, Reorienting the Early American Novel," *Early American Literature* 51.3 (2017), 655–64, for a speculative consideration of how beginning our literary histories of the early American novel with such a text changes the narrative of American history and culture we tell.

63. George Emery Littlefield, *Early Boston Booksellers, 1642–1711* (Boston: Club of Odd Volumes, 1900), 232. Accessed via *HathiTrust*, July 2, 2017.

Chapter 5

1. Naomi J. Williams, *Landfalls* (New York: Farrar, Straus, and Giroux, 2015), 198.

2. Williams, 201, 207.

3. Williams, 222.

4. Sexual, political, economic, and philosophical forms of seduction have been variously aligned in readings of Brown's *Ormond* by a number of critics. On sexual seduction, for example, see Sydney J. Krause, "*Ormond*: Seduction in a New Key," *American Literature* 44 (1973), 570–84; on philosophical seduction, W. M. Verhoeven, "Displacing the Discontinuous: Or, The Labyrinths of Reason: Fictional Design and Eighteenth-Century Thought in Charles Brockden Brown's *Ormond*," in *Rewriting the Dream: Reflections on the Changing American Literary Canon*, ed. W. M. Verhoeven (Amsterdam: Rodopi, 1992), 202–29; on sexual and philosophical seduction, Jonathan C. Tutor, "Disappointed Expectations: Artistic Strategy in *Ormond*," *Publications of the Mississippi Philological Association* (1985), 67–80; on sexual and economic seduction, Steven Hamelman, "Secret to the Last: Charles Brocken

Brown's *Ormond*," *LIT: Literature, Interpretation, Theory* 11.3 (2000), 305–26; on political seduction, Bill Christophersen, *The Apparition in the Glass: Charles Brockden Brown's American Gothic* (Athens, GA: Univ. of Georgia Press, 1993), G. St. John Stott, "Second Thoughts about Ormond," *Études Anglaises* 43.2 (1990), 157–68, and Robert Levine, *Conspiracy and Romance: Studies in Brockden Brown, Cooper, Hawthorne, and Melville* (Cambridge: Cambridge Univ. Press, 1989). For other important economic readings of *Ormond*, see Elizabeth Jane Wall Hinds, *Private Property: Charles Brockden Brown's Gendered Economics of Virtue* (Newark: Univ. of Delaware Press, 1997); Scott Ellis, "Charles Brockden Brown's *Ormond*, Property Exchange, and the Literary Marketplace in the Early American Republic," *Studies in the Novel* 37.1 (2005), 1–19; and Leonard Von Morzé, "A Massachusetts Yankee in Karl Theodor's Court: Count Rumford's Sovereign Benevolence and Charles Brockden Brown's *Ormond*," *Symbiosis: A Journal of Anglo-American Literary Relations* 15.5 (2011), 45–61. Michael J. Drexler and Ed White read the novel as a critique of republicanism; "Secret History and the Fantasy Structure of Republicanism," *Early American Literature* 44.2 (2009), 333–63. Both Matthew Garrett and Joseph Letter see the use of seriality in *Ormond* as a response to the nation; Letter, "Charles Brockden Brown's Lazaretto Chronotope Series: Secret History and 'The Man at Home,'" *Early American Literature* 50.3 (2015), 711–35; Garrett, *Episodic Poetics: Politics and Literary Form after the Constitution* (New York: Oxford Univ. Press, 2014).

5. See especially Levine. Michael J. Drexler and Ed White suggest instead that Ormond predicts the controversial figure of Aaron Burr; see *The Traumatic Colonel: The Founding Fathers, Slavery, and the Phantasmatic Aaron Burr* (New York: New York Univ. Press, 2014), 67.

6. For readings of Franklin's interest in the Pacific, see Jim Egan, *Oriental Shadows: The Presence of the East in Early American Literature* (Columbus: Ohio State Univ. Press, 2011); and Paul Giles, "Antipodean American Literature: Franklin, Twain, and the Sphere of Subalternity," *American Literary History* 20.1–2 (Spring/Summer 2008), 22–50 and *Antipodean America: Australasia and the Constitution of U.S. Literature* (Oxford: Oxford Univ. Press, 2013).

7. The American John Ledyard traveled on Cook's third expedition into the Pacific and published a popular account of the voyage in Hartford in 1783. The failure of his Philadelphia efforts may have been the result of poor economic timing, since the U.S. would not recover from its post-war debts and reconstruction costs until the following decade, when fortunes changed considerably. But it may also have been a result of Ledyard's implausible promises: while many were impressed with Morris's 25 percent return on his first mercantile trading voyage to China, Ledyard had anticipated a profit of 1000 percent. *John Ledyard's Journal of Captain Cook's Last Voyage*, ed. James Kenneth Munford (Corvallis: Oregon State Univ. Press, 1963), 15.

8. Jonathan Goldstein, *Philadelphia and the China Trade 1682–1846: Commercial, Cultural, and Attitudinal Effects* (University Park: Pennsylvania State Univ. Press, 1978), 30.

9. Carl L. Crossman, *The China Trade: Export Paintings, Furniture, Silver & Other Objects* (Princeton: The Pyne Press, 1972), xi. See also Caroline Frank, *Objectifying China, Imagining America: Chinese Commodities in Early America* (Chicago: Univ. of Chicago Press, 2011).

10. Stephen Shapiro argues that Brown's fiction must be understood in the context of America's late eighteenth-century emergence as a "re-export republic" that capitalized financially on new access to ports around the world and brought new wealth and a growing bourgeois culture to America's urban centers. Indeed, Brown's own family was involved

with the mercantile re-export business in Philadelphia during this period. I extend Shapiro's work here by including the Pacific in this geography. *The Culture and Commerce of the Early American Novel: Reading the Atlantic World-System* (University Park: Pennsylvania State Univ. Press, 2008).

11. James R. Fichter, *So Great a Proffit: How the East Indies Trade Transformed Anglo-American Capitalism* (Cambridge: Harvard Univ. Press, 2010), 2, 17, 84–5, 82, 158. Pepper offers one good example of this lucrative East Asian re-export trade; it entered the U.S. through Sumatra, and was then re-exported to Europe in amounts of about £60 million per year (Fichter, 84–5).

12. John Turnbull, *A Voyage Round the World, in the Years 1800, 1801, 1802, 1803, and 1804* (Philadelphia, 1810), 5, 135.

13. Fichter, 213.

14. Crossman, 4. Voyages that successfully combined the Pacific fur trade with the Chinese trade could bring returns as high as 200–500 percent (Fichter, 209, 211).

15. Turnbull, 57.

16. Fichter, 4, 27.

17. Shapiro notes that while there were four commercial banks in the U.S. in 1790, by the end of the decade there were twenty-six, located predominantly in Philadelphia and New York (114). Similarly, New England had only one bank in 1784, fifty-two by 1810, and 172 by 1830 (Fichter, 262). Fichter points out that "American banking and the American East Indies trade developed in tandem, were interrelated, and exhibited similar traits" (262).

18. The two Philadelphia merchants most identified with the China trade were Robert Morris and Stephen Girard. Girard in particular began to focus on Asian commerce at the end of the 1780s, and by the 1790s had shifted his primary mercantile maritime investments away from West Indian trade toward "his growing Asiatic, European, and Latin American commerce" (Goldstein, 35).

19. Goldstein, 34.

20. Paul Van Dyke, *The Canton Trade: Life and Enterprise on the China Coast, 1700–1845* (Hong Kong: Hong Kong Univ. Press, 2005), 151.

21. See Caitlin Fitz, *Our Sister Republics: The United States in an Age of Revolutions* (New York: Liveright, 2016), 164–5.

22. Goldstein, 35, 42, 43.

23. Fichter, 131, 130, 131.

24. Crossman, 4.

25. Shapiro, 134.

26. Sydney Krause, for instance, once nominated the following as *Ormond*'s most "expendable" episodes: "Craig's defrauding Dudley, Constantia's struggle with poverty, and her turning to needlework"; Krause, "'Ormond': How Rapidly and How Well 'Composed, Arranged and Delivered'," *Early American Literature* 13 (1978), 245.

27. Charles Brockden Brown, *Ormond; or the Secret Witness*, eds. Philip Barnard and Stephen Shapiro (Indianapolis: Hackett Publishing, 2009), 6, 7. Future references to the novel appear parenthetically throughout this chapter.

28. Peter Kafer has been one of the few readers to recognize *Ormond* as a book concerned with poverty and the cruel effects of market society on those in need; *Charles Brockden Brown's Revolution and the Birth of American Gothic.* (Philadelphia: Univ. of Pennsylvania Press, 2004), 159–60.

29. Ian Baucom, *Specters of the Atlantic: Finance Capital, Slavery, and the Philosophy of History* (Durham: Duke Univ. Press, 2005), 17.

30. Baucom, 55. Baucom's reference here is to the French Revolution, although I am interested in its broader, and transoceanic, application. For a recent treatment of the Haitian Revolution in *Ormond*, see Ja Yun Choi, "The Early Republic, the Haitian Revolution, and the Horrors of Slavery in Brown's *Ormond*," *British and American Fiction* 22.2 (2015), 5–33. Nicholas E. Miller develops a more sustained reading of the Haitian Revolution's connection to the novel's yellow fever episodes in "'In Utter Fearlessness of the Reigning Disease': Imagined Immunities and the Outbreak Narratives of Charles Brockden Brown," *Literature and Medicine* 35.1 (2017), 144–66.

31. Levine, 17. Levine well documents Brown's familiarity with circulating anti-Illuminati writing and sentiment in 1798 and 1799 Philadelphia, and convincingly argues that *Ormond* exposes the ways in which counter-conspiratorial discourse ostensibly aimed to warn Americans about danger actually constituted its own conspiracy. In other words, Ormond engages in "an ideologically sanctioned hedonism" (42) further supported by "an amoralism derived from Enlightenment sciences" (43).

32. Bryan Waterman, "The Bavarian Illuminati, the Early American Novel, and Histories of the Public Sphere," *The William and Mary Quarterly* 62.1 (2005), 28.

33. Christopher Lukasik, "'The Vanity of Physiognomy': Dissimulation and Discernment in Charles Brockden Brown's *Ormond*," *Amerikastudien* 50.3 (2005), 498. Craig exemplifies Chesterfieldianism, the practice of performing upwardly mobile behavior taught in Chesterfield's *Letters*, an enormously popular late eighteenth-century book that, as Lukasik notes, was also seen as "responsible for the downward distribution of gentility in America" (490). Lukaskik argues that Brown recognizes that "the market jeopardizes a system of social relations where faces externalize character...because it trades in faces as if they were commodities" (496).

34. Levine, 22.

35. Hinds, 62.

36. Ormond's seduction of Helena operates on a similar narrative logic of speculative promise and risk, leaving her bereft in the present of the security and reputation she hoped might arrive in the future form of marriage.

37. As Levine aptly describes it, Ormond turns this question of marriage into an "algebraic equation" (38).

38. Nigel Leask points out that the Pacific voyages of Wallis, Bougainville, and Cook, and their descriptions of Tahiti, Hawai'i, and other Pacific island locations, would have been well known by the time Brown was writing; "Irish Republicans and Gothic Eleutherarchs: Pacific Utopias in the Writings of Theobald Wolfe Tone and Charles Brockden Brown," *British Radical Culture of the 1790s*, ed. Robert M. Maniquis (San Marino, CA: Huntington Library, 2002), 104. Other scholars who have discussed Brown's interest in the Pacific include Giles, who focuses on Brown and Australia in *Antipodean America*; Martin Brückner, who focuses on Brown and Japan in *The Geographic Revolution in Early America: Maps, Literacy, and National Identity* (Chapel Hill: Univ. of North Carolina Press, 2006); and Hsuan Hsu, who focuses on Brown and South Pacific islands in *Geography and the Production of Space in Nineteenth-Century American Literature* (Cambridge: Cambridge Univ. Press, 2010).

39. Ledyard, 70.

40. Some have seen Ledyard's publication of his voyage with Cook as a deliberate "first step in his project to urge and promote the exploitation by American merchants of the tremendous commercial possibilities on the northwest coast"; Stephen D. Watrous, "A Biographical Sketch," *in John Ledyard's Journey Through Russia and Siberia, 1787–1788: The Journal and Selected Letters* (Madison: Univ. of Wisconsin Press, 1966), 13.

41. "Account," *The Massachusetts Magazine* (Feb. 1972), 94, 95; *American Periodical Series*. Watrous recounts Ledyard's numerous failed efforts to fund this Pacific venture. An earlier agreement by Ledyard with John Paul Jones to lead an expedition in 1785 (a plan supported by Thomas Jefferson) did not materialize, and his efforts to find investors in France also fell through. Ledyard's plan to cross the Pacific to America and then cross the continent on foot was reportedly suggested to him by Jefferson and backed in Britain by Sir Joseph Banks and Colonel William Stephens Smith (Watrous, 37). Ledyard's project failed, however, when the Russian empress Catherine had him arrested, imprisoned, and banished when he reached Kamchatka, to which he had traveled without her express permission. Although the reasons for this arrest remain unclear, one theory suggests that Russia may have been responding to the legacy of Benyowsky's 1771 uprising, especially in the wake of renewed conflict with Turkey in 1787. Benyowsky had been captured by the Russians while fighting on behalf of Polish independence, while Ormond is identified as fighting on behalf of the Cossacks, a group whose allegiances with Russia wavered considerably during the late eighteenth century. Ledyard died on a Joseph Banks-sponsored expedition to Africa.

42. "Extracts, from a letter, written by Mr. John Ledyard," *The American Magazine* 1.11 (Oct. 1788), 808; *American Periodical Series*, ProQuest. Evidence of Brown's familiarity with these ideas abound. Ledyard's comparison was later repeated, for example, in Benjamin Barton's 1798 book *New Views of the Origin of Tribes and Nations of America*. Brown's review of Barton's book, printed in the May 1799 issue of *The Monthly Magazine*, explains Barton's view that "all the natives of America, except the Esquimaux, are nearly akin to the natives of Siberia" (119). The review is signed "C.B." Comparisons between American and Asian indigenous peoples were common at the time. In their edition of *Ormond*, Barnard and Shapiro locate comparisons between the Mongols and the Sioux in Volney's 1803 *View of the Climate and Soil of the United States of America* and in Lewis and Clark's 1809 narrative (157n.1). Jonathan Carver's 1778 *Travels Through the Interior Parts of North America* appeared earlier, but nowhere in Carver's extensive descriptions of the Naudowessie (or the Sioux) does he compare them with the Tartars or Mongols. See also the *Monthly Magazine* article "Remarks upon the Russian Empire," signed "H, X" and published in April 1800, which describes Russia's enormous size and ferocious people, as well as the remarkable productivity of the Kamchatka region of Siberia.

43. "Proposals for Publishing by Subscription, (Spotswood No. 22, Marlbro'-Street,) Memoirs and Travels of Maurice Augustus Count Benyowsky." Boston, 1799. *Early American Imprints,* Readex.

44. Benyowksky designed to use a Baltimore company to facilitate trade (primarily in slaves) with Madagascar.

45. Mauritius Augustus Count de Benyowsky, *Memoirs and Travels of Mauritius Augustus Count de Benyowsky,* 2 vols. (Dublin, 1790), I.164, I.254, I.58, I.369.

46. "Proposals for Publishing by Subscription."

47. August von Kotzebue, *Count Benyowsky; or, the Conspiracy of Kamchatka,* 3rd ed., trans. Rev. W. Render (Cork, 1799). Future references to this play appear parenthetically within the text. Frequent reprintings and translations suggest the play's popularity: English

translations appeared in 1798 simultaneously in London, Dublin, and Cambridge, with subsequent 1799 editions in London and Dublin and Cork, and 1800 editions in Boston and London. The title page of the 1798 London edition notes that it was performed "at the Theatre Royal, Drury-Lane." In addition, potential subscribers to Benyowsky's *Memoirs* are assured in the 1799 Boston broadside that they will receive "a copy of Kotzebue's much admired dramatic piece, founded on the abovementioned memoirs" ("Proposals for Publishing by Subscription")—evidence that the drama was well known in the U.S. long before its first performance in 1814 in Baltimore (when the "Star-Spangled Banner" also premiered).

48. Kotzebue, *Count Benyowsky; or, the Conspiracy of Kamchatka* (London, 1799), vi.

49. "Anecdotes of distinguished Characters. KOTZEBUE," *Monthly Magazine and American Review* (Apr. 1799), 76; *American Periodical Series*. The brief biography offered in the article notes that Kotzebue left Russia where he was "appointed president of the high college of Justice" because he came under fire by many "who magnified every trifling foible of his private conduct into a crime of the first magnitude, and persecuted him with such unrelenting malignity" (76–7). It also notes that Kotzebue's departure from Russia was "chiefly on account of a work called '*The Life of Count Beniowsky*,' written by himself, which contained many private anecdotes relative to the cruelties practiced by order of the late Empress of Russia" (78).

50. Hinds, 58.

51. A brief summary of Benyowsky's rebellion in Harold McCracken's *Hunters of the Stormy Sea* (London: Oldbourne Press, 1957) includes the detail that he forged a document attesting to his courtly origins and recommending that he be treated with special favor, and points toward the violent brutality of the uprising he masterminded (92–3).

52. Benyowsky's own *Memoirs* similarly describes the island of Tonquin as a place "where the vices and wickedness of Europe are yet unknown, and the government is founded only upon the principles of humanity" (II.17), and where he promptly selects a wife from among the seven women presented to him upon his arrival (II.14).

53. Ormond and Martinette grew up in what Barnard and Shapiro describe as "the cosmopolitan, multiethnic merchant networks of the Eastern Mediterranean and Levant" (144n.20). The appearance of decorative possessions from this area in Ormond's Philadelphia house suggests that he is engaged in trade with the region.

54. Brown was familiar with two 1798 Pacific plays by Kotzebue that imagine the possibilities of a polygamous domesticity. The *Monthly Magazine and American Review* article on Kotzebue includes a footnote that recognizes the publication in 1798 of four new Kotzebue plays. One of these is singled out for more extensive attention in the note, where it is described as "A play founded on the misfortunes of La Perouse, who is supposed to have been shipwrecked in the South Seas. Malvina, a female savage, who has rescued Perouse from the waves, and by whom he has a son; his wife and son, who in search of him, arrive at the island, and find him with Malvina; and the brother of Madame La Perouse, are the principal characters" ("Anecdotes of distinguished Characters. KOTZEBUE," 78). This play, titled *La Peyrouse*, ends with an agreement between the shipwrecked explorer, his French wife, and his Native mistress to live together on the isolated island in a series of three huts.

55. Ott argues that "commercial temporal anxiety" emerged from the era's "accelerating credit clock," and gives the example of temporal anxiety in the 1819 play *Wall Street: Or, Ten Minutes before Three* as its characters attempt to ward off financial panic and an economic crash; "Reading Hamilton's Clocks: Time Consciousness in Early National and Antebellum Urban Commercial Culture," *Temporal Politics*, Multiple Publics/Civic

Voices: Online Panel Discussions. For a different analysis of such temporality in relation to labor, see E. P. Thompson's discussion of what he calls "factory time" in *Customs in Common* (London: Penguin, 1993).

56. Garrett, 113.

57. Garrett, 101, 105, 19.

58. Shapiro, 67–8.

Chapter 6

1. For discussions of obeah in literary and cultural studies, see Toni Wall Jaudon, "Obeah's Sensations: Rethinking Religion at the Transnational Turn," *American Literature* 84.4 (Dec. 2012), 715–41; Kelly Wisecup, "Knowing Obeah," *Atlantic Studies* 10.3 (2013), 406–25; Elizabeth Maddock Dillon, "Obi, Assemblage, Enchantment," *J19: The Journal of Nineteenth-Century Americanists* 1.1 (Spring 2013), 172–8; and the special *Atlantic Studies* issue "Obeah: Knowledge, Power, and Writing in the Early Atlantic World," *Atlantic Studies* 12.1 (2015), edited by Jaudon and Wisecup.

2. When George tells Charles that "I know your sentiments upon the subject" of slavery, he implies that his correspondent, like the other planters in Jamaica, supports the institution. William Earle, *Obi; or, the History of Three-Fingered Jack*, ed. Srinivas Aravamudan (1800; repr. Peterborough, ON: Broadview Press, 2005), 71. Future references to the novel will be cited parenthetically.

3. *Obi* had a far longer life and garnered much more attention as a pantomime than it did as a novel. First performed in London in 1800, the play went on to enjoy seventy-nine performances in its first four seasons there, and was performed across the Atlantic in New York and Philadelphia in 1801, and in Boston in 1802. Earle's prose version met with far less popular success, although it was reprinted in an 1804 Worcester edition. For a thorough history of the pantomime and its contexts, and a reading of the performance's containment of slave rebellion, see Peter Reed, *Rogue Performances: Staging the Underclass in Early American Theatre Culture* (New York: Palgrave Macmillan, 2010), 101–26. See also Dillon's discussion in *New World Drama: The Performative Commons in the Atlantic World, 1649–1849* (Durham: Duke Univ. Press, 2014), 242–4. For a discussion of the prose retellings of Jack's story by Earle and William Burdett, see Diana Paton, "The Afterlives of Three-Fingered Jack," in *Slavery and the Cultures of Abolition: Essays Marking the Bicentennial of the British Abolition Act of 1807*, eds. Brycchan Carey and Peter J. Kitson (Cambridge: D. S. Brewer, 2007), 42–63.

4. These included, for instance, Philibert Commerçon who, along with his assistant and cross-dressed mistress Jeanne Baret, gathered plants and seeds from around the world on board Bougainville's *La Boudeuse*; George Forster, a German botanist who accompanied Cook on his second voyage, and who was the son of John (or Johann) Reinhold Forster; and Banks's own assistants, the Swedish botanist Daniel Solander and the Finnish botanist Herman Spöring, Jr.

5. John Reinhold Forster, "The Translator's Preface," in *A Voyage Round the World*, by Lewis de Bougainville, trans. John Reinhold Forster (London, 1772), viii.

6. Alan Frost, "The Antipodean Exchange: European Horticulture and Imperial Designs," in *Visions of Empire: Voyages, Botany, and Representations of Nature*, eds. David Philip Miller and Peter Hanns Reill (Cambridge: Cambridge Univ. Press, 1996), 75.

7. Forster, viii.

8. [C. F. Kaufmann], *The Dictionary of Merchandise, and Nomenclature in all Languages; for the Use of Counting-Houses: Containing, the History, Places of Growth, Culture, Use, and Marks of Excellency, of such Natural Productions, as Form Articles of Commerce; with their names in all European languages* (Philadelphia, 1805), 14, 16, 235, 248, 260.

9. See Andrea Wulf on seed and plant exchange between English and American men during the revolutionary period; *The Brother Gardeners: Botany, Empire and the Birth of an Obsession* (New York: Knopf, 2009); on gardens during the same period, see her *Founding Gardeners: The Revolutionary Generation, Nature, and the Shaping of the American Nation* (New York: Knopf, 2011). Neil Safier's "Fruitless Botany: Joseph de Jussieu's South American Odyssey," in *Science and Empire in the Atlantic World*, eds. James Delbourgo and Nicholas Dew (New York: Routledge, 2007), 203–24, considers botanical exploration in the Americas and among the Portuguese. See also Glynnis Ridley, whose biography of Jeanne Baret furthermore indicates the often-submerged gender politics within the global expanse of botanical exploration: *The Discovery of Jeanne Baret: A Story of Science, the High Seas, and the First Woman to Circumnavigate the Globe* (New York: Crown, 2010).

10. Londa Schiebinger, *Plants and Empire: Colonial Bioprospecting in the Atlantic World* (Cambridge: Harvard Univ. Press, 2004).

11. Douglas Hall, "Planters, Farmers, and Gardeners in Eighteenth-Century Jamaica," in *Slavery, Freedom, and Gender: The Dynamics of Caribbean Society*, eds. Brian L. Moore, B. W. Higman, Carl Campbell, and Patrick Bryan (Kingston, Jamaica: Univ. of West Indies Press, 2001), 102.

12. Lewis de Bougainville, *A Voyage Round the World. Performed by Order of His Most Christian Majesty, In the Years 1766, 1767, 1768, and 1769*, trans. from the French by John Reinhold Forster (London, 1772), 442.

13. Reed, 105.

14. Elizabeth DeLoughrey, "Globalizing the Routes of Breadfruit and Other Bounties," *Journal of Colonialism and Colonial History* 8.3 (2008). Web. Para. 1.

15. M. Allewaert, "Swamp Sublime: Ecologies of Resistance in the American Plantation Zone," *PMLA* 123.2 (2008), 341, 342. Elsewhere, Allewaert reads the figure of Bashra, the obi-man, as "so infolded in the tropics' weaving of trees, animals and smells that he is not in this ecology but fully of it" (*Ariel's Ecology: Plantations, Personhood, and Colonialism in the American Tropics* [Minneapolis: Univ. of Minnesota Press, 2013], 127). My reading suggests that the same is true of Jack. Allewaert's discussion of the fetish in relation to *Obi* is worth reading in full (*Ariel's*, 126–35).

16. Earle is hardly alone in establishing such a framework: Allewaert describes the effect of tropical swamps in William Bartram's 1791 *Travels*, for example, as one of bodily disintegration, noting that this disintegration affected the bodies of free whites in quite different ways from those of enslaved Africans or escaped slaves. While swamps sundered the integrity of the former, they "sheltered diasporic Africans who, in refusing slave status, repudiated the prevailing organization of…[the] plantation economy" ("Swamp," 343).

17. George in turn tells these stories to Charles over the course of many letters, but he tells them in the voice of Amri addressing Jack. In doing so, Earle packages an oral African family narrative within a written Anglo-American business correspondence.

18. Recent developments within plant studies (which have emerged in dialogue with animal studies) engage with precisely such questions about the relations between the

human and the plant. See Randy Laist, "Introduction," in *Plants and Literature: Essays in Critical Plant Studies*, ed. Randy Laist (New York: Rodopi, 2013), 9–17 and Michael Marder, *Plant-Thinking: A Philosophy of Vegetal Life* (New York: Columbia Univ. Press, 2013).

19. William Moulton, *A Concise Extract, from the Sea Journal of William Moulton; written on board of the Onico* (Utica, 1804), iii, 129.

20. Moulton's knowledge of Cook's text is evidence of the often underestimated shipboard literacy rates during this period; see Hester Blum, *The View from the Mast-Head: Maritime Imagination and Antebellum American Sea Narratives* (Chapel Hill: Univ. of North Carolina Press, 2008).

21. Moulton, 28, 101. After hiking to another harbor in hopes of finding a different ship to board, Moulton finds his ship there and he is brought back on board. For another consideration of Moulton, see Greg Grandin, *The Empire of Necessity: Slavery, Freedom, and Deception in the New World* (New York: Metropolitan Books, 2014).

22. Moulton, 102. Erasmus Darwin has a similar model in mind when he observes that "the last method of supporting animal bodies by the destruction of other living animals, as lions preying upon lambs, these upon living vegetables, and mankind upon them all, would appear to be a less perfect part of the economy of nature than those before mentioned [such as drinking the milk supplied by animals], as contributing less to the sum of general happiness." *The Botanic Garden*, 2 vols. (1791; repr. New York: Garland, 1978), I.28. Future references to this text will appear parenthetically.

23. Amasa Delano, *A Narrative of Voyages and Travels, in the Northern and Southern Hemispheres*, 2nd ed. (Boston, 1818), 200.

24. See Douglas Oliver, "Introduction," in *Return to Tahiti: Bligh's Second Breadfruit Voyage* (Honolulu: Univ. of Hawai'i Press, 1988), 4; and Caroline Alexander, "Captain Bligh's Cursed Breadfruit," *Smithsonian Magazine* (Sept. 2009),. www.smithsonianmag.com

25. Joseph Banks popularized the notion that Tahitians did not "earn their bread with the sweat of their brow" because "their cheifest sustenance Bread fruit is procurd with no more trouble than that of climbing a tree and pulling it down." Joseph Banks, *The Endeavour Journal of Joseph Banks, 1768–1771*, ed. J. C. Beaglehole (Sydney: Angus and Robertson, 1963), 341–2.

26. Greg Dening, *Mr. Bligh's Bad Language: Passion, Power and Theatre on the Bounty* (Cambridge: Cambridge Univ. Press, 1992), 11. Jill Casid, *Sowing Empire: Landscape and Colonization* (Minneapolis: Univ. of Minnesota Press, 2005), 7. Of course, this Polynesian fantasy depends on an imperial obliviousness to the bodies and labor of Tahitians, an oblivion that recurs, Beth Fowkes Tobin notes, in the Caribbean with "even more convoluted obfuscations than those in the imperial descriptions of the Pacific." "Caribbean Subjectivity and the Colonial Archive," *Small Axe* 25 (Feb. 2008), 154.

27. Richard S. Dunn, *Sugar and Slaves: The Rise of the Planter Class in the English West Indies, 1624–1713* (Chapel Hill: Univ. of North Carolina Press, 1972), 39.

28. Edward Long, *The History of Jamaica* (1774; New York: Arno Press, 1972), 355, 356.

29. Long, 362, 363, 371. See also Krista A. Thompson's discussion of a similar "imperial picturesque" in William Beckford's 1790 *Descriptive Account of the Island of Jamaica*. Beckford's descriptions of the island's plants align with his descriptions of the island's slaves, as if they, too, have been "reworked through picturesque aesthetics" into a "naturalized" landscape, "like the colonial botanical transplants" (*An Eye for the Tropics: Tourism, Photography, and Framing the Caribbean Picturesque* [Durham: Duke Univ. Press, 2006], 41).

30. Long, 362, 447–8.

31. Bryan Edwards, *The History, Civil and Commercial, of the British Colonies in the West Indies*, Vols. 1 and 2 (New York: Arno Press, 1972), 77, 187. Edwards places the West Indians ahead of the Tahitians for seeming to generate a wider variety and abundance of food, "bread fruit excepted" (78).

32. Edwards, *The History, Civil and Commercial, of the British Colonies in the West Indies*, 3 vols. 3rd ed., with considerable additions (London, 1801), III.v.

33. Indeed, "Royal botanic gardens, in the second half of the eighteenth century, became instruments through which kings (or, more proximately, their ministers) sought to show the virtue of their authority"—such as George III's plan for Caribbean botanic gardens, which were designed to serve as an "entrepôt through which Asian and Pacific plants, brought by Bligh on the Bounty, would be introduced to the West Indies, and through which New World plants would return to Kew"; see Richard Drayton, *Nature's Government: Science, Imperial Britain, and the "Improvement" of the World* (New Haven: Yale Univ. Press, 2000), 50, 87. In his *Reflections on the Revolution in France*, Edmund Burke uses botanical taxonomy satirically to categorize revolutionary dissent, suggesting that it would be helpful to add "to the ample collection of known classes, genera and species, which at present beautify the *hortus siccus* of dissent" (13; qtd. in Theresa M. Kelley, "Romantic Exemplarity: Botany and 'Material' Culture," in *Romantic Science: The Literary Forms of Natural History*, ed. Noah Heringman [Albany: State Univ. of New York Press, 2003], 233).

34. Edwards (1972), 188; Drayton, 115.

35. Kay Dian Kris, "Curiosities, Commodities, and Transplanted Bodies in Hans Sloane's 'Natural History of Jamaica,'" *The William and Mary Quarterly* 3rd ser. 57.1 (2000), 41, 45.

36. Hans Sloane, *A Voyage to the Islands Madera, Barbados, Nieves, St. Christophers and Jamaica*, 2 vols. (London, 1707), 134, 163–4, 179, 179.

37. As Bewell insists, "during the late eighteenth century botanical description was so imbued with socio-sexual implications that no botanical description was entirely removed from these concerns" ("'Jacobin Plants': Botany as Social Theory in the 1790s," *Wordsworth Circle* 20 [1989], 134). For more on the use of analogy in Darwin, see Catherine Packham, "The Science and Poetry of Animation: Personification, Analogy, and Erasmus Darwin's *Loves of the Plants*," *Romanticism* 10.2 (2004), 191–208. On the global scope of Darwin's poem, see Alan Bewell, "Erasmus Darwin's Cosmopolitan Nature," *ELH* 76.1 (2009), 19–48.

38. Darwin's *Botanic Garden* has two parts, "The Economy of Vegetation" and "The Loves of Plants," each of which was also published separately and each of which is accompanied by extensive prose footnotes (as Pierre Danchin notes, there are 2500 lines of poetry to over 7000 lines of prose in volume one, and 2000 lines of poetry to about 3000 of prose in volume two ["Erasmus Darwin's Scientific and Poetic Purpose in The Botanic Garden," in *Science and Imagination in XVIIIth-Century British Culture*, ed. Sergio Rossi [Milan: Edizioni Unicopi, 1987], 136). These voluminous and interruptive notes function as a kind of companion prose text to the poem, offering to the latter's aesthetic lyricism a kind of technical manual counterpart. Darwin's book also appeared in an American edition in 1798, put out by Elihu Hubbard Smith, who also championed the recent publications of his close friend, Charles Brockden Brown.

39. Bewell, "Jacobin," 134.

40. Both plants and humans are subjected to the transoceanic enterprise of transplantation. While this argument seems to apply to the Atlantic slave system in

particular, it can also be extended to systems of slavery in the Pacific, as well as to the transoceanic transportation of indigenous peoples such as the Tahitian Native Mai (see Chapter 4).

41. In this regard, Earle's novel is a departure from Fawcett's pantomime, since the drama "almost completely silenc[es] its black rogue," while still foregrounding Jack's banditry (Reed, 101). For a subtle reading of Southey's anti-slavery poetry and his image of the "blood-sweetened beverage," see Timothy Morton, "Blood Sugar," in *Romanticism and Colonialism: Writing and Empire, 1780–1830*, eds. Timothy Fulford and Peter Kitson (Cambridge: Cambridge Univ. Press, 1998), 98–106. The beverage to which Southey refers is probably coffee or tea sweetened by sugar, but it could also refer to the rum produced as a by-product of sugar manufacture.

42. Bewell, "Jacobin," 135. Darwin's ideas about sexuality and gender are often aligned with those of other radical thinkers of his time. He helped to found the intellectual Lunar Society in Birmingham, and shared a book publisher with Mary Wollstonecraft, Thomas Paine, and William Godwin. Donald H. Reiman argues that Darwin pursued a conventional poetic form precisely in order to conceal his book's "revolutionary thinking," as if the former provided a safe container for his radical social and political ideas; "Introduction" to Darwin, v. As Fredrike J. Teute notes, young American intellectuals of the time turned to both Darwin and Wollstonecraft for visions of a new social order whose models originated in the natural world, and they found in botany a "medium for the exploration of heterogeneous sexuality and a conduit for politicized social commentary"; "The Loves of Plants; or, the Cross-Fertilization of Science and Desire at the End of the Eighteenth Century," *Huntington Library Quarterly* 63.3 (2002), 320, 326.

43. "The Vegetable Economy" is divided into four cantos, each devoted to one of the four elements of the natural world. In each of these cantos, the Goddess of Botany addresses one of four figures "representing the elements" (I.vii): salamanders for fire (canto one), gnomes for earth (canto two), nymphs for water (canto three), and sylphs for air (canto four). Devin S. Griffiths notes Darwin's imagery of circularity through which "'little circles' reverberate in inverted pairs that cohere in 'one revolving Whole' of correspondences and extension" ("The Intuitions of Analogy in Erasmus Darwin's Poetics," *Studies in English Literature* 51.3 [2011], 657).

44. James E. McClellan, *Colonialism and Science: Saint Domingue and the Old Regime* (Chicago: Univ. of Chicago Press, 2010), xx.

45. Christopher Iannini, *Fatal Revolutions: Natural History, West Indian Slavery, and the Routes of American Literature* (Chapel Hill: Univ. of North Carolina Press, 2012), 221, 238.

46. Allawaert, "Swamp," 353; DeLoughrey, "Globalizing," para. 14.

47. Darwin was close friends with Wedgwood, whose daughter married Darwin's son (Lydia H. Liu, "Robinson Crusoe's Earthenware Pot: Science, Aesthetics, and the Metaphysics of True Porcelain," in *Romantic Science: The Literary Forms of Natural History*, ed. Noah Heringman [Albany: State Univ. of New York Press, 2003], 161). See Liu also for a discussion of the competition between British earthenware and Chinese porcelain during this period, in relation to Defoe's *Robinson Crusoe*. Darwin also refers to a second cameo by Wedgwood made from the soil of Australia, which depicted "Hope attended by Peace, and Art, and Labour; which was made of clay from Botany Bay; to which place he sent many of them to shew the inhabitants what their materials would do, and to encourage their industry" (I.87).

48. Beth Fowkes Tobin, *Colonizing Nature: The Tropics in British Arts and Letters, 1760–1820* (Philadelphia: Univ. of Pennsylvania Press, 2005), 61. In addition to keeping slaves well fed, provision grounds provided them with knowledge about plant life, and the legacy of this syncretic herbal practice endures even today in the fluid interchanges between folk medicine and biomedicine that persist in Jamaican practice. See Arvilla Payne-Jackson and Mervyn C. Alleyne, *Jamaican Folk Medicine: A Source of Healing* (Kingston, Jamaica: Univ. of the West Indies Press, 2004), 8; they note that folk medical knowledge was likely to survive and persist beyond the Middle Passage (15), and medical knowledge may even have been "one of the rare areas of African culture whose survival and continuity in the New World were enhanced by the condition of slavery" (16), in part because slaveholders' lack of attention to the health of their slaves left medical care largely in the hands of the latter. As the Caribbean population became increasingly African and its culture increasingly Afro-Caribbean, "most treatments for most ailments more closely followed West African traditions than Galenic ones. African healers used herbs and medicinal plants, often improvising in the Caribbean" (J. R. McNeill, *Mosquito Empires: Ecology and War in the Greater Caribbean, 1620–1914* [Cambridge: Cambridge Univ. Press, 2010], 81).

49. DeLoughrey contends that "the breadfruit transfer was also an attempt on the part of Caribbean planters to alter the food preferences of the slaves and by extension, the landscape and marketability of the provision grounds" which was "increasingly controlled by slaves, particularly women" ("Globalizing," para. 37).

50. The plantain grown in these plots, for instance, was both food and medicine, for it could be used as an anti-edemic, anti-inflammatory, anti-viral, or as a laxative, bactericide, or sedative (see Payne-Jackson and Alleyne). In his work on the Caribbean, John Parry has suggested that the scholarly focus on sugar betrays the dominance of a metropolitan framework that ought to be met with an equally local focus on "the story of yams, cassava, and salt fish" ("Plantation and Provision Ground: An Historical Sketch of the Introduction of Food Crops into Jamaica," *Revista de historia de América* 39 [1955], 1).

51. Sidney W. Mintz locates the existence of what he calls peasantries in "the crevices" of Caribbean society, "in places where the plantations failed, or in places where the plantation never came" including sites where agricultural conditions were unfavorable to sugarcane cultivation ("From Plantations to Peasantries in the Caribbean," in *Caribbean Contours*, eds. Sidney W. Mintz and Sally Price [Baltimore: Johns Hopkins Univ. Press, 1985], 131). In particular, he identifies a proto-peasantry of slaves who grew their own food and sold surpluses for profit at local markets (133). For more on provision grounds, see DeLoughrey, "Yam, Roots, and Rot: Allegories of the Provision Grounds," *Small Axe* 15.1 (2011), 58–65. For a Pacific world account of a botanical garden in competition with "kitchen gardens" in early nineteenth-century Sydney, see Jim Endersby, "A Garden Enclosed: Botanical Barter in Sydney, 1818–39," *The British Journal for the History of Science* 33.3 (2000), 313–34. Endersby also argues that the botanical empire represented by Kew was in fact founded on practices of plant exchange that developed in the colonies rather than the center (333).

52. For an extensive discussion of breadfruit's historical comparison to bread (and the eucharist), see Vanessa Smith, "Give Us Our Daily Breadfruit: Bread Substitution in the Pacific in the Eighteenth Century," *Studies in Eighteenth-Century Culture* 35 (2006), 53–75.

53. Payne-Jackson and Alleyne, 144.

54. Called "Bohon-Upas" by the Malays, the tree is so toxic that only "condemned criminals are sent... to get the juice." Those who succeed in returning with the juice are

"pardoned" for their crime, but "not one in four are said to return" (II.115). This tree is evocative of Yann Martel's carnivorous island in *Life of Pi*.

55. These slave provision grounds were typically located at considerable distances from the slaves' homes in "mountainous terrain unsuitable for sugar cane production" (Tobin, *Colonizing*, 59–60). Dunn explains that yaws was "clinically similar to syphilis," and indeed its symptoms were often confused with those of the venereal disease (Dunn, 305). Yaws is also described in several early accounts of Jamaica, including Sloane's natural history and Henry Barham's *Hortus Americanus*, a medical-botanical catalog of Jamaican plants and their uses for treating a variety of diseases. Both Sloane and Barham appear as source texts in the footnotes to Darwin's *Botanic Garden*.

56. Benjamin Moseley, *A Treatise on Sugar* (London, 1799), in Earle, ed. Aravamudan, 161, 163. Because those afflicted with the highly infectious yaws were typically avoided by white doctors, treatment was left to the island's "slave nurses," the vast majority of whom were disabled or disfigured. See Payne-Jackson and Alleyne, 18, 21.

57. Moseley, 163, 163–4.

58. Lenora Warren notes that "the years immediately before and after Tacky's Rebellion witnessed some of the bloodiest incidents in the history of shipboard insurrection," with sixty-nine shipboard insurrections documented between 1760 and 1771; "Insurrection at Sea: Violence, the Slave Trade, and the Rhetoric of Abolition," *Atlantic Studies* 10.2 (2013), 199. Adding a transoceanic dimension to work on maritime slave rebellions allows us to recognize the global dimensions to what was really an amphibian age of revolution.

59. Clarkson, qtd. in Warren, 203.

60. It is also worth remembering that the breadfruit transplantation scheme was initially tied to the felon transportation scheme, as the *Bounty* was intended to stop at Botany Bay with convicts before arriving in Tahiti to pick up the breadfruit destined for the West Indies (David Mackey, *In the Wake of Cook: Exploration, Science & Empire, 1780–1801* [New York: St. Martin's Press, 1985], 131). Indeed, the uncle for whom Bligh had worked in Jamaica was also involved in the transport of felons to Australia (see DeLoughrey, "Globalizing," para. 39).

61. Dening, 63, 88. For more on Bligh's two breadfruit voyages to Tahiti, see Jennifer Newell, *Trading Nature: Tahitians, Europeans, and Ecological Exchange* (Honolulu: Univ. of Hawai'i Press, 2010), esp. 141–70. Scholars have recently pointed out that some ship captains "were reluctant to accept biocargo, especially live plants or animals that put demands on a vessel's limited supply of space and water far out of proportion to the profit they promised" (Christopher M. Parsons and Kathleen S. Murphy, "Ecosystems under Sail: Specimen Transport in the Eighteenth-Century French and British Atlantics," *Early American Studies* [2012], 514).

62. George Vancouver, *A Voyage of Discovery to the North Pacific Ocean, and Round the World*, 3 vols. (London, 1798), I.148. Cook also planted gardens in New Zealand, and distributed turnip, parsnip, and carrot seeds in Tonga (Tobin, *Colonizing*, 7). James Colnett planted celery, onions, and turnips on Cocos Island and Socorro during his 1793–4 voyage, and William Bligh planted European seeds in Tasmania and Tahiti during both of his Pacific voyages (Frost, 66).

63. Vancouver, I.147; Bougainville, 286. The bodies of women repeatedly appear at this complicated nexus of sexual and political freedom in early accounts of the Pacific. See, for example, Margaret Jolly's discussion of Johann Forster's use of the stadial theory of

development from savagery to civilization to discuss Pacific island women as well as Pacific flora, fauna, and landscapes ("Women of the East, Women of the West: Region and Race, Gender and Sexuality on Cook's Voyages," in *The Atlantic World in the Antipodes: Effects and Transformations since the Eighteenth Century*, ed. Kate Fullagar [Newcastle upon Tyne: Cambridge Scholars Publishing, 2012], 2–32). See also DeLoughrey on the breadfruit's alignment with white settler nationalism and "its extensive diasporic 'seeds,' including the mutineers' progeny with local women." These Tahitian women later revolted against the mutineers after they accompanied them to Pitcairn Island ("Globalizing," para. 8). Europe, meanwhile, experienced a vogue in botanical study among well-to-do women, for whom books like Darwin's "Loves of Plants" served as an educational textbook both in plant and sexual knowledge (Anne Shteir, *Culivating Women, Cultivating Science: Flora's Daughters and Botany in England 1760–1860* [Baltimore: Johns Hopkins Univ. Press, 1996], 4). This trend also marked the end, however, of an earlier tradition in which plants were a source of medical knowledge and practice dominated by women. As Shteir explains, by the second half of the century "many women in the gentrifying middle ranks lost or left behind their familiarity with traditional healing practices and relied more on male physicians than on female skills" (39). The fascinating story of Jeanne Baret exemplifies this shift, for Commerçon relied on her knowledge about plants (as well as her physical capabilities) to guide and perform his specimen collection (see Ridley). The sexual exploitation and infection of indigenous women as a result of these voyages is one of the most complex stories from the eighteenth-century Pacific, particularly because the details of sexual negotiation and desire transpired at the crossroads of two very different cultural systems whose encounter is recorded largely in writing produced by European visitors and observers. See Jolly and Patty O'Brien, *The Pacific Muse: Exotic Femininity and the Colonial Pacific* (Seattle: Univ. of Washington Press, 2006).

64. Included in the later sale of Hinton East's estate were thirty-nine slaves, some of whom were gardeners both in East's garden and their own (Hall, 108).

65. Another of the many layers of the breadfruit fantasy was its cultivation. As an extensive entry on "Breadfruit" in David Brewster's *The Edinburgh Encyclopaedia* would later report, breadfruit was in fact not as easy to cultivate as Banks and others imagined, for "the bread fruit tree…requires some years to bring it to maturity, [and] the mode of propagation is tedious." This propagation method involves extracting the root from the earth and "wound[ing] with a spade" "one of the branches of the root." Shortly after, a "shoot springs up from the wound," after which "the shoot is sufficiently vigorous to bear removal." Subsequently, "the young plant is then dug up, with a proper quantity of earth, and placed in a hole, in which it soon fixes itself" and three years later, it begins to bear fruit ("Breadfruit," Vol. 4. *Edinburgh Encyclopedia*, 18 vols. [Edinburgh, 1830], 447). Growing breadfruit, in other words, seems to entail a kind of violence against the plant intended to force its propagation, followed by a time-consuming replanting and waiting period before any fruit will appear. The Pacific voyages of William Dampier and James Cook (both the Hawkesworth edition of the earlier voyages and the King edition of the last voyage) are referred to and cited in Brewster's article.

66. In contrast to the complex, laborious, and time-consuming scheme for reproducing breadfruit trees, the plantain plant practically reproduces itself, as Brewster explains: "one root sends up many shoots in regular succession, and this it continues to do for many years. After the first planting of these, the cultivator has no further trouble than to cut down the

shoots on which the fruit is fit for use, and these are in their turn regularly replaced by others." Therefore "there will always be a regular succession of fruit for many years" (Brewster, "Breadfruit," 448).

67. McNeill, 24.

68. Long, 391–2.

69. Srinivas Aravamudan notes in the introduction to his edition of the novel that the form "mimics the many correspondences maintained between overseers of plantations and their absentee landlords" ("Introduction," *Obi; or, The History of Three-Fingered Jack* by William Earle, 8). By the end of the seventeenth century, when Jamaica had already been taken over by large plantations "manned by armies of slaves," the plantation owners "had withdrawn from the island as much as possible, retiring to England as absentee proprietors" (Long, 151).

70. For an analysis that emphasizes George's haunting by Jack, and the role of haunting in the novel more generally, see Keith Sandiford, "William Earle's Novella: *Obi*, Obeah and the Ideological Work of Haunting," *Symbolism: An International Annual of Critical Aesthetics* 14 (2014), 221–43.

Chapter 7

1. Junot Díaz, *The Brief Wondrous Life of Oscar Wao* (New York: Riverhead Books, 2007), 1–2.

2. On the modern world system, see Immanuel Wallerstein, *The Modern World-System: Capitalist Agriculture and the Origins of the European World-Economy in the Sixteenth Century* (New York: Academic, 1974) and *The Modern World-System II: Mercantilism and the Consolidation of the European World-Economy, 1600–1750* (New York: Academic, 1980). On its origins in the Americas, see Aníbal Quijano and Immanuel Wallerstein, "Americanity as a Concept, or the Americas in the Modern World-System," *ISSJ* 134 (1992), 549–57. On the modern/colonial world system, see Walter D. Mignolo, *Local Histories/Global Designs: Coloniality, Subaltern Knowledges, and Border Thinking* (Princeton: Princeton Univ. Press, 2000).

3. Although use of the name Santo Domingo to identify the island causes some confusion with the Spanish colony of Santo Domingo on the eastern portion of the island, I conform to the early nineteenth-century practice of Sansay and others in using that term in this chapter to refer to the island as a whole.

4. See Junot Díaz, "The Silence: The Legacy of Childhood Trauma," *The New Yorker* (Apr. 16, 2016), www.newyorker.com; and Kristine Phillips, "Pulitzer Prize-winning author Junot Díaz accused of sexual misconduct, misogynistic behavior," *Washington Post* (May 6, 2016), www.washingtonpost.com.

5. For an excellent analysis of how "matters of the intimate are critical sites for the consolidation of colonial power" (4), see Ann Laura Stoler, "Intimations of Empire: Predicaments of the Tactile and Unseen," in *Haunted by Empire: Geographies of Intimacy in North American History*, ed. Stoler (Durham: Duke Univ. Press, 2006), 1–22.

6. Sven Beckert, *The Empire of Cotton: A Global History* (New York: Knopf, 2015), 90.

7. Beckert, 91.

8. Patty O'Brien, *The Pacific Muse: Exotic Femininity and the Colonial Pacific* (Seattle: Univ. of Washington Press, 2006), 33, 57.

9. Frantz Fanon, *The Wretched of the Earth*, trans. Constance Farrington (New York: Grove Press, 1968); Albert Memmi, *The Colonizer and the Colonized*, trans. Howard Greenfield (Boston: Beacon Press, 1967); Homi K. Bhabha, ed. *The Location of Culture* (New York: Routledge, 1994); Robert J. C. Young, *Colonial Desire: Hybridity in Theory, Culture, and Race* (New York: Routledge, 1995).

10. Eve Kosofsky Sedgwick's widely employed model of homosocial triangulated desire draws from the narrative studies of Girard and describes the rerouting of desire through a third figure whose socially legitimizing presence masks the expression of otherwise illegitimate desire; *Between Men: English Literature and Male Homosocial Desire* (New York: Columbia Univ. Press, 1985). The concept of triangulated desire has been used to understand the inequalities of colonial and racial relations in addition to those of gender and sexuality; see, for example, Beth Kramer, "Postcolonial Triangles: An Analysis of Masculinity and Homosocial Desire in Achebe's *A Man of the People* and Greene's *The Quiet American*," *Postcolonial Text* 4.4 (2008), 1–14, and Susan Fraiman, "Geometries of Race and Gender: Eve Sedgwick, Spike Lee, Charlayne Hunter-Gault," *Feminist Studies* 20.1 (1994), 67–84.

11. Slavoj Žižek, *The Ticklish Subject: The Absent Center of Political Ontology* (London: Verso, 1999), 293 and *The Parallax View* (Cambridge: MIT Press, 2006), 61.

12. The movements of the two women and their letters trace out a geographical triangle between three islands in the Caribbean. The vertices of this triangle are marked by the cities of Le Cap on the northwest coast of Haiti, Kingston on the southeast shore of Jamaica, and a collection of small towns (Barracoa, St. Jago, El Cobre, and Bayam) along the southern side of Cuba (see Figure 7.1). It bears mentioning that the routes between almost any of those locations would have taken these women past the entrance to Guantánamo Bay, a location that today remains subject to land crab migrations among other, far greater, offenses.

13. Michael J. Drexler notes that "the Mary and Clara personae were always intended to have represented the split persona of Sansay herself" ("Brigands and Nuns: The Vernacular Sociology of Collectivity after the Haitian Revolution," *Messy Beginnings: Postcoloniality and Early American Studies*, eds. Malini Johar Schueller and Edward Watts [New Brunswick: Rutgers Univ. Press, 2003], 199, n.47). Gretchen Woertendyke suggests that Sansay's creation of herself "as a dual-character" allows her to be both a "body [that] gets bought and sold into marriage" and an observer able to "highlight her body as one part of a colonial exchange" ("Romance to Novel: A Secret History," *Narrative* 17.3 [Oct. 2009], 264). Sean X. Goudie aligns Mary with creoleness and Clara with creolité (209–10), the former unable "to let go of her conservative bourgeois value system" and the latter "marked by her intricate relations with oppressed peoples across the islands of the West Indies" (*Creole America: The West Indies and the Formation of Literature and Culture in the New Republic* [Philadelphia: Univ. of Pennsylvania Press, 2006], 211).

14. In 1808, when Sansay's novel was published, Aaron Burr had sailed for Europe after having just been acquitted in a trial for treason, in which he was accused of plotting to incite a revolution in the trans-Mississippi West with the purported goal of conquering and becoming emperor of Mexico. These details make Mary's hope that Burr will serve as "friend and protector" to Clara ironic at best—but if so, this irony additionally makes a point about the reliability of men in the context of military, political, and commercial power that has everything to do with Sansay's novel. On the significance of Burr to *Secret History*, see Drexler, "The Displacement of the American Novel: Imagining Aaron Burr and Haiti in Leonora Sansay's *Secret History*," *Common-place* 9.3 (Apr. 2009), www.common-place.org;

for a recent biography of Burr, see Nancy Isenberg, *Fallen Founder: A Life of Aaron Burr* (New York: Viking, 2007); for a study of Burr's significance to American cultural and political history, particularly in relation to the figure of Toussaint Louverture, see Drexler and Ed White, *The Traumatic Colonel: The Founding Fathers, Slavery, and the Phantasmatic Aaron Burr* (New York: New York Univ. Press, 2014).

15. While acknowledging that most of what we know about Sansay comes from the personal writings of Burr, Drexler describes Sansay's reputation as one of "a public woman, a coquette" who was "capricious, witty, and inconstant in her attachments" (Introduction, *Secret History; or the Horrors of Santo Domingo* and *Laura*, by Leonora Sansay, 27). Jennifer Van Bergen, whose reconstruction of Sansay's life depends heavily on a biographical reading of her novels, suggests that Sansay met Burr not through her stepfather's tavern but rather through her boyfriend, who may have turned to Burr in order to provide assistance to Sansay. Van Bergen questions the oft-repeated assumption that Sansay was Burr's lover, suggesting rather that he was a "mentor" to her, and that they may have shared political sympathies regarding abolitionism, Native American rights, and the project for revolution in Mexico known as the "Burr Conspiracy." See "Reconstructing Leonora Sansay," *Another World is Possible.* Jan. 3, 2010. www.a-w-i-p.com/index.php/2010/01/03/reconstructing-leonora-sansay.

16. Drexler, Introduction, 28.

17. Drexler, "Leonora Sansay's Anatopic Imagination," in *Urban Identity and the Atlantic World*, eds. Elizabeth Fay and Leonard Von Morzé (New York: Palgrave Macmillan, 2013), 148.

18. As Elizabeth Maddock Dillon puts it, in *Secret History* "the violence of colonialism is revealed to be closely bound together with unjust patriarchal authority" and the novel suggests that "what is most hidden within the colonial scene is not interracial violence but the violence of men turned upon women" ("The Secret History of the Early American Novel: Leonora Sansay and the Revolution in Saint Domingue," *Novel* 40.1/2 [Fall 2006/Spring 2007], 92). Joan Dayan insists that in this novel "fictions of love are inextricable from facts of conquest" (169), that "sexual conquests seemed equal in importance to military feats" (*Haiti, History, and the Gods* [Berkeley: Univ. of California Press, 1995], 170), while Woertendyke notes that the novel "joins the domestic terror of Clara's marriage to St. Louis to the revolutionary horror of Saint-Domingue" (256) and "establishes the intimacy of historical violence, on the one hand, and ... the historical significance of violence in domestic space" on the other ("Romance," 262). Drexler observes that "Clara's liberation from her husband runs parallel to the revolutionary liberation of Saint-Domingue" ("Brigands," 191). I am placing these intertwined stories of violence and desire in Clara's Saint Domingue within the larger transoceanic context of capitalist drive.

19. Leonora Sansay, *Secret History; or, the Horrors of St. Domingo*, ed. Michael J. Drexler (1808; repr. Peterborough, ON: Broadview Press, 2007), 138, 61. Future references to the novel will appear parenthetically.

20. Comparable triangles abound in the novel, from the one linking Clara, Mary, and Burr to the one between General Leclerc, Madame Leclerc, and General Boyer.

21. Christopher L. Miller, *The French Atlantic Triangle: Literature and Culture of the Slave Trade* (Durham: Duke Univ. Press, 2008), 26, 248, 17.

22. Miller, ix; Drexler, Introduction, 19.

23. Doris Garraway, *The Libertine Colony: Creolization in the Early French Caribbean* (Durham: Duke Univ. Press, 2005), 240.

24. Antonio Benítez-Rojo, *The Repeating Island: The Caribbean and the Postmodern Perspective*, trans. James E. Maraniss (Durham: Duke Univ. Press, 1992), 5, 5, 7.

25. For details about the fate of La Pérouse's voyage and his narrative, see John Dunmore, "Introduction," in *The Journal of Jean-François de Galaup de la Pérouse, 1785–1788*, 2 vols., trans. and ed. John Dunmore (London: The Hakluyt Society, 1994), I.ccvii–ccxxix. Dunmore explains that La Pérouse regularly sent written accounts of his voyage back to France, so that much of his voyage survived into print even though the ships and men on it were lost at sea. Later research confirmed that his ships were wrecked near the south Pacific island of Vanikoro, probably in a cyclone.

26. Scholars such as Dillon and Woertendyke have linked Sansay's subtitle with her novel's participation in the earlier genre of the "secret history" and its use of private details to tell a more public story. It is also tempting to think of the reference to secrecy in Sansay's title in relation to the concealed commercial instructions that often accompanied voyages of discovery like La Pérouse's into the Pacific, if only because her novel exposes precisely the commercial relations in whose cycles of violence everyone on San Domingue is ensnared.

27. James R. Gibson, *Otter Skins, Boston Ships, and China Goods: The Maritime Fur Trade of the Northwest Coast 1785–1841* (Seattle: Univ. of Washington Press, 1992), 22–3.

28. Gibson, 49, 57.

29. Beginning in the 1820s, a trade glut and a decrease in furs led to a rapid dwindling of profits; by the 1840s the fur trade was depleted and abandoned; see Gibson, 66, 82.

30. La Pérouse's narrative was published in France in 1797, and quickly appeared in an English translation in London in 1798 and in an abridged version in Boston in 1801 (where it was bound together with accounts of the Pacific voyages of the Spaniard Maurelle and the Englishman Vancouver). At least eleven editions of Cook's third voyage were published between 1793 and 1818 in North American cities, and many of these featured an opening illustration of Native women dancing and performing. Pacific islands also served as the locations for various transnational utopian fictions, including the Marquis de Sade's 1795 epistolary novel *Aline et Valcour* (which includes a character named Léonore), August von Kotzebue's 1799 two-act drama *La Peyrouse*, and Charles Brockden Brown's 1801 fragment "The Narrative of Signior Adini."

31. Jean-François de Galaup de La Pérouse, *The Journal of Jean-François de Galaup de la Pérouse, 1785–1788*, 2 vols., trans. and ed. John Dunmore (London: The Hakluyt Society, 1994), 180, 183, 183, 174. The careers of many of the mariners who led these Pacific voyages illustrate the interconnectedness of the Atlantic, Pacific, Caribbean, and even Indian oceans. Before leading the expedition into the Pacific, for example, La Pérouse spent much of his naval career supplying and defending French colonial possessions in the Atlantic—in Nova Scotia, in Newfoundland, in Hudson Bay—as well as in the Caribbean, where he captured and delivered a ship to Santo Domingo in the early 1780s. He also served on the French island colony of Île de France (now Mauritius) in the Indian Ocean, where he controversially and secretly married a lower middle class creole woman (see Dunmore, "Introduction," xliv–lviii).

32. La Pérouse, 393, 407. La Pérouse suggests that it was competition among some of the islanders for the beads given by the French that may have led to the revolt (407), although it may also have been revenge for the French crew's earlier act of throwing a disorderly islander overboard (393).

33. C. L. R. James, *The Black Jacobins: Toussaint L'Ouverture and the San Domingo Revolution*, 2nd ed., rev. (New York: Vintage Books, 1989), 46.

34. Goudie, 211; Drexler, "Brigands," 190.

35. Joan Dayan accurately points out that it is the greedy, lazy French Europeans who are the central object of Sansay's disgust and hostility in the novel. The French creoles view the French Europeans with suspicion and "a jealous eye" (66) and perceive "in the army sent to defend them, oppressors who appear to seek their destruction" by appropriating their homes and their slaves (76). But the novel also indicates that the creoles have themselves claimed and consumed such homes and slaves through forced subjection, exploitation, and appropriation.

36. Daniel Cottom, *Cannibals and Philosophers: Bodies of Enlightenment* (Baltimore: Johns Hopkins Univ. Press, 2001), 154–5. The fact that Cook, following his murder by Hawai'ian islanders, would later become a purported victim of cannibalism himself suggests how the rotating cycle of consumption and exploitation produces revolution and rebellion as well as accumulation and wealth, and how the positions of agent and victim of power can so easily be reversed.

37. Marcus Rainsford, *An Historical Account of the Black Empire of Hayti* (London, 1805), 2–3, 9, 12.

38. Rainsford, 64.

39. For a different reading of coquettes and female agency in the novel, see Melissa Adams-Campbell, "Romantic Revolutions: Love and Violence in Leonora Sansay's *Secret History, or the Horrors of St. Domingo*," *Studies in American Fiction* 39.2 (2012), 125–46.

40. Rainsford, 77.

41. Joan Dayan describes how the French sometimes had to incite the dogs to eat black flesh, and how the historical General Boyer at one point "leapt into the arena, slit open the stomach of his" own servant "and pulled out the guts in order to incite the dogs" (*Haiti*, 155). It is worth placing this historical anecdote against the anecdote describing General Boyer early in *Secret History*, in which he is seen sitting at the foot of the bored and reclining Madame Leclerc—wife of General Leclerc and sister to Napoleon Bonaparte—who lets "her slipper fall continually, which he respectfully put on as often as it fell" (Sansay, 64). In Saint Domingue, the languid compulsion of flirtation and seduction are never far from the grotesque excess of brutality and violence, desire never far from drive; as Dayan notes, "Rochambeau gave his most exceptional balls after his most horrific tortures" (156).

42. This represents a disproportionate ratio of over twelve enslaved blacks to every free white inhabitant of the colony. Citing this numerical disproportion has become a virtual trope in scholarship on the Haitian Revolution.

43. Drexler goes on to read this scene as one that "conflates enlightenment theories concerning racial and geo-temporal difference with the visceral acknowledgment of the potency of indigenous anticolonial mobilization" ("Brigands," 191). For an ecological reading of the land crabs as gothic reproductive menace, see Abby L. Goode, "Gothic Fertility in Leonora Sansay's *Secret History*," *Early American Literature* 50.2 (2015), 449–73. For an analysis of the novel that foregrounds female eroticism, see Helen Hunt, " 'Fascinate, Intoxicate, Transport': Uncovering Women's Erotic Dominance in Leonora Sansay's *Secret History*," *Legacy* 33.1 (2016), 31–54.

44. Jeremy D. Popkin warns that reports of "white women's victimization by blacks" should "be treated with caution" given "the propagandistic use that proslavery groups made" of such stories, though also acknowledges that "one can hardly doubt that many white women caught up in the maelstrom of the Haitian Revolution suffered cruelly"; *Facing*

Racial Revolution: Eyewitness Accounts of the Haitian Insurrection (Chicago: Univ. of Chicago Press, 2007), 94. One German image reprinted by Popkin depicts a field on which insurrectionary blacks commit violence against white women while setting prosperous plantations ablaze (55). For a reading of the novel that emphasizes its negrophobia, see Tessie Liu, "The Secret Beyond White Patriarchal Power: Race, Gender, and Freedom in the Last Days of Colonial Saint-Domingue," *French Historical Studies* 33.3 (2010), 387–416.

45. For some background on and visual representations of these seasonal crab migrations on Cuba, see "Cuba: Wild Island of the Caribbean; Cuban Crab Invasion." *PBS's Nature.* 2010. www.pbs.org/wnet. In present day Cuba, the crabs are routinely crushed under the wheels of cars by the thousands, leaving "the road...coated with an orange-pink layer of smashed crab, so thick in places that it is like driving through three inches of pastel toothpaste," and leading to the appearance of roadside shops during the spring to provide repairs to motorists whose tires have been split by the crabs' sharp and broken shells; Kevin Sullivan, "A Crabby Conflict at the Bay of Pigs," *Washington Post*, Mar. 27, 2001; repr. *CubaNet: CubaNews*, www.cubanet.org.

46. For a discussion of this complexity in relation to *Secret History*, see Dayan (170–82).

47. It might be possible as well to think of the entangled meanings of this scene—and of what appears to be the novel's fragmented form—in terms of Benítez-Rojo's argument about Caribbean literature: "If we look at the Caribbean's most representative novels we see that their narrative discourse is constantly disrupted, and at times almost annulled, by heteroclitic, fractal, baroque, or arboreal forms, which propose themselves as vehicles to drive the reader and the text to the marginal and ritually initiating territory of the absence of violence" (25).

Epilogue

1. Kim Tingley, "The Secrets of the Wave Pilots," *The New York Times Magazine* (Mar. 17, 2017), www.nytimes.com

2. Wave pilots distinguish permanent swells that connect land from the often larger but more temporary ones created by winds. For more on wave-piloting, see David Lewis, *We, the Navigators: The Ancient Art of Landfinding in the Pacific* (Honolulu: Univ. Press of Hawai'i, 1972) and John Mack, *The Sea: A Cultural History* (London: Reaktion Books, 2011). Mack points out that some mariners identify these persistent swells beneath "larger and more locally generated waves" only by lying down on a canoe's outrigger in order to detect the waves' motions "by the feel of the vessel as it pitches and rolls even slightly in encountering waves at different angles" (127). Lewis observes that some mariners feel these sensations most clearly in the testicles (87). Tingley describes the sensation as akin to diarrhea. Thomas Gladwin's study of navigation in the Caroline Islands points out that their methods differ from those of Marshall Islanders, as likely do those of Society Islanders, because of differences in distance between islands, number of islands, and weather systems; *East is a Big Bird: Navigation and Logic on Puluwat Atoll* (Cambridge: Harvard Univ. Press, 1970), 145–6. For a comprehensive history of navigation, see Felipe Fernández-Armesto, *Pathfinders: A Global History of Exploration* (New York: W. W. Norton, 2006).

3. Hester Blum, "Introduction: Oceanic Studies," *Atlantic Studies* 10.2 (2013), 151; Philip E. Steinberg, *The Social Construction of the Ocean* (Cambridge: Cambridge Univ. Press, 2001).

4. Nicholas D. Paige, *Before Fiction: The Ancien Régime of the Novel* (Philadelphia: Univ. of Pennsylvania Press, 2011), 24, 24–5.

5. As Ralph Bauer has pointed out, American literature anthologies have silently selected textual excerpts in their colonial content that feature material focused on territory that would only later come to be part of the United States, to the exclusion of material from other regions and nations that are nonetheless part of the same original narrative. These selections and divisions give shape to the story we tell about America, but they also prevent us from seeing other stories. Ralph Bauer, "Early American Literature and American Literary History at the Hemispheric Turn," *Early American Literature* 45.2 (2010), 221.

6. Paige, 25.

7. Jorge Cañizares-Esguerra, *Puritan Conquistadors: Iberianizing the Atlantic, 1550–1700* (Stanford: Stanford Univ. Press, 2006), 232, 233.

8. Tim Ingold, *Lines: A Brief History* (London: Routledge, 2007), 152, 73, 75. Ingold draws this description of the hurrying vs. meandering line from the artist Paul Klee (*Notebooks*, Vol. 1: *The Thinking Eye*, ed. J. Spiller, trans. R. Manheim [London: Lund Humphries, 1961], 105).

9. Ingold, 161; see David Pye, *The Nature and Art of Workmanship* (Cambridge: Cambridge Univ. Press, 1968), 4.

10. Ingold, 156.

11. Stephanie Pappas, "Fire Ants Hitched Ride Around Globe in 16th-Century Ships," *LiveScience* (Feb. 19, 2015), accessed Nov. 13, 2017, www.livescience.com; this source draws from Dietrich Gotzek et al., "Global Invasion History of the Tropical Fire Ant: A Stowaway on the First Global Trade Routes," *Molecular Ecology* 24.2 (Jan. 2015), 374–88. As I completed this Epilogue, I discovered that the Philippines issued a map with commemorative stamps celebrating the Día del Geleón Festival depicting both of these Atlantic and Pacific routes. See Brian Russell Roberts and Michelle Ann Stephens, "Introduction: Archipelagic American Studies: Decontintentalizing the Study of American Culture," in *Archipelagic American Studies* (Durham: Duke Univ. Press, 2017), 6.

12. Arturo Giraldez, *The Age of Trade: The Manila Galleons and the Dawn of the Global Economy* (Lanham, MD: Rowan and Littlefield, 2015); William Lytle Schurz, *The Manila Galleon* (New York: E. P. Dutton, 1959); Maurice G. Holmes, *From New Spain by Sea to the Californias, 1519–1668* (A. H. Clark, 1963); J. H. Parry, *The Spanish Seaborne Empire* (New York: Knopf, 1966); Carl Ortwin Sauer, *The Early Spanish Main* (Berkeley: Univ. of California Press, 1966).

13. Consider, for example, the work of Jim Egan and Geoffrey Sanborn, who have brought an awareness of the East and the Pacific to bear on their readings, respectively, of colonial writers like John Smith and Anne Bradstreet, and the early nineteenth-century James Fenimore Cooper. See Jim Egan, *Oriental Shadows: The Presence of the East in Early American Literature* (Columbus: Ohio State Univ. Press, 2011); Geoffrey Sanborn, *Whipscars and Tattoos: The Last of the Mohicans, Moby-Dick, and the Maori* (New York: Oxford Univ. Press, 2011).

14. Caroline F. Levander, *Where is American Literature?* (Malden, MA: Wiley Blackwell, 2013), 14.

15. A number of the Atlantic Ocean versions of this castaway story—such as Ambrose Evans' 1719 *The Adventures, and Surprizing Deliverances, of James Dubordieu and His Wife*, Penelope Aubin's 1721 *The Strange Adventures of the Count de Vinevil and His Family*, and

the anonymous 1767 *The Female American*—have been examined by Eve Tavor Bannet, *Transatlantic Stories and the History of Reading, 1720–1820: Migrant Fictions* (Cambridge: Cambridge Univ. Press, 2011). A 1760 periodical reprinting of a Pacific adventure by Spaniards leaving from Panama ends in shipwreck and island desolation, while the 1720 *Life and Surprizing Adventures of Don Juliani* sets a similar story in the Indian Ocean. For a discussion of the *Hayy Ibn Tufayl* text in relation to Defoe, see Srinivas Avaramudan, "East-West Fiction as World Literature: The *Hayy* Problem Reconfigured," *Eighteenth-Century Studies* 47.2 (Winter 2014), 195–231. See also Michelle Burnham, "Introduction," *The Female American*, 2nd ed., eds. Michelle Burnham and James Freitas (Peterborough, ON: Broadview Press, 2011), 14–16.

16. Roberts and Stephens' resistance to the persistent "image of the desert isle" and to the isolated insularity of island spaces is critical here to fashioning a post-continental American literary history that recognizes connections rather than divisions between islands, oceans, and continents (14, 12).

17. Meredith L. McGill, *American Literature and the Culture of Reprinting, 1834–1853* (Philadelphia: Univ. of Pennsylvania Press, 2003), 39, 2.

18. See, for example, Philip Gould's concerns about the impediment of linguistic competence to a rigorous transatlantic or hemispheric approach within early American studies; "The New Early American Anthology," *Early American Literature* 38.2 (2003), 309–11.

19. Colleen Boggs compellingly argues for the centrality of translation to a transnational American literature, and emphasizes the ways in which translation "may defamiliarize the domestic and erode the very borders of linguistic distinction." Colleen Glenney Boggs, *Transnationalism and American Literature: Literary Translation, 1773–1892* (New York: Routledge, 2007), 25.

20. James Clifford, *Routes: Travel and Translation in the Late Twentieth Century* (Cambridge: Harvard Univ. Press, 1997).

21. Absolutely none of the colonial period writers included in our current American literature anthologies identified as American and many of them wrote in languages other than English. Already a surprising number of these texts—like the diaries of Christopher Columbus, or the narratives of the *Jesuit Relations*, or the novels of Susanna Rowson—bear an oceanic and imperial, rather than a terrestrial or national, relation to America.

22. Elizabeth M. DeLoughrey, *Routes and Roots: Navigating Caribbean and Pacific Island Literatures* (Honolulu: Univ. of Hawai'i Press, 2007), 24.

23. In his review of the Stanford Literary Lab's *Canon/Archive*, Ted Underwood has rightly pointed out that it is not as yet clear at all what *narrative form* new literary histories generated through digital methods might take. Can we plot this narrative at all, and if so what shape might it take? What story might it possibly tell? See "The Stanford Literary Lab's Narrative," *Public Books* (Nov. 2, 2017), www.publicbooks.org.

24. Thomas Bender, "Historians, the Nation, and the Plenitude of Narratives," in *Rethinking American History in a Global Age*, ed. Bender (Berkeley: Univ. of California Press, 2002), 12.

25. M. Alleweart, "Swamp Sublime: Ecologies of Resistance in the American Plantation Zone," *PMLA* 123 (2008), 341.

26. Roberts and Stephens, "Introduction," 1.

27. Tingley, quoting from the work of Edward Tolman and citing unspecified anthropologists working on the western Pacific.

{ BIBLIOGRAPHY }

"Account," *The Massachusetts Magazine* (February 1972), 94, 95; American Periodicals Series Online, ProQuest.

Advertisement for Bethesda Select Boarding School. *Weekly Museum* (May 4, 1799).

Advertisement for Hardie's School. *Weekly Museum* (October 21, 1797).

Advertisement for William Pirsson's Academy. *Weekly Museum* (May 4, 1799).

"An account of the new Northern Archipelago, lately discovered by the Russians," *The Pennsylvania Magazine; or, American Monthly Museum* (Jan. 1776); American Periodicals Series Online, ProQuest.

Adams-Campbell, Melissa. "Romantic Revolutions: Love and Violence in Leonora Sansay's *Secret History, or the Horrors of St. Domingo*," *Studies in American Fiction* 39.2 (2012), 125–46.

Albree, Joe and Scott H. Brown. "A Valuable Monument of Mathematical Genius: *The Ladies' Diary* (1704–1840)," *Historia Mathematica* 36 (2009), 10–47.

Alexander, Caroline. "Captain Bligh's Cursed Breadfruit," *Smithsonian Magazine* (September 2009). www.smithsonianmag.com

Alkon, Paul K. "The Odds against Friday: Defoe, Bayes, and Inverse Probability," in *Probability, Time, and Space in Eighteenth-Century Literature*, ed. Paula R. Backscheider (New York: AMS Press, 1979), 29–61.

Allewaert, M. "Swamp Sublime: Ecologies of Resistance in the American Plantation Zone," *PMLA* 123.2 (2008), 340–57.

Allewaert, Monique. *Ariel's Ecology: Plantations, Personhood, and Colonialism in the American Tropics* (Minneapolis: University of Minnesota Press, 2013).

Amer, Sahar and Laura Doyle. "Introduction" to "Reframing Postcolonial and Global Studies in the Longer *Durée*," *PMLA* 130.2 (March 2015), 331–35.

Anderson, George William. *A New, Authentic, and Complete Collection of Voyages Round the World* (London, 1784).

"Anecdotes of distinguished Characters. KOTZEBUE," *Monthly Magazine and American Review* (April 1799), 76; American Periodicals Series Online, ProQuest.

Anonymous. *The Travels of Hildebrand Bowman* [1778], ed. Lance Bertelsen (Peterborough, ON: Broadview Press, 2017).

Aravamudan, Srinivas. "East-West Fiction as World Literature: The *Hayy* Problem Reconsidered," *Eighteenth-Century Studies* 47.2 (Winter 2014), 195–231.

Aravamudan, Srinivas. *Enlightenment Orientalism: Resisting the Rise of the Novel* (Chicago: University of Chicago Press, 2012).

Aravamudan, Srinivas. "Introduction," in *Obi; or, The History of Three-Fingered Jack* by William Earle, ed. Aravamudan. (Peterborough, ON: Broadview Press, 2005), 7–52.

Arendt, Hannah. *On Revolution* (repr.; New York: Penguin, 1963).

Armitage, David. *Declaration of Independence: A Global History* (Cambridge: Harvard University Press, 2007).

Armitage, David and Alison Bashford, eds. *Pacific Histories: Ocean, Land, People* (Houndsmills: Palgrave Macmillan, 2014).

Armitage, David and Sanjay Subrahmanyam, eds. *The Age of Revolutions in Global Context, c.1760–1840* (New York: Palgrave Macmillan, 2010).

Arthur, Paul Longley. *Virtual Voyages: Travel Writing and the Antipodes, 1605–1837* (London: Anthem Press, 2010).

Baker, Jennifer. *Securing the Commonwealth: Debt, Speculation, and Writing in the Making of Early America* (Baltimore: Johns Hopkins University Press, 2005).

Banks, Joseph. *The Endeavour Journal of Joseph Banks, 1768–1771*, ed. J. C. Beaglehole (Sydney: Angus and Robertson, 1963).

Bannet, Eve Tavor. *Transatlantic Stories and the History of Reading, 1720–1820: Migrant Fictions* (Cambridge: Cambridge University Press, 2011).

Bartholomew, J. G. *A Literary and Historical Atlas of North and South America* (1911; London: J. M. Dent & Sons, 1930).

Baucom, Ian. *Specters of the Atlantic: Finance Capital, Slavery, and the Philosophy of History* (Durham: Duke University Press, 2005).

Bauer, Ralph. "Hemispheric Studies," *PMLA* 124.1 (2009), 234–50.

Bauer, Ralph. "Early American Literature and American Literary History at the Hemispheric Turn," *Early American Literature* 45.2 (2010), 217–33.

Bayly, C. A. *Imperial Meridian: The British Empire and the World, 1780–1830* (London: Longman, 1989).

Beckert, Sven. *Empire of Cotton: A Global History* (New York: Knopf, 2015).

Belich, James. "Race," in *Pacific Histories: Ocean, Land, People*, eds. David Armitage and Alison Bashford (Basingstoke: Palgrave Macmillan, 2014), 263–81.

Bender, Thomas. "Historians, the Nation, and the Plenitude of Narratives," in *Rethinking American History in a Global Age*, ed. Thomas Bender (Berkeley: University of California Press, 2002), 1–22.

Benítez-Rojo, Antonio. *The Repeating Island: The Caribbean and the Postmodern Perspective*, trans. James E. Maraniss (Durham: Duke University Press, 1992).

Bentley, Jerry H., Renate Bridenthal, and Kären Wigen, eds. *Seascapes: Maritime Histories, Littoral Cultures, and Transoceanic Exchanges* (Honolulu: University of Hawai'i Press, 2007).

Benyowsky, Mauritius Augustus Count de. *Memoirs and Travels of Mauritius Augustus Count de Benyowsky*, 2 vols. (Dublin, 1790).

Bertelsen, Lance. "Introduction" to Anonymous, *The Travels of Hildebrand Bowman* (Peterborough, ON: Broadview Press, 2017), 9–40.

Bewell, Alan. " 'Jacobin Plants': Botany as Social Theory in the 1790s," *Wordsworth Circle* 20 (1989), 132–39.

Bewell, Alan. "Erasmus Darwin's Cosmopolitan Nature," *ELH* 76.1 (2009), 19–48.

Bhabha, Homi K., ed. *The Location of Culture* (New York: Routledge, 1994).

Bibliography of Captain James Cook, 2nd ed. (Sydney: Library of New South Wales, 1970).

Blum, Hester. *The View from the Mast-Head: Maritime Imagination and Antebellum American Sea Narratives* (Chapel Hill: University of North Carolina Press, 2008).

Blum, Hester. "Introduction: Oceanic Studies," *Atlantic Studies* 10.2 (2013), 151–55.

Boggs, Colleen Glenney. *Transnationalism and American Literature: Literary Translation, 1773–1892* (New York: Routledge, 2007).

Borofsky, Robert. "An Invitation," in *Remembrance of Pacific Pasts: An Invitation to Remake History*, ed. Robert Borofsky (Honolulu: University of Hawai'i Press, 2000), 1–30.

Boswell, James. *Boswell for the Defence, 1769-1774*, eds. W. K. Wimsatt and F. A. Pottle (New Haven: Yale University Press, 1960).

Bougainville, Lewis de. *A Voyage Round the World*, trans. John Reinhold Forster (London, 1772).

Bouvier, Virginia Marie. *Women and the Conquest of California, 1542-1840* (Tucson: University of Arizona Press, 2001).

Brewer, John. "Commercialization and Politics," in Neil McKendrick, John Brewer, and J. H. Plumb, *The Birth of a Consumer Society: The Commercialization of Eighteenth-Century England* (Bloomington: Indiana University Press, 1982), 197-262.

Brewster, David. "Breadfruit," *Edinburgh Encyclopedia*, 18 vols., vol. 4 (Edinburgh, 1830), 445-48.

Brooks, Peter. *Reading for the Plot: Design and Intention in Narrative* (New York: Knopf, 1984).

Brown, Charles Brockden. Review of Benjamin Barton's *New Views of the Origin of Tribes and Nations of America*. In *The Monthly Magazine* (May 1799), 119. American Periodicals Series Online, ProQuest.

Brown, Charles Brockden. *Ormond; or the Secret Witness*, eds. Philip Barnard and Stephen Shapiro (Indianapolis: Hackett Publishing, 2009).

Brown, Christopher Leslie. *Moral Capital: Foundations of British Abolitionism* (Chapel Hill: University of North Carolina Press, 2006).

Brückner, Martin. *The Geographic Revolution in Early America: Maps, Literacy, and National Identity* (Chapel Hill: University of North Carolina Press, 2006).

Burney, James. *With Captain James Cook in the Antarctic and Pacific: The Private Journal of James Burney*, ed. Beverley Hooper (Canberra: National Library of Australia, 1975).

Burney, James. *A Chronological History of the Discoveries in the South Sea or Pacific Ocean*, 4 vols. (London, 1803).

Burney, James. "Burney's Log," in James Cook, *The Voyage of the Resolution and Adventure, 1772-1775*, Vol. II of *The Journals of Captain James Cook on his Voyages of Discovery*, ed. J. C. Beaglehole, 4 vols. (Cambridge: The Hakluyt Society, Cambridge University Press, 1961)., 746-52.

Burnham, Michelle. "Introduction" to *The Female American*, by Anonymous, 2nd ed., eds. Michelle Burnham and James Freitas (Peterborough ON: Broadview Press, 2014), 9-32.

[Callander, John, ed.] *Terra Australis Cognita: or, Voyages to the Terra Australis, or Southern Hemisphere, during the Sixteenth, Seventeenth, and Eighteenth Centuries*, 3 vols. (Edinburgh, 1766).

Cañizares-Esguerra, Jorge. *How to Write the History of the New World: Histories, Epistemologies, and Identities in the Eighteenth-Century Atlantic World* (Stanford: Stanford University Press, 2001).

Cañizares-Esguerra, Jorge. *Puritan Conquistadors: Iberianizing the Atlantic, 1550-1700* (Stanford: Stanford University Press, 2006).

Carter, Paul. *The Road to Botany Bay: An Exploration of Landscape and History* (Chicago: University of Chicago Press, 1987).

Casid, Jill. *Sowing Empire: Landscape and Colonization* (Minneapolis: University of Minnesota Press, 2005).

Chaplin, Joyce. "The Pacific Before Empire, c.150-1800," in *Pacific Histories: Ocean, Land, People*, eds. David Armitage and Alison Bashford (Basingstoke: Palgrave Macmillan, 2014), 53-74.

Chaplin, Joyce. *Round About the Earth: Circumnavigation from Magellan to Orbit* (New York: Simon and Schuster, 2012).

Choi, Ja Yun. "The Early Republic, the Haitian Revolution, and the Horrors of Slavery in Brown's *Ormond*," *British and American Fiction* 22.2 (2015), 5–33.

Christophersen, Bill. *The Apparition in the Glass: Charles Brockden Brown's American Gothic* (Athens, GA: University of Georgia Press, 1993).

"Circumnavigator," *The Massachusetts Magazine: or, Monthly Museum of Knowledge and Rational Entertainment* (Mar. 1789); American Periodicals Series Online, ProQuest.

Cleveland, Richard J. *A Narrative of Voyages and Commercial Enterprises* (Boston, 1850).

Clifford, James. *Routes: Travel and Translation in the Late Twentieth Century* (Cambridge: Harvard University Press, 1997).

Cloyd, E. L. *James Burnett, Lord Monboddo* (Oxford: Clarendon Press, 1972).

Coclanis, Peter. "ReOrienting Atlantic History: The Global Dimensions of the 'Western' Rice Trade," in *The Atlantic in Global History 1500–2000*, eds. Jorge Cañizares-Esguerra and Erik R. Seeman (Upper Saddle River NJ: Pearson/Prentice Hall, 2007), 111–28.

Cohen, Margaret. *The Novel and the Sea* (Princeton: Princeton University Press, 2010).

Colnett, James. *A Voyage to the South Atlantic and Round Cape Horn into the Pacific Ocean* (London, 1798).

Cook, Andrew S. "Alexander Dalrymple: Research, Writing and Publication of the Account," in *An Account of the Discoveries made in the South Pacifick Ocean* by Alexander Dalrymple (1767; repr. Sydney: Hordern House, 1996), 15–47.

Cook, James. *Captain Cook's Three Voyages to the Pacific Ocean. The first performed in the years 1768, 1769, 1770 and 1771: the second in 1772, 1773, 1774 and 1775: the third and last in 1776, 1777, 1778 1779 and 1780.* 2 vols., abridged (Boston, 1797).

Cook, James. *The Voyage of the Resolution and Adventure, 1772–1775*, Vol. II of *The Journals of Captain James Cook on his Voyages of Discovery*, ed. J. C. Beaglehole, 4 vols. (Cambridge: The Hakluyt Society, Cambridge University Press, 1961).

Cooke, John. *The Macaroni Jester* (Philadelphia, 1768).

Cottom, Daniel. *Cannibals and Philosophers: Bodies of Enlightenment* (Baltimore: Johns Hopkins University Press, 2001).

Coxe, William. *Account of the Russian Discoveries between Asia and America. To which are added, the Conquest of Siberia, and the History of the Transactions and Commerce between Russia and China* (London, 1780).

Crossman, Carl L. *The China Trade: Export Paintings, Furniture, Silver & Other Objects* (Princeton: The Pyne Press, 1972).

"Cuba: Wild Island of the Caribbean; Cuban Crab Invasion," *PBS's Nature*. 2010. www.pbs.org

Cumings, Bruce. *Dominion from Sea to Sea: Pacific Ascendancy and American Power* (New Haven: Yale University Press, 2009).

Dalrymple, Alexander. *Considerations on the Present State of Affairs between England and America* (London, 1778).

Dalrymple, Alexander. *An Historical Collection of the Several Voyages and Discoveries in the South Pacific Ocean*, 2 vols. (London, 1770).

Dalrymple, Alexander. *A Letter from Mr. Dalrymple to Dr. Hawkesworth* (London, 1773).

Dampier, William. *A Collection of Voyages in Four Volumes* (London, 1729).

Danchin, Pierre. "Erasmus Darwin's Scientific and Poetic Purpose in The Botanic Garden," in *Science and Imagination in XVIIIth-Century British Culture*, ed. Sergio Rossi (Milan: Edizioni Unicopi, 1987), 133–50.

"Darcus Howe BBC Interview on Riots," youtube.com, uploaded August 9, 2011.

Darwin, Erasmus. *The Botanic Garden*, 2 vols. (1791; repr. New York: Garland, 1978).

Daston, Lorraine. *Classical Probability in the Enlightenment* (Princeton: Princeton University Press, 1988).

Davis, Lennard. *Factual Fictions: The Origins of the English Novel* (Philadelphia: University of Pennsylvania Press, 1997).

Dayan, Joan. *Haiti, History, and the Gods* (Berkeley: University of California Press, 1995).

Defoe, Daniel. *The Life and Strange Surprising Adventures of Robinson Crusoe of York, Mariner* (1719; New York: W. W. Norton, 1994).

Defoe, Daniel. *A New Voyage Round the World* (London: A. Bettesworth, 1724).

Delano, Amasa. *A Narrative of the Voyages and Travels*, 2nd ed. (Boston, 1818).

DeLoughrey, Elizabeth. "Globalizing the Routes of Breadfruit and Other Bounties," *Journal of Colonialism and Colonial History* 8.3 (2008), 1–40.

DeLoughrey, Elizabeth. *Routes and Roots: Navigating Caribbean and Pacific Island Literatures* (Honolulu: University of Hawai'i Press, 2007).

DeLoughrey, Elizabeth. "Yam, Roots, and Rot: Allegories of the Provision Grounds," *Small Axe* 15.1 (2011), 58–65.

Dening, Greg. *Islands and Beaches: Discourses on a Silent Land: Marquesas, 1774–1880* (Honolulu: University Press of Hawai'i, 1980).

Dening, Greg. *Mr. Bligh's Bad Language: Passion, Power and Theatre on the Bounty* (Cambridge: Cambridge University Press, 1992).

Díaz, Junot. *The Brief Wondrous Life of Oscar Wao* (New York: Riverhead Books, 2007).

Díaz, Junot. "The Silence: The Legacy of Childhood Trauma," *The New Yorker* (April 16 2016), www.newyorker.com

Dillon, Elizabeth Maddock. *New World Drama: The Performative Commons in the Atlantic World, 1649–1849* (Durham: Duke University Press, 2014).

Dillon, Elizabeth Maddock. "Obi, Assemblage, Enchantment," *J19: The Journal of Nineteenth-Century Americanists* 1.1 (Spring 2013), 172–78.

Dillon, Elizabeth Maddock. "The Original American Novel, or, The American Origin of the Novel," in *A Companion to the Eighteenth-Century Novel and Culture*, eds. Paula R. Backscheider and Catherine Ingrassia (Malden MA: Blackwell, 2005), 235–60.

Dillon, Elizabeth Maddock. "The Secret History of the Early American Novel: Leonora Sansay and the Revolution in Saint Domingue," *Novel* 40.1/2 (Fall 2006/Spring 2007), 77–102.

Dilworth, Thomas. *The Schoolmasters Assistant: Being a Compendium of Arithmetic, both Practical and Theoretical, In Five Parts*, 17th ed. (Philadelphia, 1773).

Dimock, Wai Chee. *Through Other Continents: American Literature across Deep Time* (Princeton: Princeton University Press, 2009).

Dimock, Wai Chee and Lawrence Buell, eds. *Shades of the Planet: American Literature as World Literature* (Princeton: Princeton University Press, 2007).

Dirlik, Arif. *What Is In a Rim? Critical Perspectives on the Pacific Region Idea* (Lanham, MD: Rowan and Littlefield, 1998).

Donegan, Kathleen. *Seasons of Misery: Catastrophe and Colonial Settlement in Early America* (Philadelphia: University of Pennsylvania Press, 2014).

Downes, Jacques M. *The Golden Ghetto: The American Commercial Community at Canton and the Shaping of American China Policy, 1784–1844* (Hong Kong: Hong Kong University Press, 2015).

Doyle, Laura. "Inter-imperiality and Literary Studies in the Longer *Durée*," *PMLA* 130.2 (2015), 336–47.

Drayton, Richard. *Nature's Government: Science, Imperial Britain, and the "Improvement" of the World* (New Haven: Yale University Press, 2000).

Drexler, Michael J. "Brigands and Nuns: The Vernacular Sociology of Collectivity after the Haitian Revolution," in *Messy Beginnings: Postcoloniality and Early American Studies*, eds. Malini Johar Schueller and Edward Watts (New Brunswick: Rutgers University Press, 2003), 175–99.

Drexler, Michael J. "The Displacement of the American Novel: Imagining Aaron Burr and Haiti in Leonora Sansay's *Secret History*," *Common-place* 9.3 (April 2009), www.common-place.org.

Drexler, Michael J. "Leonora Sansay's Anatopic Imagination," in *Urban Identity and the Atlantic World*, eds. Elizabeth Fay and Leonard Von Morzé (New York: Palgrave Macmillan, 2013), 148.

Drexler, Michael J. Introduction to *Secret History; or, the Horrors of St. Domingo* by Leonora Sansay. (Peterborough, ON: Broadview Press, 2001), 10–37.

Drexler, Michael J. and Ed White. "Secret History and the Fantasy Structure of Republicanism," *Early American Literature* 44.2 (2009), 333–63.

Drexler, Michael J. and Ed White. *The Traumatic Colonel: The Founding Fathers, Slavery, and the Phantasmatic Aaron Burr* (New York: New York University Press, 2014).

Dunmore, John. "Introduction," in *The Journal of Jean-François de Galaup de la Pérouse, 1785–1788*, 2 vols., trans. and ed. John Dunmore (London: The Hakluyt Society, 1994), 1.ccvii–ccxxix.

Dunn, Richard S. *Sugar and Slaves: The Rise of the Planter Class in the English West Indies, 1624–1713* (Chapel Hill: University of North Carolina Press, 1972).

Durant, John and Alice. *Pictorial History of the American Circus* (New York: A. S. Barnes, 1957).

Dussell, Enrique. "Beyond Eurocentrism: The World-System and the Limits of Modernity," in *The Cultures of Globalization*, eds. Fredric Jameson and Masao Miyoshi (Durham: Duke University Press, 1998), 3–31.

Earle, William. *Obi; or, the History of Three-Fingered Jack*, ed. Srinivas Aravamudan (1800; repr. Peterborough, ON: Broadview Press, 2005).

Edwards, Bryan. *The History, Civil and Commercial, of the British Colonies in the West Indies*, 3 vols., 3rd ed., with considerable additions (London, 1801).

Edwards, Bryan. *The History, Civil and Commercial, of the British Colonies in the West Indies*, 2 vols. (New York: Arno Press, 1972).

Egan, Jim. *Oriental Shadows: The Presence of the East in Early American Literature* (Columbus: Ohio State University Press, 2011).

Ellis, Scott. "Charles Brockden Brown's *Ormond*, Property Exchange, and the Literary Marketplace in the Early American Republic," *Studies in the Novel* 37.1 (2005), 1–19.

Endersby, Jim. "A Garden Enclosed: Botanical Barter in Sydney, 1818–39," *The British Journal for the History of Science* 33.3 (2000), 313–34.

Engstrand, Iris H. W. "Spain's Role in Pacific Exploration during the Age of Enlightenment," in *Enlightenment and Exploration in the North Pacific, 1741–1805*, eds. Stephen Haycox, James Barnett, and Caedmon Liburd (Seattle: University of Washington Press, 1997), 25–37.

Engstrand, Iris H. W. "Seekers of the 'Northern Mystery': European Exploration of California and the Pacific," in *Contested Eden: California Before the Gold Rush*, eds.

Ramón A. Gutiérrez and Richard J. Orsi (Berkeley: University of California Press, 1998), 78–110.

"Epitome of Captain Wallis's Voyage Around the World," *The Royal American Magazine, or Universal Repository of Instruction and Amusement* (January–February, April 1774); American Periodicals Series Online, ProQuest.

"Extracts, from a letter, written by Mr. John Ledyard." *The American Magazine* 1.11 (October 1788), 808; American Periodicals Series Online, ProQuest.

Fanon, Frantz. *The Wretched of the Earth*, trans. Constance Farrington (New York: Grove Press, 1968).

Fara, Patricia. *Sex, Botany, and Empire: The Story of Carl Linnaeus and Joseph Banks* (New York: Columbia University Press, 2003).

Fausett, David. *Writing the New World: Imaginary Voyages and Utopias of the Great Southern Land* (Syracuse: Syracuse University Press, 1993).

Fenwick, E. *The White Kitten* (Boston, 1823).

Ferguson, Robert A. "Still Not Global," *William and Mary Quarterly* 65.2 (April 2008), 365–66.

Fernández-Armesto, Felipe. "Empires in Their Global Context, ca. 1500 to ca. 1800," in *The Atlantic in Global History, 1500–2000*, eds. Jorge Cañizares-Esguerra and Erik R. Seeman (Upper Saddle River, NJ: Pearson, 2007), 93–110.

Fernández-Armesto, Felipe. *Pathfinders: A Global History of Exploration* (New York: W. W. Norton, 2006).

Fichter, James R. *So Great a Proffit: How the East Indies Trade Transformed Anglo-American Capitalism* (Cambridge: Harvard University Press, 2010).

Fisher, George. *The American Instructor: or, Young Man's Best Companion.* 15th ed. (Philadelphia, 1770).

Fitz, Caitlin. *Our Sister Republics: The United States in an Age of American Revolutions* (New York: Liveright Publishing, 2016).

Flynn, Christopher. *Americans in British Literature 1770–1832* (Aldershot: Ashgate, 2008).

Foley, Barbara. *Telling the Truth: The Theory and Practice of Documentary Fiction* (Ithaca: Cornell University Press, 1986).

Forster, George. *A Voyage Round the World.* 1777, eds. Nicholas Thomas and Oliver Berghof, 2 vols. (Honolulu: University of Hawai'i Press, 2000).

Forster, Johann Reinhold. *Observations Made during a Voyage round the World* (London, 1778).

Forster, John Reinhold. "The Translator's Preface," in *A Voyage Round the World*, by Lewis de Bougainville, trans. John Reinhold Forster (London, 1772).

Fowler, William. *He Helu Kamalii, oia ka mea eao aku aii na keiki, ma na ui ao mua o ke aritemetika* (Honolulu: Mea Pai Palapala na na Misionari, 1837).

Fraiman, Susan. "Geometries of Race and Gender: Eve Sedgwick, Spike Lee, Charlayne Hunter-Gault," *Feminist Studies* 20.1 (1994), 67–84.

Frank, Caroline. *Objectifying China, Imagining America: Chinese Commodities in Early America* (Chicago: University of Chicago Press, 2011).

Franzen, Jonathan. "Farther Away: 'Robinson Crusoe,' David Foster Wallace, and the Island of Solitude," *New Yorker* (April 18, 2011), newyorker.com.

Frost, Alan. "The Antipodean Exchange: European Horticulture and Imperial Designs," in *Visions of Empire: Voyages, Botany, and Representations of Nature*, eds. David Philip Miller and Peter Hanns Reill (Cambridge: Cambridge University Press, 1996), 58–79.

Fry, Howard T. *Alexander Dalrymple (1737–1808) and the Expansion of British Trade* (London: Frank Cass & Co., 1970).

Fullagar, Kate, ed. *The Atlantic World in the Antipodes: Effects and Transformations since the Eighteenth Century* (Newcastle upon Tyne: Cambridge Scholars, 2012).

Fullagar, Kate. *The Savage Visit: New World People and Popular Culture in Britain, 1710–1795* (Berkeley: University of California Press, 2012).

Furneaux, Tobias. "Furneaux's Narrative," in *The Voyage of the Resolution and Adventure, 1772–1775*, Vol. II of *The Journals of Captain James Cook on his Voyages of Discover* by James Cook, ed. J. C. Beaglehole, 4 vols. (Cambridge: The Hakluyt Society, Cambridge University Press, 1961), 729–45.

Gaiman, Neil. *American Gods* (New York: William Morrow, 2011).

Gallagher, Catherine. *The Body Economic: Life, Death, and Sensation in Political Economy and the Victorian Novel* (Princeton: Princeton University Press, 2008).

Gallagher, Catherine. *Nobody's Story: The Vanishing Acts of Women Writers in the Marketplace* (Berkeley: University of California Press, 1995).

Gallagher, Catherine. "The Rise of Fictionality," in *The Novel*, Vol. 1, ed. Franco Moretti (Princeton: Princeton University Press, 2006), 336–63.

Games, Alison. "Atlantic History: Definitions, Challenges, and Opportunities," *American Historical Review* 111.3 (2006), 741–57.

Garraway, Doris. *The Libertine Colony: Creolization in the Early French Caribbean* (Durham: Duke University Press, 2005).

Garrett, Matthew. *Episodic Poetics: Politics and Literary Form after the Constitution* (New York: Oxford University Press, 2014).

Gascoigne, John. *Encountering the Pacific in the Age of Enlightenment* (Cambridge: Cambridge University Press, 2014).

Genette, Gérard. *Narrative Discourse: An Essay in Method*, trans. Jane E. Lewin (Ithaca: Cornell University Press, 1980).

"Getting Lost," *Uncommon Sense—The Blog*, Omohundro Institute for Early American History and Culture, blog.oieach.wm.edu/getting-lost/

[Gibbes, Phebe]. *Friendship in a Nunnery; or, The American Fugitive*, 2 vols. (London, 1778).

Gibson, James R. *Otter Skins, Boston Ships, and China Goods: The Maritime Fur Trade of the Northwest Coast 1785–1841* (Seattle: University of Washington Press, 1992).

Giles, Paul. "Antipodean American Literature: Franklin, Twain, and the Sphere of Subalternity," *American Literary History* 20.1–2 (Spring/Summer 2008), 22–50.

Giles, Paul. *Antipodean American: Australasia and the Constitution of U.S. Literature* (New York: Oxford University Press, 2013).

Giles, Paul. "Commentary: Hemispheric Partiality," *American Literary History* 18.3 (2006), 648–55.

Gilje, Paul A. "Commerce and Conquest in Early American Foreign Relations, 1750–1850," *Journal of the Early Republic* 37.4 (Winter 2017), 735–70.

Gilroy, Paul. *The Black Atlantic: Modernity and Double-Consciousness* (Cambridge: Harvard University Press, 1995).

Giraldez, Arturo. *The Age of Trade: The Manila Galleons and the Dawn of the Global Economy* (Lanham, MD: Rowan and Littlefield, 2015).

Gladwin, Thomas. *East is a Big Bird: Navigation and Logic on Puluwat Atoll* (Cambridge: Harvard University Press, 1970).

Gniadek, Melissa. "*Mary Howard*'s Mark: Children's Literature and the Scales of Reading the Pacific," *Early American Literature* 50.3 (2015), 797–826.

Goldstein, Jonathan. *Philadelphia and the China Trade 1682–1846: Commercial, Cultural, and Attitudinal Effects* (University Park: Pennsylvania State University Press, 1978).

Goode, Abby L. "Gothic Fertility in Leonora Sansay's *Secret History*," *Early American Literature* 50.2 (2015), 449–73.

Goodwin, George G. "The Crowninshield Elephant," *Natural History* (October 1951), www.naturalhistorymag.com.

Gotzek, Dietrich, et al. "Global Invasion History of the Tropical Fire Ant: A Stowaway on the First Global Trade Routes," *Molecular Ecology* 24.2 (January 2015), 374–88.

Goudie, Sean X. *Creole America: The West Indies and the Formation of Literature and Culture in the New Republic* (Philadelphia: University of Pennsylvania Press, 2006).

Gould, Philip. "The New Early American Anthology," *Early American Literature* 38.2 (2003), 305–17.

Grandin, Greg. *The Empire of Necessity: Slavery, Freedom, and Deception in the New World* (New York: Metropolitan Books, 2014).

Greenwood, Isaac. "A New Method for Composing a Natural History of Meteors," *Philosophical Transactions of the Royal Society of London* 35 (1727), 390–402.

Griffiths, Devin S. "The Intuitions of Analogy in Erasmus Darwin's Poetics," *Studies in English Literature* 51.3 (2011), 645–65.

Grove, Philip Babcock. *The Imaginary Voyage in Prose Fiction: A History of Its Criticism and a Guide for Its Study, with an Annotated Check List of 215 Imaginary Voyages from 1700 to 1800* (New York: Octagon Books, 1975).

Guterl, Matthew and Christine Skwiot. "Atlantic and Pacific Crossings: Race, Empire, and the 'Labor Problem' in the Late Nineteenth Century," *Radical History Review* 91 (Winter 2005), 40–61.

Hackel, Steven W. *Children of Coyote, Missionaries of St. Francis: Indian-Spanish Relations in Colonial California, 1769–1850* (Chapel Hill: University of North Carolina Press, 2005).

Hall, Douglas. "Planters, Farmers, and Gardeners in Eighteenth-Century Jamaica," in *Slavery, Freedom, and Gender: The Dynamics of Caribbean Society*, eds. Brian L. Moore, B. W. Higman, Carl Campbell, and Patrick Bryan (Kingston, Jamaica: University of West Indies Press, 2001), 97–114.

Hamelman, Steven. "Secret to the Last: Charles Brocken Brown's *Ormond*," *LIT: Literature, Interpretation, Theory* 11.3 (2000), 305–26.

Hamilton, Lady Mary. *Munster Village*, 2 vols. (London, 1778).

Haselden, Thomas. *The Seaman's Daily Assistant* (Philadelphia, 1777).

Hau'ofa, Epeli. *We Are the Ocean* (Honolulu: University of Hawai'i Press, 2008).

Hawkesworth, John. *An Account of the Voyages Undertaken by the Order of His Present Majesty for Making Discoveries in the Southern Hemisphere*, 3 vols. (London, 1773).

Heilman, R. B. *America in English Fiction 1760–1800: The Influences of the American Revolution* (Baton Rouge: Louisiana State University Press, 1937; repr. New York: Octagon Books, 1968).

Hemphill, C. Dallett. "Manners and Class in the Revolutionary Era: A Transatlantic Comparison," *William and Mary Quarterly*, 3rd ser. 63.2 (April 2006), 345–72.

Heng, Geraldine. "Reinventing Race, Colonization, and Globalisms across Deep Time: Lessons from the Longer *Durée*," *PMLA* 130.2 (March 2015), 358–66.

Hill, G. B., ed. *Boswell's Life of Johnson* (Oxford, 1887).

Hinds, Elizabeth Jane Wall. *Private Property: Charles Brockden Brown's Gendered Economics of Virtue* (Newark: University of Delaware Press, 1997).

Holmes, Maurice G. *From New Spain by Sea to the Californias, 1519–1668* (A. H. Clark, 1963).

Hoock, Holger. *Scars of Independence: America's Violent Birth* (New York: Crown, 2017).

Hoskins, Janet and Viet Thanh Nguyen, eds. *Transpacific Studies: Framing an Emerging Field* (Honolulu: University of Hawai'i Press, 2014).

Houghton, Eliza. *Practical Arithmetic: Comprising all the Rules for Transacting Business* (Boston, 1810?). Manuscript, Mss. Folio Vols. H. American Antiquarian Society.

Hsu, Hsuan. *Geography and the Production of Space in Nineteenth-Century American Literature* (Cambridge: Cambridge University Press, 2010).

Huang, Yunte. *Transpacific Displacement: Ethnography, Translation and Intertextual Travel in 20th Century American Literature* (Berkeley: University of California Press, 2002).

Huang, Yunte. *Transpacific Imaginations: History, Literature, Counterpoetics* (Cambridge: Harvard University Press, 2008).

Huddert, Joseph. *The Oriental Navigator, or New Directions for Sailing to and from the East Indies* (Philadelphia, 1801).

Hulme, Peter. *Colonial Encounters: Europe and the Native Caribbean, 1492–1797* (New York: Routledge, 1992).

Hunt, Helen. "'Fascinate, Intoxicate, Transport': Uncovering Women's Erotic Dominance in Leonora Sansay's *Secret History*," *Legacy* 33.1 (2016), 31–54.

Hutton, Charles. *A Course of Book-keeping, According to the Method of Single Entry* (Philadelphia, 1801).

Iannini, Christopher. *Fatal Revolutions: Natural History, West Indian Slavery, and the Routes of American Literature* (Chapel Hill: University of North Carolina Press, 2012).

Igler, David. "Diseased Goods: Global Exchanges in the Eastern Pacific Basin, 1770–1850," *The American Historical Review* 109.3 (2004), 693–719.

Igler, David. *The Great Ocean: Pacific Worlds from Captain Cook to the Gold Rush* (New York: Oxford University Press, 2013).

Ingold, Tim. *Lines: A Brief History* (London: Routledge, 2007).

Ingrassia, Catherine. *Authorship, Commerce, and Gender in Early Eighteenth-Century England: A Culture of Paper Credit* (Cambridge: Cambridge University Press, 1998).

Isenberg, Nancy. *Fallen Founder: A Life of Aaron Burr* (New York: Viking, 2007).

Jackson, Robert H. and Edward Castillo. *Indians, Franciscans, and Spanish Colonization* (Albuquerque: University of New Mexico Press, 1995).

James, C. L. R. *The Black Jacobins: Toussaint L'Ouverture and the San Domingo Revolution*, 2nd ed., rev. (New York: Vintage Books, 1989).

Jaudon, Toni Wall. "Obeah's Sensations: Rethinking Religion at the Transnational Turn," *American Literature* 84.4 (December 2012), 715–41.

Jaudon, Toni Wall and Kelly Wisecup. "Obeah: Knowledge, Power, and Writing in the Early Atlantic World," special issue of *Atlantic Studies* 12.1 (2015).

Johnson, Kendall A. *The New Middle Kingdom: China and the Early American Romance of Free Trade* (Baltimore: Johns Hopkins University Press, 2017).

Jolly, Margaret. "Women of the East, Women of the West: Region and Race, Gender and Sexuality on Cook's Voyages," in *The Atlantic World in the Antipodes: Effects and Transformations since the Eighteenth Century*, ed. Kate Fullagar (Newcastle upon Tyne: Cambridge Scholars Publishing, 2012), 2–32.

Kafer, Peter. *Charles Brockden Brown's Revolution and the Birth of American Gothic* (Philadelphia: University of Pennsylvania Press, 2004).

Kareem, Sarah Tindal. *Eighteenth-Century Fiction and the Reinvention of Wonder* (Oxford: Oxford University Press, 2014).

[Kaufmann, C. H.] *The Dictionary of Merchandise, and Nomenclature in all Languages; for the Use of Counting-Houses: Containing, the History, Places of Growth, Culture, Use, and Marks of Excellency, of such Natural Productions, as Form Articles of Commerce; with their names in all European languages* (Philadelphia, 1805).

Kelley, Theresa M. "Romantic Exemplarity: Botany and 'Material' Culture," in *Romantic Science: The Literary Forms of Natural History*, ed. Noah Heringman (Albany: State University of New York Press, 2003), 223–54.

Kendal, David. *The Young Lady's Arithmetic* (Leominster, MA, 1797).

Kirker, James. *Adventures to China: Americans in the Southern Oceans, 1792–1812* (New York: Oxford University Press, 1970).

Klee, Paul. *Notebooks*, Vol. 1: *The Thinking Eye*, ed. J. Spiller, trans. R. Manheim (London: Lund Humphries, 1961).

Kleker, Cynthia, ed. "Reconstructing History: Literature, History, and Anthropology in the Pacific," special issue of *Eighteenth Century* 49.3 (2008), 193–96.

Klooster, Wim. *Revolutions in the Atlantic World: A Comparative History* (New York: New York University Press, 2009).

Knott, Sarah. "Narrating the Age of Revolution," *William and Mary Quarterly* 73.1 (January 2016) 3rd ser., 15, 3–36.

Kommers, J. "The Significance of 18th-Century Literature about the Pacific for the Development of Travel Literature," *Bijdrage tot de Tall-, Land- en Volkenkunde* 144.4 (1988), 478–93.

Kotzebue, August von. *Count Benyowsky; or, the Conspiracy of Kamchatka*, 3rd ed., trans. Rev. W. Render (Cork, 1799).

Kramer, Beth. "Postcolonial Triangles: An Analysis of Masculinity and Homosocial Desire in Achebe's *A Man of the People* and Greene's *The Quiet American*," *Postcolonial Text* 4.4 (2008), 1–14.

Krause, Sydney J. "*Ormond*: Seduction in a New Key," *American Literature* 44 (1973), 570–84.

Krause, Sydney J. "Ormond: How Rapidly and How Well 'Composed, Arranged and Delivered', " *Early American Literature* 13 (1978), 238–49.

Kris, Kay Dian. "Curiosities, Commodities, and Transplanted Bodies in Hans Sloane's 'Natural History of Jamaica,' " *The William and Mary Quarterly* 3rd ser. 57.1 (2000), 35–78.

Kupperman, Karen. "International at the Creation: Early Modern American History," in *Rethinking American History in a Global Age*, ed. Thomas Bender (Berkeley: University of California Press, 2002), 103–122.

Kurashige, Lon, Madeline Y. Hsu, and Yujin Yaguchi. "Introduction: Conversations on Transpacific History," *Pacific Historical Review* 83.2 (May 2014), 183–88.

La Pérouse, Jean-François de Galaup de. *The Journal of Jean-François de Galaup de la Pérouse, 1785–1788*, 2 vols., trans. and ed. John Dunmore (London: The Hakluyt Society, 1994).

Laist, Randy. "Introduction," in *Plants and Literature: Essays in Critical Plant Studies*, ed. Randy Laist (New York: Rodopi, 2013), 9–17.

Lamb, Jonathan. "Minute Particulars and the Representation of South Pacific Discovery," *Eighteenth-Century Studies* 29.3 (1995), 281–94.

Lamb, Jonathan. *Preserving the Self in the South Seas, 1680–1840* (Chicago: University of Chicago Press, 2001).

Lamb, Jonathan, Vanessa Smith, and Nicholas Thomas, eds. "Introduction," to Part One: Adventurers and Explorers, in *Exploration and Exchange: A South Seas Anthology, 1680–1900* (Chicago: University of Chicago Press, 2000), xiii–xxv.

Larkin, Ed. "Nation and Empire in the Early U.S.," *American Literary History* 22.3 (Fall 2010), 501–26.

Leask, Nigel. "Irish Republicans and Gothic Eleutherarchs: Pacific Utopias in the Writings of Theobold Wolfe Tone and Charles Brockden Brown," *Huntington Library Quarterly* 63.3 (2000), 347–67.

Ledyard, John. *John Ledyard's Journal of Captain Cook's Last Voyage*, ed. James Kenneth Munford (Corvallis: Oregon State University Press, 1963).

Letter, Joseph. "Charles Brockden Brown's Lazaretto Chronotope Series: Secret History and 'The Man at Home,'" *Early American Literature* 50.3 (2015), 711–35.

Levander, Caroline F. *Where is American Literature?* (Malden, MA: Wiley Blackwell, 2013).

Levine, Robert. *Conspiracy and Romance: Studies in Brockden Brown, Cooper, Hawthorne, and Melville* (Cambridge: Cambridge University Press, 1989).

Levy, Jonathan. *Freaks of Fortune: The Emerging World of Capitalism and Risk in America* (Cambridge: Harvard University Press, 2012).

Lewis, David. *We, the Navigators: The Ancient Art of Landfinding in the Pacific* (Honolulu: University Press of Hawai'i, 1972).

Lewis, Martin W. and Kären Wigen. *The Myth of Continents: A Critique of Metageography* (Berkeley: University of California Press, 1997).

Littlefield, George Emery. *Early Boston Booksellers, 1642–1711* (Boston: Club of Odd Volumes, 1900). Accessed via *HathiTrust*, July 2, 2017.

Liu, Lydia H. "Robinson Crusoe's Earthenware Pot: Science, Aesthetics, and the Metaphysics of True Porcelain," in *Romantic Science: The Literary Forms of Natural History*, ed. Noah Heringman (Albany: State University of New York Press, 2003), 139–71.

Liu, Tessie. "The Secret Beyond White Patriarchal Power: Race, Gender, and Freedom in the Last Days of Colonial Saint-Domingue," *French Historical Studies* 33.3 (2010), 387–416.

Locke, John. *Two Treatises on Government*, ed. Peter Laslett (New York: New American Library, 1965).

Long, Edward. *The History of Jamaica* (1774; New York: Arno Press, 1972).

Lovejoy, Arthur O. "Monboddo and Rousseau," *Modern Philology* 30.3 (1933), 275–96.

Lowe, Lisa. *The Intimacies of Four Continents* (Durham: Duke University Press, 2015).

Luedtke, Luther S. *Nathaniel Hawthorne and the Romance of the Orient* (Bloomington: Indiana University Press, 1989).

Lukasik, Christopher. "'The Vanity of Physiognomy': Dissimulation and Discernment in Charles Brockden Brown's Ormond," *Amerikastudien* 50.3 (2005), 485–505.

Mack, John. *The Sea: A Cultural History* (London: Reaktion Books, 2011).

Mackey, David. *In the Wake of Cook: Exploration, Science & Empire, 1780–1801* (New York: St. Martin's Press, 1985).

Maginess, James. *A New, Copious, and Complete System of Arithmetic, for the Use of Schools and Counting-Houses, in the United States of America* (Harrisburg, PA, 1821).

Mapp, Paul W. *The Elusive West and the Contest for Empire* (Chapel Hill: University of North Carolina Press, 2011).

Marder, Michael. *Plant-Thinking: A Philosophy of Vegetal Life* (New York: Columbia University Press, 2013).

Marshall, Samuel. *Treatise on the Law of Insurance*, 2 vols. (Philadelphia, 1810).

Martin, Andy. "Introduction: Surfing the Revolution: The Fatal Impact of the Pacific On Europe," *Eighteenth-Century Studies* 41.2 (Winter 2008), 141–47.

Matsuda, Matt K. "Afterword: Pacific cross-currents," in *Pacific Histories: Ocean, Land, People* (Houndsmills: Palgrave Macmillan, 2014), 326–34.

Matsuda, Matt K. "The Pacific," *The American Historical Review* 111.3 (June 2006), 758–80.

Matsuda, Matt K. *Pacific Worlds: A History of Seas, Peoples, and Cultures* (Cambridge: Cambridge University Press, 2012).

Mavor, William Fordyce. *An Historical Collection of the Most Celebrated Voyages, Travels, and Discoveries*, 14 vols. (Philadelphia, 1802).

McClellan, James E. *Colonialism and Science: Saint Domingue and the Old Regime* (Chicago: University of Chicago Press, 2010).

McCormick, E. H. *Omai: Pacific Envoy* (Auckland, NZ: Auckland University Press, 1977).

McCracken, Harold. *Hunters of the Stormy Sea* (London: Oldbourne Press, 1957).

McDonnell, Michael A. "Facing Empire: Indigenous Histories in Comparative Perspective," in *The Atlantic World in the Antipodes: Effects and Transformations since the Eighteenth Century*, ed. Kate Fullagar (Newcastle upon Tyne: Cambridge Scholars, 2012), 220–36.

McGill, Meredith L. *American Literature and the Culture of Reprinting, 1834–1853* (Philadelphia: University of Pennsylvania Press, 2003).

McKeon, Michael. *The Origins of the English Novel, 1600–1740* (Baltimore: Johns Hopkins University Press, 1987).

McKeown, Adam. "Movement," in *Pacific Histories: Ocean, Land, People* (Houndsmills: Palgrave Macmillan, 2014), eds. Armitage and Bashford, 143–65.

McNeill, J. R. *Mosquito Empires: Ecology and War in the Greater Caribbean, 1620–1914* (Cambridge: Cambridge University Press, 2010).

Meek, Ronald L. *Social Science and the Ignoble Savage* (Cambridge: Cambridge University Press, 1976).

Memmi, Albert. *The Colonizer and the Colonized*, trans. Howard Greenfield (Boston: Beacon Press, 1967).

Mignolo, Walter D. *Local Histories/Global Designs: Coloniality, Subaltern Knowledges, and Border Thinking* (Princeton: Princeton University Press, 2000).

Miller, Christopher L. *The French Atlantic Triangle: Literature and Culture of the Slave Trade* (Durham: Duke University Press, 2007).

Miller, Gwenn A. *Kodiak Kreol: Communities of Empire in Early Russian America* (Ithaca: Cornell University Press, 2010).

Miller, Nicholas E. "'In Utter Fearlessness of the Reigning Disease': Imagined Immunities and the Outbreak Narratives of Charles Brockden Brown," *Literature and Medicine* 35.1 (2017), 144–66.

Mintz, Sidney W. "From Plantations to Peasantries in the Caribbean," in *Caribbean Contours*, eds. Sidney W. Mintz and Sally Price (Baltimore: Johns Hopkins University Press, 1985), 127–53.

Molesworth, Jesse. *Chance and the Eighteenth-Century Novel: Realism, Probability, Magic* (Cambridge: Cambridge University Press, 2010).

Monboddo, James Burnett, Lord. *Of the Origin and Progress of Language*, vol. 1 (New York: AMS Press, 1973), 6 vols.

Moore, John Hamilton. *The New Practical Navigator* (Newburyport, 1799).

Moorthy, Shanti and Ashraf Jamal. *Indian Ocean Studies: Cultural, Social, and Political Perspectives* (New York: Routledge, 2009).

Morrison, Dane A. *True Yankees: The South Seas and the Discovery of American Identity* (Baltimore: Johns Hopkins University Press, 2014).

Morton, Timothy. "Blood Sugar," in *Romanticism and Colonialism: Writing and Empire, 1780–1830*, eds. Timothy Fulford and Peter Kitson (Cambridge: Cambridge University Press, 1998), 98–106.

Moseley, Benjamin. *A Treatise on Sugar* (London, 1799), in *Obi; or, the History of Three-Fingered Jack* by William Earle, ed. Srinivas Aravamudan (1800; repr. Peterborough, ON: Broadview Press, 2005), 160–67.

Mosier, Jennifer L. "The Big Attraction: The Circus Elephant and American Culture," *Journal of American Culture* 22.2 (Summer 1999), Humanities Full Text.

Moulton, William. *A Concise Extract, from the Sea Journal of William Moulton* (Utica, 1804).

Muthu, Sankar. *Enlightenment Against Empire* (Princeton: Princeton University Press, 2003).

Neill, Anna. *British Discovery Literature and the Rise of Global Commerce* (London: Palgrave, 2002).

Neville, Henry. *The Isle of Pines*, in *Three Early Modern Utopias*, ed. Susan Bruce (Oxford: Oxford University Press, 1999), 187–212.

Newell, Jennifer. *Trading Nature: Tahitians, Europeans, and Ecological Exchange* (Honolulu: University of Hawai'i Press, 2010).

Newsom, Paul. *A Likely Story: Probability and Play in Fiction* (New Brunswick: Rutgers University Press, 1988).

O'Brien, Patty. *The Pacific Muse: Exotic Femininity and the Colonial Pacific* (Seattle: University of Washington Press, 2006).

O'Quinn, Daniel. *Staging Governance: Theatrical Imperialism in London, 1770–1800* (Baltimore: Johns Hopkins University Press, 2005).

Ojibwa. "Indian Resistance to the California Missions." Native American Netroots. Nativeamericannetroots.net 2013.

Okihiro, Gary Y. *Common Ground: Reimagining American History* (Princeton: Princeton University Press, 2001).

Okihiro, Gary Y. "Toward a Pacific Civilization," *The Japanese Journal of American Studies* 18 (2007), 73–85.

Oliver, Douglas. "Introduction," in *Return to Tahiti: Bligh's Second Breadfruit Voyage* (Honolulu: University of Hawai'i Press, 1988), 1–9.

"On the Impracticability of a Passage into the Pacific Ocean Round the N.W. Part of America," *The New-Haven Gazette, and the Connecticut Magazine* (August 17, 1786); American Periodicals Series Online, ProQuest.

Ott, Julia. "Reading Hamilton's Clocks: Time Consciousness in Early National and Antebellum Urban Commercial Culture," *Temporal Politics*, Multiple Publics/Civic Voices: Online Panel Discussions.

Packham, Catherine. "The Science and Poetry of Animation: Personification, Analogy, and Erasmus Darwin's *Loves of the Plants*," *Romanticism* 10.2 (2004), 191–208.

Paige, Nicholas D. *Before Fiction: The Ancien Régime of the Novel* (Philadelphia: University of Pennsylvania Press, 2011).

Pappas, Stephanie. "Fire Ants Hitched Ride Around Globe in 16th-Century Ships," *LiveScience* (February 19, 2015), www.livescience.com

Park, James Allen. *System of the Law of Marine Insurances* (Boston, 1799).

Parry, J. H. *The Spanish Seaborne Empire* (New York: Knopf, 1966).

Parry, John. "Plantation and Provision Ground: An Historical Sketch of the Introduction of Food Crops into Jamaica," *Revista de historia de América* 39 (1955), 1–20.

Parsons, Christopher M. and Kathleen S. Murphy. "Ecosystems under Sail: Specimen Transport in the Eighteenth-Century French and British Atlantics," *Early American Studies* 10.3 (2012), 503–29.

Patel, Samir S. "Castaways," *Archeology* (September 15, 2014), www.archeology.org

Paton, Diana. "The Afterlives of Three-Fingered Jack," in *Slavery and the Cultures of Abolition: Essays Marking the Bicentennial of the British Abolition Act of 1807*, eds. Brycchan Carey and Peter J. Kitson (Cambridge: D. S. Brewer, 2007), 42–63.

Payne, Anthony. "The Publication and Readership of Voyage Journals in the Age of Vancouver, 1730–1830," in *Enlightenment and Exploration in the North Pacific 1741–1805*, eds. Stephen Haycox, James Barnett, and Caedmon Liburd (Seattle: University of Washington Press, 1997), 176–86.

Payne-Jackson, Arvilla and Mervyn C. Alleyne. *Jamaican Folk Medicine: A Source of Healing* (Kingston, Jamaica: University of the West Indies Press, 2004).

Percy, Carol E. "In the Margins: Dr. Hawkesworth's Editorial Emendations to the Language of Captain Cook's Voyages," *English Studies* 77.6 (1996), 549–78.

Pfaelzer, Jean. *Of Human Bondage: The History of Slavery in California* (Berkeley: University of California Press, forthcoming).

Phillips, Kristine. "Pulitzer Prize-winning author Junot Díaz accused of sexual misconduct, misogynistic behavior," *Washington Post* (May 6, 2016), www.washingtonpost.com.

Pike, Nicolas. *A New and Complete System of Arithmetic, composed for the use of the citizens of the United States* (Newburyport, MA, 1788).

Piketty, Thomas. *Capital in the 21st Century* (Cambridge: Harvard University Press, 2014).

Pincus, Steven. "Placing the American Revolution in Global Context," *Age of Revolutions* (June 20, 2016), ageofrevolutions.com.

Pollock, Sarah. *Practical Arithmetic: Comprising all the Rules for Transacting Business* (Boston, 1810?). Manuscript, Mss. Folio Vols. H. American Antiquarian Society.

Poovey, Mary. *A History of the Modern Fact: Problems of Knowledge in the Sciences of Wealth and Society* (Chicago: University of Chicago Press, 1998).

Poovey, Mary. *Genres of the Credit Economy: Mediating Value in Eighteenth and Nineteenth-Century Britain* (Chicago: University of Chicago Press, 2008).

Popkin, Jeremy D. *Facing Racial Revolution: Eyewitness Accounts of the Haitian Insurrection* (Chicago: University of Chicago Press, 2007).

Porter, David. *Journal of a Cruise made to the Pacific Ocean*, 2 vols. (Philadelphia, 1815).

Porter, Theodore M. *The Rise of Statistical Thinking, 1820–1900* (Princeton: Princeton University Press, 1986).

Pratt, Mary Louise. "Language and the Afterlives of Empire," *PMLA* 130.2 (March 2015), 348–57.

Pratt, Samuel Jackson (writing as Courtney Melmoth). *The Pupil of Pleasure*, 2 vols. (London, 1776).

"Proposals for Publishing by Subscription, (Spotswood No. 22, Marlbro'-Street,) Memoirs and Travels of Maurice Augustus Count Benyowsky." Boston, 1799. *Early American Imprints*, Readex.

Pye, David. *The Nature and Art of Workmanship* (Cambridge: Cambridge University Press, 1968).

Quijano, Aníbal and Immanuel Wallerstein. "Americanity as a Concept, or the Americas in the Modern World-System," *ISSJ* 134 (1992), 549–57.

Rainsford, Marcus. *An Historical Account of the Black Empire of Hayti* (London, 1805).

Reed, Peter. *Rogue Performances: Staging the Underclass in Early American Theatre Culture* (New York: Palgrave Macmillan, 2010).

Reiman, Donald H. "Introduction" to *The Botanic Garden* by Erasmus Darwin, 2 vols. (1791; repr. New York: Garland, 1978), vol 1., v–xiv.

"Remarks upon the Russian Empire," *Monthly Magazine* (April 1800). *American Periodicals Series*, ProQuest.

Rennie, Neil. *Far-Fetched Facts: The Literature of Travel and the Idea of the South Seas* (Oxford: Clarendon Press, 1995).

Rennie, Neil. "The Point Venus 'Scene,'" in *Science and Exploration in the Pacific: European Voyages to Southern Oceans in the Eighteenth Century*, ed. Margarette Lincoln (Suffolk: Boydell Press, 1998), 135–46.

"Report of Ivan Solov'ev to T.I. Schmalev," in *Russian Discoveries in the Pacific Ocean and North America in the 18th Century*, ed. A. I Andreev (Moscow: cosudarstvennoe izdatelstovo geographfischeskoi literatury, 1948), 238r–239v.

Review of *The Travels of Hildebrand Bowman*. *The London Review of English and Foreign Literature* 7 (June 1778), 499–500.

Review of *The Travels of Hildebrand Bowman*. *The Monthly Review* 59 (1778), 409.

Ridley, Glynis. *The Discovery of Jeanne Baret: A Story of Science, the High Seas, and the First Woman to Circumnavigate the Globe* (New York: Crown, 2010).

Rivington, James. "Whosoever would purchase the English edition of *The Late Voyage Round the World*," March 16, 1774. *America's Historical Imprints*, Readex.

Roberts, Brian Russell and Michelle Ann Stephens, eds. *Archipelagic American Studies* (Durham: Duke University Press, 2017).

Roberts, Brian Russell and Michelle Ann Stephens. "Introduction: Archipelagic American Studies: Decontinentalizing the Study of American Culture," in *Archipelagic American Studies* (Durham: Duke University Press, 2017), 1–54.

Rogers, Pat. "The Noblest Savage of Them All: Johnson, Omai, and Other Primitives," *The Age of Johnson* 5 (1992), 281–301.

Roney, Jessica Choppin. "1776, Viewed from the West," *Journal of the Early Republic* 37.4 (Winter 2017), 655–700.

Root, Erastus. *An Introduction to Arithmetic for the use of Common Schools* (Norwich CT, 1795).

Rosenthal, Caitlin. "Storybook-keepers: Narratives and Numbers in Nineteenth-Century America," *Common-place* 12.3 (April 2012), www.common-place-archives.org

Rosenthal, Caitlin. "Numbers for the Innumerate: Everyday Arithmetic and Atlantic Capitalism," *Technology and Culture* 58.2 (April 2017), 529–44.

Russell, Gillian. "An 'entertainment of oddities': Fashionable Sociability and the Pacific in the 1770s," in *A New Imperial History: Culture, Identity and Modernity in Britain and the Empire, 1770–1840*, ed. Kathleen Wilson (Cambridge: Cambridge University Press, 2004), 48–70.

Safier, Neil. "Fruitless Botany: Joseph de Jussieu's South American Odyssey," in *Science and Empire in the Atlantic World*, eds. James Delbourgo and Nicholas Dew (New York: Routledge, 2007), 203–24.

Salesa, Damon Ieremia. "The Pacific in Indigenous Time," in *Pacific Histories: Ocean, Land, People*, eds. David Armitage and Alison Bashford (Basingstoke: Palgrave Macmillan, 2014), 31–52.

Salesa, Damon Ieremia. "Afterword: Opposite Footers," in *The Atlantic World in the Antipodes: Effects and Transformations since the Eighteenth Century*, ed. Kate Fullagar (Newcastle upon Tyne: Cambridge Scholars, 2012), 283–300.

Salmond, Anne. "'Their Body is Different, Our Body is Different': European and Tahitian Navigators in the 18ᵗʰ Century," *History and Anthropology* 16.2 (June 2005), 167–86.

Sanborn, Geoffrey. *Whipscars and Tattoos: The Last of the Mohicans, Moby-Dick, and the Maori* (New York: Oxford University Press, 2011).

Sandiford, Keith. "William Earle's Novella: *Obi*, Obeah and the Ideological Work of Haunting," *Symbolism: An International Annual of Critical Aesthetics* 14 (2014), 221–43.

Sandos, James A. *Converting California: Indians and Franciscans in the Missions* (New Haven: Yale University Press, 2004).

Sansay, Leonora. *Secret History; or, the Horrors of St. Domingo*, ed. Michael J. Drexler (1808; repr. Peterborough, Ontario: Broadview Press, 2007).

Sauer, Carl Ortwin. *The Early Spanish Main* (Berkeley: University of California Press, 1966).

Saunt, Claudio. *West of the Revolution: An Uncommon History of 1776* (New York: W. W. Norton, 2014).

Schaffer, Simon. "In Transit: European Cosmologies in the Pacific," in *The Atlantic World in the Antipodes: Effects and Transformations since the Eighteenth Century*, ed. Kate Fullagar (Newcastle upon Tyne: Cambridge Scholars Publishing, 2012), 70–93.

"Scheme of a Lottery," Handbill for Hartford Woollen Manufactory Lottery (Hartford, 1791), *Early American Imprints*, Readex.

Schiebinger, Londa. *Plants and Empire: Colonial Bioprospecting in the Atlantic World* (Cambridge: Harvard University Press, 2004).

Schurz, William Lytle. *The Manila Galleon* (New York: E. P. Dutton, 1959).

Sedgwick, Eve Kosofsky. *Between Men: English Literature and Male Homosocial Desire* (New York: Columbia University Press, 1985).

Sekora, John. *Luxury: The Concept in Western Thought, Eden to Smollett* (Baltimore: Johns Hopkins University Press, 1977).

Shapiro, Stephen. *The Culture and Commerce of the Early American Novel: Reading the Atlantic World-System* (University Park: Pennsylvania State University Press, 2008).

Shteir, Anne. *Cultivating Women, Cultivating Science: Flora's Daughters and Botany in England 1760–1860* (Baltimore: Johns Hopkins University Press, 1996).

Shu, Yuan and Donald E. Pease, eds. *American Studies as Transnational Practice: Turning Toward the Transpacific* (Lebanon, NH: Dartmouth College Press, 2015).

Silver, Lynette Ramsay. *The Battle of Vinegar Hill: Australia's Irish Rebellion, 1804* (Sydney: Doubleday, 1989).

Skwiot, Christine. *The Purposes of Paradise: U.S. Tourism and Empire in Cuba and Hawai'i* (Philadelphia: University of Pennsylvania Press, 2010).

Sloane, Hans. *A Voyage to the Islands Madera, Barbados, Nieves, St. Christophers and Jamaica*, 2 vols. (London, 1707).

Smith, Bernard. *European Vision and the South Pacific*, 2nd ed. (New Haven: Yale University Press, 1989).

Smith, Stacey. *Freedom's Frontier: California and the Struggle over Unfree Labor, Emancipation, and Reconstruction* (Chapel Hill: University of North Carolina Press, 2013).

Smith, Vanessa. "Give Us Our Daily Breadfruit: Bread Substitution in the Pacific in the Eighteenth Century," *Studies in Eighteenth-Century Culture* 35 (2006), 53–75.

Smith, Vanessa. *Intimate Strangers: Friendship, Exchange, and Pacific Encounters* (Cambridge: Cambridge University Press, 2010).

Spate, O. H. K. *Monopolists and Freebooters* (Minneapolis: University of Minnesota Press, 1983).

Spate, O. H. K. *Paradise Lost and Found* (Minneapolis: University of Minnesota Press, 1988).

Spate, O. H. K. *The Spanish Lake* (Minneapolis: University of Minnesota Press, 1979).

Steinberg, Philip E. *The Social Construction of the Ocean* (Cambridge: Cambridge University Press, 2001).

Steinberg, Philip E. "Of Other Seas: Metaphors and Materialities in Maritime Regions," *Atlantic Studies* 10.2 (2013), 156–69.

Stoler, Ann Laura. "Intimations of Empire: Predicaments of the Tactile and Unseen," in *Haunted by Empire: Geographies of Intimacy in North American History*, ed. Ann Laura Stoler (Durham: Duke University Press, 2006), 1–22.

Stott, G. St. John. "Second Thoughts about Ormond," *Études Anglaises* 43.2 (1990), 157–68.

Sullivan, Kevin. "A Crabby Conflict at the Bay of Pigs," *Washington Post*, March 27, 2001; repr. *CubaNet: CubaNews*, www.cubanet.org.

Taketani, Etsuko. *The Black Pacific Narrative: Geographic Imaginings of Race and Empire between the World Wars* (Hanover: Dartmouth College Press, 2014).

Tarling, Barbara Frances. "Representations of the American War of Independence in the Late Eighteenth-Century English Novel," PhD diss. (Open University, 2010).

Taylor, Alan. *American Colonies: The Settling of North America* (New York: Viking, 2001).

Taylor, Alan. *American Revolutions: A Continental History, 1750–1804* (New York: W. W. Norton & Co., 2016).

Teute, Fredrike J. "The Loves of Plants; or, the Cross-Fertilization of Science and Desire at the End of the Eighteenth Century," *Huntington Library Quarterly* 63.3 (2000), 319–45.

Thell, Anne M. *Minds in Motion: Imagining Empiricism in Eighteenth-Century British Travel Literature* (Lewisburg: Bucknell University Press, 2017).

Thomas, Nicholas. *Entangled Objects: Exchange, Material Culture, and Colonialism in the Pacific* (Cambridge: Harvard University Press, 1991).

Thomas, Nicholas. *Islanders: The Pacific in the Age of Empire* (New Haven: Yale University Press, 2010).

Thompson, E. P. *Customs in Common* (London: Penguin, 1993).

Thompson, James. *Models of Value: Eighteenth-Century Political Economy and the Novel* (Durham: Duke University Press, 1996).

Thompson, Krista A. *An Eye for the Tropics: Tourism, Photography, and Framing the Caribbean Picturesque* (Durham: Duke University Press, 2006).

Thornton, Cliff. "The Hunt for Hildebrand Bowman," *Cook's Log* 33.4 (2010), 1–2; 34.1 (2011), 1–3; 34.2 (2011), 1–2; 34.3 (2011), 6–9.

Tingley, Kim. "The Secrets of the Wave Pilots," *The New York Times Magazine* (March 17, 2017), nyti.ms/1UC6hyu.

Tobin, Beth Fowkes. *Colonizing Nature: The Tropics in British Arts and Letters, 1760–1820* (Philadelphia: University of Pennsylvania Press, 2005).

Tobin, Beth Fowkes. "Caribbean Subjectivity and the Colonial Archive," *Small Axe* 25 (February 2008), 145–56.

Turnbull, John. *A Voyage Round the World, in the Years 1800, 1801, 1802, 1803, and 1804* (Philadelphia, 1810).

Tutor, Jonathan C. "Disappointed Expectations: Artistic Strategy in *Ormond*," *Publications of the Mississippi Philological Association* (1985), 67–80.

Underwood, Ted. "The Stanford Literary Lab's Narrative," *Public Books* (November 2, 2017), www.publicbooks.org.

Underwood, Ted, Hoyt Long, and Richard Jean So. "Cents and Sensibility," *Slate* (December 14, 2014), www.slate.com

Van Bergen, Jennifer. "Reconstructing Leonora Sansay," *Another World is Possible*. January 3, 2010, http://www.a-w-i-p.com/index.php/2010/01/03/reconstructing-leonora-sansay#more1291, February 11, 2010.

Van Dyke, Paul. *The Canton Trade: Life and Enterprise on the China Coast, 1700–1845* (Hong Kong: Hong Kong University Press, 2005).

Van Ittersum, Martine and Jaap Jacobs. "Are We All Global Historians Now? An Interview with David Armitage," *Itinerario* 36.2 (August 2012), 7–28.

Vancouver, George. *A Voyage of Discovery to the North Pacific Ocean, and Round the World*, 3 vols. (London, 1798).

Vancouver, George. *A Voyage of Discovery to the North Pacific Ocean, and Round the World*, 3 vols. (London, 1804).

Verhoeven, W. M. "Displacing the Discontinuous: Or, The Labyrinths of Reason: Fictional Design and Eighteenth-Century Thought in Charles Brockden Brown's Ormond," in *Rewriting the Dream: Reflections on the Changing American Literary Canon*, ed. W. M. Verhoeven (Amsterdam: Rodopi, 1992), 202–32.

Von Morzé, Leonard. "A Massachusetts Yankee in Karl Theodor's Court: Count Rumford's Sovereign Benevolence and Charles Brockden Brown's *Ormond*," *Symbiosis: A Journal of Anglo-American Literary Relations* 15.5 (2011), 45–61.

Wahrman, Dror. *The Making of the Modern Self: Identity and Culture in Eighteenth-Century England* (New Haven: Yale University Press, 2004).

Wallace, Lee. *Sexual Encounters: Pacific Texts Modern Sexualities* (Ithaca: Cornell University Press, 2003).

Wallerstein, Immanuel. *The Modern World-System: Capitalist Agriculture and the Origins of the European World-Economy in the Sixteenth Century* (New York: Academic, 1974).

Wallerstein, Immanuel. *The Modern World-System II: Mercantilism and the Consolidation of the European World-Economy, 1600–1750* (New York: Academic, 1980).

Walsh, Michael. *A New System of Mercantile Arithmetic* (Newburyport, MA, 1801).

Walsh, Michael. *A New System of Mercantile Arithmetic*, 2nd ed. (Newburyport, MA, 1803).

Walsh, Michael. *A New System of Mercantile Arithmetic*, 3rd ed. (Newburyport, MA, 1804).

Warner, Marina. *Stranger Magic: Charmed States and the Arabian Nights* (Cambridge: Harvard University Press, 2011).

Warren, Lenora. "Insurrection at Sea: Violence, the Slave Trade, and the Rhetoric of Abolition," *Atlantic Studies* 10.2 (2013), 197–210.

Waterman, Bryan. "The Bavarian Illuminati, the Early American Novel, and Histories of the Public Sphere," *The William and Mary Quarterly* 62.1 (2005), 9–30.

Watrous, Stephen D. "A Biographical Sketch," in *John Ledyard's Journey Through Russia and Siberia, 1787–1788: The Journal and Selected Letters*, ed. Stephen D. Watrous (Madison: University of Wisconsin Press, 1966), 3–87.

Watson, George, ed. *New Cambridge Bibliography of English Literature*, Vol. II: 1660–1800 (Cambridge: Cambridge University Press, 1971).

Watt, Ian. *The Rise of the Novel* (Berkeley: University of California Press, 1957).

"The Ways to Raise a Fortune; or, the Art of Growing Rich," *Universal Magazine of Knowledge & Pleasure* (June 1, 1748), 285. American Antiquarian Society Historical Periodicals Collection.Weyler, Karen. *Intricate Relations: Sexual and Economic Desire in American Fiction, 1789–1814* (Iowa City: University of Iowa Press, 2004).

Weyler, Karen A. and Michelle Burnham. "Reanimating Ghost Editions, Reorienting the Early American Novel," *Early American Literature* 51.3 (2017), 655–64.

White, Ashli. *Encountering Revolution: Haiti and the Making of the Early Republic* (Baltimore: Johns Hopkins University Press, 2010).

White, Hayden. *The Content of the Form: Narrative Discourse and Historical Representation* (Baltimore: Johns Hopkins University Press, 1987).

Wigen, Kären. "Introduction" to Forum on "Oceans of History," *American Historical Review* 111.3 (June 2006), 717–21.

Williams, Glyn. *Voyages of Delusion: The Quest for the Northwest Passage* (New Haven: Yale University Press, 2003).

Williams, Naomi J. *Landfalls* (New York: Farrar, Straus, and Giroux, 2015).

Wills, Jr., John E. "A Very Long Early Modern?: Asia and Its Oceans, 1000–1850," *Pacific Historical Review* 83.2 (2014), 189–203.

Wilson, Kathleen. *The Island Race: Englishness, Empire, and Gender in the Eighteenth Century* (New York: Routledge, 2003).

Wisecup, Kelly. "Knowing Obeah," *Atlantic Studies* 10.3 (2013), 406–25.

Woertendyke, Gretchen. "Romance to Novel: A Secret History," *Narrative* 17.3 (October 2009), 255–73.

Wonderful Advantages of Adventuring in the Lottery! (Boston, 1802).

Workler, Robert. "Apes and Races in the Scottish Enlightenment: Monboddo and Kames on the Nature of Man," *Philosophy and Science in the Scottish Enlightenment* (1998), 145–68.

Wulf, Andrea. *The Brother Gardeners: Botany, Empire and the Birth of an Obsession* (New York: Knopf, 2009).

Wulf, Andrea. *Founding Gardeners: The Revolutionary Generation, Nature, and the Shaping of the American Nation* (New York: Knopf, 2011).

Yokota, Kariann Akemi. *Unbecoming British: How Revolutionary America Became a Postcolonial Nation* (New York: Oxford University Press, 2014).

Young, Robert J. C. *Colonial Desire: Hybridity in Theory, Culture, and Race* (New York: Routledge, 1995).

Zabin, Serena R. "Writing To and From the Revolution," *William and Mary Quarterly*, 3rd ser. 74.4 (October 2017), 753–64.

Zagarri, Rosemarie. "The Significance of the 'Global Turn' for the Early American Republic: Globalization in the Age of Nation-Building," *Journal of the Early Republic* 31.1 (2011), 1–37.

Žižek, Slavoj. *The Ticklish Subject: The Absent Center of Political Ontology* (London: Verso, 1999).

Žižek, Slavoj. *The Parallax View* (Cambridge: MIT Press, 2006).

{INDEX}

Note: Figures are indicated by an italic *t* following the page number.